IT'S
TIME
FOR
AFRICA

IT'S
TIME
FOR
AFRICA

Embracing Our Ancient Roots and
Charting a Prosperous Tomorrow

JOSHUA CHIMAKULA NGOMA

First published in 2024 by Dean Publishing
PO Box 119
Mt. Macedon, Victoria, 3441
Australia
deanpublishing.com

DEAN PUBLISHING

Cataloguing-in-Publication Data
National Library of Australia
Title: It's Time For Africa — Embracing Our Ancient Roots and Charting a Prosperous
Tomorrow
Edition: 1st edition
ISBN: 978-1-925452-80-8
Category: Business & Economics/Sustainable Development/Leadership

This book is lovingly dedicated to the foundational figures in my life, whose influence and teachings have shaped my journey and inspired these pages.

To my parents, Joshua and Elina, who are no longer with us but whose legacy lives on in every step I take. Dad, your early lessons in entrepreneurship and Mom, your extraordinary strength and values, continue to guide me like stars in the night sky. Your principles of resilience, integrity, and respect have been the bedrock upon which I stand.

To my beloved wife, Susan, who has been my rock and constant companion through all of life's ebbs and flows. Your unwavering support and partnership have been my anchor in both storms and calm seas. Together, we have crafted a life filled with love and shared purpose, a journey I cherish deeply.

To our children, Daliso and Natasha, you are the living embodiments of the values we treasure. The pride I feel in your achievements and the lives you lead is immeasurable. You continue to inspire me every day with your integrity, kindness, and dedication.

To Sage, our granddaughter, whose youthful spirit and remarkable growth remind us of the endless possibilities and hope the future holds. You are a beacon of joy and a testament to the enduring legacy of our family.

And to Trent, our son-in-law, your devotion to our daughter and your role as a father to our granddaughter are exemplary. Thank you for being an integral part of our family and for contributing to the fabric of our shared lives with such grace and commitment.

Each of you has played an indispensable role in my life, and this book is a tribute to your unwavering love, guidance, and inspiration.

CONTENTS

CHAPTER 20

FOREWORD
JAMES EHRLICH

I met Joshua Ngoma in Helsinki, Finland in 2019 when I presented a keynote for the Singularity University Nordic conference on the topic of regenerative and resilient, self-reliant village developments. What I came to understand about Joshua's background is inspiring: how he came to build a successful career and create a beautiful family life, travelling the world in constant pursuit of indigenous wisdom that he relates back to his rich cultural experiences in Africa, and the ways in which he applies these experiences and principles as a role model to improve the lives of others. Joshua's profound commitment to educating young Africans on organic and regenerative agricultural practices, as well as teaching the financial feasibility of sustainable farming as a livelihood, attained my instant respect and established our lifelong friendship.

In *It's Time for Africa*, Joshua paints an immense horizon across a diverse continent through the epochs of time, spanning from the cradle of our species' origins, through the evolution of humanity's earliest successful civilisations.

This book also posits a fascinating and poignant perspective on imagining what our modern world would be like if continental Africa had gone a different course from being overcome by its early colonial domination. Taking us on a journey towards economic empowerment and cultural renaissance that allows us to consider an alternate time line of history, where the scales of immense wealth and prosperity tipped in favour of Africa and its people.

The narrative weaves a tapestry of the past and present, of a continent so often misunderstood and purposefully divided, conquered, and depleted to literally disable generations from standing on their own. While, remarkably, Joshua captivates us with an optimistic vision of a bright future of hope and capability, based on the unified African spirit, inspired by collective ingenuity.

It's a fact that every human on planet Earth has Africa's story embedded within them. Africa is literally coded in our DNA, with overwhelming scientific evidence debunking any lingering notions of racial hierarchy, proving that human ancestry and diversity are intrinsically linked.

Joshua does not wax over the painful history of Africa. Marred by exploitation and stereotypes, with the scars of the transatlantic slave trade and abject theft of resources by colonial powers still reverberating across the continent's socio-economic and ecological landscape. Rather, this book places a mirror on our global consciousness, reflecting the impact of colonial wealth predicated on the kidnapping of human beings from their homelands for seemingly eternal subjugation, coupled with the unmitigated stealing of natural resources that literally lined the pockets and crowns with Africa's precious soul. Yet again, Joshua's tone rises above the adversities of past and present to boldly envision an emergent Africa that reclaims its rich cultural heritage, guiding us toward a positive and proactive future for the whole continent to aspire to.

This book is methodical in offering up each chapter as a stepping stone in understanding the intricate layers that is African history and culture, bringing us through to a place where innovative solutions are being brought forward for the benefit of regenerative and sustainable communities. Joshua captures the real essence of Africa, which lies in its people – vibrant, diverse, and resilient, poised to rewrite their destiny.

Delving into critical areas such as leadership, education, technology, and environmental stewardship, drawing parallels with other nations' success stories, this book provides a road map for how African nations can navigate their unique paths towards equitable prosperity.

From his very real and profound personal experiences, Joshua shares his pivotal role in the shaping of young minds to learn from his successful entrepreneurial background. Embodying initiatives like those embarked upon by the Enterprising Africa Regional Network (Pty) Ltd (EARN). These partnerships are not mere theoretical concepts; they are practical, actionable strategies that can propel Africa towards a brighter future.

In essence, this book is a journey – a journey through Africa's past hardships, its present challenges, and its potential for a remarkable future. It's an invitation to view Africa not as a continent defined by its problems but as a land of endless possibilities.

As you turn each page, I invite you to join in this journey of discovery, reflection, and, ultimately, transformation.

James Ehrlich
Director, Compassionate Sustainability
Stanford University School of Medicine/CCARE Institute
Faculty, Singularity University
Sr Fellow, NASA Ames Research Center
Founder, ReGen Villages Holding, BV

PREFACE

From my earliest memories, curiosity has been a steadfast companion, guiding my journey through life. Now, in my 60s, this curiosity remains undiminished. With each discovery about our world, I find myself humbled by the vastness of what I have yet to learn. My lifelong fascination with the world and its diverse inhabitants has been the driving force behind this book.

As a teenager, my world was a sketchpad where I drew borderless maps, imagining the interconnectedness of different lands and peoples. This early interest blossomed into a passion for travel, a journey I have been fortunate to share with my family. Together, we've traversed all six habitable continents, immersing ourselves in local cultures, from bustling cities to tranquil countrysides. These travels have enriched us with friendships that span the globe, teaching us, including our two children, the invaluable lesson of seeing every person as an equal, irrespective of race, religion, or nationality.

Through these experiences, a profound realisation took root:

beneath our superficial differences lie striking similarities – shared emotions, dreams, and aspirations. This realisation sparked a question that has lingered in my mind, especially as an African: Why is a continent as rich in resources as Africa, with its youthful energy and fertile lands, still perceived as impoverished? Why aren't these abundant resources being harnessed to uplift all its people, bring prosperity, and earn the continent the respect it rightfully deserves, all while safeguarding our environment?

This book is born from a desire to illuminate Africa's true essence – a continent often misunderstood, yet overflowing with culture, history, and potential. As the cradle of humanity, Africa plays an integral role in our collective history and future. My goal is to present a nuanced, comprehensive portrait of Africa, highlighting its complexity and importance on the world stage.

I delve into the 'Out of Africa' theory to underscore our shared African roots, a narrative that dispels notions of racial hierarchy and celebrates our common heritage. This perspective is crucial for Africa and its diaspora in reclaiming and reshaping their narratives in the global context.

However, Africa's journey is not without its challenges. The scars of the transatlantic slave trade and colonialism linger, compounded by contemporary issues, such as youth unemployment and food insecurity. This book outlines pivotal economic growth pillars: leadership, infrastructure, education, governance, economic diversification, innovation, and environmental sustainability. These elements, when effectively harnessed, can be catalysts for Africa's transformative growth.

Furthermore, I emphasise the importance of regional cooperation, global partnerships, and prioritising youth development, as exemplified in our organisation, Enterprising Africa Regional

Network (Pty) Ltd (EARN). Africa's youth, the continent's greatest asset, hold the key to its future.

This book has been written from an observer's perspective on the critical issues facing Africa, and I acknowledge that some views may be subject to debate. I encourage this discussion, hoping it sparks action towards positive change. The chapters from 5 to 19, detailing key economic growth pillars, can be read in any sequence, offering flexibility to the reader. For those interested in further details, additional material will be available on our website, itstimefor.africa.

Trimmed to its essence by my editors, this book aims to broaden the reader's understanding of Africa – to appreciate its rich history, dynamic present, and promising future. It is a call to deepen our understanding, ignite action, and commit to building a prosperous, inclusive, and sustainable Africa. With this knowledge, we can all contribute to the continent's renaissance, shaping a future where every African citizen has the opportunity to thrive.

INTRODUCTION

Our continent of Africa is often referred to as the cradle of humanity, a distinction that highlights its rich and enduring historical significance. The first theory, known as the 'out of Africa' model, is that Homo sapiens developed first in Africa and then spread around the world between 100,000 and 200,000 years ago, superseding all other hominid species. The implication of this argument is that all modern people are ultimately of African descent, an idea supported by a vast amount of scientific data, including genetic, archaeological, and fossil evidence. The 'out of Africa' theory helps us recognise that all human beings share a common ancestry, thereby debunking any false notions of racial inferiority or superiority. This understanding can help those in Africa and other parts of the world who were once colonised to reject the negative stereotypes that have been imposed on them and to embrace their unique cultural heritage and identity with pride.

All too often, people in far-flung corners of the world, perhaps due to limited exposure or understanding, mistakenly talk about Africa as if it is a single country. Africa is **NOT** a country. Being the origin of all modern people, Africa is a diverse, complex, and vibrant **CONTINENT**. It is the second largest continent on Earth, and is home to an incredible **55 countries**, each with its own unique identity and story. The continent has significant variations in natural resources, human development, and political and economic systems. The land area of Africa is approximately 30.37 million km², which is larger than China, Europe, and the United States combined.

Beyond its cultural and anthropological importance, it is accurate to state that Africa is endowed with:

1. An astounding 65 percent of the world's uncultivated arable land
2. An impressive 90 percent of the world's raw material reserves
3. A glittering 40 percent of the world's gold reserves, a symbol of wealth and power throughout history
4. A sparkling cache representing 33 percent of global diamond reserves nestled in its depths
5. A whopping 80 percent of the world's coltan reserves, a vital component of our digital age
6. An essential 60 percent of global cobalt reserves.

Africa is rich in oil and natural gas, is culturally diverse, and has contributed many art forms to the world, including dance, music, architecture, and sculpture.

While it is difficult to attribute exact quantities of natural resources to specific African countries, as resources are often spread across multiple countries and estimates can vary depending on the source, according to the latest Economist Intelligence Unit report, South Africa, Nigeria, Algeria, Angola, and Libya produce more than two-thirds of Africa's mineral wealth.[1]

While the statement that Africa accommodates 30,000 recipes for medicines and herbs is difficult to verify, it is true that traditional medicines continue to play an important role in many African communities, and there is growing interest in studying their potential therapeutic benefits. Africa, as a land of immense natural resources and untapped potential, has the potential to become a global economic powerhouse. With a rapidly growing population, abundant arable land, and a wealth of mineral resources, Africa has the potential to transform itself into a prosperous continent capable of competing on the global stage.

However, Africa, resplendent with diversity and brimming with potential, has been entangled in the chains of historical injustices and contemporary challenges. The transatlantic slave trade, colonialism, and subsequent political and economic exploitation have cast long shadows over the continent's history. These past traumas have shaped the trajectory of Africa's development, often leading to political instability, corruption, and widespread poverty.

In the present day, Africa is grappling with problems such as youth unemployment and food insecurity. As reported by the International Labour Organisation, an estimated 26 percent of the youth labour force aged 15–24 is unemployed.[2] This situation is especially stark in South Africa, where unemployment rates for young people hover at alarming highs. Concurrently, nearly 280 million of our African population battle hunger and malnutrition due to food insecurity stemming from factors such as climate change, population growth, and political instability.[3]

Yet, amid these challenges, Africa stands poised at the cusp of a new dawn. The path to prosperity lies in identifying key pillars of economic growth and nurturing them effectively. While the journey may differ for each country, certain common elements stand out:

1. **Leadership essential for economic development**: Africa needs leaders who champion diversity, unity, and transparency. Leaders can promote social justice and catalyse sustainable development by creating strong institutions and governance structures.

2. **Unveiling Africa's cultural renaissance**: Africa must celebrate its rich heritage, arts, and traditions. As Africans, we need to foster a sense of pride, identity, and self-worth by reviving indigenous languages, music, and literature, and promoting natural beauty.

3. **Infrastructure development**: Just as South Korea's and Singapore's economic growth was fuelled by substantial infrastructure investments, Africa must prioritise sectors like transportation, energy, water, and telecommunications to enhance economic productivity.

4. **Education and human capital development**: Quality education is the backbone of development. As Africans, we need to navigate our destiny with knowledge and confidence by fostering critical thinking, scientific literacy, and a sense of shared history.

5. **Rule of law and good governance**: A stable legal and regulatory environment, along with transparent and efficient public institutions, can facilitate high levels of economic development.

6. **Diversifying economies and embracing open markets**: Africa should diversify its economies and reduce its reliance on raw material exports. Open markets, free trade, and competition will stimulate innovation, efficiency, and growth.

7. **Innovation and technological advancements**: Investment in research and development as well as fostering a conducive environment for innovation can drive significant economic growth, as seen in countries like the United States, Germany, and Japan.

8. **Social safety nets and inclusive growth**: To ensure that economic growth benefits all, social safety nets and equal opportunities should be promoted. Countries like Sweden, Norway, and Finland exemplify this approach.

9. **Fiscal responsibility and sound monetary policy**: Fiscal discipline, low inflation, and stable currency provide a conducive environment for investment and growth, contributing to stable and growing economies.

10. **Environmental sustainability**: Balancing economic development with environmental protection ensures long-term growth and wellbeing. Costa Rica's strides in renewable energy and forest conservation stand as a shining example that African countries can learn from.

11. **Regional cooperation and integration**: African nations can leverage their collective strengths, overcome shared challenges, and stimulate economic growth through fostering greater collaboration and integration.

12. **Attracting foreign direct investment (FDI)**: By creating an attractive investment climate, African nations can draw in foreign direct investment, which can spur economic growth, create jobs, and facilitate the transfer of technology and

skills.

13. **Cultivating global partnerships:** Constructive and equitable partnerships can help Africa access resources, technology, and expertise necessary for development, while maintaining a sense of agency.

14. **Adaptability and resilience:** Fostering adaptability and resilience is essential for sustainable development in African nations. African nations should ensure that their development is sustainable in the face of changing circumstances and potential setbacks, thus promoting long-term economic stability and growth through building adaptable and resilient systems.

15. **Health and wellness development:** Robust health systems form the cornerstone of societal progression. By promoting comprehensive healthcare, disease prevention, and overall wellbeing, we Africans can live more productive, satisfying lives. This focus on health not only contributes to increased longevity but also enhances quality of life, allowing individuals to contribute more effectively to their communities and economies.

16. **Youth training and development partnerships:** Collaborations with purpose-driven organisations like the Enterprising Africa Regional Network (Pty) Ltd (EARN) can provide valuable training in entrepreneurship, technology, and smart agriculture.

These interdependent pillars form a solid foundation for Africa's journey towards sustainable economic growth and prosperity. Our African nations can take effective strides towards a brighter, more prosperous future by learning from the experiences of successful countries and tailoring strategies to each country's unique circumstances. The road may be long and winding, but the potential rewards – a thriving Africa where economic sectors flourish and the youth find meaningful employment – make it a journey worth undertaking.

This is the story I'm about to tell. A story of change, transformation, and the promise of a prosperous future for Africa.

In Chapter 1, we will dig deeper into understanding Africa's rich history and cultural diversity. We start by viewing our beautiful planet from space to get the 'overview effect'. We will then zoom in to our continent of Africa, the centre of the universe and the cradle of humankind. We will then travel across the continent to examine its diverse history and culture, and how this would contribute to Africa's economic development.

CHAPTER 1

UNDERSTANDING AFRICA'S RICH HISTORY AND CULTURAL DIVERSITY

On the momentous date of 12 September 1962, the then president of the United States, John F. Kennedy, impassioned the nation with his "we choose to go to the Moon" address, a landmark speech in galvanising public support for the Apollo programme – the collective endeavour intended to place a man on the lunar surface within the decade. What unfolded post this speech radically transformed our perception of our own home, Earth.

The Blue Dot and Our Shared Fate

In 1969, an indelible mark was made in human history as astronauts Neil Armstrong and Edwin 'Buzz' Aldrin set foot on the Moon. From their unique vantage point, they beheld an awe-inspiring sight: our planet, a breathtaking blue sphere, serenely existing in the boundless expanse of space. They saw a world without borders, a single entity floating in the cosmos, reinforcing the idea of a global family living on a fragile planet. This profound experience, known as the 'overview effect', redefined our understanding of Earth as not merely an assemblage of nations but as a unified global community residing on a delicate sphere.[1]

I believe in one race, the human race, which we need to preserve and protect at all costs. We must either embrace full cooperation and coexistence or risk our own extinction. The results of our actions, or inaction, will be inherited by the generations that follow us. Therefore, the solutions for a sustainable future hinge on our collective efforts, on every individual, community, and nation working in harmony.

As we gaze upon the horizon, one area of the world that presents an enormous opportunity for the global sustainable future is our African continent. Known for its diverse cultures, rich history, and abundant resources, Africa has tremendous potential. The question that arises is: "How can we, as a global community, collaboratively utilise these resources to not only benefit Africa but also contribute positively to the world economy?"

In addressing this, we should prioritise a sustainable and equitable approach. This means developing an economic model that does not exploit Africa's resources at the expense of its environment and people but instead fosters shared prosperity. Africa's abundant natural resources, from minerals to its vast agricultural potential, should be developed responsibly, taking into account the needs of its local communities and the planet's ecological balance.

At the same time, we need to invest in Africa's most valuable resource: its people. This includes bolstering education, healthcare, and infrastructure to foster innovation and technological growth. The aim should be to build a self-sustaining, diversified economy that empowers Africans while also contributing to the global market.

Sustainable development in Africa is not just about economic growth; it's about ensuring equitable access to resources, opportunities, and benefits. It's about creating systems that respect and protect the environment, and about building societies that uphold human rights and promote social justice. Achieving this vision will require concerted efforts from us Africans and the global community.

Africa – the Heart of Our World

Africa is at the centre of our planet Earth. The Earth's surface, where the prime meridian and the equator intersect, is located on a unique spot known as Null Island, which is located about 600 km off the coast of West Africa, nestled in the Gulf of Guinea.

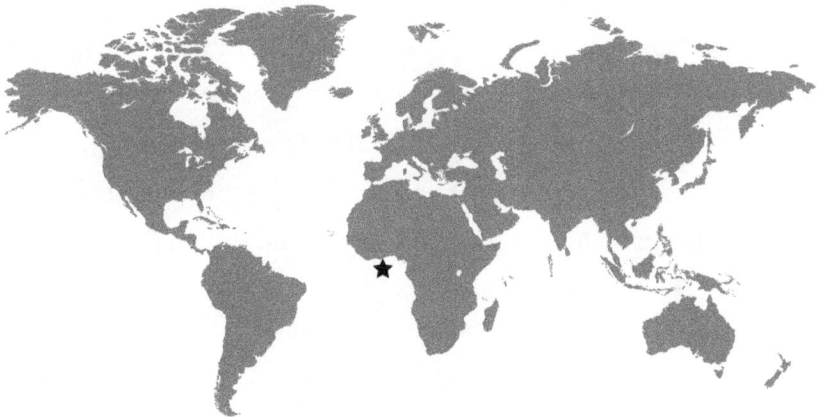

Africa as the Cradle of Humanity

As mentioned earlier, Africa, a vast continent rich in history, stands as the cradle of humanity, hosting our earliest ancestors and tales of Homo sapiens' evolution. Anthropologist Ian Tattersall has underscored the significance of Africa's archaeological treasures, pointing to their pivotal role in shaping our understanding of human evolution.

Africa is recognised as the birthplace of humankind, with notable discoveries like 'Lucy', an Australopithecus afarensis from Ethiopia, that link us to our ancestral past and emphasise that, genetically, all humans have African origins.

But Africa's importance isn't just in fossils. The continent boasts some of the earliest manifestations of human creativity and spirituality, evident in its prehistoric rock art. Southern Africa's cave paintings reveal our ancestors' artistic capabilities, while Algeria's Tassili n'Ajjer region offers a deeper dive into early human beliefs. This region's rock art chronicles the Sahara's transformation from a green landscape filled with wildlife to the desert we recognise today. As the environment shifted, so did the art, marking a transition from hunting to pastoral lifestyles. Intriguingly, the 'Round Head' paintings in the region hint at ancient spiritual practices and rituals.

Furthermore, the diverse art styles in Tassili n'Ajjer suggest it was a melting pot of cultures, where various communities converged and shared ideas. Together, the work of scholars, ancient remains, and Africa's rock art paint a vivid picture of early human history, highlighting our intrinsic artistic and spiritual tendencies.

Africa's Blossoming Heritage of Cultures and Economies Poised to Shape the Future

Appreciating Africa's deep historical relevance is not merely an intellectual pursuit. It signifies a journey of self-understanding, an opportunity to value the myriad of cultures and societies that have flourished on this primeval terrain. It brings to light that this continent, often misconstrued or underestimated, has immense potential, vibrant economies, innovative minds, and a youthful demographic that holds the keys to the future.

The diversity of Africa is proof of the rich cultural expressions that exist within its bounds. With over 2,000 ethnic groups, each with its own unique language, traditions, and societal structures, the continent offers a rich spectrum of heritage and ways of life.[2] Let's start our journey across the continent.

West Africa

West Africa is a region celebrated for its ethnic diversity and cultural vibrancy, which are particularly evident in its artistic and musical traditions that have significantly enriched the world's cultural tapestry. The Kingdom of Benin, located in modern-day Edo State, Nigeria, was renowned for its advanced lost-wax cast bronze sculptures dating from the 13th to the late 19th century. These bronzes were not mere art; they chronicled the Benin Kingdom's history, capturing court life, rituals, battles, and the monarchy's grandeur. They also portrayed Portuguese traders, indicating the historical importance of trade, and featured mythological elements reflective of spiritual beliefs. As *Treasures of Ancient Nigeria* by Ekpo Eyo and Frank Willett reveals, these pieces are windows into Benin's societal intricacies and artistic influence.[3]

The Ashanti people of Ghana are also known for their kente cloth, a fabric woven with complex geometric patterns, each symbolising particular aspects of Ashanti wisdom and history. Initially exclusive to royalty, kente has become a broader emblem of African identity and is worn on significant occasions to signify pride and connection to African heritage – a sentiment echoed worldwide, even by US politicians showing solidarity with the Black community.

In the realm of expression, West African literature from Nigeria and beyond has been instrumental in portraying the region's oral traditions, historical narratives, and cultural legacies while often critiquing contemporary social and political issues. The region's music has equally stamped its mark globally, with artists like Fela Kuti, Ali Farka Touré, and Youssou N'Dour introducing the world to diverse sounds ranging from Afrobeat to desert blues and Mbalax, all of which have captivated a worldwide audience.

This cultural output is a continuum that not only honours its past but also actively shapes the present and future of global arts, literature, and music. The spirit of West Africa, manifested in its culture, is a living testament to the region's resilience, creativity, and diversity. Now, let us turn our attention to the cultural landscapes of East Africa.

East Africa

East Africa is another vibrant region that offers a rich tapestry of cultural heritage. The Maasai community, primarily in Kenya and Tanzania, is one of the most globally recognised African ethnic groups. The Masai are known for their distinct customs, attire, and semi-nomadic pastoralism. Despite modern influences, they've preserved their traditions, which promote the sustainability of the savannah ecosystem. Their vibrant attire, the shuka, and detailed beadwork symbolise East African culture.

The Swahili Coast reflects Africa's role as a melting pot of cultures – Bantu, Arab, Persian, and Indian. The resultant Swahili culture boasts the Kiswahili language, a blend of Bantu and Arabic, unique architectural designs, and UNESCO World Heritage Sites like Kilwa Kisiwani. Kiswahili, a product of cultural fusion, unifies many East African nations. Let's turn our gaze to Southern Africa.

Southern Africa

Southern Africa is a melting pot of cultures, notably exemplified by the Zulu, Ndebele, and Xhosa communities.

The Zulus of KwaZulu-Natal are pivotal in the region's cultural landscape, from their rich oral traditions like 'izinganekwane' (folktales) and 'izisho' (proverbs) to their musical expressions and dance, such as the Indlamu. Zulu ceremonies, including the 'umemulo' (coming-of-age) and 'umkhosi woMhlanga' (reed dance), emphasise communal interconnectedness and respect for life's cycles.

The Ndebele people too are celebrated for their vibrant visual arts. Their murals, 'uMgwalo', painted by women, signify family lineage and status. Their beadwork, 'amaprojwana', also has significant cultural connotations, marking various life events and statuses. This artistic tradition encapsulates Ndebele identity and has evolved, reflecting societal changes and creativity.

The Xhosa, from South Africa's Eastern Cape, blend oral traditions with symbolic beadwork. Their praise poems, 'izibongo', extol virtues and critically reflect on leadership. Folktales in Xhosa culture, laden with moral lessons, have been instrumental in guiding younger generations. The life and leadership of Nelson Mandela exemplified the synthesis of these traditions with contemporary ideals. His Xhosa roots deeply influenced his inclusive vision for South Africa, as evident in his memoir, *Long Walk to Freedom*.

In summary, Southern Africa's cultural richness is evident in the practices and traditions of the Zulu, Ndebele, and Xhosa communities. These traditions not only celebrate individual identities but also emphasise communal values and leadership. Let's move to Central Africa.

Central Africa

Central Africa is a mosaic of distinctive cultures, such as the Baka, Mbuti, Twa, Aka, and the inhabitants of the Kuba Kingdom.

Indigenous peoples like the Baka, Mbuti, Twa, and Aka share an intrinsic bond with the Central African rainforests. This bond is evident in their vast knowledge of the environment, particularly in their sustainable hunting methods and understanding of medicinal plants. Their spirituality seamlessly blends with daily life, with their 'forest music' – a polyphonic singing style – being a testament to their profound connection with nature. This music has not only influenced world music genres but also experimental segments in popular music, highlighting its universal appeal and the global influence of indigenous people and the rainforest's harmonies.

Meanwhile, the Kuba Kingdom, in present-day Democratic Republic of Congo, is celebrated for its intricate textiles and masks. Kuba textiles, crafted from raffia palm leaves, are more than aesthetic marvels; they encapsulate historical narratives, societal values, and are emblematic in ceremonies. Their masks, deeply spiritual in nature, bridge the gap between the material and spiritual realms. These masks, along with dance and music, play essential roles in ceremonies, ensuring the continuity of traditions and reinforcing societal roles.

In essence, Central Africa's cultures highlight the deep bond between humans and nature, the transformative power of music, and the role of art in expressing societal beliefs and structures. Let's turn to North Africa.

North Africa

North Africa is also a blend of diverse cultures, shaped by history and external influences.

The Berbers, or Amazigh, are the ancient inhabitants of North Africa. Their Tamazight languages, unique Tifinagh script, and earth-and-stone architecture like the Kasbahs reflect a deep-rooted identity. They have a vibrant oral tradition filled with songs, tales, and proverbs. Their craftsmanship, seen in jewellery and rugs, is rich in symbolism.

Egypt too, a beacon of ancient civilisation, is renowned for the pyramids, a testament to their architectural prowess. Additionally, the Egyptian solar calendar showcases their astronomical knowledge. Modern-day Egypt blends ancient customs with Islamic traditions, seen in celebrations like the 'moulid' festivals. Literature, cinema, and traditional dance forms, like belly dance, highlight Egypt's cultural depth.

Then there are the Tuareg people of the Sahara who are known for their indigo-dyed garments, desert knowledge, and a unique matrilineal society. Their rich oral traditions encompass poetry and folk tales, and their crafts, particularly silver jewellery and leatherwork, are intricately designed with deep cultural significance.

In essence, North Africa's cultures are a blend of ancient traditions and modern influences, each contributing uniquely to the region's rich heritage.

Beyond Cultural Richness

Beyond cultural richness, Africa houses burgeoning economies. Nigeria, Africa's most populous country, is home to Nollywood, the world's second largest film industry by output, following Bollywood. Nollywood contributes significantly to the country's GDP and employment, demonstrating the power of creative industries in driving economic growth.[4]

The tech sector is another fast-growing industry in Africa, particularly in South Africa. Cape Town has emerged as a leading tech hub, often referred to as the 'Silicon Cape'. The city's tech industry has attracted both domestic and international investment and fostered startups that offer innovative solutions in fields such as fintech, health tech, and education tech.[5]

Kenya is a global pioneer in mobile money services, most notably through M-Pesa. Launched by mobile network operator Safaricom in 2007, M-PESA has revolutionised banking in a region where traditional banking infrastructure is sparse. The service allows users to deposit, withdraw, and transfer money, as well as pay for goods and services, using a mobile device. This has greatly increased financial inclusion, particularly for people in rural areas.[6]

Africa's economic potential is bolstered by its young and rapidly growing population. According to the African Development Bank, the continent's youth population is projected to double by 2050, presenting enormous opportunities for economic growth and innovation.[7] However, this also poses challenges in terms of

creating sufficient jobs and providing quality education and training to equip young people with the skills needed for the labour
market.

The rise of digital technologies and the increasing connectivity
of Africa provide promising pathways for addressing these challenges. Digital platforms can offer innovative solutions for education, training, and job matching, and foster entrepreneurship and
creativity among Africa's youth.[8]

Both literary and practical instances affirm Africa as a melting pot of vibrant cultures and innovative economies, overflowing
with youthful vitality ready to shape the future. Africa's story is
one of diversity, resilience, and enormous potential. Recognising
this echoes the continent's historical importance as humanity's
birthplace and its contemporary significance as a crucial partici-
pant in the global narrative.

As we envisage Africa's promising future, let us remember its
past, for it resonates with our own echoes. In the skeletal remains
of Lucy, in the ancient brushstrokes, in the soil of this remarkable
continent, we unearth not just our beginnings but also the promise
of our potential.

In Chapter 2, we will delve deeper into the impact of race,
racism, slavery, and colonialism on Africa's economic and social
development. We will explore how European powers exploited
Africa's resources and its people for their own gain. We will also
discuss how this exploitation has contributed to the current state
of poverty and underdevelopment on the continent. We will also
look at how some African countries have overcome or are overcoming this legacy.

CHAPTER 2

THE IMPACT OF RACISM, SLAVERY, AND COLONIALISM ON AFRICA

Despite being the 'cradle of humanity', the profound and long-lasting impacts of racism, slavery, and colonialism have had significant effects on the African continent, shaping its modern-day sociopolitical and economic landscapes.

Race

The human brain's innate ability to categorise the world around us has contributed significantly to our understanding of race and the subsequent development of racism, slavery, and colonialism. The human brain's tendency to categorise is rooted in our evolutionary past, and this ability has both served and hindered our progress as a species.

Evolutionary Basis for Categorisation

Our human ancestors, like other animals, depended on the ability to quickly recognise and react to threats. A lion on the horizon wasn't just a beautiful animal – it was also a potential threat. Deciding whether an entity was friend or foe, edible or toxic, could make the difference between life and death. Thus, the ability to categorise and recognise patterns became an evolutionary advantage.

For example, there's the theory of 'in-group versus out-group'. Humans, being social animals, relied on their tribes or groups for survival. Recognising and favouring members of your own group (in-group) while being wary of or even hostile to those outside of it (out-group) provided security and ensured that resources were shared among group members. Unlike today, when resources are in abundance, this form of recognising made sense in a time when resources were scarce and where unknown individuals could pose a threat to the survival of in-group members.[1]

Categorisation and Modern Implications

As societies grew and became more complex, this natural instinct to categorise didn't disappear but instead took on new forms. In the context of social structures and human interactions, this categorisation instinct has manifested in various ways. One of the most evident and consequential forms it has taken is the categorisation of people based on perceived differences like race and ethnicity. At a glance, such classifications might appear as mere reflections of biological differences. However, deeper introspection reveals that they are more social constructs than they are biological realities.

Gordon W. Allport's work underscores the significance of our tendency to group and differentiate. In our prehistoric past, this may have been a mechanism to identify in-group members from potential threats. A tribe or group could easily recognise and cooperate with those who looked, behaved, and spoke similarly. On the other hand, strangers or those who seemed different posed unknown risks, and it was adaptive to be cautious or even hostile.[2]

In contemporary societies, though, this instinct has intermingled with sociopolitical dynamics, cultural beliefs, and historical narratives, leading to the creation of racial and ethnic categories. Over time, these categories have come to bear significant weight and meaning, often beyond mere physical distinctions. They have become imbued with stereotypes, prejudices, and societal expectations, which shape individuals' identities, opportunities, and experiences.

The modern implications of this categorisation are manifold. On the one hand, racial and ethnic classifications have fostered rich cultural traditions, community bonding, and a sense of belonging among members of specific groups. On the other hand, they've also been the basis for discrimination, prejudice, and systemic inequities.

Jay Van Bavel and Dominic J. Packer's *The Power of Us* delves into the profound dynamics of social identities, highlighting their ability to unite and divide. This understanding is pivotal when examining the longstanding impacts of racism and slavery on the African continent. Bavel and Packer underscore that social identities are shaped not just by individual perceptions but also by external influences, often leading to an 'us vs. them' mentality.[3] This mindset can further harmful biases, discrimination, and violence.

Over time, the perception and classification of race have shifted.

There's now a broader understanding that race is mainly a social construct without a biological foundation for notions of superiority or inferiority. For instance, the Human Genome Project revealed that genetic variation within a single race often exceeds that between different races. Although humans are about 99.9 percent genetically identical, the 0.1 percent difference is far more complex than previously believed, with environment and lifestyle interacting with our DNA.[4]

Recognising our genetic diversity should push us towards unity and debunk harmful stereotypes. Understanding that race is a product of our tendency to categorise can help in proactively addressing biases and promoting inclusivity.

We need to always remember that while the brain may naturally categorise, it is also remarkably plastic, capable of learning and evolving. We can train ourselves to be more open-minded and less prejudiced by leveraging this plasticity. By challenging these categorisations and promoting a more nuanced understanding of human diversity, we will be able to work towards a more inclusive and equitable society.

Racism

As discussed in the previous section, racism is a complex issue deeply rooted in socio-economic factors, political power, and how we perceive differences. It thrives on stereotypes related to our most cherished values, painting the 'other' group in negative hues while uplifting our own racial group. As mentioned earlier, these biased perceptions often arise from limited information, leading to the categorisation of people into 'good vs. bad' or 'friend vs. foe' and anxiety towards those who differ from us.

While racism is usually seen in terms of colour, some scholars have examined it from a broader perspective. For instance, Ramon Grosfoguel, an associate professor in the Department of Ethnic Studies at UC Berkeley, delves into the nuanced, multifaceted nature of racism as a concept and its role in both historical and contemporary global systems of power. He frames racism as a hierarchy of superiority and inferiority, with 'markers' of this hierarchy varying depending on regional and historical context. These markers might be colour, ethnicity, language, culture, or religion.[5]

Racism has profound impacts on its victims, particularly regarding self-esteem. Historically, Africans were dehumanised by enslavers and colonisers, a sentiment that continues globally in many forms today. Such ongoing prejudices lead to self-doubt among affected groups. Tackling racism requires a deep understanding of its roots in socio-economic, political, and cultural realms. It's perpetuated by stereotypes and institutional biases. Additionally, privilege grants unseen advantages to certain groups, making it hard for beneficiaries to recognise or relinquish it. While applying scientific methods to understand racism and privilege is enticing, the complexity of human behaviour makes it challenging compared to more predictable physical sciences.

Using a scientific approach could entail systematic observation, data collection, and analysis to better understand the underlying causes and effects of racism and privilege. This could help in identifying bias, both implicit and explicit, and in measuring the impacts of systemic racism. This evidence-based approach could help us devise effective strategies to counter racism and dismantle privilege.

However, such an approach would need to be coupled with emotional intelligence and empathy. The complexity of human behaviour and the deep-seated emotions involved in discussions of racism and privilege mean that logical argumentation alone is unlikely to be sufficient.

That said, as we become more connected through technological advances, changes in behaviour, and meaningful interactions among equals from different racial backgrounds, we will reduce prejudice. As familiarity grows, the realisation that we share more similarities than differences will become evident, and, slowly but surely, stereotypes will be dismantled. This is my hope, anyway.

Slavery

The transatlantic slave trade was one of the most devastating periods in Africa's history. It significantly altered the conception and system of slavery that had previously existed in various forms in both Europe and Africa. This shift was prompted primarily by the significant profits reaped from plantation agriculture in the Americas, which necessitated a substantial labour force.

People argue that there was slavery in Africa even before the advent of the transatlantic slave trade. This may be true, but, in the African context, while the enslaved individuals often occupied diverse roles – from working as agricultural labourers in fields, to miners extracting valuable minerals, to artisans producing a variety of goods – the system wasn't static but flexible, allowing room for social mobility. Often, individuals could transition from a state of enslavement to emancipation, and sometimes even rise in social status.

One of the fundamental differences between African systems of slavery and the chattel slavery that would later be instituted in the Americas was the nature of the social relationships. In many African societies, enslaved people were not merely seen as property but were incorporated into the familial and social structures of those who enslaved them. They could marry, have children, and their children were not automatically enslaved. This incorporation into the kinship group provided a level of social protection, despite their lower social status.[6]

The situation was different in Europe, where serfdom was prevalent. In Europe, particularly during the Middle Ages, the prevailing system of serfdom was a significant component of the broader feudal system. Serfdom is often contrasted with slavery, as, while they share some similarities, there are key differences that distinguish the two.

Serfs were integral to medieval Europe, working on land owned by lords in return for protection and the right to farm a section for themselves. Though bound to the land, serfs weren't personal property; they couldn't be traded as slaves. They held specific rights, such as inheritance of their holdings and protection against unwarranted displacement. While lords could demand their labour, they also had duties, like ensuring serfs' subsistence rights and providing communal facilities. Serfdom's prevalence varied across Europe; it faded in Western Europe by the Late Middle Ages but lingered in Eastern Europe until the 19th century. Despite having more rights than slaves, serfs still experienced significant constraints, with limited freedom and opportunities.

The transatlantic slave trade brought these two African and European systems of labour exploitation into direct contact, which fundamentally transformed the practice and conception of slavery. The transatlantic slave trade represented a stark departure from earlier forms of slavery in both Africa and Europe.[7]

The transatlantic slave trade had a profound influence on both sides of the Atlantic, with its repercussions still felt today. The unique nature of chattel slavery saw enslaved Africans treated as property, devoid of rights, laying the foundation for a racial hierarchy and deep-seated racial discrimination. Africa suffered a massive demographic blow as millions were taken as slaves, severely stunting its economic development and contributing to its modern-day challenges. The trade also sparked extensive conflict and societal disruptions, with the fear of slave raids causing widespread instability that lingered into postcolonial times. As for the legacy, the historical injustices and resulting systemic racial discrimination led to notable disparities in areas like education, health, and income, especially in the Americas. Meanwhile, the African diaspora saw enslaved Africans influencing their new homes in music, cuisine, and language. Yet, they faced identity challenges due to displacement and continued racial discrimination.

Understanding the transatlantic slave trade and its implications is paramount. Works by scholars like Walter Rodney and Hilary Beckles underscore this importance.[8] Recognising the profound effects of this trade is not just an academic exercise; it's pivotal in contemporary efforts aimed at rectifying racial inequalities and fostering a just society where the dignity of every individual is acknowledged and upheld.

Colonialism – the Scramble for Africa

Colonialism followed slavery, with European powers carving up Africa and exploiting its resources for their own benefit.

In the late-19th and early-20th centuries, a fevered race among European powers to stake a claim in Africa, known as the 'Scramble for Africa', deeply scarred the continent.

Before we discuss the Scramble for Africa, let's step back to the 15th century, when the nation-states emerged in Europe. If there were no nation-states, the Scramble for Africa, and the colonisation of other nations, may have taken a different form from what we know today.

In the late medieval period, the black plague destabilised the feudal system by significantly reducing the population, leading to increased labour demand and fostering social mobility. This upheaval was bolstered by the growth of towns and cities, which shifted Europe's primarily agrarian society towards urbanisation. Cities became centres of trade, nurturing a new social class, the bourgeoisie – wealthy merchants and artisans – which held interests divergent from the feudal nobility. Their wealth, untethered from land-based feudal systems, and their desires for trade-friendly reforms further weakened traditional power structures. The urban concentration facilitated the exchange of ideas, promoting shared identities, thus laying the groundwork for the nation-state concept.

Power centralisation became paramount as monarchs allied with the merchant class and established expansive administrative systems. The invention of the printing press in the mid-15th century, introduced by Johannes Gutenberg, was instrumental in this cultural shift. Mass production and dissemination of printed materials helped standardise language and spread shared narratives, reinforcing the sense of a larger collective identity.

The Enlightenment era further accelerated this shift, with philosophers like Locke, Rousseau, and Montesquieu challenging traditional notions of governance. They argued that rulers' authority should stem from the people's consent, rather than divine right, emphasising the state's responsibility towards its citizens. The emergence of the nation-state, therefore, was a result of intertwined economic, political, and cultural evolutions, transitioning from local allegiances to centralised authority and national identity, profoundly influencing the modern world order.

In the tumultuous 17th century, Europe was also a hotbed of religious passion due to the spread of the church. The church's origins trace back to Jesus Christ's teachings in the 1st century AD. Early Christian communities, initially Jewish, evolved and spread rapidly throughout the Roman Empire, with figures like Peter and Paul being instrumental in their establishment. These communities later distanced themselves from Judaism, attracting non-Jews, particularly after the Edict of Milan in 313 AD sanctioned Christianity, mainly through the Catholic Church, leading to its dominance by the 4th century.

By the dawn of the 17th century, the Catholic Church's authority was under threat from Martin Luther's Protestant Reformation. The Holy Roman Empire, under Charles V, was a mosaic of territories, each with unique religious and political affiliations. The empire faced internal challenges from the rise of Protestantism and external threats from France and the expanding Ottoman Empire. With religious tensions escalating, Ferdinand II's attempt to enforce Catholicism on the Protestants led to the Thirty Years' War. The Peace of Westphalia in 1648, which ended this war, laid the groundwork for the modern nation-state, emphasising territorial integrity and national sovereignty.

Now coming back to the Scramble for Africa – people have wondered why, initially, Europeans travelled all the way to the Americas to conquer those nations when Africa was so close. Firstly, while Africa was geographically closer to Europe than the Americas, the continent's challenging geography, deadly diseases, and powerful indigenous empires with strong armies deterred early large-scale European colonisation. Secondly, the existing trade relations, where Europeans exchanged goods for African commodities, were more lucrative than potential conquests. The discovery of the Americas and their vast riches further diverted European imperial ambitions westward.

However, by the late 19th century, various factors would change Europe's stance towards Africa. With advancements in technology and a desire for new markets and resources, and with each of the European nation-states considered equal and independent, it was time to pounce on weaker empires or nations far afield that held a lot of resources. One such place happened to be in Africa. European powers met in 1884–1885 at the Berlin Conference, a gathering infamous for not inviting a single African representative, to carve up Africa like a cake at a children's party. This blatant act of imperialism saw powerful nations split ethnic groups and families across different colonies, planting seeds of discord that continue to sprout conflicts today.[9]

In *The United States and Africa: A History*, Peter Duignan highlights that these arbitrarily drawn borders disrupted established African communities and cultures, leading to discord that persists till today. The seeds sown by this intrusive colonial invasion continue to yield conflict, chaos, and suffering. He describes this as a significant historical tragedy that transformed the African continent's sociopolitical landscape.

Duignan further highlights the lasting implications of the Scramble for Africa. The hasty and inconsiderate partition of Africa, he argues, is at the root of many of the ethnic tensions, civil wars, and political instabilities that have plagued African nations in the postcolonial era.

In his comprehensive analysis, Duignan vividly captures the brutality and ruthlessness of the Scramble for Africa. His work serves as a grim reminder of the devastating impact of imperialism and the long-lasting scars it has left on the African continent.

The Scramble for Africa also resulted in the current Africa's strangest borders. In Central Africa, the Democratic Republic of Congo (DRC) has two distinct panhandles. The Congo Pedicle stretches into Zambia, a result of colonial-era negotiations between the British and Belgians. Unable to agree, the two consulted the Italian king, who decided the boundary, causing a travel anomaly for Zambians who must cross two borders to stay within their own country.[10] The second panhandle, Congo Central, was created by Belgian King Leopold II so the Belgians could access this massive colony from the Atlantic Ocean to facilitate the shipment of slaves, minerals, ivory, and rubber back to Europe.

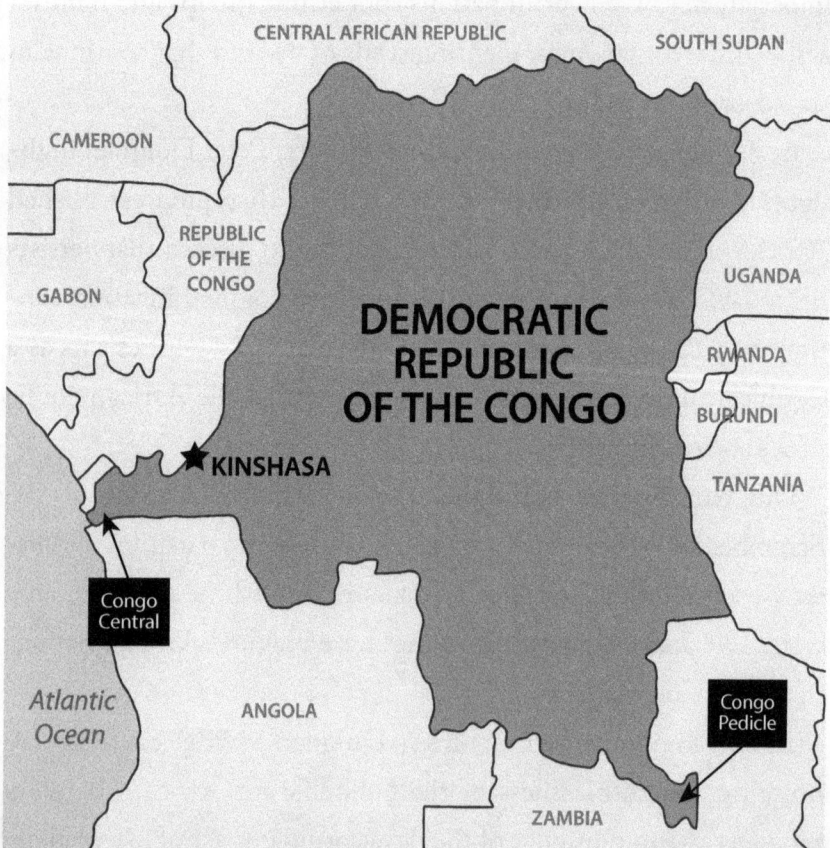

In Southern Africa, the Caprivi Strip in Namibia extends towards Zambia. It was acquired by Germany in exchange for Zanzibar. Germany intended to use the Zambezi River for trade, overlooking the river's unnavigable nature due to massive waterfalls. The strip also resulted in the world's only international 'quadripoint' where Zambia, Namibia, Zimbabwe, and Botswana converge.[11]

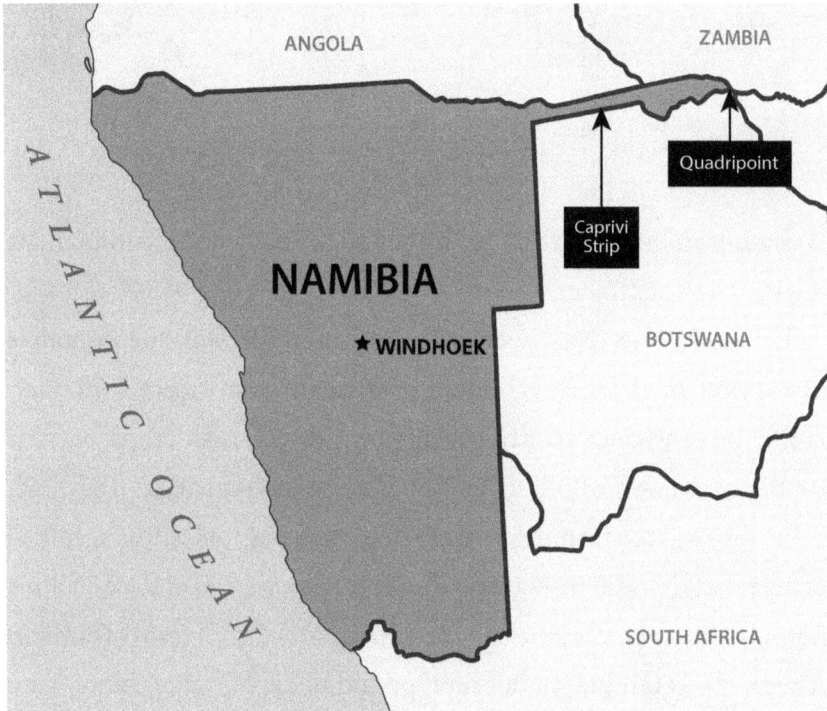

The Gambia in West Africa, almost entirely surrounded by Senegal, is a narrow stretch along the Gambia River. Its shape is allegedly attributed to a British warship that navigated up the Gambia River, firing cannonballs off either side, with the British claiming the land within cannon range. While the story seems far-fetched, it contains elements of truth. The resulting shape has left Senegal with an unusual-looking map, split by the long strip of the

Gambia that causes Senegalese travelling from north to south, or vice versa, to cross two borders.[12]

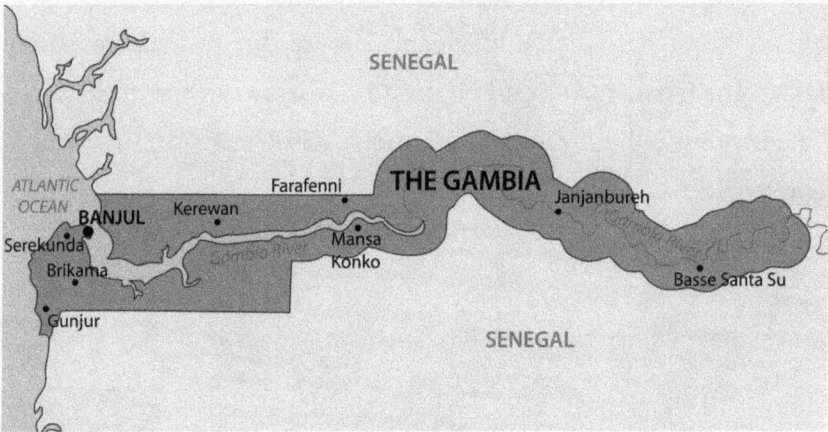

Such borders in Africa highlight the arbitrary decisions made during the colonial era.

The economic consequence of the scramble was the complete disruption of African economies. Africans were forced off their lands, turning once fruitful fields into sites for cash crops, such as rubber and palm oil, destined for European industries. This shift from subsistence farming to cash crop farming caused widespread poverty and food insecurity. As the historian Caroline Elkins notes in *Imperial Reckoning: The Untold Story of Britain's Gulag in Kenya*, the scramble was a brutal period of exploitative colonialism that triggered an economic downturn from which Africa has never fully recovered.

Elkins delves into how fertile African lands, once used by locals for subsistence farming, were seized by European powers. These lands were repurposed for the cultivation of cash crops, such as rubber and palm oil, primarily intended for export to feed burgeoning industries in Europe during the industrial revolution.

With their lands taken away, many were forced into poorly paid labour on the same farms they once owned. The entrenched systems of exploitation left a lasting legacy of economic instability and underdevelopment, issues that continue to plague the African continent today.[13]

In his illuminating work, *The Black Man's Burden*, historian Basil Davidson argues that the root cause of Africa's present-day political instability lies in the historical irony that Africa's liberators, reluctant to embrace Africa's own history, chose to form nation-states based on fundamentally flawed European models. He maintains that African leaders, in their rush to liberation and in their alienation from African culture, which they viewed as savage and primitive, agreed to construct new nation-states based on European models imposed upon them by departing colonial authorities.

Davidson further laments the fact that European powers, in their rush to control Africa, disregarded the continent's existing ethnic, cultural, and political boundaries. In his view, they created a series of artificial states that bore little resemblance to the complex mixture of societies that existed prior to colonisation.

These new borders, he points out, often split ethnic groups, creating situations where people who shared a common language, culture, and history found themselves in different countries. Conversely, groups with little in common were thrown together, leading to a lack of cohesion and shared identity within these new countries. These arbitrary divisions led directly to ethnic conflicts and civil wars in many African countries.[14]

In Sudan, for instance, the division of the country into North and South led to decades-long civil wars, as explained by historian Douglas H. Johnson in *The Root Causes of Sudan's Civil Wars*.

According to Johnson, the division of Sudan into North and

South by European powers was done largely along religious and ethnic lines. The North was predominantly Arab and Muslim, while the South was made up of several ethnic groups, most of which practised Christianity or indigenous religions.

Johnson argues that these imposed divisions laid the groundwork for decades-long civil wars in Sudan. The South felt marginalised and underrepresented in the central government, which was dominated by Northern Arab elites. This resulted in feelings of resentment and demands for greater autonomy or independence, leading to the First Sudanese Civil War, which lasted from 1955 to 1972.

Following a decade of unstable peace, the same unresolved issues of cultural, ethnic, and religious differences reignited conflict in the Second Sudanese Civil War from 1983 to 2005. The 2005 signing of the Comprehensive Peace Agreement (CPA) officially ended the North-South conflict and set the date for a referendum on South Sudan's self-determination in January 2011. Voters overwhelmingly chose independence, and the Republic of South Sudan declared independence on 9 July 2011. Johnson suggests that these conflicts were not inevitable but were the direct result of the artificial division of the country by colonial powers.

Furthermore, Johnson discusses the devastating impact of these wars on the people of Sudan. Millions were displaced, and countless lives were lost. The wars also severely hindered economic and social development, leaving the country impoverished and unstable.[15]

In West Africa, Nigeria's post-independence history is also replete with conflicts, the most notable being the Biafra War, sparked by ethno-regional tensions rooted in colonial rule.

The Biafra War, also known as the Nigerian Civil War, was a

grim chapter in Nigeria's history that unfolded from 1967 to 1970. It was a conflict deeply rooted in the colonial legacy left by Britain and is best understood through the prism of several notable literary works.

British historian Frederick Forsyth's *The Biafra Story* provides a detailed account of the war's origins and progression. As Forsyth points out, the conflict was sparked by ethno-regional tensions that had been simmering since the colonial period. In 1914, the British amalgamated diverse ethnic groups into one entity called Nigeria, creating a tinderbox of competing interests and identities.

The most prominent of these groups were the Hausa-Fulani in the north, the Yoruba in the west, and the Igbo in the east. The colonial administration governed the country with a policy of indirect rule, which amplified regional and ethnic divisions. The north, predominantly Muslim and feudal, was ruled differently from the Christian and more westernised south. These differences sowed the seeds of post-independence conflict.

After independence in 1960, political and economic power was disproportionately held by the northern elites. Accusations of corruption and electoral malpractice sparked widespread discontent. This discontent culminated in a bloody military coup in 1966 led predominantly by Igbo officers, leading to retaliatory massacres of Igbos in the north.

The secession of Biafra, predominantly inhabited by the Igbo, was declared in May 1967 by Lieutenant Colonel Odumegwu Ojukwu in response to these massacres. The Nigerian government, unwilling to see the country disintegrate, responded with military force, sparking a civil war that lasted for two and a half years.[16]

The war was brutal, marked by widespread atrocities and a humanitarian crisis. *Half of a Yellow Sun* by Nigerian author Chimamanda Ngozi Adichie brings the war's human cost into sharp focus, telling the story of the conflict through the eyes of those who lived through it. By January 1970, the secessionist movement had been quelled, leaving an estimated one to three million people dead, many from starvation due to a blockade imposed by the Nigerian government.[17]

The Biafra War serves as a stark reminder of the lasting damage inflicted by colonial rule. Its legacy continues to influence Nigeria's political landscape and the relationship between its diverse ethnic groups.

Then there was the case of the 1994 genocide in Rwanda. The Rwanda genocide is one of the most chilling episodes in human history, a stark reminder of the catastrophic consequences of unchecked hate, divisiveness, and international apathy.

In *We Wish to Inform You That Tomorrow We Will Be Killed with Our Families*, Philip Gourevitch recounts this horrifying event, providing a vivid, personal, and detailed account that brings the tragedy to life in a deeply human context.

Rwanda, a small, densely populated nation in East Africa, is predominantly made up of two ethnic groups: the Hutus and Tutsis. While there were always differences and occasional tension between the two, their relationships were complex and often more a result of occupational rather than strict ethnic differences, until the arrival of European colonial powers.

The first Europeans to colonise Rwanda were the Germans, followed by the Belgians after World War I. These colonial powers, influenced by a now discredited form of science called eugenics, regarded the Tutsis as being racially superior to the Hutus. They formalised the distinctions between the two groups, issuing identity cards that labelled Rwandans as either Hutu, Tutsi, or Twa (a smaller indigenous group).

The Tutsis, making up about 15 percent of the population, were favoured by the Belgians, which created deep resentment among the Hutu majority. The Belgians used the classic colonial strategy of 'divide and rule', deepening the rift between Hutus and Tutsis.

In the wake of decolonisation in the 1960s, the Hutus took power in Rwanda. The decades that followed were marked by sporadic violence and systematic discrimination against the Tutsis. In 1994, the situation reached a boiling point when the plane carrying Rwanda's Hutu president, Juvenal Habyarimana, was shot down.

What followed was a 100-day massacre, in which Hutu extremists killed between 800,000 and 1 million Tutsis and moderate Hutus. This brutal event was characterised by the horrific speed and efficiency with which it was carried out. Encouraged by a hate-filled radio station, Radio Television Libre des Mille Collines (RTLM), and armed with machetes and crude weaponry, the Hutu militias known as the Interahamwe ('those who attack together') unleashed a spree of violence primarily against Tutsis but also against moderate Hutus.[18]

Despite the alarming signs of an impending catastrophe, international bodies and influential nations largely turned a blind eye to the atrocities. Roméo Dallaire's *Shake Hands with the Devil: The Failure of Humanity in Rwanda* serves as a poignant chronicle of these dark days. As the Canadian general in charge of the United Nations peacekeeping force in Rwanda, Dallaire was a firsthand witness to the mounting violence and the international community's hesitance to take decisive action. In his book, Dallaire paints a harrowing picture of the complexities he faced, the bureaucratic hurdles, the lack of resources, and the overriding sense of international apathy. His narrative not only captures the brutality of the genocide but also serves as an indictment of the world's collective failure to step in when humanity was most in need.[19]

The effects of the Rwanda genocide continue to resonate today, a reminder of how colonial policies can have lasting and devastating impacts long after the colonisers have left. It underlines the importance of fostering ethnic harmony, building strong institutions, and the vital role of the international community in preventing such atrocities.

The Scramble for Africa set the continent on a tortuous path of economic underdevelopment and social unrest. The effects continue to echo through the continent's modern history, serving as a harsh reminder of the destructive power of imperialism and racism.

The Aftermath of Independence: Challenges and Opportunities

Post-independence, many African nations inherited economies designed for extraction and export, not for internal development. As we have seen, European colonialism significantly transformed Africa's economic and social landscapes, with effects that continue to shape the continent's development trajectory.

Colonial economic policies in Africa primarily aimed to benefit the colonising nations, resulting in a pattern of economic exploitation that impacted Africa's development. The economic model imposed by the colonisers often involved the extraction of raw materials for export to the home countries, where they were used in the production of industrial goods. These goods were then often sold back to the colonies, thus stifling local industry and reinforcing economic dependency. This is still happening today, with most African nations continuing to export raw materials and later import, at higher prices, the finished products made from the very raw materials they exported.

Walter Rodney's groundbreaking work *How Europe Underdeveloped Africa* illuminates this pattern of economic exploitation. Rodney argues that European colonial powers intentionally exploited and underdeveloped Africa, creating the conditions for the continent's current economic challenges. The economies of many African nations remain heavily dependent on the export of raw materials, a legacy of the colonial economic model.

The colonisation of Zambia (formerly known as Northern Rhodesia) by the British stands out as a classic instance of the colonial extractive model. Rather than investing in diverse sectors of the colony's economy or its human capital, the British primarily homed in on the vast copper deposits, recognising the potential profitability of this resource. Copper, consequently, became not just a significant export but the very backbone of Northern Rhodesia's economy.

Most of the profits generated from the copper mines, instead of being reinvested in the local economy or infrastructure, were channelled back to Britain. This system ensured that while the colonial powers prospered, Northern Rhodesia experienced a continuous outflow of wealth, further exacerbating economic inequalities.[20]

Following its independence in 1964, Zambia found itself in a challenging predicament. The economic structures established during colonial rule persisted, and the nation's heavy reliance on copper exports carried on. While copper can be lucrative during periods of high global demand, the flip side is its susceptibility to volatile global market conditions. This dependency made Zambia's economy particularly sensitive to the ebbs and flows of global copper prices, leading to periods of economic boom and bust.

Such economic unpredictability hinders long-term planning, discourages diverse investments, and can exacerbate social challenges. According to Alastair Fraser's and Miles Larmer's 2010 book, *Zambia, Mining, and Neoliberalism,* this legacy of dependence on a single resource, a direct outcome of British colonial priorities, continues to influence Zambia's economic trajectories.[21]

The Belgian colonisation of the now Democratic Republic of Congo followed a similar pattern. The vast mineral wealth of the DRC, especially its significant cobalt reserves, drew the attention of Belgian colonisers. These resources became a beacon for intensive and often brutal exploitation.

Under the leadership of King Leopold II, and later the Belgian state, the DRC underwent some of the most severe forms of colonial subjugation. Local populations were coerced into labour, often under brutal conditions, to extract the valuable minerals that would enrich Belgium. These activities were marked by both environmental degradation and immense human suffering, with untold numbers of Congolese losing their lives or facing debilitating conditions due to the harsh work environment.

In the postcolonial era, despite gaining independence, the DRC has continued to grapple with the economic structures and imbalances instilled during the Belgian rule. The vast cobalt reserves remain a significant component of the country's economy. However, instead of these resources acting as a boon, they have often been a curse. The profits from the cobalt industry, rather than elevating the general populace, have disproportionately flowed to multinational corporations, which have continued the extraction and export patterns set during colonial times. Simultaneously, a select group of local elites has reaped significant benefits, thereby perpetuating economic disparities within the nation. Severine

Autesserre's 2012 study underscores this point, highlighting how a nation so rich in resources continues to witness vast sections of its population living in poverty, largely due to the legacies of its colonial past and the continued dominance of external actors in its resource sectors.[22]

Both examples of Zambia and the DRC highlight the lasting impact of colonial economic policies on African development. They underscore the need for economic diversification, domestic industrial development, and more equitable profit distribution as key strategies for breaking the cycle of economic dependency and underdevelopment in postcolonial African nations.

Colonial rule in Africa also had a profound and long-lasting social impact. The colonisers often imposed their own languages, educational systems, religious beliefs, and cultural norms on the societies they governed. The imposition of foreign languages, for example, was not merely a tool of communication but also served as a medium for the propagation of the coloniser's culture, worldview, and values. This linguistic domination often led to the marginalisation of indigenous languages. As Ngũgĩ wa Thiong'o discusses in *Decolonising the Mind*, the result was a disconnection of many Africans from their native languages and, by extension, their cultural heritage.[23]

The imposed education systems also served as an important tool for cultural indoctrination. They were often designed to promote the cultural superiority of the colonisers and relegate African cultures and knowledge systems to a position of inferiority. In many instances, these systems of education failed to reflect the local context and history, thereby creating a form of cultural alienation.

I'm reminded of someone telling me of one African leader who once declared, "Picture a Frenchman, a Spaniard, a Portuguese, a

Chinese, a Russian – someone from any corner of the world outside Africa. When they stumble in their English in an English-speaking country, we, Africans, nod in understanding. We extend our respect, acknowledging the linguistic challenges that come with cross-cultural communication.

"Now, cast your eyes upon an African man or woman wrestling with English words. Suddenly, we lose our empathy. We scorn our own. We brand them as a laughing-stock, illiterate, intellectually deficient. It's as though our ability to speak English has become the litmus test of our intelligence – a tool not just for communication, but also for measuring one's worth.

"The tragedy isn't confined to adults. We use this same yardstick on our children, instilling in them the notion that fluency in English – an alien language to their ancestral roots – is synonymous with intelligence.

"This is the scale of the psychological scar we bear as a people! We have unwittingly submitted to the chains of linguistic imperialism. We belittle our languages, dismiss them as 'vernacular', surrendering the richness of our diverse linguistic heritage. But it's time we broke free from this mental servitude.

Let's return dignity to our languages. Let's teach our children their mother tongue. Let's encourage everyone to speak their native language free from prejudice or shame. It's high time we stopped serving as the unwitting accomplices in our own oppression."

Specifically, the African leader's discussion of the psychological and cultural impacts of colonialism on African societies highlights a form of cultural imperialism, where the colonial language (in this case, English) is valued above indigenous languages, leading to a certain level of internalised racism or cultural self-deprecation.

Colonialism was not just about economic exploitation and political control; it was also about cultural domination. The colonisers often aimed to replace or subjugate the local cultures and languages with their own. This was a method to consolidate power and maintain control over the colonised peoples.

The call to action from the African leader under discussion is for Africans to reclaim their indigenous languages and to stop using proficiency in a colonial language as a yardstick for measuring intelligence. This is seen as an essential step towards reversing the psychological damage caused by colonialism and fostering cultural pride and self-esteem among Africans. This change would also promote linguistic diversity and the survival of local languages, many of which are endangered.

Colonial rule didn't merely extract resources; it fundamentally transformed the very fabric of the societies it dominated. By introducing Western systems of governance and administration, colonial powers often inadvertently (or intentionally) destabilised existing societal norms and structures that had evolved over centuries, if not millennia.

Traditional leadership structures, which were typically rooted in indigenous cultural practices, rituals, and beliefs, were frequently supplanted by bureaucratic systems that favoured European methods and ethos. This imposition often led to power vacuums as native leaders and institutions found themselves either marginalised or replaced. As a result, internal conflicts, as communities grappled with these new power dynamics, became a common occurrence, laying the groundwork for future political instability in many postcolonial states.

Overall, while colonial rule formally ended decades ago, its economic and social impacts continue to reverberate across Africa, shaping the continent's development trajectory and the challenges it faces today. For instance, France's relationship with its former colonies, especially those in Africa, remains intertwined through a complex matrix of historical, political, economic, and cultural ties, often referred to as 'Françafrique'.

As you may know, historically, from the late-19th to the mid-20th century, France established colonies across West and Central Africa. During this period, these regions underwent economic exploitation, cultural assimilation policies, and political domination. Unlike some other colonisers, France viewed its colonies as an essential part of the French Republic. This perception led to a deeply ingrained relationship that continued even after these territories achieved independence in the 1960s following waves of nationalist movements spurred by the end of World War II.

The term 'Françafrique' encapsulates these enduring ties. Politically, France has maintained a close relationship with its former colonies, sometimes supporting leaders or regimes that were seen as authoritarian or corrupt in the name of stability or to safeguard French interests. Over the years, there have been several allegations of France's involvement in coups, elections, and other internal affairs in these countries.

Economically, the relationship has been exemplified by the CFA Franc. The acronym CFA stands for Communauté Financière Africaine or African Financial Community. The CFA Franc, a currency established in the 1940s, is used by several former French colonies in West and Central Africa. It's divided into the West African CFA Franc and the Central African CFA Franc. The currency is pegged to the Euro (formerly the French Franc) to ensure monetary stability. Additionally, these African nations must deposit 50 percent of their foreign reserves in the French treasury, with France guaranteeing the CFA Franc's convertibility to the

Euro.

There are many other detractors who agree that the CFA Franc is a symbol of continued neo-colonial influence by France over its former colonies. The debate over the CFA Franc, its benefits, and its drawbacks reflect broader conversations about the nature of postcolonial relationships between African nations and their former European colonisers. As Africa charts its course in the 21st century, discussions around instruments like the CFA Franc highlight the complexities of navigating historical ties while forging new economic and political paths.

Furthermore, France's military presence is palpable in many of its former colonies, whether to protect its nationals, economic interests, or at the behest of African states facing internal issues. France has been deeply involved in the security landscape of its former African colonies, notably through military interventions in Mali, Chad, and the Central African Republic.

In Mali, France launched Operation Serval in 2013 to assist the government in combating Islamist militants and later expanded this to Operation Barkhane, a broader counterterrorism effort involving several Sahel countries. While the operation has had some success, it has also been criticised for potential human rights abuses and concerns that it may inadvertently fuel extremism.

In Chad, France's military intervention in 2019 helped thwart a potential coup against President Idriss Déby, showcasing the country's commitment to preserving its interests and alliances in the region. Critics argue, however, that such support may prop up authoritarian regimes at the expense of democracy and human rights.

Finally, in the Central African Republic, France launched Operation Sangaris in 2013 under a UN mandate to curb escalating violence. Although the operation ended in 2016, France continues to play a significant role in diplomatic efforts and peacekeeping missions in the country.

On the cultural front, the influence of the French language and culture looms large in many of these countries. French education systems continue to have a significant impact, and many students from these countries pursue their higher education in France.

Lastly, like many former colonial powers, France's perceived failure to fully acknowledge or redress past wrongs during the colonial era remains a sticking point.

I was listening to a speech addressed to France's President Macron by a young Kenyan media personality, Adelle Onyango, at the New Africa-France Summit held in Montpellier on 8 October 2021. The aim of this event was to address new challenges and arrive at a new perspective on the relationship between Africa and France to offer new generations a new framework for reflection and action.

Throughout her speech, Adelle maintained a tone that was assertive yet respectful. While she addressed sensitive issues, she did so in a manner that invited dialogue rather than confrontation, which is the approach required when you're looking for solutions. Adelle began by humorously highlighting her limited knowledge of the French language before delving into the crux of her speech – the complex relationship between Africa and France. She emphasised the need to critically examine this relationship by addressing three main questions concerning its efficiency, ethics, and integrity gaps.

Adelle's speech focused on the lingering impacts of colonisation on Africa. Central to her address was the enduring impact of colonisation on Africa. She stressed how the effects of colonisation, both economic and personal, continue to resonate with Africans daily. She particularly emphasised the need for acknowledgement of the wrongs done to Africans by the colonisers and the trust building that needs to occur between former colonisers like France and African nations. She highlighted the emotional and economic scars still felt by Africans and pointed out the contradictions between France's professed values and its actions in Africa. She further underscored the imbalanced nature of the current relationship, which, in her view, lacked genuine collaboration and, at times, appeared exploitative. Adelle criticised initiatives that were designed without input from relevant African organisations, stressing the potential value such entities bring to solution-driven endeavours. However, the speech was not just about highlighting challenges. Adelle emphasised that solutions existed. To foster a more equitable relationship, she suggested several steps, including open dialogue about the painful past, genuine acknowledgement of wrongdoings, and consistent actions that align with stated values. Additionally, Adelle stressed the importance of mutual respect, inclusive development involving local organisations, and education that provided a balanced historical perspective. Her speech serves as a significant call to action, urging the need for both understanding and tangible steps towards a more equitable and respectful relationship between Africa and its former colonisers.

In the context of colonialism and slavery, it is crucial that Africa is able to define its own path to development. This involves not only drawing lessons from other countries but also addressing the structural imbalances and injustices caused by colonialism and slavery. This may involve efforts such as land reform, transitional justice, and reduction of inequality. The challenge and opportunity for Africa is to take the lessons of the past and use them to build a future that is equitable, sustainable, and prosperous.

We all know that the African continent, rich with diversity and potential, has been shackled by a tumultuous history fraught with colonial exploitation, political strife, and economic injustices. However, as Nelson Mandela, pointedly observed, "As I walked out the door toward the gate that would lead to my freedom, I knew if I didn't leave my bitterness and hatred behind, I'd still be in prison."[24] This quote serves as a poignant reminder of the psychological chains that can bind individuals and nations, stifling growth and development.

For Africa, the journey to sustained economic development and prosperity begins with the mind. By choosing to step out of the shadow of a bitter past, Africa can redefine its narrative. The decolonisation of the mind is an important step towards realising Africa's potential.

We should remember that Africa's path to liberation from its historical chains and sustained economic prosperity is multifaceted. It requires psychological emancipation, investment in education, economic inclusivity, good governance, and embracing technological innovation. As the continent moves forward, it must carry Mandela's wisdom in its heart – to let go of bitterness and hatred, for the greatest prison is indeed in our minds.

In Chapter 3, we will look at Africa's immense valuable collection of natural resources. We will explore Africa's resources, from the vast stretches of fertile land to the mineral-laden subsoils and the untapped renewable energy potential. We will then look at how Africa can utilise these vast resources to spur exponential growth and development if appropriately harnessed.

CHAPTER 3

AFRICA'S NATURAL RESOURCES AND ECONOMIC POTENTIAL

Africa, often dubbed the 'sleeping giant', holds an immense and valuable collection of natural resources waiting to be unlocked and utilised optimally.

Land of Endless Potential

Africa, known for its diverse cultures and awe-inspiring land-scapes, is also the cradle to an incredible 65 percent of the world's uncultivated arable land.[1] This staggering statistic holds the prom-ise of a brighter, greener future, a transformative journey from bar-ren lands to bountiful harvests.

Imagine the vast, sun-soaked expanses of Africa as a canvas yet to be painted. As the first rays of dawn sweep across the Zambian plains, they illuminate fields of golden grain, undulating in the morning breeze. The valleys of South Africa, brimming with rich, fertile soils, hold within their depths the potential for verdant growth, promising abundant harvests of maize, grapes, and rooibos tea. When awakened from its slumber, the arable expanse of the Democratic Republic of Congo can transform into an agricultural powerhouse, feeding not just its people but also a significant portion of the world.

But the story of Africa's agricultural potential doesn't end with mere images of flourishing farmlands. Agriculture is not just about food production; it represents the opportunity for economic growth and the promise of livelihoods for millions of African men and women.

Consider the story of Rwanda, a small landlocked country known as the 'land of a thousand hills'. Despite its tumultuous past and limited geographic size, Rwanda has made exceptional strides in its agricultural sector. Rwanda's agricultural success story bears witness to what can be achieved with the right policies, investments, and commitment to change. With a predominantly agrarian economy, the importance of agriculture to Rwanda's development cannot be overstated. It not only provides livelihoods for a significant proportion of the population but also holds the key to the nation's food security.[2]

The Crop Intensification Programme (CIP) introduced in 2007 has been a key driver in transforming Rwanda's agricultural sector. The initiative encouraged farmers to use improved seeds and fertilisers, along with modern farming techniques, to increase their productivity. It also promoted the cultivation of specific crops on a large scale in areas where they would grow best, leading to increased yields and profits for farmers.[3]

Under this programme, Rwanda's crop yields have seen a significant increase. For instance, maize yields increased from less than 1 ton per hectare to over 5 tons per hectare in some areas. Such improvements in productivity have not only boosted food security but also increased farmers' incomes, lifting many out of poverty.

Further aiding this transformation is the government's emphasis on investing in rural infrastructure, such as irrigation and post-harvest facilities, and promoting cooperatives, which have allowed farmers to pool resources, share knowledge, and access credit and markets more easily.

Furthermore, the Rwandan government has also focused on diversifying its agricultural sector by promoting non-traditional, high-value crops and investing in value addition. This diversification has opened up new markets and created opportunities for employment in the agro-processing sector.

A crucial aspect of Rwanda's agricultural transformation has been its focus on sustainability. The government has integrated climate-smart agricultural practices into its policies, recognising the need to adapt to and mitigate the effects of climate change. Practices such as terracing, agroforestry, and the use of organic fertilisers are being promoted to ensure long-term sustainability.

Rwanda's agricultural transformation demonstrates that, with the right strategies, countries can overcome even the most significant challenges. Through its focused agricultural policies, Rwanda has managed to significantly increase its agricultural productivity, improve food security, and raise farmers' incomes, setting a promising precedent for other African nations.

Africa's agricultural potential, though vast, remains untapped.

With the right policies, investments, and focus on sustainable practices, this potential can be harnessed to alleviate poverty, create jobs, drive economic growth, and ensure food security for millions. The promise of Africa's agricultural revolution is not just a story of economic transformation but a testament to the resilience and tenacity of its people.

Powering the Future

Africa's energy potential is another noteworthy asset. A symphony of power awaits discovery and harmonious coordination across the African continent. The African landscape is a dynamic fabric composed of windswept coasts, gushing rivers, the scorching Sahara, and vast reserves of oil and gas. Like a sleeping giant, it holds enormous potential for energy, especially renewable energy.

Imagine the relentless sun that graces the Sahara, the world's largest hot desert. If efficiently harnessed, the radiant energy could be a game changer. Morocco is a shining example of a nation riding the wave of this potential. They've constructed the world's largest concentrated solar farm, the Noor Complex. This gargantuan testament to ingenuity doesn't merely stand as a monument in the desert; it powers over a million homes, a beacon of solar power that lights up the night.

As one travels further south, the dramatic East African coasts unveil themselves, their winds singing songs of untapped potential. Wind turbines could stand tall and proud along these coasts, transforming gusts of wind into power, much like the Lake Turkana Wind Power project in Kenya, the largest of its kind in Africa.

Venturing into the heart of Africa, the Congo Basin's might is evident in its thunderous rivers. If utilised effectively, these waters could propel hydro-electric projects, providing a steady, renewable power source, reminiscent of the Grand Inga Dam, a proposed hydro-electric dam on the Congo River, expected to power millions of homes across Africa.

The ground beneath Africa also hides wealth, with significant oil and gas reserves in countries like Nigeria, Algeria, and Angola. However, the challenge is to manage these reserves sustainably and equitably, transitioning towards cleaner energy sources over time.

Unleashing Africa's full energy potential isn't just about harnessing the power of the elements. It will require robust infrastructure, investment in technology, and upskilling local workforces. The rhapsody of Africa's energy potential is composed of many notes, and only with careful orchestration can Africa strike the perfect chord for sustained economic development. I will expand more on the issue of power infrastructure in Chapter 7.

Treasure House Beneath the Soil

Dig a little deeper, and you'll find Africa's subsoil glistening with valuable minerals. The continent is world-renowned for its gold, diamonds, and rare earth metals. Take a journey with me, and let's look at the top ten African countries wealthiest in minerals:

1. **Niger Republic:** Labelled the 'land of uranium', Niger Republic is an interesting place to start. A landlocked country nestled in the heart of West Africa, Niger stands as a beacon for its immense uranium deposits. Despite its challenging desert environment and relatively sparse rainfall, it holds significant reserves of valuable natural resources. The country is globally recognised for its abundant uranium deposits.

Uranium mining in Niger started in the 1970s, following the discovery of sizeable reserves. These deposits are mainly located in the north-western part of the country, in areas such as Arlit and Akouta. The uranium mined from these areas powers nuclear reactors worldwide, making Niger one of the top uranium producers globally. In fact, according to the World Nuclear Association, Niger accounts for up to 5 percent of the world's total uranium production.[4] But the story of Niger's natural resources does not end with uranium. Beneath its soil, the country also has considerable reserves of coal, limestone, and gold. Coal mining has not been extensively developed, but the proven reserves offer potential for future exploitation. Gold mining, on the other hand, has become a vital part of Niger's economy, with artisanal gold mining in particular providing an important source of income for many Nigeriens. Gold deposits are mostly located in the western and southern parts of the country.

Furthermore, Niger has an extensive cement industry, spurred by the discovery of limestone deposits, which are a primary ingredient in cement production. Cement manufacturing has the potential to support infrastructure development within the country and also serves as an important export.

2. **Namibia:** Namibia, often referred to as the 'gem of Africa', is indeed a powerhouse of natural resources. Situated in south-western Africa, it is the world's third largest producer of uranium, with its mining industry forming the backbone of the country's economy.[5]

The uranium deposits in Namibia are found predominantly in the Namib Desert, an ancient geological feature of the country. The nation's largest uranium mine, the Rössing mine, has been in operation since the 1970s and is one of the longest-running and largest open pit uranium mines in the world. In recent years, the Husab mine, owned by the China General Nuclear Power Company, has also started production, which has significantly increased Namibia's uranium output.

Uranium mining plays a vital role in Namibia's economy. It generates substantial export earnings, provides jobs, and has led to the development of infrastructure, such as roads, power lines, and towns. The government has also implemented policies to ensure that a portion of the earnings from uranium mining goes back to the communities affected by mining operations.

But uranium is not the only jewel in Namibia's crown. The country's rich mineral resources also include diamonds, zinc, lead, sulphur, salt, tantalite, and copper. The mining of these resources has also contributed significantly to Namibia's economy. The diamond industry, in particular, is a major contributor to the country's GDP and export earnings. Namibia's diamond deposits are mostly offshore, making it one of the leading countries in marine diamond mining.

3. **Democratic Republic of Congo:** Journeying to the heart of the continent, we find the Democratic Republic of Congo. The DRC is a country of immense natural wealth. The vast and diverse landscapes, ranging from dense rainforests to

active volcanoes, give a hint of the country's geological riches hidden beneath.

The DRC's mineral sector is among the most prolific globally, with its subsoil overflowing with an assortment of minerals, such as copper, coltan (used in electronics), cobalt (crucial in electric vehicle batteries), diamonds, gold, and tin. Additionally, the country also has a burgeoning oil production industry. According to the Extractive Industries Transparency Initiative, these resources potentially make the DRC one of the wealthiest countries on the planet 'on paper'.[6]

Copper and cobalt mining form the backbone of the DRC's economy, with the south-eastern Katanga region being the main producer. The DRC reportedly contains half of the world's cobalt reserves and is the world's largest cobalt producer. This positions the DRC strategically in the global economy, particularly considering the increasing demand for batteries in electric vehicles and renewable energy storage.

Meanwhile, the eastern regions of the DRC, particularly the provinces of Kivu and Orientale, are rich in gold and coltan. The latter mineral has seen surging demand with the rise of the digital era, as it is an essential component of capacitors used in electronic devices.

4. **Zambia**: Crossing the border from the DRC into Zambia, we find the beating heart of Africa's copper industry. Situated in the southern part of Africa, Zambia is richly endowed with mineral resources, particularly copper, which has been instrumental in shaping its economic and social landscape.

The country's Copperbelt and North Western provinces, stretching across the north of the country, are one of the world's most significant copper-producing regions, contributing an impressive 70 percent of Africa's total copper production.[7]

Zambia's prowess in copper mining is rooted in its history. With commercial mining dating back to the 1920s, the copper industry has become deeply entwined in Zambia's economy, politics, and society. Copper isn't the only valuable mineral found in Zambia's generous geology. The nation is also globally known for its high-quality emeralds and sizeable cobalt reserves.

The emerald mines of Zambia, particularly the Kagem Emerald Mine – the single largest emerald mine in the world – are famed for producing beautiful, high-quality stones with a distinctive deep green hue. These emeralds, sought after by gemstone connoisseurs worldwide, add an extra dimension to Zambia's mineral wealth, contributing to its export earnings and providing employment opportunities to local communities.

In recent years, the global demand for cobalt has risen. Zambia, with its abundant cobalt reserves, mostly found in association with copper ores on the Copperbelt, stands to gain from this burgeoning demand.

5. **South Africa**: Moving south to the tip of the continent, South Africa's mineral wealth lies shimmering in its veins. South Africa is blessed with an abundance of mineral resources, contributing significantly to its economy and establishing it as a key player in the global mining industry.

The country's rich mineral endowment was instrumental in shaping its historical and economic trajectory. The discovery of diamond in Kimberley in 1867 and the subsequent gold rush in the Witwatersrand Basin in 1886 led to a surge in the country's economy, prompting the establishment of mining towns and infrastructure networks and leading to an influx of migrant workers and settlers.

Gold mining, in particular, has been central to South Africa's economic development. Despite dwindling reserves, the gold industry remains a vital part of the country's economy, contributing to its gross domestic product and providing employment opportunities.

In addition to gold, South Africa is also the world's largest producer of platinum, and it holds significant reserves of other minerals, including copper, uranium, vanadium, coal, chromium, iron, zirconium, and nickel. The platinum industry, in particular, is important both for its economic value and its role in reducing air pollution through its use in catalytic converters. The extraction of these minerals forms a critical part of the country's industrial landscape, with the mining sector being a major employer and a significant contributor to the country's export revenue.

6. **Mozambique:** Crossing the border from South Africa, our voyage continues to Mozambique, a nation primarily known for its aluminium production. Located on the south-eastern coast of Africa, Mozambique is a land brimming with abundant mineral resources that hold immense economic potential. In recent years, the country has emerged as one of the world's significant producers of aluminium, primarily due

to the presence of the Mozal smelter, one of Africa's largest aluminium smelters, which has significantly contributed to the nation's GDP.[8]

However, the vast mineral wealth of Mozambique goes far beyond aluminium. The country is endowed with a diverse range of mineral resources, some of which remain largely untapped. Beryllium and tantalum, for instance, are two critical minerals found in Mozambique. Beryllium is used in the production of high-speed aircraft, missiles, spacecraft, and communication satellites because of its light weight and ability to withstand high temperatures. Tantalum, on the other hand, is a key component in the electronics industry, particularly in the manufacturing of capacitors for mobile phones, computers, and automotive electronics.

Additionally, Mozambique has substantial reserves of limestone and marble. These minerals play a crucial role in the construction industry, with limestone used for making cement and marble serving as an essential material for flooring, countertops, and sculptures.

Further enhancing its mineral repertoire, Mozambique is also home to gemstones like tourmaline, aquamarine, morganite, and various types of garnet and topaz. These precious and semiprecious stones significantly contribute to the country's export revenues.

Coal resources in Mozambique, particularly in the Tete province, are among the world's largest. The extracted coal is primarily used for power generation and steel production.

Furthermore, the discovery of significant offshore natural gas fields in the Rovuma Basin has opened up new prospects for Mozambique. With the right investment and infrastructure, the oil and gas sector could potentially transform the country's economy, positioning it as a leading global LNG (liquefied natural gas) exporter.[9]

7. **Guinea:** Let's sail to West Africa. Situated on the west coast of Africa, Guinea, the 'bauxite powerhouse', is home to the world's largest reserves of bauxite, a sedimentary rock that is the main source of aluminium. Aluminium is used in a vast array of products, from cars and planes to packaging and household items, making it a crucial global commodity.

Guinea has made the most of this natural endowment. The country's mining industry is dominated by bauxite extraction, making up 80 percent of Africa's total bauxite production since 1950.[10] This significant output has positioned Guinea as a vital player in the global aluminium industry.

Bauxite mining has been a key driver of economic growth in Guinea. Revenues from bauxite have been used to fund infrastructure projects, education, healthcare, and other social services.

8. **Tanzania:** We fly to East Africa. Tanzania, the East African nation known for its spectacular landscapes, including the highest peak in Africa, Mount Kilimanjaro, is also endowed with immense mineral wealth, making it a key player in the global mining industry. Its geological treasures span a wide range of precious and semiprecious gemstones, industrial minerals, and precious metals, with a significant part of the country's wealth lying beneath its surface.

The crown jewel of Tanzania's mineral resources is

undoubtedly its gold reserves. Tanzania ranks as the fourth largest gold reserve holder in Africa, with gold mining contributing a substantial portion to the country's GDP and export revenues.[11] Major gold mining companies operate in the country, capitalising on the substantial deposits found primarily in the greenstone belt around Lake Victoria.

Equally significant is the presence of tanzanite, a deep blue-violet gemstone that is found almost exclusively in the foothills of Mount Kilimanjaro. This rare gemstone's scarcity, combined with its captivating colour, makes it a highly sought after commodity in global jewellery markets. The tanzanite mines of Tanzania offer a significant source of employment and have an important role in the country's economy.

Additionally, Tanzania's mineral wealth extends to diamonds, silver, and a host of other minerals, contributing to the country's economic growth and providing employment opportunities. The diamond deposits located in the Williamson Diamonds Mine have been a significant source of gem-quality diamonds for the global market.

9. **Ghana:** We take a drive to West Africa. Ghana's former name, the Gold Coast, is a testament to its rich gold reserves. Gold mining has been part of Ghana's story for centuries. Even today, it's a major contributor to the country's economy. Ghana is the largest gold producer in Africa and the seventh largest in the world. Large-scale mining operations coexist with small-scale or artisanal gold mining, which, while economically important, poses environmental and safety challenges.[12]

However, Ghana's geological wealth is not limited to gold. The country has substantial deposits of other minerals that play a significant role in its economy. Ghana has one of the world's largest bauxite reserves. The government has established the Ghana Integrated Aluminium Development Corporation to develop and promote this resource.

Ghana's diamond deposits, mainly in the Birim and Tarkwa regions, have also been commercially exploited. Although not as significant as gold, diamond mining has contributed to the local economies of these areas.

Furthermore, manganese mining is crucial for the steel industry, as manganese is an essential ingredient in steel production. Ghana's manganese reserves are primarily located in the western region in the city of Tarkwa, making it one of the top manganese producers globally.

The country's geological wealth extends to crude oil as well. After oil was discovered in commercial quantities in 2007, production has rapidly become a critical part of Ghana's economy. The Tano Basin, particularly the offshore Tano fields, has been the focus of oil exploration and production.

10. **Botswana:** We jet back to Southern Africa. Botswana is the crown jewel of the diamond industry. Renowned for its diamond resources, it sparkles on the global stage as one of the world's largest diamond producers. Botswana stands out as a beacon of economic stability and growth in the African continent, primarily due to its judicious management of its rich mineral resources. With approximately one-third of the world's gem-quality diamonds extracted from its mines,

Botswana has used its diamond wealth to transform from one of the poorest countries in the world at the time of its independence in 1966 to one of the fastest-growing economies globally.[13]

While diamonds have been the linchpin of Botswana's economy, the country also possesses significant deposits of other minerals like copper, coal, soda ash, and nickel. The government has sought to leverage these resources to further diversify its economy, particularly through the development of value-added industries related to mining.

In countries like Nigeria, Angola, and Algeria, oil and gas reserves have been central to their economic development. Nigeria, for instance, is the largest oil producer in Africa and the 11th largest globally, with petroleum accounting for more than 90 percent of its export revenue.[14]

Angola is the second largest oil producer in Africa, with oil constituting over 90 percent of its exports. Meanwhile, Algeria, the largest country in Africa, has the third largest oil reserve on the continent and is the ninth largest exporter of natural gas in the world. The revenue from these resources has played a pivotal role in Algeria's economy, supporting its social welfare programmes and infrastructure development.

In addition, the coastal and marine resources in Africa present another avenue for economic development. For instance, Namibia and South Africa have highly productive fishing industries that contribute significantly to their economies. Namibia's fishing industry, largely based on hake, horse mackerel, and pilchard, provides employment, promotes food security, and is a key contributor to GDP.

South Africa, with its extensive coastline, also boasts a diversified marine economy. Its commercial fishing industry, which includes species such as sardines, hake, and lobster, contributes significantly to the country's exports. South Africa is also exploring the potential of aquaculture for economic growth and job creation.

Overall, these African nations provide a snapshot of the continent's extensive mineral wealth. This wealth, if managed responsibly and sustainably, has the potential to drive economic development and improve the living standards of Africa's populations. These nations can learn from countries like Botswana and Namibia, which have been recognised for their successful resource management, translating mineral wealth into broad-based economic growth.

The story of Africa's mineral wealth is a complex one, marked by immense potential but also significant challenges. To realise this potential fully, our African countries will need to invest in human capital, improve governance and accountability, and ensure that the benefits of mining are shared equitably among Africa's people. This is the path to transforming mineral wealth into real wealth – a better life for all Africans.

In Chapter 4, we will look at the bulging youthful population Africa is experiencing and the potential it has to transform the continent's future. Africa, with a striking 60 percent of its population under the age of 25, is indisputably the youngest continent on Earth.[15] This youth bulge represents a potentially transformative force that could shape the continent's trajectory in the decades to come.

CHAPTER 4

AFRICA'S YOUTH DEMOGRAPHIC AND THE CHALLENGE OF YOUTH UNEMPLOYMENT

In the previous chapter, I touched on Africa's abundant natural resources. Africa has a second advantage: the continent is experiencing a unique demographic shift that has potential to transform the continent's future.

Current Demographic Trend of Africa's Young Population

Africa's burgeoning youth population, set against the backdrop of its rich cultures, traditions, and abundant natural resources, presents a fascinating confluence of opportunities that could significantly elevate the continent's status on the global stage. The continent's demographic profile, marked by the prominent 'youth bulge', is poised to be its defining feature in the forthcoming decades. But when juxtaposed with Africa's natural wealth, this combination becomes a compelling engine for potential growth, transformation, and ascendancy.[1]

To begin with, the sheer dynamism of a young population is synonymous with innovation and adaptability. A youthful populace is more likely to embrace new technologies, adapt to global trends, and pioneer breakthroughs in various fields. This innovative drive can be directed towards optimising and refining the extraction and utilisation of Africa's vast natural resources, such as minerals, oil, and agricultural lands. Harnessing modern technologies and sustainable practices could lead to a more efficient and ecologically responsible exploitation of these resources.

Furthermore, the interconnectedness of today's world economy implies that Africa's youth, if equipped with the right skills and knowledge, can attract global investments. International stakeholders recognise the value of combining a young, trainable workforce with rich natural resources. Investment not just in extraction but also in refining, processing, and adding value to raw materials within the continent itself could drive industrial growth, thereby multiplying job opportunities and boosting economic activity.

However, the interplay between youth and resources is not just about extraction and industry. The youth's perspective on sustainability, conservation, and ethical utilisation of resources is crucial. Younger generations globally are becoming increasingly conscious of the environment, ethical sourcing, and the long-term impact of today's decisions. Africa's youth, with their intrinsic connection to the continent's natural beauty and wealth, could champion sustainable models of growth, ensuring that the exploration of natural resources doesn't come at the expense of the environment or future generations.

Moreover, the intertwining narratives of youth and resources can shape Africa's cultural and soft power. Stories of young entrepreneurs using local resources to craft global brands, artists drawing inspiration from Africa's natural beauty, or tech innovators leveraging the continent's materials to develop new products can enhance Africa's image, showcasing it as a hub of innovation, tradition, and opportunity.

However, the demographic trend of Africa's expanding youth population is a two-edged sword, holding the power to reshape the continent's future in myriad ways. With projections indicating that, by 2030, Africa will be home to the world's largest young workforce, surpassing even population giants like the Chinese and Indian subcontinents, the implications are both profound and multifaceted.

At the heart of this massive demographic shift is a vibrant and energetic generation, eager to make their mark on the world. With the right nurturing, this demographic dividend can catalyse transformative change, driving innovation, entrepreneurship, and economic growth. Yet, alongside these optimistic possibilities lies a set of formidable challenges. Without proper education, training, and opportunities, this young population might face unemployment, underemployment, and disenfranchisement. A vast, young workforce without adequate avenues to apply their skills and passion could lead to widespread dissatisfaction, social unrest, and even political instability. It underscores the importance of holistic and forward-thinking policies that not only aim at immediate employment but also foster an environment of continuous learning, innovation, and engagement.

Furthermore, as Africa's youths shape the continent's social fabric, the values, beliefs, and aspirations they carry with them will define the continent's cultural and moral compass. The narratives they construct, the stories they tell, and the legacies they wish to leave behind will be instrumental in dictating Africa's position on the global stage. This isn't just about economic prosperity or political power – it's also about how Africa sees itself and how the world perceives Africa in return.

Imagine the sheer magnitude of this human capital. Think about millions of youthful, vibrant, innovative, and driven individuals eager to make a difference in our world. This wave of human potential could be the engine that powers Africa's development in the 21st century, driving innovation, growth, and societal transformation.

The demographic dividend, as economists term it, is the economic growth potential that can arise when the share of the working-age population (15 to 64) is larger than the non-working-age share of the population (14 and younger, and 65 and older). Although this concept appears straightforward, translating it into tangible prosperity is a complex process that requires strategic planning, careful investment, and the creation of appropriate policy frameworks. In essence, these young individuals must be moulded into a productive workforce that can catapult Africa into an era of unprecedented economic prosperity.

To harness this demographic dividend, Africa's strategy must revolve around three critical cornerstones: education, health, and job creation.

Let's embark on a journey to explore this exciting potential. The narrative of progress within Africa starts with the transformative power of education. Take Rwanda, for instance. The vibrant nation of Rwanda stands as a beacon of progress in this regard. Despite the gruesome shadows of its past, as we saw in Chapter 2, the nation is blooming into a symbol of educational progress. With an awe-inspiring commitment to knowledge, it achieved a remarkable feat with a primary school enrolment rate reaching 98 percent.[2] This level of commitment is shaping the country's future, fostering a generation of dreamers, innovators, and global competitors.

Rwanda's remarkable commitment to growth and development has made headlines, but it is not the sole African nation demonstrating an unwavering belief in the transformative potential of education. Take Botswana, for example, a nation that has strategically positioned education at the forefront of its national agenda. By earmarking an impressive 20 percent of its annual budget for educational pursuits, Botswana sends a clear message about its priorities.[3] Such a significant financial commitment is both a reflection of the nation's understanding of the role of education in sustainable development and proof of its long-term vision.

The fruits of this investment are palpable. Boasting a literacy rate exceeding 88 percent places Botswana among the top-ranking African countries in this metric.[4] But beyond just numbers, this high literacy rate heralds a multitude of advantages for the nation. Literacy, often seen as the cornerstone of personal empowerment, paves the way for a populace that is better informed, more critical in its thinking, and equipped with the foundational skills needed to further its education and training. This, in turn, elevates the quality of the workforce, making it more competitive both regionally and globally.

Furthermore, Botswana's dedication to education can attract

foreign investment and partnerships. Multinational companies and institutions are often on the lookout for regions with a skilled and educated workforce, conducive to setting up operations that require specialised skills. Thus, Botswana's educational commitment not only serves its immediate population but also positions the country as an attractive destination for global collaborations and ventures.

Parallel to the importance of education is the essential aspect of health. Youthful vigour and wellbeing fuel the nation's progress. Ghana, in this context, has been making strides in promoting the health of its youth. The National Health Insurance Scheme (NHIS) in Ghana, a trailblazer in the region, has expanded healthcare access significantly, ensuring its younger generations remain robust and ready to propel the nation forward. The NHIS gets most of its funds from the National Health Insurance Levy, which is a 2.5 percent charge on goods and services included in the value added tax.[5] Started in 2004, the NHIS now uses this levy, along with other contributions, to finance healthcare in Ghana. By 2018, about 36 percent of Ghanaians were covered by it.[6] Thanks to this programme, more people in Ghana, especially the youth, have access to healthcare, helping them stay healthy and contribute to the country's progress.

Ghana's pursuit of universal health coverage is mirrored by Rwanda, which, through its successful community-based health insurance system, has managed to cover almost 90 percent of its population.[7] This remarkable achievement has resulted in improved health outcomes, paving the way for a stronger, healthier Rwanda. Rwanda's community-based health insurance system stands as a beacon of what is achievable when a nation commits to prioritising the health of its people. Initiated as a response to the country's pressing health challenges, the system is rooted in the principle of inclusivity, aiming to bridge the gap between the urban elite and rural populations.

Central to the system's success is its grassroots approach. By embedding the health insurance at the community level, Rwanda has tapped into the power of local structures and networks. This not only ensures wide coverage but also fosters a sense of owner-ship among communities. Residents are more likely to invest in a system they see as their own and one that directly caters to their specific needs.

To make the programme financially accessible to all, premiums are set based on a sliding scale tied to an individual's or family's income. This means that while everyone contributes, the system doesn't place an undue burden on the poorest. Furthermore, by pooling resources on a community level, the system can negotiate better prices and services with healthcare providers.[8]

Beyond the financial mechanics, the community-based approach has had ripple effects on the healthcare infrastructure. There's been a noticeable improvement in healthcare delivery, with facili-ties ramping up their services and standards to cater to the insured population. This has led to the rise of a positive feedback loop. As healthcare services improve, more residents see the value in joining the insurance scheme, which in turn injects more funds into the system, leading to further enhancements in service delivery and a healthy youth population.

Last, but by no means least, comes the critical challenge of job creation. Kenya, often referred to as the 'Silicon Savannah', is a shining example of the power of strategic investments in the right sectors. This technological hub is not just a centre of innovation but also a thriving ecosystem that provides thousands of jobs, fostering youthful inspiration and fuelling national progress.

Similarly, Ethiopia's strategic focus on industrialisation, particularly in textiles and garments, has spurred the creation of industrial parks and, consequently, thousands of jobs. This initiative paves the way for other nations to learn, diversify their economies, and open up avenues for employment.

In a nutshell, the African continent's potential is vast and ripe with possibilities. Countries such as Rwanda, Botswana, Ghana, Kenya, and Ethiopia are leading the way in areas such as education, health, and job creation. Their efforts are not just improving the lives of their citizens but are also providing valuable models that other nations can emulate as they work to unlock their potential and shape a brighter future for Africa.

However, to truly reap the benefits of this demographic dividend, Africa must extend its strategic investments beyond education, health, and job creation. Infrastructure development is a crucial area that can facilitate economic growth. Countries like Morocco have made significant headway here, with large-scale projects such as the Noor Ouarzazate Solar Complex, the world's largest concentrated solar power plant. More detail on this in Chapter 7.

The Scale of Youth Unemployment in Africa

Despite the potential of Africa's young population, the continent faces a high rate of youth unemployment. On average, approximately 26 percent of young Africans 15–24 years old are out of work.[9]

This challenge is exacerbated by the fact that many young people are underemployed or working in the informal sector, which offers limited job security, social protection, and opportunities for skill development. This is partly due to a rapidly growing youth population, limited job opportunities, and a mismatch between education and labour market needs.[10] These issues are complex and interrelated, and they include, as mentioned, a mismatch between the skills obtained through education and the demands of the labour market, limited access to financial resources and credit for young entrepreneurs, and insufficient investment in sectors with high job creation potential, such as agriculture, manufacturing, and renewable energy.

Mismatch between Education and Labour Market Demands

A significant factor contributing to youth unemployment on our continent of Africa is the mismatch between the skills acquired through education and the needs of the labour market.

Imagine this scene – a jubilant, young graduate, dressed in a flowing robe and mortarboard, proudly clutching a degree. The symbolic parchment, an emblem of years of dedication and late-night study sessions, is more than just a certificate. It's a passport to the future, a ticket to the world of work, an assurance of an affluent life ahead. Yet, as they enthusiastically dive into the job market, ready to transform the theoretical knowledge acquired over the years into practical expertise, they hit an invisible but impenetrable wall. Their theoretical learning, as it turns out, doesn't translate neatly to the practical skills that employers are hunting for. This is not a dystopian novel or a grimly spun tale. It's the harsh reality for many young Africans today.

In a significant swath of Africa, the educational structure remains firmly anchored in traditional pedagogical approaches, which focus heavily on theoretical knowledge. Although these methodologies build a robust academic foundation, they often fall short of equipping learners with practical vocational skills, which are critical in the ever-evolving job market. It's akin to relying on a static, grainy, black-and-white photograph to navigate a world that's swiftly transforming into a full-colour, high-resolution video.

The disconnection between theoretical knowledge and practical, employable skills is a significant challenge many parts of Africa face today. In an era marked by the fourth industrial revolution, this gap creates a particularly problematic situation where the fast-paced transformation of the job market far outstrips the ability of traditional educational institutions to adapt.

This rapid technological advancement is revolutionising the way we work, creating roles that were unthinkable just a decade ago. Occupations such as AI specialists, digital health experts, and sustainability managers are rapidly rising in demand. However, the educational institutions, held back by a combination of bureaucratic restrictions and limited resources, find it difficult to keep pace with these changes.

As a result, many graduates, despite being well-versed in theory, find themselves lacking the digital literacy and practical skills the contemporary job market demands. For example, in Nigeria, despite a large number of university graduates, there is a significant shortage of workers equipped with the necessary technical and problem-solving skills.[11]

This reflects a broader issue across the continent – a gap between the skills acquired through education and those needed for employment. It's not a minor hurdle but a substantial chasm that has serious implications for Africa's economic development and the future of its youth.

Confronting this challenge requires a comprehensive, multi-pronged approach:

1. **Educational reforms**: Academic curricula need to evolve to incorporate more practical skills training. This includes integrating digital literacy into core education and offering courses that focus on the applied aspects of learning. Education should not merely be about imparting knowledge but also equipping students with skills that make them job ready.

2. **Improved collaboration**: There needs to be a stronger alliance between educational institutions and industries. By collaborating closely, industries can communicate their requirements to the institutions, which can then tailor their programmes accordingly. Work placements and internships could be encouraged, offering students hands-on experience and an understanding of industry demands.

3. **Investment in technology and infrastructure**: Limited resources should not inhibit educational advancement. Increased investment in technology and infrastructure, particularly in supporting digital education, is crucial. This will not only broaden the scope of learning but also make education more accessible, particularly in remote areas.

4. **Educator training**: Educators should be trained in modern pedagogical approaches, especially those emphasising practical skill development. This will enable them to guide students effectively in an evolving educational landscape.

While the transformation of Africa's education system is a pressing need, if we bridge the gap between academic learning and employment skills, Africa can unlock its immense potential, fuel economic growth, and secure a prosperous future for its youth.

Limited Access to Financial Resources and Credit for Young Entrepreneurs

The dynamic continent of Africa is a powerhouse of creativity and entrepreneurial spirit, an uncharted canvas poised to be filled with the vibrant hues of innovation. Yet, for many young Africans bursting with revolutionary ideas and the enthusiasm to carve out their entrepreneurial paths, actualising their dreams often feels like an unattainable quest. This struggle primarily stems from one major roadblock: access to capital.

The wealth of entrepreneurial visions across the continent is as diverse as the continent itself. From disruptive tech startups to agribusinesses aiming to tackle food security and sustainability, Africa's youth aspire to establish businesses that solve critical societal challenges while generating wealth. However, the gateways to the capital necessary to realise these visions often remain closed, particularly for young entrepreneurs.

Let's imagine a young South African with an innovative business idea. This individual has done the requisite market research, identified a market need, and stands ready to make their entrepreneurial dream a reality. However, this dream faces a significant barrier when the individual approaches a bank for a loan. Deemed a high-risk borrower due to a lack of a substantial track record or collateral, their application is likely to be declined.

But the lack of financial resources is only one part of the problem. Another obstacle confronting many young Africans is a lack of financial literacy. With comprehensive financial education not commonplace in many African nations, our young entrepreneurs often find themselves trying to navigate the complex world of finances without a guide. This absence of knowledge about financial management, investment strategies, and loan applications can compound the challenges faced when attempting to secure capital.

Think about the process of approaching investors for funding. An entrepreneur needs to understand how to pitch their idea, negotiate a deal, and manage investment relations. Without financial literacy, this process can turn into an intimidating maze, further limiting an entrepreneur's chances of securing much-needed funding.

Nonetheless, despite this formidable set of challenges, there are reasons for optimism. Across our continent of Africa, innovative solutions are emerging to overcome these barriers.

Take the fintech sector, for example. These companies have been revolutionary in bridging the financial inclusion gap. Traditional banks often have strict requirements and might be hesitant to lend to young entrepreneurs without a consistent financial history or collateral. However, fintech solutions, such as Kenya's M-PESA, have dramatically transformed this landscape. M-PESA began as a mobile money transfer service and has evolved into a fully-fledged financial ecosystem, enabling users to save, borrow, and even access micro-insurance products. This provides young Kenyan entrepreneurs with the necessary tools to launch and grow their businesses.

Similarly, in Nigeria, platforms like Flutterwave and Paystack are simplifying the process of online payments, enabling a younger generation of digital-savvy entrepreneurs to easily accept payments both domestically and from abroad. This means a young fashion designer in Lagos can now effortlessly sell her designs to a customer in Paris or New York without the complexities that once marred such transactions.

Crowdfunding, too, has been a game changer. Before its advent, sourcing funds for a venture was primarily limited to personal savings, bank loans, or local angel investors. Now, platforms like Afrikstart and Thundafund are democratising access to capital. An entrepreneur in Cape Town with an innovative idea can pitch to thousands across the globe, accessing diverse pools of funds and resources that were once unthinkable. This not only aids in capital generation but also offers young entrepreneurs a chance to gauge global interest in their products or services, helping them refine their offerings accordingly.

These shifts, driven by technology and the globalised nature of today's economy, signal that Africa's youth, despite current challenges, have a plethora of tools at their disposal to carve out a brighter future. Through these innovative platforms, there's a renewed sense of hope and a clear pathway towards tapping into the vast potential that Africa's young population holds.

Moreover, initiatives to enhance financial literacy are gaining momentum across the continent. Several NGOs, governments, and international organisations are implementing programmes focused on equipping young entrepreneurs with essential financial skills. These initiatives, often in the form of workshops, online courses, and mentoring programmes, aim to guide young entrepreneurs through the intricate world of finance, thereby enhancing their prospects of securing capital.

While the road to entrepreneurial success in Africa has its share of obstacles, the continent's potential for innovation and prosperity is enormous. By enabling access to capital and enhancing financial literacy, we can empower Africa's youth to turn their entrepreneurial visions into reality. This could transform the continent's socio-economic landscape, turning the canvas of Africa into a vibrant masterpiece of innovation and prosperity.

Insufficient Investment in High Job Creation Sectors

Lastly, there's often insufficient investment in sectors with high job creation potential, such as agriculture, manufacturing, and renewable energy. Much like the continent's burgeoning young population, these sectors can blossom into powerful pillars of economic growth and employment generation if given the right nurturing environment and sufficient investment.

Agriculture, for instance, is too often perceived solely in the context of subsistence farming. Viewed as a labour-intensive activity at the mercy of environmental conditions, it's commonly associated with minimal sustenance for farming families. This perspective, however, overlooks the vast potential inherent in this sector. With the right amount of investment and innovation, agriculture could metamorphose from a subsistence activity into a vibrant industry, creating massive employment opportunities and fostering sustainable business models.

From using technology to enhance farming techniques to developing efficient food processing and storage methods and promoting value addition activities, the agriculture sector holds tremendous scope for innovation, productivity enhancement, and job creation. Investments in agriculture can also foster increased food security, sustainable use of resources, and resilience to climate change, making it a sector with significant socio-economic and environmental implications.

Next, consider the renewable energy sector, a realm overflowing with untapped potential. Due to a combination of insufficient awareness and inadequate investment, renewable energy's potential to transform Africa's economic landscape is often overlooked. Picture an Africa where the continent's abundant sunshine not only sustains life but powers it. Envision a land filled with solar panels soaking up the radiant African sun and wind turbines rhythmically slicing through the breeze, a beacon of a clean, sustainable future.

Renewable energy is not just a means to power homes and industries; it's also an opportunity to foster a vibrant sector that generates jobs, drives economic growth, and contributes to global carbon reduction efforts. The renewable energy industry requires a wide range of skills and roles – from engineers and technicians for the installation and maintenance of equipment to researchers developing better technologies and entrepreneurs establishing new businesses in the sector. By harnessing Africa's immense renewable energy resources, the continent can make a significant stride towards self-sustaining, environmentally friendly, and job-rich economic growth.

The challenge lies in channelling appropriate investments into these sectors, fostering innovation, improving sectoral skills and knowledge, and creating supportive policy environments. By doing so, the seeds of potential within these sectors can grow into thriving industries, not only creating jobs for Africa's youth but also propelling the continent towards sustainable economic development. The prospect of an Africa where its young population thrives and its economic sectors flourish is not only an inspiring vision but also a realisable future if these opportunities are seized.

In the chapters that follow, I will focus on the key pillars of economic growth that will play a pivotal role in shifting Africa's psyche, cultivating a mindset that fosters creativity, innovation, and prosperity. It's time to nourish the seeds of potential that lie within Africa, let them take root, and witness the continent's transformation into a land of economic opportunity and unprecedented prosperity.

CHAPTER 5

LEADERSHIP ESSENTIAL FOR ECONOMIC DEVELOPMENT

In the first pillar of economic growth, we look at leadership. For our continent of Africa to truly thrive and develop economically, it's vital to have leaders at the helm who deeply value and actively care for the people they lead and promote diversity, unity, and honesty. These leaders play a pivotal role in shaping the trajectory of their nations. When they prioritise creating strong, reliable organisations or nations and implement sound governance, they lay the groundwork for a fairer society where opportunities are widespread. In such an environment, sustainable growth is not just an aspiration but a tangible reality in which the continent realises its vast potential and all citizens benefit.

What Is Leadership?

The late pastor Dr Myles Munroe put it eloquently when he said leadership is a complex and multifaceted series of interconnected elements: purpose, conviction, vision, passion, and inspiration. Let's go deeper into each component.

Purpose

The foundation of effective leadership is purpose. Purpose in leadership refers to a clear and meaningful reason for taking action or making decisions. It's the core guiding principle that drives leaders, fuelling their determination and giving them a sense of direction. A purpose is not a set of goals or objectives; it's a profound understanding of why an organisation exists and what it ultimately seeks to achieve.

Simon Sinek's book *Start with Why* significantly emphasises the power of purpose in leadership. Sinek introduced the concept of the Golden Circle, a model that codifies the three distinct and interdependent elements (why, how, and what) that make any person or organisation function at its best.

In the model, **why** stands for purpose. It's the reason to get out of bed in the morning. It's why an organisation exists, why it does what it does.

How represents the actions taken to realise the why.

What refers to the results of those actions – the products, services, and so on.

Sinek argues that most organisations operate from the outside in; they first explain what they do, then how they do it, but often fail to mention why they do what they do. However, the most successful and influential organisations operate from the inside out; they start with their 'why'.[1]

Conviction

A purpose fuels conviction, which is a firmly held belief or opinion. Conviction in leadership pertains to the deep-seated beliefs and principles that inform a leader's actions and decisions. It's a form of unwavering certainty that comes from knowing not just what you do but why you do it. This conviction often becomes the defining trait of influential leaders, as it instils confidence and inspires trust among their followers.

Albert Mohler, in his book *The Conviction to Lead*, emphasises the critical role conviction plays in leadership. He coins the term 'convictional leadership' to describe leadership driven by firmly held beliefs. According to Mohler, these leaders are different because they're driven by a set of beliefs and principles that dictate their actions, decisions, and the way they influence others. Their convictions form the foundation upon which their leadership is built, and their followers find their certainty and consistency inspiring.[2]

Today, convictional leadership is considered essential for successful leaders across all sectors. These leaders stand firm in their beliefs even when faced with challenges or resistance, motivating others with their unwavering commitment to their purpose. They display courage in making difficult decisions, taking risks, and staying the course in the face of adversity.

However, convictional leadership also requires humility and openness to learn, grow, and adapt. Leaders must ensure their convictions are informed by truth, justice, and the wellbeing of those they lead. They must be open to constructive criticism and willing to re-evaluate their convictions in the light of new evidence or changing circumstances.

Vision

Conviction, in turn, births a vision, an aspirational image of what the future could be. Vision is the image or idea of the desired future that a leader or an organisation strives to realise. It's an aspirational projection of what could be achieved or realised in the future. A compelling vision helps direct efforts, fosters unity, and inspires perseverance among team members.

A well-articulated vision also serves as a communication tool that aligns stakeholders, employees, and customers. It inspires people to commit to the organisation's purpose, and it provides a roadmap that guides the organisation's strategies and decisions. The same is true regarding leaders who lead communities or even nations.

Hence, vision is a critical element of effective leadership. It creates a sense of purpose, aligns efforts, motivates stakeholders, and sets the stage for sustainable success.

Passion

A leader's vision should ignite passion, an intense enthusiasm or desire. Passion in leadership refers to a deep, intense enthusiasm or excitement for one's work or cause. It's more than mere interest or inclination; it's a profound, driving force that pushes leaders to strive for excellence and inspires others to do the same.

When leaders demonstrate genuine passion, it can be contagious, sparking enthusiasm and dedication among team members. Passionate leaders often inspire their followers to go above and beyond, fostering a high-performing and committed workforce.

This can lead to increased productivity, improved morale, and lower turnover rates.

However, it's important to remember that passion should be guided by a clear vision and grounded in deep-seated convictions. Unchecked passion without direction can lead to burnout or misguided efforts. On the other hand, passion that is aligned with an organisation's vision and driven by a leader's conviction can be a powerful force for innovation, growth, and success.

Moreover, passion in leadership also relates to empathy and emotional intelligence. Passionate leaders often care deeply about their team members, showing interest in their wellbeing and development. They can create an environment where individuals feel valued and motivated to contribute their best work. When leaders bring passion to their work, they can inspire their teams, overcome challenges, and drive their organisations towards their vision. The same is true regarding leaders who lead communities or even nations.

Inspiration

Finally, inspiration is the means through which leaders influence others. Inspiration in leadership encompasses the ability of leaders to energise, motivate, and guide others towards achieving common goals. These inspirational leaders not only set the direction but also ignite an inner drive, stimulating enthusiasm, fostering creativity, and encouraging individuals to go beyond their personal interests and limitations for the collective good.

Inspirational leadership extends beyond mere charisma or enthusiasm; it involves setting a strong example, making people feel capable and appreciated, and creating an atmosphere where individuals are encouraged to strive for excellence.

The father of the democratic South African nation, Nelson Mandela, famously said, "Lead from the back – and let others believe they are in front." This quote underscores Mandela's belief in the importance of empowering others, fostering collective leadership, and enabling individuals to realise their potential. Mandela's style of leadership wasn't about asserting authority from a position of power; instead, it was about inspiring, motivating, and fostering growth among the people he led. His leadership philosophy was based on the idea of leading by example, showing empathy, and promoting unity and collaboration.

Inspirational leaders employ various strategies to motivate their teams. They start by setting a clear and compelling vision, painting a vivid picture of the future that motivates their team. This vision aligns efforts and provides a direction towards success. Moreover, they lead by example, embodying the behaviours and attitudes they expect from their team. This not only sets the standard but also builds trust and respect.

The golden key to catalysing economic growth anywhere on the globe is robust and dynamic leadership. The imprints of effective leadership are intricately woven into the fabric of progress and prosperity. Africa is not exempt from this universal truth.

Principles of Leadership

With a plethora of challenges, including sociopolitical unrest, economic inequality, and corruption, African leaders are tasked with the responsibility of fostering unity and inclusivity while steering their nations towards prosperity. Here, we dive deeper into the principles of visionary and inclusive leadership and how they could potentially reshape the African landscape. This leadership depends on the unique circumstances of each nation. It's not a one size fits all. Let's look at the types of leadership that have positively impacted economic development on our continent of Africa and elsewhere in the world.

Forward-Looking Leadership

The pivotal role that forward-thinking leadership plays in carving the pathway for a nation's future is an absolute necessity, an incontestable truth that rings throughout the annals of history. These far-sighted leaders are not simply tethered to the ebb and flow of the present circumstance. Instead, their vision pierces the murkiness of the present, their minds voyaging into the uncharted territory of the future. Their ability to make projections, based on both empirical evidence and nuanced intuition, is what separates them from the pack.

Such leaders carry the heavy mantle of strategic planning and decision-making, performing an intricate dance between the needs of the present and the wellbeing of the unborn generations. They consistently maintain this delicate balance, all the while shouldering the weight of the nation's expectations and the unpredictability of the future.

The mark of truly forward-looking leaders lies in their capacity to think beyond the constraints of their time in office. They craft policies not just for the applause of the now but also for the sighs of relief in the decades to come. They lay down plans and initiatives with a consideration that transcends the immediacy of their term, ensuring the sustenance and progression of the nation far beyond their tenure.

Rather than solely focusing on the dazzling flash of immediate success, they persistently stoke the slow-burning flame of sustainable growth. Their strategies are geared not only towards temporary triumphs but also target the robustness and resilience of the future state. They labour to leave an enduring legacy that will continue to shape the nation's destiny long after they have vacated the office.

In a world where the present often eclipses the future, these leaders offer an alternate narrative. They remind us that true leadership is not just about navigating the currents of the present but about charting a course for an enduring, prosperous future. A future that promises a safe haven for the generations yet to come, ensuring that the nation continues to thrive, echoing their strategic foresight and timeless vision.

One striking example of such visionary leadership can be seen in the transformation of Rwanda under President Paul Kagame. Born in 1957, Paul Kagame, president of Rwanda since 2000, has played a pivotal role in transforming Rwanda from a nation traumatised by the 1994 genocide against the Tutsis into an African success story. Kagame, a former refugee in Uganda, led the Rwandan Patriotic Front (RPF) to end the genocide.

Post genocide, Kagame's leadership emphasised national reconciliation. The Gacaca courts, a traditional justice system, facilitated justice and reconciliation by allowing perpetrators and victims to confront past horrors. His administration's stance on good governance, particularly its zero-tolerance policy on corruption, positioned Rwanda as one of Africa's least corrupt countries, spurring economic growth.

Kagame also prioritised long-term developmental plans. His 'education for all' policy transformed Rwanda's education system, elevating primary school enrolment rates from 62 percent in 1991 to 97 percent by 2016.[3] The 'one laptop per child' initiative embedded technology in education, equipping students with digital skills. Kagame's vision for Rwanda as an information and communications technology (ICT) hub led to initiatives like the National Information Communications Infrastructure (NICI) plan, ensuring high-speed internet coverage across the country and the development of Kigali as a 'smart city' for digital innovation.

In healthcare, Kagame introduced the Rwandan Health Insurance Scheme, providing over 90 percent of Rwandans access to affordable healthcare, resulting in significant improvements in child and maternal mortality rates.[4]

Kagame's visionary leadership has redefined Rwanda, emphasising the power of strategic planning in driving sustainable growth and development in a resource-constrained setting.

All in all, forward-looking leadership is crucial to navigate the challenging landscape of economic development. Leaders such as Kagame can inspire a shared vision for the future, motivating individuals to contribute towards the realisation of that vision. This is especially critical in the African context, given the pressing socio-economic challenges facing many African nations.

Inclusive Leadership

Inclusive leadership, a leadership trait that fosters a sense of belonging among all individuals within a society or an organization, is particularly vital in a diverse and multicultural setting, such as that found in many of our African nations. This form of leadership serves as the linchpin that holds together the multifaceted mosaic of ethnicities, languages, cultures, and beliefs. It is the cornerstone upon which a harmonious and productive community is built.

Such leaders are adept at navigating the rich tapestry of diversity, weaving together the threads of different perspectives into a single, unified narrative. They possess an intuitive understanding that strength lies in diversity, and they tap into this reservoir of varied human experience to enrich decision-making processes. By valuing each voice, by ensuring that no member of the community is left unheard or marginalised, inclusive leaders cultivate an environment where equity and mutual respect are not just aspirational goals but lived realities.

In the African context, where colonial legacies have often drawn sharp lines between different groups, the inclusive leader stands as a bridge builder. They understand that the path to national unity and progress does not involve the suppression of diversity but its celebration. These leaders work tirelessly to dismantle the barriers erected by prejudice and inequality, replacing them with pillars of unity and shared purpose.

Their approach to leadership is characterised by empathy and compassion. They are able to step into the shoes of others to understand their needs, fears, and aspirations. This empathy enables them to craft policies that are sensitive to the needs of all, not just a privileged few. By championing inclusivity, they ensure that everyone has a stake in the society's prosperity, thereby fostering a sense of ownership and responsibility across the board.

Inclusive leadership is also proactive. It recognises the potential for divisions and tensions in a society as dynamic and varied as those found on the African continent. Therefore, such leaders do not wait for conflicts to erupt but actively seek to anticipate and address the underlying issues that could lead to discord. Through dialogue, outreach, and representation, they strive to keep the fabric of the nation intact, promoting a culture of understanding and tolerance.

Moreover, inclusive leaders are transformative figures. They do not only react to the present but also look to the future, paving the way for a society that continually evolves towards greater inclusivity. Their legacy is measured not by the monuments they erect but by the societal norms they help shift – the intangible yet profound advancement of social justice and equality.

This attribute in leadership has been widely exhibited by great leaders but perhaps none more strikingly than Nelson Rolihlahla Mandela. Not only was he an inspirational leader, but he was also an inclusive leader.

Nelson Mandela, born in 1918 in Mvezo, Eastern Cape, is an iconic figure celebrated for his fight against apartheid in South Africa. As a key member of the African National Congress, his opposition to the regime led to 27 years of imprisonment. Released from prison in 1990, Mandela spearheaded the end of apartheid, culminating in his historic election as South Africa's first black president in 1994.

Emerging from apartheid's shadows, Mandela championed unity, inclusivity, and reconciliation. He envisioned South Africa as a 'rainbow nation', harmoniously woven together from its diverse racial and ethnic threads. He established the Truth and Reconciliation Commission, which, instead of seeking revenge, promoted understanding, forgiveness, and healing.

Mandela's impact wasn't limited to social and political realms; he also transformed the economic landscape. He believed in inclusive economic growth, underlined by initiatives like the National Skills Authority (NSA) for workforce skill development and the Sector Education and Training Authorities (SETAs). His administration introduced education reforms like the South African Schools Act and Curriculum 2005, emphasising quality and learner-centric approaches. To address apartheid-era economic disparities, the

Broad-Based Black Economic Empowerment policy was introduced, prioritising skills development, employment equity, and black entrepreneurship.

Under Mandela's leadership, South Africa took great strides towards creating an inclusive society where every citizen could contribute to the nation's economic growth. His initiatives laid the groundwork for a more equitable future, making him a beacon of inclusive leadership.

Inclusive leaders like Nelson Mandela show that leadership is not just about making decisions and governing; it's about understanding the diverse needs of a multicultural society, empathising with all citizens, and taking actions that consider the wellbeing of all. Their leadership serves as a shining beacon of what inclusive leadership looks like in practice, providing inspiration for other leaders worldwide.

Transformational Leadership

Transformational leadership, a dynamic approach that inspires change and motivates individuals to exceed their own limitations, is an invaluable asset within any organisation or society that aspires to move beyond the status quo. This brand of leadership does not only seek to manage or navigate the existing systems but also to revolutionise them, to forge a new path that leads to higher levels of achievement and fulfilment for all involved.

Transformational leaders are visionaries, equipped with an uncanny ability to see the potential for a future that others have yet to imagine. They are driven by a deep conviction that the world they interact with is malleable, ripe for innovation and progress. Their eyes are not fixed on the world as it is but on the world as it could be. They share this vision with such persuasive passion that it becomes a shared goal, igniting the collective imagination of their followers.

In the throes of this shared vision, transformational leaders are catalysts for growth. They create an atmosphere charged with enthusiasm and energy, where the seeds of new ideas can sprout and take root. By challenging traditional beliefs and encouraging out-of-the-box thinking, they promote an environment where creativity and innovation are not only welcomed but expected. They are not content with incremental improvements; they aim for breakthroughs that redefine the very metrics of success.

The approach of transformational leaders is inherently inclusive. They foster an environment where each individual feels valued and inspired to contribute. Through their charisma and compelling nature, they are able to connect with people on a profound level, stimulating their intrinsic motivation and empowering them to take initiative. This empowerment is key – it transforms passive participants into active agents of change, cocreators of a shared future.

Furthermore, transformational leaders are characterised by their integrity and high ethical standards. They lead by example, demonstrating the values and behaviours that reflect their vision for the organisation or society. Their consistency in word and action garners trust and respect, creating a strong foundation for enduring change. Their leadership transcends mere transactional exchanges; it is about forging meaningful, transformative relationships.

In addition, these leaders are change agents who possess the fortitude to confront existing realities and are resilient in the face of the challenges that accompany major shifts. They understand that transformation is often a disruptive, uncomfortable process, yet they maintain an unwavering commitment to guiding their followers through the turbulence of change. They are adept at managing the dynamics of change, balancing the need for a new direction with the realities of human adaptation.

In a world that is continuously evolving, transformational leadership is not a luxury but a necessity. Such leaders do not just adapt to change; they are the harbingers of change, redefining what is possible. Their influence extends far beyond their immediate sphere of control and continues to resonate long after their direct involvement. By aligning the aspirations of individuals with a collective purpose, they unlock the potential for dramatic shifts in culture, productivity, and, ultimately, the human condition itself.

Within Africa, this style of leadership is embodied by Ellen Johnson Sirleaf. Sirleaf, born on 29 October 1938 in Monrovia, Liberia, was the first elected female head of state in Africa, serving as Liberia's president from 2006 to 2018. Assuming leadership after years of civil conflict, she was tasked with the monumental challenge of rebuilding a war-torn nation.

Sirleaf initiated economic reforms to revitalise major sectors like agriculture, mining, and forestry. She emphasised modern agriculture, value-added mining, and sustainable forestry management. To boost the economy, her government created legislation that attracted foreign investments, leading to significant economic growth, particularly in the mining sector.

In education, Sirleaf's government implemented the Free and Compulsory Primary Education policy in 2007, ensuring all Liberian children had access to schooling, resulting in a surge in enrolment rates. Healthcare was another focus, with investments in facility rehabilitation, healthcare provider training, preventive care, and essential services. This led to marked improvements in health indicators, such as reduced child and maternal mortality rates.

Recognising corruption as a key barrier to progress, Sirleaf established the Liberia Anti-Corruption Commission in 2008, aiming to restore public trust in government. She also addressed Liberia's staggering external debt of $4.6 billion through negotiations and meeting the Heavily Indebted Poor Countries Initiative's requirements. In 2010, the majority of this debt was cancelled, allowing more resources for public services and development.[5]

Sirleaf's transformative leadership was pivotal for Liberia's post-conflict recovery, fostering growth, stability, improved human rights, and rule of law. Her tenure ushered in hope, national unity, and set Liberia on a trajectory towards sustainable development.

The examples of Sirleaf underline the immense potential of transformational leadership in driving economic development. When leaders can inspire and mobilise their citizens towards a shared vision, they can effect significant positive change, even in the face of seemingly insurmountable challenges.

Ethical Leadership

Ethical leadership, a beacon of integrity and principled decision-making, stands as a cornerstone for organisations and societies that prioritise moral conduct and accountability. It is a brand of leadership that embeds fairness, respect, and honesty at the heart of all policies and practices and is particularly critical at a time when ethical considerations are as important as economic outcomes.

Ethical leaders are the moral compasses of their organisations or nations, guiding them through the murky waters of modern ethical dilemmas. They hold fast to the belief that the right thing to do is also the best thing to do for long-term success. Their decision-making process is transparent and rooted in a clear set of values; they make choices not based on expediency or personal gain but on what is just and good for the collective.

These leaders possess a deep understanding of the complex tapestry of societal norms, cultural diversity, and human psychology. They use this knowledge to foster environments where ethical behaviour is the norm, not the exception. They do not simply enact rules but create a culture that supports ethical ideals, where individuals are encouraged to speak up without fear of retribution and where ethical behaviour is recognised and rewarded.

In an age where every action is scrutinised and the court of public opinion can decree judgement instantaneously, ethical leaders remain steadfast in their commitment to doing what is right. They acknowledge their role as examples, understanding that their actions set a precedent for others to follow. Their leadership is not characterised by lofty pronouncements of ethical behaviour but by the quiet consistency of their everyday actions.

Ethical leadership extends beyond avoidance of wrongdoing. It actively promotes a positive impact on individuals, communities, and the environment. It involves taking responsibility for the welfare of others and striving to make a difference. These leaders work tirelessly to ensure that they leave their charges better than they found them, serving the greater good and inspiring others to do the same.

The efficacy of ethical leadership is particularly evident in times of crisis. When faced with challenging situations, ethical leaders can provide a clear and principled path forward, maintaining the trust and confidence of their followers. They do not waver from their principles for short-term gain but remain focused on long-term, sustainable success.

Ethical leaders are also skilled communicators, articulating their values and the reasoning behind their decisions in a way that is both persuasive and accessible. They engage in dialogue with various stakeholders, considering different perspectives and the impact of decisions on a broad spectrum of interests. Through open communication, they build consensus and foster an inclusive atmosphere where diverse viewpoints are valued.

In the realm of ethical leadership, the measure of success is not just in balance sheets or productivity metrics but in the level of trust and respect leaders garner from their followers, peers, and even competitors. It is reflected in the organisation's reputation and the legacy it creates, a legacy that outlives products, services, or political terms. It's a legacy of integrity, reliability, and principled action.

Sir Seretse Khama, born on 1 July 1921 in Serowe, Bechuanaland (now Botswana), stands as an emblematic figure in the discourse on ethical leadership, particularly in the context of post-colonial Africa. His leadership qualities have been studied and praised for establishing a legacy of good governance, economic prosperity, and social cohesion in Botswana. Assuming leadership in 1966, Khama transformed one of the world's poorest nations through principled governance, focusing on integrity, transparency, and people's welfare.

Recognising Botswana's diamond wealth, Khama ensured its benefits were not solely reaped by foreign corporations. Partnering in a 50-50 joint venture with De Beers to form Debswana, he channelled the resultant revenue into sectors like education, healthcare, and infrastructure. Khama's emphasis on education led to the establishment of schools nationwide and the creation of the University of Botswana, a leading African institution.

Healthcare was expanded under Khama, with medical facilities reaching even remote areas. His leadership marked a period of remarkable democratic governance, low corruption, and inclusive decision-making, making Botswana a model of stability in Africa. On the global stage, Khama's ethical leadership shone when Botswana opposed South Africa's apartheid policy, facing significant pressures as a result.

Khama's legacy, marked by astute economic policies, prioritisation of education and healthcare, and commitment to democracy, has been pivotal in shaping Botswana into one of Africa's most prosperous nations.

In a nutshell, the examples of Sir Seretse Khama demonstrate that ethical leadership – characterised by transparency, accountability, and a commitment to social justice – can contribute significantly to political stability, social cohesion, and economic development.

Servant Leadership

Servant leadership, a paradigm of leadership that inverts the traditional power hierarchy, posits the leader as a steward of the resources of the organisation or nation and a servant to its constituents. This leadership philosophy is grounded in the desire to serve first and lead second and prioritise the growth and wellbeing of others over the aggrandisement of personal power.

The essence of servant leadership lies in the genuine commitment to fostering an environment where the leader serves the needs of their team members, empowering and uplifting them to realise their full potential. It's a style deeply embedded in empathy and altruism, resonating particularly well within communities and organisations that value collective success and individual development.

Servant leaders are characterised by their focus on collaboration, trust, and ethical use of power. They engage in deep listening and remain attuned to the needs of others, ensuring that their policies and practices are responsive and adaptive to the needs of those they lead. In this model, the leader is a facilitator whose authority comes from a shared sense of mission and the earned respect of their peers and subordinates.

This leadership approach is transformative, often in the way it fosters an inclusive culture that honours diverse perspectives and backgrounds. Servant leaders are dedicated to creating a sense of community and shared purpose, recognising that the strength of a group comes from its unity and the mutual respect of its members. They see the potential in every individual and situation and work tirelessly to unlock that potential for the common good.

In practice, servant leadership manifests in a variety of ways. Leaders who adopt this style are active listeners, empathetic and mindful communicators, and strong advocates for their team. They lead by example, often rolling up their sleeves and working alongside their team to achieve collective goals. Their leadership is not about accumulating personal accolades but about ensuring that the group thrives and each member feels valued and heard.

Moreover, servant leaders are foresighted, looking beyond the immediate to the long-term health and success of the organisation or community. They understand that by investing in people – providing opportunities for learning and growth, encouraging autonomy, and building a supportive culture — they are investing in the future of the enterprise or the community itself.

In an era that is increasingly complex and fraught with challenges, servant leadership offers a path that is both ethical and effective. It shows that power does not have to corrupt and leadership can be a force for good. It engenders an environment where success is measured not only in profit margins or victories but also in the growth and wellbeing of individuals and the community.

Born on 28 April 1924 in Chinsali, Zambia, Dr Kenneth David Kaunda, the father of the Zambia nation, who served from 1964 to 1991, stands as a shining example of servant leadership on the African continent.

Kaunda was a champion for independence and equality. Beginning his public service career as a teacher, he soon found his true calling in politics, fuelled by his passion for social justice. He played a vital role in the formation of the United National Independence Party (UNIP), which became instrumental in Zambia's fight for independence from colonial rule.

In Kaunda's case, his leadership was grounded in humility and selflessness, with a clear focus on the welfare of the Zambian people. When he assumed office in 1964, Zambia had just gained independence and was dealing with the challenges of nation-building. Divisions along tribal and regional lines were prevalent, and national unity was far from guaranteed. Undeterred by these challenges, Kaunda implemented the policy of 'one Zambia, one nation' to encourage unity among Zambians regardless of their tribal or regional background. This policy had a tremendous impact on social cohesion and instilled a sense of national unity among Zambians.

Kaunda's administration also tackled economic inequality through policies like the nationalisation of key industries, notably copper mining. Although his term faced challenges, including economic downturns, Kaunda's dedication to his people never wavered.

Furthermore, Kaunda's leadership was characterised by a commitment to progressive social and economic reforms. Understanding the transformational power of education, he introduced universal primary education, resulting in a significant increase in school enrolment rates. Healthcare was also a priority, with a particular focus on underserved rural areas. Kaunda's economic policies, while subject to criticism, were rooted in a philosophy of 'humanism', which emphasised social and economic equity.

Lastly, Kaunda was a promoter of peace both within Zambia and in the wider Southern African region. His approach to governance ensured that Zambia remained peaceful despite regional instability. He played a significant role in regional diplomacy, most notably in the negotiation of the Lancaster House Agreement in 1979, which led to the end of white minority rule in Zimbabwe. Kaunda was also an anti-apartheid stalwart, contributing to the formation of the Frontline States, an alliance aimed at coordinating the regional response to apartheid South Africa, a significant development.

Kaunda's leadership, rooted in servant leadership principles, made him a beacon of hope and an example of dedication to the welfare of the people he led. His impact was felt not only in Zambia but also in the broader Southern African region, cementing his legacy as one of Africa's great servant leaders.

Therefore, in terms of fostering sustainable economic development in Africa, it's essential to choose leaders who embody the previously mentioned traits. This involves educating the electorate on the importance of their vote and engaging them in political processes, including elections and public debates. The electoral process must be free, fair, and transparent, with efforts to uphold its integrity against malpractices. Diversity and inclusion should be emphasised, making room for marginalised groups in leadership roles. Accountability in leadership can be promoted through legal frameworks and policies that keep a check on corruption. Finally, a culture of servant leadership should be fostered through community-based initiatives that identify and nurture future leaders with the right values.

I will end with what former President Mbeki of South Africa said at the 'Leadership for the Africa We Want' gathering in Kigali, Rwanda on 22 May 2015. President Mbeki started with one critical question, "What is the Africa we want?"

In his speech, President Mbeki highlighted the vital need for self-evaluation, internal reform, and effective, service-oriented leadership for Africa's progress. He set forth a vision of an Africa free from conflict, poverty, corruption, and gender inequality, emphasising that achieving these goals requires a specific kind of leadership distinct from the current style.

Mbeki emphasised the importance of 'truthful self-assessment' in evaluating the performance of Africa's leaders and criticised the underutilisation of the African Peer Review Mechanism, a tool designed to promote good governance within the African Union. He argued that self-centred leadership hinders the realisation of a prosperous and equitable Africa and called for a shift towards service-oriented leadership.

Furthermore, Mbeki addressed the need to instil values of unity and strength in the face of diversity within the population and political parties. He criticised the current leadership's failure to understand the importance of economic emancipation and highlighted the irony of Africa's natural resources being exploited for the benefit of others.[6]

As we end this chapter, in the words of President Mbeki, we Africans should all ask ourselves, "What kind of leadership do we need to create for the Africa we want?"

Chapter 6 will look at cultural renaissance as the second pillar of economic growth. We will look at why Africans should celebrate African heritage, arts, and traditions to help strengthen a sense of identity, pride, and self-worth in the global arena. This includes promoting African indigenous languages, music, literature, and other forms of cultural expression.

CHAPTER 6

UNVEILING AFRICA'S CULTURAL RENAISSANCE

The African cultural renaissance... what is it? Picture a reawakening, a rekindling of Africa's cultural legacy – that's what the African cultural renaissance is about. It's about bringing back to life indigenous languages and traditions, promoting African arts, literature, music, and creating a sense of pride and identity among Africans. This shift in narrative, a counter to the negative stereotypes, has the power to grip global attention and unlock the economic potential hidden in Africa's creative and cultural industries.

In Chapter 1, I touched on the African cultures across the African continent. This chapter explores the concept of a 'cultural renaissance' in Africa and how it can serve as a driver for sustainable development and transformation.

Celebrating Africa's Cultural Diversity

Despite a history scarred by the tragedy of slavery and the oppression of colonialism, Africa is a continent that boasts an astonishing wealth of cultural diversity. This variety is a beautiful symphony of human expression and creativity, encapsulating over 3,000 distinct ethnic groups and more than 2,000 languages. This wealth of cultural diversity isn't just a testament to Africa's deep, multi-layered history; it's also the bedrock of its vibrant traditions, beliefs, and practices.

Imagine a vast quilt made of vibrant patches, each patch representing a unique culture, a unique language, a unique way of life. Each patch tells a story of a community, of their joys, their struggles, their traditions, and their dreams. Stitched together, these patches form a dazzling mosaic that is much greater than the sum of its parts – the mosaic of African culture.

For instance, take the Yoruba people of West Africa, one of Africa's largest ethnic groups. The Yoruba people, residing primarily in Nigeria, Benin, and Togo in West Africa, represent one of the largest ethnic groups in Africa. Their culture is vibrant and rich in folklore and tradition, forming a cornerstone of their identity.

One of the most captivating elements of the Yoruba culture is their religious belief system, which revolves around an elaborate pantheon of deities known as orishas. Each orisha embodies specific natural elements and human characteristics, creating a rich, interconnected spiritual universe. These deities are revered through traditional rituals, ceremonies, and festivals that are an integral part of Yoruba society. For instance, Ogun, the god of iron, war, and labour, is believed to be the deity that crafts tools for human survival, while Osun is revered as the goddess of love, beauty, and fertility.[1]

The Yoruba culture's vibrancy extends into their music, dance, and art, which are deeply intertwined with their religious beliefs. Yoruba music is dominated by the use of traditional percussion instruments like the 'bata' drum, which often serves to summon and pay homage to the orishas. Songs are used not just as a means of entertainment but also as a way to pass down their folklore and religious beliefs from one generation to another.

Dance too plays a critical role in Yoruba culture, with specific dances associated with different orishas. During religious ceremonies and festivals, these dances are performed to invoke the deity's presence and seek their blessings.

Yoruba art, especially sculpture, is globally renowned for its aesthetic and symbolic value. Much of their sculpture serves religious purposes, representing the orishas or ancestors. One of the most recognised forms of Yoruba art is the creation of intricate 'Ife heads', naturalistic terracotta or brass sculptures that depict royal figures.

Yoruba culture, with its sophisticated spiritual system and rich artistic heritage, provides a fascinating insight into the diversity and depth of African cultures. The cultural expressions of the Yoruba people, from their music and dance to their artwork, form a significant part of their identity and offer a profound connection to their past, shaping their present and future.[2]

Or consider the Maasai of East Africa, renowned for their distinctive customs and dress. The Maasai people are a Nilotic ethnic group residing primarily in Kenya and Tanzania, known for their distinctive customs, clothing, and resilience against cultural erosion. Their vivid cultural practices and enduring traditions serve as a testament to the rich cultural mosaic of East Africa.

One of the most identifiable aspects of Maasai culture is their distinct clothing. The Maasai are known for their brightly coloured shuka (a plaid, wrapped cloth), beaded jewellery, and the intricate beadwork that both men and women display. These elements are more than just fashion – they carry deep cultural significance, representing identity, status, and personal history.

Among the Maasai's many traditions, the 'Adumu' or 'jumping dance' is perhaps the most famous. Performed during the Eunoto ceremony, marking the transition of morans (Maasai warriors) to elderhood, the Adumu is more than just a dance. It is a rite of passage, a test of strength, and a deeply communal event. The morans gather in a circle and, one by one, leap into the air with straightened backs, their feet barely seeming to touch the ground. The height of one's jump is often seen as a measure of one's strength and virility. The dance is accompanied by rhythmic chants and low, harmonious singing, creating an immersive and powerful experience.

Despite the pressures of modernity and globalisation, the Maasai have managed to maintain their cultural identity. They have accomplished this through a strong sense of community, deep respect for traditions, and a commitment to passing these practices down to younger generations. This resilience is not just a reflection of their dedication to their culture but also a statement of their adaptability. For instance, while the Maasai have embraced changes like education and technology, these changes have often been incorporated in ways that align with and respect Maasai culture and values.

In essence, the Maasai, with their vivid clothing, deeply communal dances, and resilience against cultural erosion, offer a fascinating glimpse into the enduring richness and dynamism of African cultures. Their traditions and customs, from the Adumu dance to their dress, not only form a crucial part of their identity but also symbolise their strength and resilience in maintaining their cultural heritage.[3]

Africa's cultural wealth is also showcased in its numerous languages. Language, an essential aspect of human culture, not only serves as a tool for communication but also encapsulates a society's history, identity, and worldview. Africa, home to an estimated 2,000 languages, is a testament to this diversity and richness in linguistic heritage. Among these languages, Kiswahili, also known as Swahili, has emerged as an influential lingua franca across much of East Africa and parts of Central Africa.

Originating from the Bantu language family, Kiswahili is believed to have developed in East Africa's coastal regions through a fusion of local Bantu languages with Arabic, influenced by the region's historical trade connections with Arab countries. Today, Kiswahili is spoken by millions across Tanzania, Kenya, Uganda, Rwanda, Burundi, Mozambique, and the Democratic Republic of Congo. It's also one of the African Union's official languages.

But Kiswahili is more than just a common language. It acts as a cultural bridge, connecting different ethnic communities across the region. By providing a common medium of communication, Kiswahili helps foster mutual understanding and unity among diverse groups, transcending ethnic and regional boundaries. For instance, it has played a vital role in nation-building in Tanzania, where more than 120 languages are spoken. The adoption of Kiswahili as the national language has helped foster a sense of Tanzanian identity that rises above ethnic affiliations.

Furthermore, Kiswahili is a vibrant carrier of culture, reflecting in its proverbs, poetry, music, and literature the philosophy, wisdom, and worldview of the people who speak it. Taasisi ya Uchunguzi wa Kiswahili (TUKI) at the University of Dar es Salaam and other institutions continue to promote the development, research, and recognition of Kiswahili on a global scale.

This vibrant blend of cultures, languages, and traditions is a source of strength and resilience for Africa. By embracing and celebrating this cultural wealth, Africa can foster a sense of unity and pride. This unity in diversity could prove to be Africa's most potent tool in overcoming the lingering shadows of its past and paving the way for a future marked by sustainable development and shared prosperity.

Cultural Diversity as a Driver of Economic Development

In addition to fostering unity and resilience, Africa's cultural diversity can also be a driver of economic development. Cultural industries, such as music, film, fashion, and tourism, can generate jobs, stimulate local economies, and promote sustainable development.

Film Industry

When one speaks of Africa's cultural resurgence, Nollywood, Nigeria's booming film industry, is impossible to ignore. Since its rebirth in the 1990s, Nollywood has grown exponentially, now proudly standing as the world's second largest film industry by volume, outpacing even Hollywood and trailing just behind India's Bollywood. This rapid growth is not merely an industrial triumph; it is a testament to the remarkable cultural and creative vibrancy of Nigeria and Africa at large.[4]

Nollywood's strength lies in its authentically Nigerian narrative.

Unlike Hollywood movies that often rely on high budgets and special effects, Nollywood films have etched a place in viewers' hearts through their compelling storytelling, relatable characters, and authentic portrayal of Nigerian culture. By focusing on local themes and experiences – love, betrayal, community, tradition, and transformation – these films provide a unique lens through which to understand and appreciate Nigerian society.

Moreover, Nollywood actors, often locally sourced, bring these narratives to life with performances that reflect their cultural milieu. From seasoned actors like Genevieve Nnaji and Ramsey Nouah to newer talents, these performers have become cultural ambassadors, introducing Nigerian and African cultures to global audiences.

The success of Nollywood also holds significant economic implications. Nollywood is not just an entertainment powerhouse; it is a significant job creator and contributes substantially to Nigeria's GDP. The industry has spawned an entire ecosystem of directors, producers, scriptwriters, actors, and technicians who are promoting local talent and generating economic growth.[5]

However, Nollywood's influence goes beyond the boundaries of Nigeria. Its movies have found an audience across the rest of Africa and in the African diaspora, shaping perceptions of African culture worldwide. Therefore, Nollywood serves as a beacon of Africa's cultural renaissance, exemplifying how local culture, when portrayed with authenticity and creativity, can resonate globally, promote cultural understanding, and drive economic growth.

Music, Dance, and Fashion

The ripples of Africa's cultural resurgence are felt globally through its music, dance, and fashion.

In the realm of music, Afrobeat, a genre that beautifully blends West African musical styles with American jazz and funk, has truly swept the globe. Fela Kuti, often considered the godfather of Afrobeat, used music as a medium to express social and political views, creating a lasting legacy. Contemporary artists like Burna Boy and Wizkid are further popularising Afrobeat, ensuring its beats reverberate in clubs and music festivals worldwide.

Meanwhile, East Africa's contribution to the world's music landscape includes the hypnotic rhythms of modern taarab. Originating from coastal areas in Kenya and Tanzania, taarab is an intoxicating blend of Swahili tunes, Arabic instrumentation, and Indian melodic structures. The lyrical depth and rhythmic intricacy of taarab have gained international recognition, highlighting the cultural richness of East Africa.

From the Democratic Republic of Congo, rhumba music has found its way into global music charts. With its infectious rhythms and sensual dance accompaniments, rhumba has not only dominated the African music scene but also found popularity in Europe and the Americas.

Dance, a vital form of cultural expression in Africa, has also caught the world's attention. African dance forms are deeply rooted in tradition and community and are as diverse as the continent itself. From the high-energy dance styles accompanying Afrobeat and rhumba music to the symbolic Adumu dance of the Maasai, these dance forms have gained international fame, often featuring in global dance competitions and festivals.

African influence is also prominent in the world of fashion. African fashion designers are making their mark in international fashion weeks with their bold prints, vibrant colours, and innovative designs inspired by traditional African aesthetics. African textiles, like the Ghanaian kente or the Nigerian aso oke, are increasingly sought after in global fashion markets.

Southern Africa has also made significant contributions to the global fashion scene. Here, local designers are drawing upon their rich heritage to create unique fashion pieces that incorporate traditional elements into modern designs, showcasing the region's diversity and cultural wealth.

One of the most internationally recognised fashion trends from Southern Africa is the traditional 'shweshwe' fabric, originating from Lesotho and South Africa. This vibrant, intricately patterned fabric has been incorporated into modern fashion designs, resulting in a unique blend of traditional and contemporary styles. Designers such as Laduma Ngxokolo of the brand MaXhosa have even brought shweshwe-inspired designs to international fashion weeks, turning heads with their bold and colourful patterns.

In Lesotho, the seshoeshoe, a printed fabric featuring colourful geometric designs, has become a fashion staple. It is used in a variety of clothing items, from everyday wear to elaborate wedding dresses, underscoring the region's fashion versatility.

The Ndebele people, known for their stunning wall art and unique beadwork, also influence South African fashion. Their traditional geometric patterns and vibrant colours have inspired numerous modern designs and fashion accessories.

Zimbabwe's fashion industry is also making waves, with designers like Farai Simoyi gaining international recognition for her fashion line that integrates traditional African textiles with contemporary silhouettes.

The fashion scene in Southern Africa is a vibrant fusion of traditional elements and modern aesthetics. Through their designs, Southern African designers are not only showcasing their cultural heritage but also making significant contributions to global fashion, underscoring Africa's role as a dynamic and influential player in the international fashion industry.

Additionally, the Afrocentric aesthetics and 'Wakanda' style popularised by the global hit movie *Black Panther* have further sparked a global interest in African fashion.

In essence, the influence of Africa's cultural resurgence is far-reaching, shaping global film, music, dance, and fashion trends. This not only underscores the richness of African culture but also its dynamism and its ability to innovate and inspire globally. Through these cultural exports, Africa is leaving an indelible mark on the global cultural landscape.

Tourism

Tourism is undeniably a powerful engine for economic development and cultural preservation in Africa. As international and local tourists flock to Africa's stunning cultural heritage sites, vibrant festivals, and awe-inspiring natural wonders, they not only stimulate economic growth but also contribute to the safeguarding of Africa's cultural and natural heritage.

North Africa, for instance, is home to the majestic pyramids of Egypt, the ancient Roman ruins of Leptis Magna in Libya, and the charming medinas of Morocco. These heritage sites, coupled with unique experiences like cruising down the Nile or wandering through the Sahara Desert, attract millions of tourists each year, providing crucial income to local communities and businesses.

In East Africa, tourists are drawn by the annual Great Migration in the Serengeti-Mara ecosystem in Tanzania and Kenya, where over a million wildebeest and other migratory species travel across vast savannahs in an awe-inspiring spectacle of life.

Ethiopia's rock-hewn churches of Lalibela, Kenya's historic Lamu Island, and Uganda's sacred tombs of Buganda's kings are other key cultural attractions in the region.

West Africa offers a rich cultural experience, from the historic slave forts of Ghana and Senegal to the mudbrick mosques of Mali. The cultural festivals, like the Voodoo Festival in Benin or the Fête des Masques in Burkina Faso, provide visitors with a profound understanding of local customs and traditions.

In Southern Africa, the awe-inspiring Victoria Falls on the border of Zambia and Zimbabwe, the ancient San rock paintings in South Africa, the Okavango Delta in Botswana, and the picturesque islands of Seychelles and Mauritius are major tourist attractions.

Central Africa, though less traversed by mainstream tourism, houses incredible attractions like the rainforests and gorilla sanctuaries of Rwanda and Uganda, the active Nyiragongo volcano in the Democratic Republic of Congo, and the enchanting Waza National Park in Cameroon.

Beyond these natural and cultural attractions, Africa's vibrant cities – from the cosmopolitan Cape Town, with its blend of cultures and the imposing Table Mountain backdrop, to Dakar's bustling markets and vibrant art scene, to the bustling streets of Lagos, pulsating with music and arts – offer unique urban experiences that draw tourists.

Promoting sustainable tourism practices is crucial to ensure that tourism development benefits local communities, preserves cultural assets, and protects the environment. This includes employing locals, sourcing local products, respecting cultural traditions, and limiting environmental impact.

Tourism, when harnessed sustainably, can be a significant driver of socio-economic development and cultural preservation in Africa, contributing to the creation of jobs, generation of income, and safeguarding of Africa's cultural and natural heritage.

African Diaspora

Furthermore, the African diaspora, with its connections to diverse cultural heritages, can play an important role in promoting Africa's cultural wealth and fostering international collaborations in trade, innovation, and education. The African diaspora represents a significant portion of the global population. Dispersed through historical migrations, the transatlantic slave trade, and more recent waves of emigration, African diasporic communities have established a substantial presence on every continent. These diaspora communities, with their deep ties to African heritage and global locales, can and do play a crucial role in promoting Africa's cultural wealth and fostering collaborations across a range of sectors.

In the realm of culture, the African diaspora has been instrumental in sharing and promoting African traditions, art, music, and cuisine in their host countries. For instance, Afro-Caribbean communities have shaped the musical and cultural landscapes of countries like Jamaica, Haiti, and Cuba, blending African rhythms with local influences to create new genres like reggae and salsa. In the United States, African American communities have profoundly influenced music, art, and literature, from blues and jazz to hip-hop.[6]

The African diaspora also fosters economic ties and collaborations. For example, diaspora remittances to Africa substantially exceed official development aid, contributing to poverty reduction, economic stability, and investment in sectors like health and education.[7] The diaspora also facilitates trade and investment links between their host countries and Africa. African diaspora entrepreneurs, like Ethiopian-born Bethlehem Tilahun Alemu, founder of the sustainable footwear brand soleRebels, are creating jobs, promoting local craftsmanship, and connecting African products to global markets.

The African diaspora is also increasingly playing a significant role in education and innovation, both within Africa and globally. With a considerable number of the diaspora engaged in academic, research, and technological sectors in their host countries, they serve as crucial bridges for knowledge exchange, capacity building, and innovation. This transnational network of academics and professionals enhances the quality of education and research within Africa, exposing African institutions and scholars to global advancements and standards in various fields.

One example is the African Institute for Mathematical Sciences (AIMS), an innovative, pan-African network of postgraduate training and research institutes that leverages the expertise of African diaspora academics.[8] AIMS offers advanced training in mathematical sciences, a critical area for Africa's development, to talented students across the continent. Through its 'Next Einstein' initiative, AIMS aims to build a critical mass of scientific and technical talent in Africa, essential for driving economic growth and innovation.

Another example is the Carnegie African Diaspora Fellowship Programme (CADFP). This programme facilitates collaborations between African diaspora academics in the United States and Canada and their counterparts in Africa. The collaborations involve curriculum co-development, research, graduate teaching, training, and mentoring activities.[9]

Beyond formal education and research, the diaspora also plays a role in promoting innovation and entrepreneurship in Africa. Many diaspora members are involved in launching startups, introducing new technologies, and investing in Africa's burgeoning tech hubs, like those in Nairobi, Lagos, and Cape Town.

Furthermore, diaspora networks like the African Diaspora Network (ADN) offer platforms for members to connect, share ideas, and collaborate on initiatives aimed at fostering innovation and development in Africa. ADN organises events like the annual 'African Diaspora Investment Symposium', which promotes entrepreneurship and attracts investments for businesses in Africa.[10]

The African diaspora, with its academic prowess, professional expertise, and transnational networks, is a potent catalyst for education, innovation, and capacity building in Africa. Leveraging this potential can significantly contribute to Africa's journey towards sustainable development and global competitiveness.

Reviving Indigenous Knowledge

One of the crucial facets of Africa's cultural renaissance is the resurgence and recognition of indigenous knowledge and practices. These systems, honed over millennia and deeply intertwined with local cultures and environments, can offer sustainable and locally appropriate solutions to contemporary challenges.

In the field of agriculture, traditional farming techniques are increasingly recognised for their resilience and adaptability to local ecosystems. For example, agroforestry practices, which integrate trees into crop and livestock farming systems, have been traditionally employed in many African farming communities for centuries. With its roots in traditional land-use systems, agroforestry is a fine example of how indigenous knowledge and practices can offer sustainable solutions for contemporary challenges like food security and climate change.

Agroforestry practices can take various forms. For instance, in the 'parklands' agroforestry system common in West Africa's Sahel region, farmers retain and manage certain tree species in their cereal fields, providing shade and improving soil fertility.[11] In East Africa, the 'homegarden' agroforestry system involves growing a diversity of trees, crops, and livestock around homesteads, creating a microcosm of a forest ecosystem that provides food, fodder, fuel, and other products.[12]

The benefits of agroforestry are manifold. For starters, trees can improve soil fertility by fixing nitrogen, recycling nutrients from deeper soil layers, and adding organic matter through leaf litter. This not only enhances crop yields but also reduces the need for synthetic fertilisers, contributing to sustainable, organic farming.

Moreover, by increasing biodiversity, agroforestry systems promote ecological resilience. The presence of trees and the variety of crops can attract a range of beneficial insects, birds, and other fauna, which contribute to pest control and pollination. This biodiversity can also make farming systems more resilient to pests, diseases, and climatic shocks like droughts or floods.[13]

Furthermore, trees in agroforestry systems sequester carbon, thus mitigating greenhouse gas emissions and combating climate change. In fact, agroforestry is recognised as a significant nature-based solution for climate change, with the potential to deliver 23 percent of the total cost-effective mitigation potential across the global agricultural sector by 2030.[14]

Agroforestry also contributes to socio-economic sustainability. It can diversify farm income, as trees provide timber, fruits, nuts, and other products that can be sold or used by the household. This diversification can reduce vulnerability to crop failures and market fluctuations, enhancing food and income security for smallholder farmers.[15]

However, promoting agroforestry requires overcoming several challenges. These include land tenure insecurity, which can discourage farmers from investing in trees, and lack of access to quality tree seeds and technical knowledge. Policies and programmes that address these barriers and support agroforestry can help harness its potential for sustainable agriculture in Africa.

Another agricultural practice indigenous to Africa is conservation agriculture. Conservation agriculture is an indigenous farming method that has gained recognition for its potential to address many of the contemporary challenges that agriculture faces. This approach, which is particularly prevalent in countries like Zambia and Zimbabwe, focuses on improving long-term, sustainable agricultural productivity while simultaneously preserving and enhancing the environment upon which agriculture depends.

Conservation agriculture is grounded in three core principles that aim to maintain a healthy and sustainable farming ecosystem. First, the practice of minimal soil disturbance, often known as 'no-till' farming, advises farmers to minimise the disruption of the soil's natural structure and biological processes. By avoiding ploughing and tilling, farmers can preserve the soil's organic make-up, conserve its moisture levels, diminish erosion, and boost the activity of beneficial microbes within the soil.[16]

Second, the principle of permanent soil cover emphasises the importance of keeping a consistent protective layer on the soil surface. This can be achieved either through the use of crop residues or by planting specific cover crops. This cover not only shields the soil from the erosive forces of wind and water but also improves its water retention capacity.[17] Additionally, it can help to suppress weeds and offers a conducive environment for beneficial insects and microorganisms. As this cover decomposes over time, it further enriches the soil with organic matter.

Lastly, the principle of diversified crop rotations is aimed at enhancing the soil's health and fertility. By alternating different types of crops in a planned sequence, farmers can interrupt the life cycles of various pests and diseases. This reduces the need for chemical interventions like pesticides and fertilisers. For example, incorporating leguminous crops into the rotation can naturally fix nitrogen in the soil, which in turn benefits the crops that follow in the rotation.

In practice, these principles contribute to enhanced soil health, improved crop yields, and increased resilience to climatic shocks, such as droughts and heavy rains. By helping to retain soil moisture, improve soil fertility, and control pests and diseases, conservation agriculture provides a robust and sustainable system that is well adapted to the smallholder farming contexts of many African countries.

Moreover, by reducing the need for synthetic fertilisers and pesticides, conservation agriculture can also reduce farming costs and the environmental footprint of agriculture. It aligns with the principles of climate-smart agriculture, contributing to climate change mitigation by sequestering carbon in the soil and reducing greenhouse gas emissions.

However, promoting conservation agriculture also entails challenges. It requires a paradigm shift from conventional tillage-based farming, necessitating training and extension support for farmers. Issues of labour demands, especially for weed control, and the need for specialised equipment for no-till planting can also pose obstacles. Overcoming these barriers requires supportive policies, farmer training, and innovations in farm machinery adapted to smallholder contexts.[18]

The indigenous knowledge is not confined to farming; it extends to healthcare as well. Traditional African medicine, underpinned by centuries of experience and cultural understanding, continues to be a primary source of healthcare for a large portion of the African population.

The perception of traditional African medicine has been historically influenced by the colonial era, during which it was often erroneously linked to malevolent or evil practices. This has, in some ways, marginalised the practice, confining it primarily to herbalists or traditional medicine men. Despite this, traditional African medicine remains a cornerstone of healthcare for a large segment of the population across the continent. It offers a wealth of knowledge, refined over centuries, and is deeply rooted in the specialised wisdom of various communities, including those inhabiting the rainforests.

Today, the challenge lies in integrating this rich tradition into modern, mainstream healthcare systems. This integration is complicated but crucial, particularly because a substantial part of the African population has grown accustomed to pharmaceutical solutions offered by modern medicine. Bridging this divide requires a nuanced approach that recognises the invaluable diversity and specialised local understanding embedded in traditional African medicine.

To effect this change, firstly, it's essential to combat lingering stigmas that stem from colonial-era mischaracterisations, while also conducting rigorous scientific research to validate the efficacy and safety of traditional treatments. This way, the wealth of medical wisdom that has been honed through generations can find its rightful place alongside modern medical practices, leading to a more holistic and culturally sensitive healthcare system.

Secondly, comprehensive documentation of these traditional practices, possibly through ethnographic studies and oral histories, is crucial for preserving this knowledge for future generations and facilitating its wider dissemination. This documentation can serve as an educational resource for healthcare practitioners in both traditional and mainstream medicine.

Thirdly, regulatory frameworks must be developed to certify and standardise traditional medical practices, ensuring they meet set quality and safety standards. This would help in creating a bridge between traditional practitioners and mainstream healthcare providers and ensuring patient safety.

Fourthly, educational curricula for healthcare professionals should incorporate a component on traditional African medicine. This would allow doctors, nurses, and other healthcare providers to have a nuanced understanding of these practices and how they can complement modern medical treatments.

Fifthly, public awareness campaigns should be initiated to educate the broader population about the validated benefits of traditional medicine, eradicating any existing stigmas and facilitating acceptance in mainstream healthcare settings.

Finally, partnerships between government agencies, healthcare organisations, academic institutions, and community leaders can offer a multidisciplinary approach to the integration process. These collaborations could facilitate resource allocation, research, and the implementation of pilot programmes aimed at assessing the efficacy of merging traditional and mainstream healthcare practices.

Traditional African medicine could be effectively incorporated into mainstream healthcare systems by taking these measures, thereby creating a more holistic and culturally sensitive approach to health and wellbeing.

Already, recognising its value, the WHO has emphasised integrating traditional medicine into national health systems in a culturally sensitive and scientifically validated manner.[19] Notable examples include the use of the *Artemisia annua* plant in the treatment of malaria, a practice rooted in traditional Chinese medicine that has led to the development of modern antimalarial drugs.[20]

Beyond these examples, indigenous knowledge systems encompass a vast array of practices and insights in fields ranging from natural resource management to conflict resolution. It is crucial to recognise, document, and apply this knowledge in ways that respect and uphold the rights of indigenous communities.

Reviving and harnessing indigenous knowledge and practices can therefore be a powerful tool for sustainable development in Africa. Emphasising their role not only respects and revitalises cultural heritage but also can provide practical, locally adapted solutions to contemporary challenges.

In Chapter 7, we will dig deeper into another crucial element of Africa's path to prosperity – infrastructure development. Africa must prioritise investment in resource and infrastructure development to enhance economic productivity.

CHAPTER 7

INFRASTRUCTURE DEVELOPMENT

As Africa continues to experience its cultural renaissance, a fundamental factor that would determine its economic prosperity and social progress is the quality and extent of its infrastructure. Infrastructure, in its various forms – be it transportation, energy, water, or digital – plays a critical role in enabling commerce, facilitating access to essential services, and enhancing quality of life. This chapter explores the importance of infrastructure development in Africa, provides examples of significant projects, and discusses the challenges and opportunities it presents.

Essentially, infrastructure is the physical and organisational setup that helps a society function smoothly. It's like the backbone of a country, supporting its economy and helping communities grow. In simple terms, infrastructure includes things like roads, bridges, and ports that help move goods and people around. These physical systems are crucial for businesses and the overall economy because they help goods get to where they need to go, creating jobs and opportunities along the way.

But infrastructure isn't just about economics. It's also vital for improving people's lives in other ways. For example, having reliable electricity in homes means people can study, stay comfortable, and access healthcare. Clean water and good sanitation systems protect people from diseases and make communities healthier.

In today's digital age, infrastructure also includes things like internet connectivity and data centres. These are the building blocks of the digital economy, making it possible for people to access services like online healthcare and shopping.

Let's look at specific examples of infrastructure developed or being developed across Africa.

Transportation Infrastructure

Economic activities, from the everyday exchange of goods to the global trade, largely depend on reliable infrastructure. Take a moment to imagine goods produced in a factory. These goods, whether agricultural produce, manufactured items, or raw materials, need to reach various markets – local, regional, or international. Here's where the transportation network swings into action. A well-maintained road or efficient railway line can make the journey quick and cost-effective. Airports and seaports further widen this network, connecting the landlocked regions to global markets and fostering economic integration. The following are some examples.

Mombasa-Nairobi Standard Gauge Railway (Kenya)

The Mombasa-Nairobi Standard Gauge Railway (SGR) is a shining example of a transformative infrastructure project in Kenya, leaving a broad imprint on multiple sectors of the economy. The SGR is more than just a railway; it's also a tangible symbol of Africa's commitment to infrastructural advancement, economic progress, and regional integration.

Spanning 472 km, it connects Mombasa, a key trade port, to the capital, Nairobi. Prior to the SGR, freight trains took 36 hours for this journey; now, it's reduced to 8 hours, enhancing transport efficiency.

This efficiency has spurred numerous benefits: quicker goods transit boosts sectors like manufacturing and agriculture; reduced freight costs make Kenyan products more competitive and benefit consumers. Furthermore, the SGR promotes trade integration, a cornerstone of Africa's economic strategy. It also generated employment during construction and continues to indirectly support various sectors. Enhanced connectivity along the route will stimulate regional development, and the railway offers a boost to tourism, allowing easier access to Kenya's attractions.

Standard Gauge Railway (Tanzania)

The Tanzania Standard Gauge Railway (SGR) is another exemplary infrastructure project underway in East Africa that underlines the region's commitment to improving connectivity, facilitating trade, and fostering economic development. The ongoing project signifies one of the key steps towards Tanzania's aspiration to position itself as a strategic regional transport hub.

Central Corridor Project (East Africa)

The Kenya and Tanzania Standard Gauge Railway will eventually feed into the Central Corridor Project. The Central Corridor is a multimodal transport route encapsulating road, rail, and lake networks. The project is a transformative infrastructure initiative designed to strengthen trade routes and connectivity within East Africa, notably connecting the port of Dar es Salaam in Tanzania to landlocked nations like Uganda, Rwanda, and Burundi.

This venture symbolises East Africa's commitment to integration, aiming to boost both trade and socio-economic development. By enhancing connections to the port of Dar es Salaam, the project promotes regional trade, reduces transportation costs, and supports the economic development of landlocked nations.

The initiative also aligns with global sustainability efforts, emphasising energy-efficient transport like rail and lake over road transportation. Furthermore, the Central Corridor fortifies regional ties, as the enhanced economic interdependence promotes cooperation among member states.

In essence, the project epitomises the potential of joint infrastructure development to usher in widespread regional advancement.

Addis Ababa–Djibouti Railway and Djibouti Multipurpose Port (Ethiopia & Djibouti)

The Addis Ababa–Djibouti Railway, a 759-km conduit connecting Ethiopia's capital to Djibouti's port, is a testament to the benefits of cross-border collaboration. Operational since 2018, it provides landlocked Ethiopia with crucial access to global trade through the strategic Djibouti port.

The railway's introduction has been transformative, streamlining trade between Ethiopia and global markets. Prior challenges of time-consuming and expensive road transportation between the two destinations have been mitigated, leading to lower consumer costs and boosting economic activities in both countries. Additionally, it's a catalyst for job creation and poverty reduction.

Furthermore, the Djibouti Multipurpose Port, equipped with modern facilities, plays a pivotal role in amplifying trade for Djibouti and neighbouring countries. Linked to the Addis Ababa–Djibouti Railway, it serves as a vital maritime gateway, especially for landlocked nations like Ethiopia. The port's operations not only create jobs and stimulate local industries but also elevate Djibouti's position in global maritime affairs, particularly given its strategic location on the Gulf of Aden. Alongside other infrastructural projects like the Djibouti International Free Trade Zone, the port embodies Djibouti's ambition to emerge as a leading commercial hub in East Africa.

Kazungula Bridge (Zambia & Botswana)

The Kazungula Bridge, connecting Botswana and Zambia over the Zambezi River, stands as a significant symbol of regional cooperation in Southern Africa.

Inaugurated in 2021, this bridge enhances the North-South Corridor, a major trade route from South Africa's Durban port to landlocked Southern African nations. By facilitating trade and simplifying transit, the bridge bolsters economic growth, cutting down the previously cumbersome and costly ferry crossings. Its construction and ensuing operations offer local job opportunities, boost tourism, and promote local businesses. Beyond just infrastructure, the bridge emphasises environmental sustainability, ensuring minimal disruption to the Zambezi River and its ecosystem.

The Kazungula Bridge epitomises Africa's infrastructural advancements and the potential of collaborative efforts, driving regional integration and shared economic progress.

Port of Durban (South Africa)

The Port of Durban, situated on the eastern seaboard of South Africa, is one of the busiest and most strategic ports in Africa. It plays a critical role in facilitating international trade, supporting the South African economy, and fostering regional integration. As a key node in global maritime networks, the Port of Durban is an engine of economic growth and a testament to South Africa's strategic importance in international logistics and supply chains.

The Port of Durban, overseen by Transnet's National Ports Authority, is undergoing key developmental projects to boost its capacity and efficiency, aiming to accommodate increased maritime traffic and streamline goods processing. This enhancement is pivotal for stimulating South Africa's economy and facilitating trade for regional landlocked countries like Botswana, Zimbabwe, and Zambia. The developments promise significant job creation, both in construction and long-term operations. Serving as a vital link to global markets, the upgraded port will strengthen South Africa's connection to international trade and attract diverse investments due to reduced logistics costs.

As highlighted by Transnet in 2021, these upgrades reinforce South Africa's leadership in maritime trade and logistics, with far-reaching economic and regional impacts.[1]

Bole International Airport Expansion (Ethiopia)

The completion of Bole International Airport's expansion in 2019 marked a significant milestone in Ethiopia's infrastructural development. Located in the nation's capital, Addis Ababa, the expanded airport now boasts increased capacity to handle both passengers and cargo, setting the stage for the city to become a key aviation hub on the African continent.

With its modernised terminal and facilities, it now ranks among Africa's busiest airports, significantly enhancing Ethiopia's connectivity. Serving numerous international airlines, it provides extensive links to destinations across the globe, fostering trade, tourism, and cultural interactions. The expansion has economically benefitted Ethiopia by strengthening Ethiopian Airlines, attracting foreign investments, and boosting tourism. Moreover, it has generated numerous job opportunities across sectors, from construction to airline services. The revamped airport not only positions Ethiopia as a major aviation hub in Africa but also promotes its appeal as a tourist hotspot. As highlighted by Addis Fortune in 2019, Bole International Airport's growth epitomises Ethiopia's ambition in global aviation and its drive towards greater economic and regional integration.[2]

OR Tambo International Airport (South Africa)

Named after liberation leader Oliver Reginald Tambo, OR Tambo International Airport stands as a major strategic asset for Johannesburg and South Africa. As one of Africa's busiest airports, it links South Africa to over 60 global destinations, serving millions of passengers annually.

Significant upgrades, including a new central terminal and improved infrastructure, were undertaken for the 2010 FIFA World Cup, elevating the airport to a world-class status. OR Tambo International Airport offers travellers streamlined terminals, diverse services, and luxurious lounges to enhance convenience.

Economically, it's a significant job creator, promoting international tourism, trade, and investment in South Africa. Beyond its economic contributions, the airport symbolises national pride, modernity, and South Africa's global integration, exemplifying the nation's ambitions and potential.

Energy Infrastructure

Infrastructure's influence extends far beyond economic contributions, fostering social progress by enhancing access to vital services and amenities. The impact on societies varies widely, but one key area is access to reliable electricity, which is paramount to improving societal standards. Electricity in homes, schools, and hospitals has the capacity to significantly uplift the quality of life and socio-economic conditions of individuals and communities. In households, electricity facilitates better lighting, heating, and the use of appliances, improving comfort and freeing up time for productive activities. For example, the simple act of using electric cooking appliances can reduce the time spent on meal preparation, offering more opportunities for employment, education, or leisure.

In schools, electricity supports an enhanced educational environment. It enables the use of computers and other digital tools that are becoming increasingly critical in modern education. Beyond basic literacy and numeracy, these tools help to develop digital literacy and other crucial 21st-century skills, thereby preparing students for a technologically advanced workplace.

In hospitals, reliable electricity is a matter of life and death. It powers essential equipment, from lighting to life support machines, and supports the cold storage of medicines and vaccines. In many developing countries, such as those on our continent of Africa and elsewhere in the world, lack of reliable power can be a significant barrier to providing effective healthcare services.

Africa, a continent known for its extensive mineral, oil, and gas reserves, is often overlooked for its abundant renewable energy potential, which it can provide to its citizens both in urban and rural areas. Blessed with bountiful solar, wind, hydro, and geothermal resources, Africa presents a golden opportunity for the world's green energy transition.

Solar Energy

Blessed with abundant sunlight, Africa holds immense potential for solar energy, with the Noor Ouarzazate Solar Complex in Morocco exemplifying this capability. Located in the Drâa-Tafilalet region, this complex is the world's largest concentrated solar power (CSP) plant, boasting a capacity of nearly 580 MW and a project cost of about $2.5 billion. Spanning an area equivalent to over 3,500 football fields, the facility utilises both photovoltaic and innovative CSP technologies. More than just a power generator, it's pivotal to Morocco's goal of sourcing 52 percent of its energy from renewables by 2030.[3] The complex not only addresses Morocco's energy needs but also fosters job creation, supports local industries, and reduces the nation's carbon footprint. The success of the Noor Ouarzazate Solar Complex serves as a powerful model for leveraging renewable energy resources in Africa and globally.

Wind Energy

The consistent winds across Africa, especially in regions like the Horn of Africa, North Africa, and West Africa's coasts, offer vast wind energy potential. The Lake Turkana Wind Power project in Kenya exemplifies this promise. Located in Marsabit County, this

310 MW capacity wind farm is Africa's largest, boosting Kenya's power generation by about 13 percent.[4]

Beyond energy, it's a catalyst for local economic growth, providing jobs and spurring infrastructure investments. This project underscores how, by tapping into natural resources like wind, African nations can meet energy demands and foster local development, setting a precedent for the continent's sustainable future.

Hydroelectric and Geothermal Energy

Africa's vast rivers, notably the Congo, Nile, and Zambezi, present significant hydroelectric potential. A prime example is the Grand Ethiopian Renaissance Dam (GERD) on the Nile, a central figure in Ethiopia's energy strategy. Once complete, GERD will offer an impressive 6,450 MW capacity, bolstering Ethiopia's energy supply and positioning it as an electricity exporter.[5] Besides power generation, GERD promises socio-economic development, job creation, agricultural advancement, and improved water access.

Meanwhile, the East African Rift Valley harbours significant geothermal energy potential. Ethiopia's geothermal reserves, estimated at 10,000 MW, could revolutionise its energy sector.[6] Unlike intermittent renewables, geothermal energy provides consistent power and is environmentally friendly. It promises to enhance energy security, drive economic growth, create jobs, and extend electricity to remote areas. Projects like Corbetti and Tulu Moye are pivotal in realising Ethiopia's geothermal ambitions.

Together, these hydroelectric and geothermal initiatives symbolise Africa's commitment to renewable energy, pointing towards sustainable growth, economic advancement, and enhanced quality of life for its people.

Renewable Energy Independent Power Producer Procurement Programme (REIPPPP).

In Africa's quest to harness renewable energy, South Africa has pioneered renewable energy adoption through its Renewable Energy Independent Power Producer Procurement Programme (REIPPPP) launched in 2011. The initiative encourages independent power producers to bid for renewable energy project developments. Notably, the country has seen a rise in wind and solar energy sectors, with significant projects like the Jeffreys Bay Wind Farm and Kathu Solar Park.

The Jeffreys Bay Wind Farm, one of the country's largest, occupies 3,700 hectares in the Eastern Cape. Benefitting from optimal onshore wind conditions and proximity to an existing power grid, it generates roughly 460,000 MWh annually, powering around 100,000 homes and contributing to job creation and community upliftment.[7]

Meanwhile, the Northern Cape boasts the expansive Kathu Solar Park. Harnessing the region's abundant sunlight, it produces enough electricity to power approximately 179,000 homes annually, offsetting 300,000 tons of CO_2.[8] Beyond electricity generation, the park has stimulated job opportunities and skills development in the community.

The REIPPPP's success is attributed to a solid policy foundation, competitive bidding, and robust regulatory structures, emphasising the importance of public-private collaborations. Having attracted significant investment and diversified the energy landscape away from coal, this programme offers an exemplary model for other African nations aiming to bolster their renewable energy portfolios.

Unlocking Africa's renewable energy potential can mitigate

energy access issues, decrease fossil fuel dependency, and contribute to climate change solutions. However, barriers persist, including high up-front capital costs, inadequate policy frameworks and incentives, and limited technical expertise.

To overcome these obstacles, Africa can look to countries like Germany and Denmark, who have successfully transitioned to renewable energy. Germany's 'Energiewende' (energy transition) policy has successfully encouraged private investment and public participation, leading to a surge in renewable energy production. Denmark, the world's leader in wind energy, has shown how strong policy support, incentives, and local participation can drive renewable energy deployment.

For Africa, a blend of supportive policy frameworks, investment in technical training, and financial mechanisms to reduce up-front costs are needed to realise its renewable potential. With the right mix of factors, Africa could not only meet its energy needs sustainably but also become a frontrunner in the global green energy revolution.

Continental Power Transmission

Building a comprehensive power transmission network across Africa is akin to weaving a grand fabric that stretches from the shores of North Africa to the southern tip of the continent. It's an ambitious vision that requires the integration of strategic planning, advanced technology, and regional collaboration.

Central to this mission is the creation of high-voltage transmission lines, akin to the mega highways of electric power. These vast networks would span thousands of kilometres, traversing diverse terrains and connecting power plants to urban centres, remote villages, industrial hubs, and mining areas. A key example of this ambitious infrastructural endeavour is the Inga-Kolwezi high-voltage direct current (HVDC) transmission line in the Democratic Republic of Congo. Stretched across approximately 1,700 kilometres, this line stands as one of the longest of its kind in the world.[9] It is the physical embodiment of human tenacity, technological advancement, and strategic vision, navigating the diverse and challenging geographical conditions of Africa.

The story of the Inga-Kolwezi line begins at the Inga dams, located along the Congo River, which boasts one of the world's largest hydropower potentials. From these power plants, the transmission line weaves its way across the vast landscapes of the Democratic Republic of Congo, ferrying the generated electricity to the bustling mining town of Kolwezi.

The construction of the Inga-Kolwezi transmission line was an engineering feat of monumental proportions. Given the challenging terrain and vast distances, the implementation of this project required meticulous planning, careful engineering, and robust technology. The line's HVDC technology was crucial in this regard. Unlike alternating current (AC) transmission, HVDC allows for efficient long-distance transmission of power with lower losses, making it a practical solution for the unique challenges posed by the Inga-Kolwezi project.

Since its inauguration, the Inga-Kolwezi line has revolutionised the power landscape of the region. It has not only strengthened the reliability of the power supply to the mining industry in Kolwezi but has also bolstered the national grid. Moreover, the project has set a compelling precedent for long-distance power transmission in Africa, demonstrating that geographical vastness and diversity are not insurmountable obstacles but challenges that can be overcome with vision, ingenuity, and technology.

The Inga-Kolwezi HVDC line is more than just a physical structure. It's a symbol of Africa's potential for energy self-sufficiency and regional integration, a testament to human achievement against all odds, and a beacon illuminating the path towards a robust, interconnected power sector that can light up the entire continent.

However, the physical transmission lines are only one piece of the puzzle. Alongside the visible, tangible facets, an invisible revolution is taking place – the integration of smart grid technologies. These systems are bringing in a new age of efficiency and reliability in the power sector, and Egypt is at the forefront of this transformation.[10]

The concept of a 'smart grid' refers to an electricity network that employs digital technology to monitor and manage the production, transmission, and consumption of electricity in real time. It's like having a nervous system for the power grid, enabling instant response and adaptation to changes in electricity usage and system conditions.

In Egypt, a nationwide initiative is underway to metamorphose the traditional grid into a smart grid. This ambitious project is a testament to the country's commitment to harnessing cutting-edge technology to improve its energy sector. The transformation touches every aspect of the grid, from generation to consumption, painting a comprehensive picture of a modern, efficient, and resilient power system.

At the core of this initiative is the upgrade of grid infrastructure. Old and outdated components are replaced or modernised, laying the groundwork for a more reliable and efficient grid. However, the transformation goes beyond physical changes. It's as much about information as it is about electricity.

Advanced metering systems are a key feature of Egypt's smart grid. These devices do more than just record energy consumption; they provide detailed, real-time data that allows for better demand management and accurate billing. Imagine knowing exactly when and where electricity is being used in your home or business, enabling you to manage and even reduce your energy usage.

The role of cross-border interconnections is critical in this vast power network. The power systems of individual countries, much like the countries themselves, are not islands unto themselves. They are part of a larger, interconnected world, and harnessing these connections can yield significant benefits. In the realm of power systems, these connections take the form of cross-border interconnections, powerful conduits that extend across national boundaries, linking separate power systems into a cohesive whole.

Imagine the countries of a region as houses in a neighbourhood, each with its own power supply. Now, imagine if these houses were to connect their power supplies to each other, creating a network that could share, distribute, and balance power across the entire neighbourhood. This is essentially what cross-border interconnections do for power systems. They serve as electrical bridges between countries, allowing them to share and exchange electricity, balance supply and demand across a larger area, and improve the overall resilience, flexibility, and efficiency of their power systems.

A prime example is the West African Power Pool (WAPP), an agency under ECOWAS, connecting 14 West African nations. This vast electric grid facilitates power trading, optimising resource use, reducing electricity costs, and ensuring a reliable supply. Beyond its physical infrastructure, WAPP symbolises cooperation and regional integration. Since its 2000 inception, WAPP has significantly integrated West Africa's power systems, with numerous cross-border lines established and an evolving regional electricity market. It envisions a borderless West Africa with uninterrupted electricity flow.

Financing the development of transmission infrastructure requires substantial investment. Public-private partnerships (PPPs) can play a critical role in this context, leveraging private sector capital and expertise for public infrastructure projects. The Lake Turkana Wind Power project in Kenya, the largest wind farm in Africa, was developed using a PPP model, illustrating the potential of this.

Finally, capacity building is a crucial component of this grand vision. Developing the technical and regulatory skills to manage complex power systems is a pressing need. In South Africa, the Eskom Academy of Learning has been a pioneer in this regard, offering technical and managerial training programmes for the power sector.

Building a continent-wide power transmission network in Africa is indeed a monumental task, but with strategic planning, advanced technology, regional collaboration, innovative financing, and capacity building, it is an achievable goal. This grand under-taking has the potential to bring light and power to millions, stimulate economic growth, and set Africa on a sustainable development pathway.

Water and Sanitation Infrastructure

Water and sanitation infrastructure is essential for public health and sustainable development. Imagine a world where turning on a tap didn't guarantee clean, drinkable water, or where safe and sanitary toilet facilities were a luxury, not a right. For many on our continent, this isn't just a thought exercise – it's reality. Access to reliable water and sanitation infrastructure, while often taken for granted in developed countries, remains a significant challenge in many parts of the world, including many of the countries on our continent, especially in rural and underprivileged areas. This is where the transformative power of water and sanitation infrastructure should take centre stage.

Take a moment to visualise the journey of a single drop of water from a reservoir or a river to your tap. It's not a simple path. The water must be collected, treated to remove impurities, and then transported through a complex network of pipes to reach its final destination. Similarly, sanitation infrastructure serves the critical function of collecting, treating, and disposing or reusing waste in a sanitary manner. Together, they form a vital backbone of public health and socio-economic development.

Let's delve into the potential of effective water and sanitation systems. Clean water is the elixir of life. It is essential for drinking, cooking, personal hygiene, and has a host of other purposes. Reliable access to clean water can dramatically improve health outcomes, reducing the prevalence of waterborne diseases like cholera and dysentery, which can ravage communities.[11]

Beyond health, the ripple effect of clean water access touches every aspect of community life. Children, free from water-related illnesses, can attend school more consistently and acquire knowledge that can break the cycle of poverty. Adults, enjoying better health, can work more productively and contribute more significantly to the local economy.

Turning our attention to sanitation, the benefits are just as profound. Sanitation facilities, such as toilets and sewer systems, play a critical role in enhancing public health by preventing contact with harmful waste, thereby reducing disease spread. The establishment of such facilities can notably reduce the incidence of diarrheal diseases, especially among children, leading to better school attendance and overall health.

Ethiopia's Health Extension programme (HEP), initiated in 2003, was transformative. Beyond just establishing latrines, it delivered comprehensive health services to underserved populations. The programme trained local women as health extension workers (HEWs) who promoted sanitation and hygiene at the grassroots level. Their efforts saw national basic sanitation coverage leap to 66 percent, leading to reduced waterborne diseases and lower child mortality.[12]

South Africa's eThekwini Municipality, encompassing Durban, adopted an innovative approach to sanitation with Urine Diverting Dry Toilets (UDDTs). These toilets, besides enhancing sanitation, addressed water scarcity and facilitated waste recycling as fertilisers. With community engagement at its core, over 85,000 UDDTs were installed by 2013, serving around 500,000 residents.[13]

West Africa's Senegal championed the Community-led Total Sanitation (CLTS) programme, emphasising behavioural change and community ownership. Instead of relying on externally imposed solutions, it empowered communities to realise the consequences of open defecation and encouraged them to find local solutions. This approach led to many villages becoming open defecation free, with consequent health improvements.

All in all, water and sanitation infrastructure is far more than pipes, taps, and toilets. It is a catalyst for public health, an enabler of socio-economic development, and a cornerstone of dignified living. The journey towards universal access to clean water and improved sanitation may be arduous, but its destination – a healthier, more sustainable world – is well worth the effort.

Telecommunication and Digital Infrastructure

Telecommunication infrastructure and digital infrastructure are two terms that are often used interchangeably, but they refer to different, albeit related, concepts.

Telecommunication infrastructure primarily concerns the physical and hardware facets of communication systems. These include the vast network of equipment and technologies that facilitate the transmission of voice, data, text, video, and multimedia across various media. Concrete examples of these are the telephone lines that zigzag across our cities, the mobile networks that keep our smartphones buzzing, the intricate lattice of satellite systems that hover above our heads, the undersea fibre-optic cables that connect continents, and the broadcasting towers that pepper our skylines. This network of structures forms the backbone of traditional telephony services like landlines and mobile networks, as well as internet-based communication services.

On the other hand, digital infrastructure paints a broader canvas. It envelopes not just the telecommunication infrastructure but also the myriad software, platforms, and services that enable and enhance digital activities. Digital infrastructure extends its reach beyond the physical. It touches the humming data centres that store our digital lives, the cloud computing resources that fuel our online applications, the vast data repositories that hold the secrets of big data, and the digital platforms that have become the agora of modern society. But it's not just about technology. Digital infrastructure also spans areas like digital literacy, regulations, and policies that help manage and govern the digital ecosystem.

In this interconnected tapestry, the two are tightly interwoven, each one vital for the functioning and prosperity of modern societies. Their robustness and reach form the bedrock of a country's digital readiness and inclusivity, underpinning the ability of its citizens to participate in the digital age.

Telecommunications Infrastructure

The vast African continent has been carving out a unique trajectory in the telecommunications landscape. Over the past few decades, Africa has leapfrogged traditional developmental stages of telecommunications infrastructure, making the transition from minimal fixed-line telephony directly to widespread mobile technology. This has created a paradigm shift, bringing about unprecedented connectivity and laying a solid foundation for digital growth.

At the helm of this transformation is mobile technology. Mobile technology is a key driver of transformation in Sub-Saharan Africa, with GSMA predicting 615 million unique mobile subscribers by 2025 due to the spread of 5G networks.[14] Nigeria, Africa's largest economy, exemplifies the potential of telecom infrastructure for economic growth. By 2020, mobile subscriptions exceeded 180 million, reaching approximately 222.6 million by December 2022, attributed to the broad 4G network rollout by companies like MTN, Airtel, and Globacom.[15] This boom has enhanced internet speed, reshaping work, education, and entertainment in Nigeria.

Ecommerce has especially thrived, with platforms like Jumia, Konga, and Jiji transforming the retail landscape and significantly contributing to Nigeria's GDP. Moreover, fintech platforms like Paystack and Paga are revolutionising financial transactions, increasing financial inclusion, particularly for the previously unbanked population. Digital hubs, including Co-Creation Hub and Ventures Platform, have bolstered tech entrepreneurship, leading to innovative solutions addressing local challenges, from healthcare to agriculture.

Turning to South Africa, with a 2023 population of 60.14 million, the story is equally compelling. With telecom giants Vodacom and MTN expanding 4G coverage, mobile broadband subscriptions have seen a significant rise. By early 2023, there were 112.7 million cellular connections, representing around 187 percent of the population (likely due to singular people using multiple connections).[16] This increased connectivity is driving the digital economy. Ecommerce platforms like Takealot and Zando are prospering, and a thriving tech startup culture is emerging. The broader impact, however, lies in the democratisation of digital access, narrowing the digital divide and allowing more South Africans to benefit from online services, from education to health.

Not just limited to mobile connectivity, Africa's telecommunication revolution extends to the deployment of undersea fibre-optic cables. These underwater information highways have been instrumental in linking the African continent to the global digital grid, reshaping the contours of Africa's digital landscape.

The East African Submarine Cable System (EASSy) has reshaped the telecom dynamics, spanning approximately 10,000 km and enhancing Africa's international bandwidth since 2010. Similarly, the West Africa Cable System (WACS) and the Main One Cable have been instrumental in magnifying digital connections, leading to innovation and socio-economic growth in their regions.

Beyond these physical cables, Africa is also tapping into satellite communication to bridge infrastructure gaps, especially in remote areas. Ethiopia's launch of the Ethiopian Remote Sensing Satellite-1 (ETRSS-1) in 2019 marked its initiation into the spacefaring nations club, utilising the satellite to improve agricultural planning. South Africa's ZACUBE-2 satellite, launched in 2018, aids in disaster management and marine traffic monitoring. Similarly, Ghana, Angola, and Egypt have launched satellites to bolster their disaster management, telecommunication, and digital services capabilities, showcasing Africa's commitment to harnessing space technology for development.

As 5G technology emerges, pilot projects in countries like South Africa and Gabon signal the commencement of a new era in Africa's telecommunication narrative.

All in all, from widespread mobile networks to undersea fibre-optic cables, and from satellite communications to the dawn of 5G, the telecommunication infrastructure across Africa is experiencing an evolution. As these digital highways continue to expand and mature, they carry the promise of driving economic development, fostering innovation, and bridging the digital divide. As the African proverb goes, "If you want to go fast, go alone. If you want to go far, go together." The journey towards a digitally inclusive Africa is a collective one, and telecommunications infrastructure provides the necessary path.

Digital infrastructure

Digital infrastructure serves as the vital arteries through which data flows and digital transactions occur. As our world stitches together tighter webs of interconnection, these networks are woven into the fabric of our everyday lives and the global economy, growing in importance with each passing day.

At the crossroads of healthcare and technology, digital infrastructure orchestrates the melody of e-health services. These services, empowered by robust internet connectivity, throw open the doors to healthcare access, especially in the remotest corners of the globe. Telemedicine erases geographical barriers, enabling patients to consult with healthcare professionals at the tap of a button. Digital platforms streamline the healthcare journey, from booking appointments to refilling prescriptions and accessing medical records. In essence, digital infrastructure holds the reins of health information systems and research, shaping a future of improved healthcare delivery and outcomes.

In the realm of education, digital infrastructure clears the path for e-learning, transforming physical classrooms into virtual learning environments. It's the magic carpet that carries education to students in far-off places or during challenging times, like the COVID-19 pandemic. It's the key that unlocks online learning resources, from educational platforms to digital libraries, unfurling opportunities for learning like never before.

For the economic landscape, digital infrastructure lays the foundation for ecommerce. It is the bridge that connects businesses to customers far beyond their geographical confines. It is the catalyst that sparks online transactions, dismantling barriers for businesses and offering consumers an array of choices at their fingertips. In recent times, the pulse of economic activity has throbbed along these digital pathways, particularly during lockdowns imposed during COVID-19.

Digital infrastructure also serves as the champion of digital inclusion. It ensures that the doors of the digital economy swing open for all individuals and communities. This inclusion is paramount today, when digital skills and connectivity are intrinsically tied to economic opportunities and social integration.

Moreover, digital infrastructure redefines the delivery of government services, moulding them into efficient online processes. From filing taxes to applying for essential documents or benefits, a multitude of government services are now a click away, revolutionising efficiency and user experience.

Robust digital infrastructure plays a pivotal role in modern society. It stands as an enabler, propelling economic growth, fuelling social progress, and ensuring equitable access to services.[17] Therefore, the task of investing in and developing digital infrastructure stands tall on the agenda for governments and societies worldwide.

At the heart of this revolution lies the financial sector. Traditionally, banking and financial services have been anchored to physical institutions – concrete and glass structures often beyond reach for those dwelling in remote or rural areas. But mobile technology has disrupted this paradigm, breaking the chains of traditional banking. It has sowed the seeds of mobile money services, a digital oasis in the desert of financial exclusion. Imagine a rural farmer in Kenya, far from the nearest town and even farther from the nearest bank. Traditional banking infrastructure has long overlooked such individuals, with the distance and the cost of travelling to a bank branch making financial services inaccessible. Yet, in today's digital age, the farmer holds a powerful banking tool right in his hand – his mobile phone.

This transformation is primarily driven by mobile money services, a novel application of mobile technology that has taken the financial world by storm. The advent of platforms such as M-PE-

SA in Kenya and MTN Mobile Money in Ghana has birthed a new landscape of financial inclusion. These services enable users to deposit money into an account linked to their mobile devices, withdraw cash, transfer funds to other users, pay bills, and even access credit and savings products.

Mobile money services stand out for their simplicity and convenience. With a few phone taps, a Kenyan farmer can manage finances without travel, queues, or complex paperwork, making it user-friendly even for those with limited literacy or tech experience.

The impact of mobile money services extends beyond convenience. It holds profound socio-economic implications. In Kenya, access to M-PESA has lifted an estimated 194,000 households out of poverty, with the impacts particularly pronounced among female-headed households.[18]

The gates of economic participation have swung open, and the future of finance in Africa is likely to be written not in the ledgers of banks but in the data packets of mobile networks.

The power of mobile connectivity doesn't stop at finance. It also serves as a beacon of knowledge, piercing through the fog of information asymmetry. Consider agriculture, for example. Farmers, once at the mercy of unpredictable weather, can now access real-time meteorological data to guide their cultivation practices. This information, delivered directly to their mobile devices, enables them to plan their cropping cycles, manage irrigation, and reduce the risk of crop failures, potentially improving yields and incomes.[19]

Let's turn our gaze to Malawi, a nation nestled in the south-eastern region of Africa, where the power of mobile technology is reshaping the agricultural landscape. Imagine a smallholder farmer in the lush Shire Highlands of southern Malawi. Traditionally, their farming practices were a gamble with nature, the skies above dictating the rhythm of their agricultural activities. However, with the advent of mobile technology, the tables have turned.

Thanks to innovative services like the National Smallholder Farmers' Association of Malawi's (NASFAM) Farmbook, farmers can access critical weather data in real time. This foreknowledge enables the farmer to make informed decisions. Will rain arrive to nourish newly sown seeds, or should they hold off sowing in anticipation of a dry spell? Such timely information helps them optimise their cultivation cycles and manage irrigation efficiently, reducing the risk of crop failure.

The cascading effects of this digital integration are considerable. When farming activities align with weather patterns and resources are used effectively, crop yields can increase significantly. This, in turn, means a more bountiful harvest, leading to improved income for farmers and greater food security for the wider community.

As mobile connectivity continues to penetrate the farthest corners of the continent, it promises a future where agriculture and technology thrive symbiotically, fostering sustainable development and food security.

Similarly, in the realm of education, mobile connectivity extends the reach of learning resources beyond brick-and-mortar classrooms. It enables students, even in the remotest corners of the continent, to access educational materials, participate in interactive lessons, and collaborate with peers, effectively bringing the school to the student. Take Egypt, for example, where the Alemni platform has been reshaping the educational landscape. This homegrown ed-tech startup is leveraging mobile technology to break down barriers in education and extend learning opportunities far beyond traditional classrooms.

Alemni, which means 'teach me' in Arabic, offers a mobile learning platform that allows students across Egypt and beyond to access a wealth of educational resources at their fingertips. It delivers comprehensive and curriculum-aligned lessons to students through their mobile devices, making education accessible irrespective of location or time constraints.

The transformative effects of mobile technology can also be seen vividly in the health sector across Africa. In a continent where healthcare facilities are often concentrated in urban centres, mobile technology is helping to bridge the rural-urban divide.

For example, in Rwanda, the Babyl telemedicine service allows patients in remote areas to consult with qualified doctors through their mobile devices. Before Babyl, many of Rwanda's rural residents often had to travel long distances to reach the nearest health centre. This situation was exacerbated by the high cost of transport and the time it took to get there, which often discouraged people from seeking medical help.

Mobile technology is also facilitating the continual professional development of health workers. The Uganda-based app mTrac, for instance, provides health workers with real-time data on disease outbreaks, stock levels of essential medicines, and other crucial health service indicators.

Before the advent of mTrac, the health information system in Uganda was largely paper-based. This led to delays in data reporting and acted as a barrier to prompt decision-making. With mTrac, real-time data is now at the fingertips of health workers and decision-makers. Health workers across the country can report on disease outbreaks, drug stock-outs, and service delivery issues directly from their mobile phones. This data is then collected and analysed in real time, ensuring that swift and informed decisions can be made at the local, district, and national levels.

mTrac offers an anonymous hotline for reporting healthcare delivery issues, promoting accountability and community involvement. It also boosts health workers' professional growth through SMS training, updates, and quizzes on health policies. This has elevated Uganda's health system efficiency and exemplifies how digital tools can enhance health services and outcomes.

In Ghana, the Mobile Midwife solution, launched in 2010 by the Grameen Foundation with Ghana Health Service, aids pregnant women and caregivers. It consists of two apps: one provides expectant mothers with tailored advice and reminders in their local language, while the other helps healthcare professionals manage patient care, track health indicators, and communicate with patients. A 2016 study showed Mobile Midwife increased antenatal and postnatal visits along with skilled deliveries, improving maternal and newborn health.[20] This initiative underscores how digital advancements can elevate healthcare access and community empowerment.

In essence, digital infrastructure is rapidly emerging as a critical pillar of Africa's development. As the threads of mobile connectivity continue to weave their way across the continent, they carry with them the promise of economic growth, social development, and a brighter future, one signal bar at a time.

These infrastructural projects showcase Africa's aspirations for development, integration, and global scientific leadership. They underscore the transformative potential of strategic infrastructure development in stimulating economic growth, fostering regional integration, and enhancing the quality of life for communities. Not only do these projects stimulate trade and economic activity, but they also foster regional integration and create a more interconnected Africa.

The benefits of such infrastructure are far-reaching. For businesses, it means more accessible markets and reduced operating costs. For consumers, it ensures a steady supply of goods. For the workforce, it creates job opportunities – not only during the construction phase but also in the long term through auxiliary services like logistics, maintenance, and operations.

However, realising such transformative potential requires substantial investment, meticulous planning, and sustained maintenance. Challenges such as funding gaps, governance issues, and technical expertise will need to be addressed.[21]

In Chapter 8, we will explore another essential pillar of Africa's journey to prosperity: education and human capital development. Quality education is the backbone of development. By going beyond traditional education to fostering critical thinking, scientific literacy, and a sense of shared history, Africans will navigate their destiny with knowledge and confidence.

CHAPTER 8

EDUCATION AND HUMAN CAPITAL DEVELOPMENT

As Africa makes strides in infrastructure development, it also needs to invest in its most significant resource – its people. This chapter delves into the pivotal role of quality and relevant education in empowering the continent's youth and driving economic growth.

Importance of Education

One of the most famous education-related quotes of the revered Nelson Mandela is, "Education is the most powerful weapon which you can use to change the world."

Studies suggest a strong correlation between a country's human capital and its economic performance. For instance, Eric

Hanushek, a renowned economist, has written extensively on the impact of education quality on development goals. In his work, he argues that the quality of education, as measured by cognitive skills, is a key driver of economic growth. If we go deeper into the arguments laid out in Hanushek's research, we learn that education is not a mere metric of literacy or numeracy but a broad domain that impacts every facet of a nation's socio-economic fabric.[1]

At the heart of this is the concept of human capital – the sum of the skills, knowledge, and competencies of a nation's population. Hanushek establishes that a nation's human capital stands as a significant determinant of its economic prowess. A well-educated workforce, armed with the necessary skills and knowledge, can optimise productivity, innovate, and drive economic expansion. This not only improves individual lives but also propels the nation on a trajectory of sustained economic growth.

Furthermore, quality education also provides the foundation for a robust democracy. It fosters civic participation, making the populace more likely to engage in democratic processes, uphold democratic values, and advocate for justice and equality. This active citizenry contributes to the stability and harmony of a society – factors that attract investment and further stimulate economic growth.

However, the key to unlocking these benefits lies in the quality of education. Hanushek emphasises that merely providing access to education is not enough; the education must be of high quality. Quality education equips students with critical thinking skills, problem-solving abilities, and creativity, which are necessary for the complexities of the modern world. It prepares students not just for the existing job market, but also for industries of the future.

Hanushek also underscores the need for the education system to be adaptable and responsive to the changing economic landscape. As the world evolves, so too must the skills and competencies taught in schools. This necessitates continuous investment in education, curriculum updates, teacher training, and the incorporation of technology in learning.

Hanushek's analysis affirms the transformative power of quality education. It reiterates that investment in education is indeed an investment in a nation's future – in its economic growth, social stability, and democratic strength. It serves as a call to action for policymakers worldwide to prioritise education as a strategic lever for national development.

For a glimpse of how prioritising education can transform a nation, let's look at other African nations, other than Botswana and Rwanda, that have done just as well in the area of education.

Ghana

In West Africa, Ghana stands out for its strategic emphasis on education as a tool for national development. Highlighting this commitment was the launch of the Free Senior High School (Free SHS) programme in 2017, ensuring secondary education accessibility for all, regardless of socio-economic backgrounds.

Beyond broadening access, Ghana has prioritised educational quality through initiatives like comprehensive teacher training and curriculum overhauls. In 2018, a teacher licensure exam was introduced to uphold teaching standards. Consequently, the nation has witnessed rising literacy rates, a surge in secondary school enrolments, and enhanced learning outcomes.

These educational advancements are not just academic; they're shaping a skilled youth populace ready to propel economic growth and innovation. Ghana's inclusive educational model promotes both social equity and a culture of continuous learning, offering a template for other nations prioritising education.

Mauritius

Mauritius, an Indian Ocean island nation, stands as a testament to the transformative power of prioritising education for national development. Since its independence in 1968, the country has transitioned from a low-income agrarian base to a diversified, upper-middle-income status, attributing much of this growth to its emphasis on education. One of the standout features of Mauritius's approach has been free education across all levels, resulting in an impressive literacy rate of over 92 percent, one of the highest in Africa.[2]

But the country's commitment isn't just to accessibility; Mauritius equally values quality. The curriculum is holistic, imparting both academic proficiency and essential soft skills. A notable focus has been on STEM fields, aligning with the nation's economic aspirations. Investments in teacher training, infrastructure, and technology have further bolstered the education quality. Additionally, the nation emphasises inclusivity with measures for special education needs and gender parity.

This comprehensive approach to education has cultivated a skilled workforce, fuelling sectors like information and communications technology (ICT), finance, and tourism. Besides economic growth, the educational strides have enhanced social mobility and diminished inequalities. In essence, Mauritius showcases how a nation, through a well-rounded and inclusive education system, can achieve both economic advancement and societal equity, serving as an inspiration for other countries.

Seychelles

Seychelles, an Indian Ocean archipelago, boasts notable successes in education, with a literacy rate approaching 96 percent, making it one of the highest in Africa.[3] The nation's focus on education is evident through its policy of free and compulsory education for ages 6 to 16, emphasising equal opportunity for all children, irrespective of their socio-economic status.

The Seychellois government's commitment goes beyond mere access; it has also poured resources into enhancing the quality of education. This includes infrastructure upgrades, consistent teacher training, and a diverse curriculum that integrates academic subjects with life skills, arts, and a significant focus on environmental education.

The returns on this educational investment are manifold. Economically, it has translated into a well-educated workforce, fuelling growth in sectors like tourism and fisheries, catapulting Seychelles to a high-income nation with a remarkable GDP per capita. From a social standpoint, this emphasis on education promotes upward mobility and narrows income disparities. Furthermore, the curriculum's stress on environmental awareness has ingrained a conservation mindset in the Seychellois, crucial for an economy anchored in the nation's natural beauty.

Tunisia

Tunisia, a North African nation, stands out for its strong emphasis on education, dedicating a significant portion of its budget to this sector – among the highest in Africa. Since its post-independence era, Tunisia has been proactive in reshaping its education system, achieving universal primary education and elevating literacy rates and enrolment numbers. Recognising the global economy's evolving demands, the country has expanded its focus to secondary, tertiary, and vocational education.

Central to Tunisia's educational strategy is a commitment to quality and inclusivity. The nation has undergone curriculum reforms, prioritised teacher training, and integrated digital tools in classrooms. Additionally, a notable aspect of its educational approach is the emphasis on gender equality, ensuring that females have equal access to learning opportunities. This has seen its literacy rate rise to 84 percent in 2022, marking a significant increase from 2014.[4]

Despite economic hurdles, Tunisia's consistent focus on education has fortified its social stability and spurred economic progress. An educated populace is more adept at weathering economic challenges, contributing to advanced sectors, and engaging in democratic processes. Moreover, education in Tunisia has been a beacon of social mobility and equality.

Morocco

Morocco, renowned for its rich heritage, has shown significant dedication to revitalising its education system over recent decades. Recognising the pivotal role of education in socio-economic growth, the government has championed reforms that both widen educational access and elevate its quality. These reforms have been influenced by the global economy's evolving requirements, emphasising 21st-century skills such as critical thinking, digital proficiency, and entrepreneurial acumen.

A highlight of Morocco's strategy has been its investment in teacher training, affirming that quality education is closely linked to adept teaching. In addition to mainstream education, Morocco has spotlighted vocational training, syncing it with labour market demands to assure graduates have industry-relevant skills.

As a result of these efforts, literacy rates, especially among the youth and women, have risen markedly. Furthermore, the emphasis on skills training has produced a cadre of competent graduates contributing to diverse economic sectors. Morocco's educational endeavours signal its commitment to shaping an informed citizenry primed for socio-economic advancement.

Gabon

Gabon, a prosperous Central African nation, primarily due to its oil reserves, has recognised the crucial role of education in sustaining its economy and reducing oil reliance. The government has made education mandatory for children aged 6 to 16, reflecting its dedication to imparting essential skills to the youth. Notably, initiatives to expand educational access in rural areas, such as constructing schools and incentivising teachers to work in remote regions, demonstrate the nation's commitment to universal quality education.

These endeavours have resulted in a commendable literacy rate in Gabon, signifying the effectiveness of its educational policies. This educational foundation supports the 'Emerging Gabon' strategy, which seeks to elevate Gabon to an emerging economy by 2025. With a focus on a well-educated workforce, Gabon aspires to diversify its economic landscape and ensure long-term growth.

Zambia

Zambia, located in Southern Africa, has prioritised education as a tool for national development. Post-independence in 1964, under President Kenneth Kaunda's leadership, free primary education was introduced, greatly benefiting the population, including individuals like me. While this policy boosted enrolment, it also strained resources, leading to overcrowded classrooms and resource shortages.

During the economic hardships of the 1980s and 1990s, due to falling copper prices and surging external debt, Zambia faced pressure from international entities like the IMF and World Bank. These challenges prompted the succeeding president, Frederick Chiluba, in 1993, to introduce school fees at the primary level, abandoning the free education legacy. This decision decreased enrolment, particularly among the less privileged.

In 2002, President Levy Mwanawasa revived free primary education, bolstering the goal of universal primary education in alignment with the Millennium Development Goals. This policy direction has continued under President Hakainde Hichilema, emphasising both primary and secondary education quality.

Recognising the critical role of quality instruction, Zambia revamped its curriculum to foster 21st-century skills and heavily invested in teacher training and development. These initiatives have resulted in improved literacy, enrolment rates, and overall student performance, cementing education as pivotal for Zambia's economic growth and societal progress.

Zambia's journey offers lessons for other nations: consistent political commitment is vital; expanding access and maintaining quality is crucial, and robust financial backing is necessary to sustain free education policies. Comprehensive education systems must also emphasise secondary and tertiary levels, ensuring holistic development opportunities for students.

Strategic Investing in Education

Undoubtedly, education stands as a cornerstone for economic development and prosperity. For Africa, with its young and burgeoning population, it becomes even more crucial. Strategically investing in specific types of education can propel the continent towards sustainable development and economic growth.

STEM Education

In today's rapidly evolving global landscape, science, technology, engineering, and mathematics (STEM) education holds the key to equipping future generations with the skills needed to drive innovation and technological advancement. This sector of education emphasises critical thinking, problem-solving, creativity, and digital literacy – all necessary skills in the contemporary workforce and key elements in driving economic growth and development.

For our African nations, promoting and investing in STEM education have become increasingly important as they seek to harness the immense potential of their youthful populations. By focusing on STEM, these nations can foster a generation of innovators, inventors, and leaders who can steer technological revolutions, drive economic growth, and solve complex societal problems.

Rwanda serves as an inspiring example of how an emphasis on STEM education can dramatically reshape a nation's prospects. The government of Rwanda has placed significant emphasis on developing STEM skills in its population, leading to the creation of tech-focused initiatives like the Kigali Innovation City, a platform designed to nurture digital innovation and technology.

Further south, South Africa's commitment to STEM education has also yielded impressive results. The nation's focus on cultivating a strong foundation in STEM subjects has led to an increase in skilled workers adept at navigating the complex landscape of today's digital economy. This has attracted global tech giants such as Google and Amazon to establish innovation centres in the country, contributing to job creation and economic growth.

However, promoting STEM education on our continent is not without its challenges. It requires substantial investment in infrastructure, teacher training, and curriculum development. It also requires efforts to eliminate gender disparities in STEM, as girls and women in many African societies are often underrepresented in these fields.

Yet, the payoff from investing in STEM education is significant. As digital technologies continue to transform economies worldwide, African nations with a strong emphasis on STEM education will be better positioned to take advantage of these changes. Through fostering a strong STEM-educated workforce, these nations can catalyse technological innovation, drive sustainable economic growth, and assert themselves more prominently on the global stage.

Vocational and Technical Training

Vocational and technical training represents a critical aspect of education that equips students with practical skills and knowledge directly applicable to the workforce. This form of education has the potential to significantly improve the employability of youth, providing them with specific skills tailored to the needs of various industries.

African nations can learn from the efficacy of vocational and technical training seen in Germany's dual vocational training system. This innovative approach combines theoretical education in classrooms with hands-on work experience, providing students with a well-rounded education that directly prepares them for the demands of their chosen fields. The success of this model is evidenced by Germany's comparatively low youth unemployment rates. Youth unemployment rate in Germany remained unchanged at 5.6 percent in October from 5.6 percent in July of 2023, attesting to the ability of vocational and technical training to facilitate smoother transitions from school to work.[5]

This model's potential benefits for Africa are immense, particularly in the context of its burgeoning youth population and the challenge of youth unemployment. By aligning education more closely with labour market demands, vocational and technical training can equip our African youth with the skills they need to secure employment and drive economic growth.

Ethiopia provides a compelling example of how this approach can be successfully implemented in an African context. The government's efforts to improve the quality of technical and vocational education and training (TVET) has yielded promising results. The revamped TVET system has shown significant success in improving youth employability and fostering entrepreneurship, demonstrating the transformative potential of high-quality vocational and technical training.[6]

However, scaling up vocational and technical training in Africa would require substantial investments, not only in terms of financial resources but also in developing high-quality curricula, training teachers, and establishing partnerships with industries. Moreover, societal attitudes towards vocational and technical education need to change. Too often, such education is viewed as a less desirable alternative to academic education. But as the German and Ethiopian examples show, vocational and technical training can offer a valuable pathway to employment and should be seen as a crucial part of the education landscape.

Thus, prioritising vocational and technical training can play a pivotal role in addressing youth unemployment in Africa, enhancing the continent's human capital, and driving its economic development. The benefits of such a focus would extend beyond the individual students, leading to more robust, resilient, and inclusive economies.

Entrepreneurship Education

Entrepreneurship education serves a pivotal role in fostering an entrepreneurial mindset, equipping learners with a unique set of skills that extend beyond the confines of traditional academic education. These skills include opportunity recognition, innovative problem-solving, risk management, resilience, strategic thinking, and more. When taught effectively, entrepreneurship education can spark creativity, promote ambition, and, most importantly, cultivate an entrepreneurial spirit among students.

In the context of our continent of Africa, where many countries face high rates of unemployment, particularly among the youth, entrepreneurship education can be a vital tool in promoting self-reliance, job creation, and economic growth. By nurturing entrepreneurial talent, African countries can foster the growth of small, micro, and medium-sized enterprises (SMMEs), which are recognised as key engines of economic growth, innovation, regional development, and employment globally.

Uganda provides a potent example of the transformative potential of entrepreneurship education. In this East African country, the introduction of an entrepreneurship curriculum in secondary schools has yielded encouraging results. Studies conducted by Educate!, a social enterprise in Uganda, found that exposure to entrepreneurship education led to an increase in business knowledge, entrepreneurial attitudes, and entrepreneurial intentions among students. These students were more likely to start their own businesses and create jobs, contributing to economic growth and poverty reduction.[7]

Such positive outcomes underline the importance of integrating entrepreneurship education into national education systems across Africa. However, implementing effective entrepreneurship education requires a comprehensive approach. This involves developing context-specific curricula, training teachers, fostering partnerships with the business community, and creating supportive environments that encourage entrepreneurial initiatives.

In a nutshell, entrepreneurship offers a pathway to tackling youth unemployment, driving economic growth, and transforming Africa's development trajectory. It is, therefore, imperative that African countries invest in entrepreneurship education as a core component of their broader education and economic development strategies.

Digital Literacy

In the age of the Fourth Industrial Revolution, where advancements in technology are transforming all aspects of human life, digital literacy has emerged as an essential skill. Digital literacy refers to the ability to use digital technology, communication tools, or networks to locate, evaluate, use, and create information. It goes beyond simply knowing how to use specific pieces of technology and includes a critical understanding of the ethical, social, and security implications of digital technologies.

Incorporating digital literacy into education equips learners with competencies that are increasingly in demand in today's digital economy. These competencies include, but are not limited to, coding, data analysis, digital communication, online collaboration, and digital content creation. Moreover, fostering digital literacy can unlock innovation potential by enabling individuals to leverage technology to solve problems, create value, and drive societal and economic progress.

Africa's burgeoning youth population presents an immense opportunity to harness digital technology's transformative potential. However, this calls for substantial investments in digital infrastructure, the integration of digital literacy into national curricula, and teacher training.

Kenya serves as an exemplary case of proactive efforts in cultivating digital literacy. The country's Digital Literacy Programme, launched by the Ministry of Education in 2016, aimed to integrate ICT into primary education. The programme involves the distribution of digital learning devices to schools, training teachers in ICT, and developing digital content for the curriculum.

The example of Kenya underscores the importance of digital literacy in the 21st-century education landscape. For Africa to effectively ride the wave of the Fourth Industrial Revolution, digital literacy needs to be at the forefront of education policy and curriculum development. With a digitally literate population, Africa can unlock the full potential of digital technology to drive economic growth, enhance social inclusion, and transform its development trajectory.

Inclusive Education

Inclusive education is an approach that aims to transform education systems to accommodate all learners, regardless of their backgrounds, abilities, or circumstances. It implies recognising and respecting the diverse needs, abilities, and characteristics of learners and eliminating all forms of discrimination in the learning environment.

Inclusive education is crucial for achieving social and economic development. It helps to reduce social inequalities by ensuring that all individuals have an equal opportunity to acquire education and skills, which are key to economic participation and mobility. It also fosters social cohesion by promoting understanding, tolerance, and solidarity among diverse groups of learners.

Moreover, inclusive education is an essential component of sustainable development. It is explicitly recognised in the United Nations' Sustainable Development Goals, particularly Goal 4, which aims to "ensure inclusive and equitable quality education and promote lifelong learning opportunities for all."[8]

South Africa's approach to inclusive education provides an example of how this concept can be operationalised. The country's inclusive education policy, introduced in 2001, reflects a commitment to ensuring that all learners, particularly those who are marginalised and excluded, have access to quality education. The policy acknowledges the diverse range of learner needs and calls for flexible teaching strategies, an adaptable curriculum, and a supportive and accepting learning environment.[9]

The pursuit of inclusive education requires sustained commitment, resources, and collaborative efforts among all education stakeholders. However, the potential payoff – in terms of reduced inequality, social cohesion, and sustainable economic growth – makes these efforts a worthwhile investment. As Africa seeks to harness its demographic dividend, inclusive education needs to be a key component of its education and development strategy.

Improving Quality and Relevance of Education

However, our current education system that we use to acquire skills is deficient because it is largely still based on rote learning. Rote learning is the process of memorising to remember material verbatim. As a result, students don't learn how to think critically, analyse, or solve real-world problems.

Furthermore, beyond traditional subjects, there is a growing consensus on the importance of fostering so-called '21st-century skills' mentioned earlier. As one great man once said, "Education is not a name of any degree or certificate that can be shown to others as proof. Education is the name of our attitude, actions, language, and behaviour with others in real life." While this quotation may not be directly attributed to a specific person, it is a philosophical statement often echoed in discussions about education, emphasising that the essence of education goes beyond formal certifications or degrees. Instead, it points out that education should be viewed as a holistic development process that influences attitudes, actions, language, and behaviour.

Applying this concept to education and human capital development in Africa suggests a need for a broader, more comprehensive approach to education that doesn't solely focus on academic achievements but also includes character development, practical skills, emotional intelligence, and moral values.

In line with this thinking, African countries, and others around the world, need to consider placing an emphasis on holistic education. Holistic education is a pedagogical philosophy that believes education should foster the overall development of a person, including intellectual, social, emotional, and physical aspects.[10] It values experiential learning, critical thinking, creativity, and character development.

Furthermore, given the diverse range of environments and contexts across Africa, practical skills and vocational training mentioned earlier should be integral parts of education systems. This includes skills such as entrepreneurship, agriculture, craftsmanship, and digital literacy, which could help empower individuals to create their own opportunities and contribute meaningfully to their communities.[11]

Going beyond traditional subjects, we need to teach our young populace more advanced skills. These skills should encompass a range of abilities known as the six Cs – that is, critical thinking, creativity, collaboration, communication, citizenship, and character. Together, they equip individuals to navigate an increasingly complex, interconnected, and rapidly changing world. Let's examine their role in Africa's education system and economic development.

Critical Thinking

Critical thinking, as a key component of a modern educational curriculum, equips learners with the ability to assess information thoughtfully and objectively, analyse complex situations, identify underlying assumptions, draw out implications, and ultimately make informed decisions.

In today's increasingly complex and interconnected world, this skill is more crucial than ever. From discerning fake news from facts and making everyday decisions to solving complex problems in the workplace, critical thinking plays a pivotal role in multiple aspects of life.

In the context of entrepreneurship and business, critical thinking takes on even more significance. It empowers entrepreneurs to assess market scenarios, identify opportunities, analyse risks, and make strategic decisions. It enables them to question assumptions, recognise biases, weigh various solutions, and make decisions that optimise business outcomes. In other words, critical thinking is the bedrock of strategic thinking and effective decision-making in business.

One illustrative example of how critical thinking can drive entrepreneurial success is the case of M-PESA in Kenya. The founders of M-PESA employed critical thinking to assess the Kenyan financial market's landscape. They identified a significant gap – a vast majority of Kenyans lacked access to formal banking services but had access to mobile phones. This led them to innovate a mobile money solution that revolutionised financial services in Kenya and other markets.[12]

While the technology behind M-PESA is significant, it is the critical thinking – the ability to identify an unmet need, envision a solution, and bring it to life – that led to its success. This highlights the importance of embedding critical thinking in education systems, not just for the sake of individual cognitive development but also for fostering innovation, entrepreneurship, and economic development.

As Africa aspires to be a continent of innovation and economic growth, critical thinking needs to be at the core of its educational agenda. This requires incorporating critical thinking in curricula, training teachers to foster critical thinking, and creating a learning environment that encourages questioning, curiosity, and thoughtful reasoning. By doing so, Africa can nurture a generation of critical thinkers who can drive innovation, entrepreneurship, and economic progress.

Creativity

Creativity, as an essential pillar of education and personal development, is the force that drives innovation, progress, and problem-solving. In essence, it is the capacity to think unconventionally, perceive the world in new ways, find hidden patterns, connect unrelated phenomena, and generate solutions. It's not just about artistic expression but also about the ability to think outside the box, challenge the status quo, and innovate.

When applied to entrepreneurship, creativity plays an instrumental role. It's the driving force behind the development of novel products, unique services, and innovative business models. Creative entrepreneurs can spot opportunities that others overlook, find unique solutions to problems, and offer products or services that stand out in the marketplace. In this way, creativity leads to competitive advantage, business growth, and market evolution.

One shining example of creativity in entrepreneurship in Africa is Khula in South Africa. Khula is an innovative mobile application that significantly revolutionises the agricultural supply chain by connecting small-scale farmers directly with the formal market. The application offers a fresh produce marketplace that enables farmers, particularly those in remote or rural areas, to pool their crops together to sell in bulk directly to the market.

This example underscores the importance of nurturing creativity in Africa's education systems. This involves not just integrating creativity in the curriculum but also creating a learning environment that encourages curiosity, risk-taking, and experimentation. Furthermore, it requires recognising and encouraging diverse talents and multiple intelligences beyond traditional academic skills. Africa can empower its youth to become not just job seekers but also job creators – entrepreneurs who can drive economic growth and social progress by fostering creativity.

Collaboration

Collaboration, a skill closely tied to success in the modern world, entails the ability to work efficiently and effectively in a team, leveraging a range of skills, backgrounds, and perspectives towards the achievement of a common goal. In the sphere of entrepreneurship and business, collaboration often enables a pooling of resources, a sharing of knowledge, and an exchange of ideas. It is an avenue through which diversity is harnessed, yielding more innovative, efficient, and effective solutions.

This concept of collaboration extends beyond just interpersonal dynamics and team building. It also applies at the level of organisations, sectors, and even nations. Cross-sector collaborations, such as those between the government and private entities, non-profit organisations, and businesses, or between businesses themselves, can unlock immense value. By joining forces, these entities can tackle challenges more holistically, access new resources, enter new markets, and drive innovation.

A vivid example of this kind of productive collaboration in Africa is the partnership between the Rwandan government and Zipline, a California-based drone delivery company. Recognising the challenge of swiftly and reliably delivering crucial medical supplies across its diverse terrain, the Rwandan government partnered with Zipline to implement a drone delivery system.[13]

The drones, known as 'Zips', are loaded with medical products and launched to various health facilities at speeds of up to 100 km/h. This groundbreaking collaboration has significantly reduced delivery times, ensuring that even remote areas have access to essential medical supplies. It demonstrates the power of collaboration in leveraging technology for social good, drastically enhancing the healthcare delivery system, and saving lives.

Such examples highlight the need for education systems in Africa to prioritise teaching and fostering collaboration skills. This could involve team projects, group problem-solving activities, and learning methods that stress interaction, cooperation, and mutual respect. With these skills, the future African workforce would be well-equipped to thrive in an increasingly interconnected global economy and drive forward innovative, collaborative solutions to the continent's challenges.

Communication

Communication is an indispensable skill, both in the everyday realm of interpersonal relationships and in the complex dynamics of the business world. It involves not only the effective conveyance of ideas, information, and expectations but also the art of listening and comprehending the perspectives of others. In a business setting, effective communication is the bedrock of diverse operations: from internal team management and project coordination to external customer relationships, stakeholder engagement, and marketing.

Clear and effective communication is crucial for entrepreneurs and businesses seeking to establish a strong brand identity, build customer trust, and create an enduring market presence. It helps organisations clearly articulate their value proposition, define their mission and vision, and consistently deliver their brand message to the target audience. Furthermore, it enables them to engage effectively with various stakeholders, including customers, employees, investors, partners, and the community at large.

An African company that exemplifies the power of effective

communication is Jumia, often hailed as Africa's first unicorn startup. Launched in Lagos, Nigeria, in 2012, Jumia has grown exponentially to expand its operations across several African countries. At the core of its growth strategy is its ability to communicate its value proposition effectively across different African markets.[14]

Jumia positioned itself as an online marketplace that addresses the needs of the African consumer, offering a wide range of products, providing convenient payment options (including cash on delivery), and overcoming logistical hurdles to deliver products to the customer's doorstep. The company's communication strategy, which was tailored to the local context in each of its markets, played a crucial role in enabling it to establish its brand, grow its customer base, and expand its operations.

The Jumia story underscores the need for education systems in Africa to place a strong emphasis on developing communication skills. This could include curricula components on verbal and written communication, presentation skills, negotiation techniques, and digital communication, among others. By nurturing strong communication skills, Africa's future workforce will be well-equipped to convey ideas effectively, foster mutual understanding, and drive successful business operations in the global marketplace.

Citizenship

Citizenship involves an understanding of societal issues and contributing positively to the community. Citizenship, in an entrepreneurial context, extends beyond the legal status of an individual in a community. It is about active participation and contribution to the community and society at large. Entrepreneurs who exhibit a strong sense of citizenship don't just focus on their businesses' economic prosperity but also consider their enterprises' impact on societal challenges. They seek to add value not only to their shareholders but also to the community, environment, and society at large.

A prime example of an entrepreneur who epitomises good citizenship is Mo Ibrahim, a Sudanese-British businessman. He is the founder of Celtel, a telecommunications company that significantly contributed to Africa's telecommunications revolution. Celtel, which was sold for $3.4 billion in 2005, brought mobile communication to millions of people across Africa, driving connectivity, enabling business opportunities, and enhancing quality of life.[15]

However, Ibrahim's contribution to Africa extends far beyond his entrepreneurial ventures in the telecom sector. Recognising the critical role of governance and leadership in Africa's development, he established the Mo Ibrahim Foundation in 2006. The foundation is committed to supporting great African leadership that will drive economic development, social progress, and prosperity on the continent. It offers the Ibrahim Prize for Achievement in African Leadership, which is awarded to a former African executive head of state or government who has demonstrated exceptional leadership.

Furthermore, the Mo Ibrahim Foundation publishes the Ibrahim Index of African Governance, a tool that measures and monitors governance performance in African countries. By doing so, the foundation promotes transparency, accountability, and good governance, contributing significantly to Africa's socio-economic development.

Mo Ibrahim's journey encapsulates the power of business leaders who embody citizenship. His story serves as a model for aspiring African entrepreneurs, demonstrating that successful entrepreneurship is not merely about economic prosperity. Instead, it's about leveraging business as a force for good, driving societal change, and making a lasting, positive impact on the community and the wider society. This further underscores the need for African education systems to foster a strong sense of citizenship among learners, preparing them to be not just successful professionals but also responsible and active contributors to society.

Character

Character refers to the collective qualities and traits that define an individual. These qualities could include honesty, integrity, resilience, empathy, and a strong work ethic, among others. In the business realm, character is often underlined as a vital aspect of successful entrepreneurship. Good character in business leadership fosters trust, builds long-term business relationships, and ultimately drives sustainable business success.

An example of this principle in the African context is Zimbabwean billionaire Strive Masiyiwa, the founder of Econet Wireless, a global telecommunications group with operations and investments in Africa, Europe, North America, Latin America, and the Asia-Pacific.

Masiyiwa, widely respected as one of Africa's most successful entrepreneurs, is celebrated not just for his business acumen and success but also for his character and commitment to ethical business practices. Throughout his entrepreneurial journey, he has demonstrated a consistent commitment to integrity, even when faced with significant obstacles.

For instance, Masiyiwa fought a five-year legal battle in Zimbabwe to obtain a telecoms licence for Econet, resisting corruption and upholding the principles of transparency and fairness.

His resilience and commitment to integrity paid off, with Econet becoming a leading telecom provider in Zimbabwe and expanding its operations across Africa and beyond.[16]

Furthermore, Masiyiwa's empathy and sense of social responsibility have driven him to make substantial philanthropic contributions. His family foundation provides scholarships to orphaned and underprivileged children. He is also a founding member of the Giving Pledge, a commitment by the world's wealthiest individuals and families to dedicate the majority of their wealth to giving back.

Masiyiwa's journey underscores the importance of character in entrepreneurship. His story illustrates that success is not just about innovative ideas or business strategies but also about who you are as an individual, how you treat others, and the values you uphold. His experience is a powerful testament to the notion that character is a crucial determinant of long-term business success, trust, and respect.

Masiyiwa's example also highlights the need to nurture character development within African education systems. By fostering traits such as integrity, resilience, and empathy, education can equip learners to become not just successful professionals but also ethical leaders and responsible citizens.

Furthermore, in an era marked by technological advancement and rapid changes, it's crucial to equip young people with 21st-century skills that go beyond traditional academic subjects. Learner-centred pedagogies and experiential learning are often most effective in cultivating these skills.

Learner-centred pedagogy refers to instructional approaches that prioritise and respond to the needs of the student. It focuses on developing students' knowledge and skills through interactive and practical learning experiences. This might involve project-based learning, inquiry-based learning, or cooperative learning, among other methods.

Experiential learning, meanwhile, refers to 'learning by doing' and then reflecting on the experience. For instance, entrepreneurship education could involve students setting up and running a small business, while digital literacy could be enhanced through coding workshops or creating digital content.

Inclusive curriculums also play a vital role in fostering these skills. Such curriculums take into account students' diverse backgrounds, abilities, and learning needs, ensuring that all students, regardless of their circumstances, have the opportunity to develop these critical skills. An inclusive curriculum could involve using inclusive teaching strategies, diversifying learning materials, or providing additional support to learners who need it.

As Alvin Eugene Toffler, an American writer, futurist, and businessman, once said, "The illiterate of the 21st century will not be those who cannot read and write, but those who cannot learn, unlearn, and relearn." Toffler's quote emphasises the importance of adaptability and lifelong learning in a rapidly changing world. In the context of Africa's economic development, there are several key takeaways:

1. **Embracing change and continuous learning**: Toffler's point highlights the need for adaptability in today's ever-evolving world. For Africa, this could mean embracing new technologies, innovations, and ways of doing things, as well as discarding outdated practices that may be hampering progress. Education systems should emphasise critical thinking, creativity, and problem-solving, equipping students with the

skills to adapt and thrive in a changing world.[17]

2. **Fostering a culture of innovation**: In a rapidly changing global economy, innovation is a key driver of economic development. This requires a culture of unlearning, learning, and relearning, where new ideas are welcomed and failure is seen as a learning opportunity rather than a setback. Policies that support research and development, entrepreneurship, and startups will help foster such a culture.

3. **Overcoming misconceptions and stereotypes**: Overcoming misconceptions, biases, and stereotypes that are holding back development is crucial. For instance, this could involve challenging misconceptions about Africans' abilities to develop homegrown systems and technological advances, traditional gender roles that limit opportunities for women, or addressing negative stereotypes about Africa that may deter investment. Education and public awareness campaigns should play a crucial role here.

The potential payoff from investing in quality and relevant education is enormous. As Africa's youthful population continues to grow, the continent has a unique opportunity to reap a 'demographic dividend'. By investing in their education, Africa will equip its youth with the skills and knowledge they need to drive economic growth, innovation, and social progress.

However, the journey is far from over. Many African countries still face significant challenges in providing quality education to all their citizens. These challenges include inadequate funding, poor infrastructure, lack of trained teachers, and high dropout rates, particularly among girls.

Addressing these challenges requires holistic and innovative approaches. These include boosting public investment in education, promoting public-private partnerships, leveraging technology to enhance learning, and implementing policies to ensure inclusive, equitable, and quality education.

As we move to the next chapter, we will explore another vital aspect of Africa's journey to prosperity – the rule of law and good governance. A strong education system and an enlightened citizenry provide the foundation for a society where laws are respected and good governance is the norm.

CHAPTER 9

RULE OF LAW AND GOOD GOVERNANCE

Strong institutions, accountability, and transparency are the pillars of any prosperous nation. This chapter focuses on the role of rule of law and good governance in Africa's economic development, exploring how these elements are not only crucial for stability but also catalysts for growth and prosperity.

The Rule of Law

The rule of law, as a cornerstone of democratic societies, embodies a commitment to a system of self-government that places high value on equality, predictability, and accountability. It is not rule by law where law is simply an instrument of the government, but rather rule under law where everyone, including the government itself, is subject to the law.

One of the key aspects of the rule of law is accountability. This means that everyone, from government officials and corporations to private individuals, is subject to the law.

Moreover, the rule of law requires that the laws themselves are just. This means they should be clear, predictable, uniformly enforced, and protect fundamental rights. For instance, the European Convention on Human Rights and the Human Rights Act 1998 in the UK ensure that laws do not infringe upon the basic human rights of citizens.

In addition to this, the principle of the rule of law posits that government operations should be open. Laws must be publicly promulgated and openly administered, and judicial decisions should be accessible to the public. The Freedom of Information Act (FOIA) in the United States exemplifies this principle, allowing public access to information from the federal government, thus emphasising transparency and accountability.

On our continent of Africa, the equivalent to the United States' FOIA is found in several countries. For instance, South Africa has the Promotion of Access to Information Act (PAIA) of 2000. This law gives effect to the constitutional right of access to any information held by the state, as well as any information held by another person that is required for the exercise or protection of any rights.[1]

Nigeria also has a similar law known as the Freedom of Information (FOI) Act, which was enacted in 2011. The Nigerian FOI Act grants public access to public records and information, protects public records and information to the extent consistent with the public interest and the protection of personal privacy, protects serving public officers from adverse consequences of disclosing certain kinds of official information without authorisation, and establishes procedures for the achievement of those purposes.[2]

The existence of these laws in African countries demonstrates their commitment to transparency, accountability, and the rule of law, similar to the values embodied in the US FOIA. However, the effective implementation of these laws varies and depends on factors such as political will, societal norms, and infrastructural capacities.

The rule of law also provides for accessible and impartial dispute resolution. This requires a system where disputes can be resolved efficiently by independent, competent, and ethical adjudicators. The independent court systems in many democratic countries serve as good examples of this principle, ensuring that judgments can be made impartially, free from governmental influence.

Historically, discussions of the rule of law can be traced back to Aristotle, who, in his work Politics stated, "It is more proper that law should govern than any one of the citizens."[3] This sentiment was later encapsulated in the Magna Carta in 1215, a document that laid the groundwork for the concept that the king is not above the law.

From there, the principle of the rule of law has been further developed by a variety of legal and philosophical thinkers. In the 19th century, British constitutional scholar Albert V Dicey defined three principles that constitute the rule of law:

1. **No punishment without law:** This means that no one can be punished unless they have broken a law that is established in the ordinary legal manner before the ordinary courts of the land.
2. **Equality before the law:** This means that everyone is subject to the same laws and treated equally by the legal system.

3. **Constitutional law being incorporated within the rights of individuals:** This means that the rights and freedoms of individuals are protected by the constitution and cannot be taken away by the government.[4]

In more recent years, scholars like Joseph Raz and Brian Z Tamanaha have contributed significantly to our understanding of the rule of law. Raz argues that the rule of law has instrumental value in maintaining democratic processes and safeguarding human rights, while Tamanaha suggests that for the rule of law to be effectively implemented, a clear understanding of it is necessary.[5]

Apart from its philosophical dimensions, the rule of law carries practical implications for everyday life. It provides citizens with an understanding of the laws that govern their lives, allows them to plan their affairs with certainty, empowers them to hold their government accountable, and enables them to seek redress from independent courts when their rights are violated. Consequently, the rule of law is not only a philosophical ideal but also a critical framework for governance and societal organisation.

Rule of Law and Economic Development

The rule of law and economic development are inextricably linked, as the rule of law provides the structural basis necessary for a thriving and stable economy. It's the legal foundation that allows businesses to operate with confidence, secure in their property rights and contract enforcement. A robust rule of law provides an environment of predictability, which is essential for economic development, as it reduces uncertainties and risks for businesses and investors.

The World Bank's 'Doing Business' report highlights this connection, showing that countries with stronger adherence to the rule of law typically have better business environments. The reason for this is quite straightforward: investors and entrepreneurs are more likely to invest their resources where they believe contracts will be upheld and legal rights will be protected. In countries with weak rule of law, businesses may be reluctant to invest due to fear of arbitrary government action, corruption, or instability.[6]

Mauritius provides a concrete example of how the rule of law can stimulate economic development. It is often cited as one of Africa's success stories, having made significant strides in terms of economic progress over the past few decades. Mauritius is frequently lauded for its strong rule of law and stable political environment. According to the World Bank, this island nation has a well-regulated economy and a high degree of transparency, factors that contribute to its favourable business climate.

One of the keys to Mauritius's success has been the government's commitment to upholding property rights, a critical aspect of the rule of law. The security of property rights has encouraged both domestic and foreign investment, which in turn has stimulated economic growth. For example, the sugar cane industry in Mauritius, historically a major part of the country's economy, has benefitted from secure property rights that allow farmers to make long-term investments and plans.

In addition, Mauritius's judicial system is independent and efficient, and it has been effective in enforcing contracts. This has created a trustworthy and dependable environment for businesses and has been instrumental in Mauritius's development as a major global financial centre.

More than that, the government of Mauritius has made significant efforts to combat corruption, another critical aspect of the rule of law. The Independent Commission Against Corruption (ICAC) in Mauritius plays a key role in maintaining a clean public sector, which further enhances the business environment. The functions of the ICAC include educating the public against corruption, enlisting and fostering public support in combating corruption, receiving and considering any allegation that a corruption offence has been committed, detecting and investigating any act of corruption, and monitoring the implementation of any contract awarded by a public body.[7]

Rule of Law, Social Justice, and Stability

The rule of law is central to the realisation of social justice and stability in any society. It fosters a sense of fairness and equity among citizens by ensuring that all individuals are treated equally under the law and by providing mechanisms for the peaceful resolution of disputes. This not only promotes social justice but also contributes significantly to societal stability.

A clear example of this principle at work can be seen in the civil rights movement in the United States. The civil rights movement that unfolded in the United States during the mid-20th century is a monumental instance in the fight for equality and justice under the rule of law. It marked a critical shift towards the abolition of legal racial segregation and discrimination, largely sustained by the so-called 'Jim Crow' laws that had been in place since the post-Civil War Reconstruction era.

Under Jim Crow, African Americans were subjected to a broad range of discriminatory practices. This segregation was enforced through both law and social custom, leading to significant racial inequalities in education, housing, employment, and all areas of public life. The system also disenfranchised Black citizens, severely limiting their voting rights through mechanisms such as literacy tests and poll taxes.

The Civil Rights Act of 1964 represented a significant step towards rectifying these injustices. This act outlawed segregation in public places and banned employment discrimination on the basis of race, colour, religion, sex, or national origin. Title VII of the act, which focused on employment discrimination, led to the creation of the Equal Employment Opportunity Commission (EEOC), a federal agency tasked with enforcing these provisions.[8]

The act also carried provisions enabling the federal government to intervene in cases where states were not upholding the rights of citizens, serving to strengthen the enforcement of the 14th and 15th Amendments, which promise equal protection and the right to vote.

The Voting Rights Act of 1965 further advanced the cause of social justice. It prohibited racial discrimination in voting, effectively removing the barriers, such as literacy tests, that had been used to disenfranchise Black voters. The act had immediate and transformative effects, leading to a significant increase in African American voter registration, especially in the South.

On our African continent, a typical example was seen at work in South Africa. Apartheid was a policy of systemic racial segregation and discrimination enforced by the National Party government between 1948 and 1994. Under apartheid, the rights of the majority black African inhabitants were severely curtailed, while white supremacy and Afrikaner minority rule were maintained.

The struggle against apartheid featured several notable milestones towards the establishment of the rule of law and social justice. The efforts of activists, both within and outside of South

Africa, eventually led to the dismantling of the apartheid system.

A significant stride towards the rule of law and social justice was the introduction of the interim constitution in 1993, which marked the end of apartheid. The interim constitution provided for a transitional period of coalition governance until a new constitution, which was to be drafted by a freely elected constitutional assembly, could be adopted.

The final constitution of South Africa was enacted in 1996, marking the culmination of a four-year, inclusive, participatory, and transparent constitution-making process. The constitution was a groundbreaking document, embodying principles of human dignity, equality, and freedom. It is known for its comprehensive bill of rights, which includes not only civil and political rights but also social, economic, and cultural rights. The Constitutional Court was also established to ensure adherence to the constitution and the rule of law. This transition marked a pivotal moment in South African history, demonstrating the transformative power of the rule of law in promoting social justice and equality.

In addition to promoting social justice, the rule of law plays a pivotal role in ensuring societal stability and peace. By providing a structure within which conflicts can be resolved peacefully and fairly, it serves as a mechanism to prevent disputes from escalating into violence. Looking at Africa again, the post-conflict experiences of South Africa and Rwanda provide clear examples of this.

As stated earlier, following the end of apartheid in 1994, South Africa set up the Truth and Reconciliation Commission (TRC) to help the nation move forward by confronting its painful past. The TRC allowed victims of human rights violations to share their experiences and for perpetrators to testify and request amnesty.

By encouraging truth-telling and facilitating reconciliation, the TRC played a key role in helping South Africa transition towards a democratic society governed by the rule of law.[9]

The TRC's process was underpinned by the principles of restorative justice, which emphasise healing, forgiveness, and reparations, rather than punitive justice. This approach acknowledged the systemic nature of apartheid-era abuses and aimed to restore the dignity of victims, foster social healing, and prevent a recurrence of such atrocities. The South African TRC has since served as a model for similar commissions in other countries transitioning from conflict or repression to peace and democracy.

In Rwanda, the aftermath of the 1994 genocide led to the establishment of the International Criminal Tribunal for Rwanda (ICTR) and the Gacaca courts. The ICTR, established by the United Nations, aimed to bring those responsible for the genocide to justice. It played a critical role in creating a historical record of the genocide, holding leaders accountable and developing international humanitarian law.

In parallel, Rwanda also established the Gacaca courts, a justice system based on community and traditional dispute resolution mechanisms. The term 'gacaca' can be translated as 'short grass', referring to the public space where neighbourhood male elders (abagabo) used to meet to solve local problems. The Gacaca courts aimed to process the vast number of genocide-related cases and promote community healing and reconciliation. Despite some criticisms, these courts played a crucial role in Rwanda's peace-building and nation-building processes by providing a measure of justice to victims and reintegrating perpetrators into society.[10]

The examples of post-apartheid South Africa and post-genocide Rwanda underscore the importance of the rule of law in promoting social stability. South Africa and Rwanda showed how the rule of law can help societies heal from past atrocities and build a more peaceful and stable future.

In a broader perspective, the United Nations' Sustainable Development Goal (SDG) 16 underlines the profound recognition at the international level of the indispensable role that peace, justice, and strong institutions play in achieving sustainable development. This SDG, titled 'Peace, Justice, and Strong Institutions', includes a set of targets to be achieved by the year 2030, which collectively aim to reduce violence, deliver justice, combat corruption, and ensure inclusive participation in decision-making processes globally.

One crucial aspect of SDG 16 is its recognition of the close interlinkages between peace, justice, inclusivity, and strong institutions. Peaceful societies are prerequisites for justice, while justice, in turn, is essential for maintaining peace. Strong institutions that are effective, accountable, and inclusive are necessary for upholding justice and maintaining peace. This interconnectedness underscores the need for a holistic approach in working towards achieving SDG 16.

SDG 16, like all SDGs, applies to all countries, underscoring the universal relevance of the rule of law, peace, and good governance to sustainable development. While the goal provides a broad framework, countries are encouraged to set their national targets guided by the global level of ambition but taking into account national circumstances.

The inclusion of the rule of law, peace, and governance in the SDG framework signifies the global consensus that sustainable development cannot be realised without peaceful, just, and inclusive societies that are free from fear and violence.

Good Governance

Good governance refers to the process by which public institutions conduct public affairs, manage public resources, and make decisions. It is the cornerstone of effective public administration and management. It is characterised by the responsible stewardship of public resources and decision-making that prioritises the public interest and adheres to the rule of law. It implies fair, efficient, and effective public institutions and processes that serve all citizens and protect their rights.

Participation, both direct and indirect, is a key tenet of good governance. It ensures that citizens have a voice in decision-making, either directly or through legitimate intermediate institutions that represent their interests. Such broad participation is built on freedom of association and speech, as well as capacities to participate constructively. This helps ensure that decisions made reflect the collective will of the population, promoting societal cohesion and reducing the potential for conflict.

Transparency is also essential so information is freely available and directly accessible to those who will be affected by such decisions and their enforcement. It involves sharing information and acting in an open manner. Transparency helps prevent corruption, promote trust in government, and ensures the effective use of public resources.

Accountability is also a fundamental requirement of good governance. Public officials must be answerable for governmental behaviour and responsive to the entity from which they derive their authority. Governmental institutions, as well as the private sector and civil society organisations, must be accountable to the public and their institutional stakeholders.

Effectiveness and efficiency in good governance involve processes and institutions producing results that meet the needs of society while making the best use of resources at their disposal. This includes sustainable use of natural resources and the protection of the environment.

Equity and inclusiveness require that all members of society feel that they have a stake in it and do not feel excluded from the mainstream. This requires that all groups, particularly the most vulnerable, have opportunities to improve or maintain their wellbeing.

Rule of law is another key attribute of good governance. It involves legal frameworks being fair and enforced impartially, particularly the laws on human rights.

Good governance leads to better development outcomes, including poverty reduction, economic growth, and social justice.

Good Governance and Economic Development

Good governance can foster economic development by promoting efficient and effective use of resources, improving service delivery and creating a trustworthy environment for economic activities. Good governance lays the groundwork for economic prosperity by enhancing the efficiency and effectiveness of public resource use, improving service delivery, and creating a predictable environment for economic activities.

One notable example of good governance driving economic growth in Africa can be found in Botswana. As mentioned earlier, since gaining independence in 1966, Botswana transformed itself from one of the poorest countries in the world into a middle-income country with one of the world's fastest-growing economies. Botswana's success can be largely attributed to the country's commitment to good governance principles.

Botswana's leaders have focused on ensuring stability, promoting economic diversification, and maintaining sound fiscal policies. Unlike many resource-rich countries that have fallen prey to the 'resource curse', Botswana has managed its diamond resources effectively and responsibly, investing revenues in infrastructure, education, and healthcare.

The country has consistently been ranked as one of the least corrupt in Africa by Transparency International. This can be attributed to strong anti-corruption measures and a culture of accountability and transparency in public affairs.

Botswana has also prioritised inclusive growth and social equality. Despite its resource wealth, the government has made significant efforts to ensure that the benefits of growth are widely shared among its population. As a result, Botswana has seen substantial improvements in indicators of human development, including health, education, and income levels.

Good Governance and Social Inclusion

Good governance also plays a critical role in promoting social inclusion and equity. It provides avenues for all members of society, especially the marginalised and vulnerable, to have a say in decision-making processes. In this way, the policies and initiatives that are implemented are likely to be more representative of and responsive to a wider range of societal needs.

In practice, good governance can help drive social inclusion in numerous ways. It can ensure that laws are designed and implemented in a way that respects all citizens' rights, preventing discrimination based on gender, race, ethnicity, or any other characteristic. Moreover, good governance can provide mechanisms for citizens to challenge decisions they perceive to be unjust, further promoting social inclusion and equity.

One notable example of good governance fostering social inclusion is the case of Brazil's participatory budgeting experiment in Porto Alegre. It provides a compelling example of how democratic innovations can enhance citizen participation and the accountability of public authorities.

Porto Alegre, the capital city of the Brazilian state of Rio Grande do Sul, introduced participatory budgeting in 1989 as part of a broader effort to democratise public administration and ensure that municipal resources were allocated in a manner that was more responsive to citizens' needs.

The participatory budgeting process in Porto Alegre was structured around a series of regular meetings held at the neighbourhood, regional, and citywide levels. These meetings were open to all residents and offered an opportunity for citizens to debate and prioritise public spending projects. The main areas of expenditure included infrastructure, such as roads, sewage, and schools, and social services, such as health and education.[11]

Over the years, this process of participatory budgeting has resulted in a more equitable allocation of public resources, with a larger share of the city's budget directed towards poorer neighbourhoods. For instance, a World Bank study found that participatory budgeting led to significant improvements in sanitation and water services in the city's poorest regions.[12]

Additionally, participatory budgeting in Porto Alegre has been associated with a rise in tax compliance and increased transparency in municipal finances. The direct involvement of citizens in the budgeting process has resulted in a higher level of trust in local government and enhanced accountability.

Furthermore, the participatory budgeting process has also empowered traditionally marginalised citizens by giving them a voice in decision-making. It has fostered a culture of active citizenship, with residents becoming more engaged in the public sphere and more knowledgeable about public finances.

The Porto Alegre model of participatory budgeting has since been replicated in hundreds of cities worldwide, reflecting its success and the growing recognition of the role of citizen participation in promoting good governance.

It should be borne in mind that good governance, characterised by participation, equity, and inclusiveness, plays a pivotal role in promoting social inclusion. Good governance can ensure that policies are more reflective of and responsive to the needs of all citizens by creating avenues for the marginalised and vulnerable to participate in decision-making processes.

Building the Rule of Law and Good Governance

Building and promoting the rule of law and good governance is indeed a complex task that requires comprehensive reforms at multiple levels of society. Enhancing the efficiency and accountability of public institutions, fostering transparency, promoting citizen participation, and strengthening legal frameworks are all crucial components of this process.

International organisations play a significant role in promoting the rule of law and good governance. The United Nations, for instance, has established the United Nations Development Programme (UNDP), which supports countries in their efforts to achieve sustainable development through good governance and rule of law. It provides expertise and resources to help countries strengthen their institutions, uphold the rule of law, and promote inclusive participation.

The World Bank's Governance Global Practice (GGP) is another initiative that helps countries build capable, efficient, open, inclusive, and accountable institutions. The GGP provides financial resources, expertise, and coordination among other development partners to assist countries in implementing governance reforms.[13]

On a regional level, the African Governance Architecture (AGA), under the auspices of the African Union, is a significant regional initiative that works towards promoting good governance across the African continent. The AGA is underpinned by the African Charter on Democracy, Elections, and Governance, a normative framework that emphasises democratic governance and human rights.[14]

The AGA essentially serves as a platform where diverse stakeholders – both state and non-state actors – engage in dialogue on governance, democracy, and human rights issues. This involves representatives from African Union member states, civil society organisations, academia, the private sector, and regional economic communities. The idea is to foster constructive discussions, exchange ideas, learn from each other's experiences, and coordinate efforts in the promotion of democratic governance.

The AGA thus plays a crucial role in fostering a collective commitment to democratic governance across our African continent by promoting dialogue, peer learning, and shared standards.

Specific examples of these efforts can also be seen in numerous governance reform initiatives worldwide. As mentioned earlier, international bodies like the United Nations Development Programme (UNDP) and the World Bank have often been at the forefront of these initiatives, offering technical and financial support to countries aiming to enhance their governance structures and practices.

In Jordan, for instance, UNDP has played a key role in supporting the development and implementation of a national anti-corruption strategy. This comprehensive strategy aimed to tackle corruption through enhancing legal frameworks, institutional capacities, and public awareness. As part of this strategy, the Jordan Integrity and Anti-Corruption Commission (JIACC) was established in 2016 as the primary institution responsible for preventing and combating corruption. JIACC's functions include investigating corruption-related crimes, promoting integrity and transparency in public and private sectors, and raising awareness about the dangers of corruption. The establishment of JIACC marked a crucial step in strengthening the rule of law and promoting accountability in Jordan.[15]

The example of Jordan demonstrates how international organisations can support countries in promoting the rule of law and enhancing good governance. These organisations will help foster environments conducive to economic development, social justice, and stability by providing technical assistance, financial resources, and platforms for dialogue and cooperation. Such initiatives, though context-specific, will offer valuable lessons for other countries embarking on similar governance reform journeys.

Challenges in Africa and the Path Forward

Despite some success stories, many African nations continue to struggle with corruption, weak institutions, and limited respect for the rule of law.

Corruption remains a major concern in many African nations. According to Transparency International's 2021 Corruption Perceptions Index, Sub-Saharan Africa is the lowest scoring region on the index, reflecting a situation of rampant bribery, lack of punishment for corruption, and inadequate public services.[16]

Weak institutions also pose a significant challenge. In many countries on the continent, institutions that are critical to upholding the rule of law and ensuring good governance – such as the judiciary, the police, and various regulatory bodies – are often under-resourced, lack independence, and are susceptible to political interference.

Despite these challenges, there are encouraging signs of progress and potential paths forward. Efforts to combat corruption and strengthen institutions are being undertaken at various levels. For instance, in Nigeria, the Economic and Financial Crimes Commission has been working to combat corruption by prosecuting high-profile cases.[17]

On a regional level, the African Peer Review Mechanism (APRM) aims to foster the adoption of policies, standards, and practices that lead to political stability, high economic growth, sustainable development, and accelerated regional and continental economic integration. Countries voluntarily submit to evaluation by other member countries in an effort to identify strengths and weaknesses in governance.

Efforts to strengthen institutions are also being supported by international bodies. The World Bank, for instance, has several initiatives aimed at strengthening institutions in African countries to promote good governance and economic development.

Addressing the challenges facing Africa will require concerted efforts at all levels – from local communities to national governments and regional and international bodies. Through collective action and commitment to good governance and the rule of law, African nations will work towards more prosperous, equitable, and stable societies.

The rule of law and good governance are not just about economic growth. They are also about justice, dignity, and respect for all individuals. They are about building societies where everyone can thrive and contribute their talents to the common good.

In the next chapter, we will delve into the benefits of economic freedom and open markets. As we will see, the rule of law and good governance are also vital for creating an environment where businesses can flourish, trade can thrive, and economies can grow.

CHAPTER 10

DIVERSIFYING ECONOMIES AND EMBRACING OPEN MARKETS

Open markets, free trade, and competition stimulate innovation, efficiency, and economic growth. This chapter focuses on the benefits of economic freedom and open markets in Africa's economic development, exploring how these elements are catalysts for growth and prosperity.

Definitions of Diversifying Economies and Embracing Open Markets

'Diversifying economies' and 'embracing open markets' are terms often used in discussions of economic development strategy. Let's break down each one.

Diversifying Economies

Economic diversification refers to the process whereby a country expands the range of economic activities it engages in. It involves a shift away from a single income source or narrow set of activities towards a wider array of sectors and revenue sources. This could mean expanding from raw material production to include more processing or manufacturing activities, developing new sectors like tourism or ICT, or diversifying within a sector, such as a farmer growing a wider variety of crops.

The benefits of economic diversification are numerous. It helps in risk mitigation, as economies heavily dependent on a single sector are susceptible to demand and price shocks associated with that sector. When you diversify, you help maintain stability if one sector faces a downturn. Diversification can also lead to job creation as new industries emerge and existing ones expand. Furthermore, it stimulates innovation, as new sectors may bring fresh ideas, techniques, and technologies. Lastly, a diverse economy can support more balanced, sustainable growth by reducing dependence on non-renewable resources.

Achieving diversification is a complex process often necessitating strategic public policy and investment. This includes investing in education and skills development to ensure the workforce can meet the needs of a diversifying economy, and improving infrastructure, such as transportation, energy, or digital networks, to support new industries. It also requires promoting research and development. Governments can stimulate innovation and diversification by investing in these areas and providing incentives for businesses to do the same. Lastly, fostering a conducive business environment through regulatory reforms can attract a wider array of investments and stimulate the growth of new sectors.

A prime example of economic diversification is the United Arab Emirates (UAE). Traditionally heavily reliant on oil exports, the UAE recognised the associated risks and has made significant efforts to diversify its economy away from the petroleum sector.

The process of economic diversification began in earnest during the late 20th century and has accelerated over the past few decades. Sheikh Zayed bin Sultan Al Nahyan, the founder of the UAE and its first president, set the foundation for this diversification. He invested heavily in infrastructure, healthcare, and education, using the wealth generated from the oil sector to modernise the country.[1]

Sheikh Khalifa bin Zayed Al Nahyan was the second president of the UAE and the ruler of Abu Dhabi from November 2004 until his passing in May 2022.[2]

As a leader, Khalifa played a pivotal role in transforming the UAE into a regional economic powerhouse. He was known for diversifying the nation's economy beyond its oil reserves. Under his guidance, the non-oil economy experienced significant growth. In Abu Dhabi, Khalifa was instrumental in the establishment of key cultural, academic, and transportation hubs, including the Louvre Abu Dhabi, New York University Abu Dhabi, Sorbonne University Abu Dhabi, and Etihad Airways.

The ruler of Dubai, Sheikh Mohammed bin Rashid Al Maktoum, who has been the prime minister and vice president of the UAE since 2006, has also played a significant role in the economic diversification of the UAE. The UAE, under the leadership of Sheikh Mohammed bin Rashid Al Maktoum, has successfully transformed itself into a significant international hub for finance and trade.[3] A key element of this transformation has been the establishment of the Dubai International Financial Centre (DIFC), which serves as a gateway for global finance and offers an independent regulation and judicial system. Dubai is also home to the Dubai Financial Market (DFM), a stock exchange that lists shares of UAE companies and encourages foreign investment. Alongside DFM, the Abu Dhabi Securities Exchange further strengthens the UAE's role in the region's financial sector.

The UAE's ambitions are not just restricted to the financial sector. Its real estate ventures, particularly in Dubai, have captured international attention and investment. The Burj Khalifa, developed by Emaar Properties, stands as the world's tallest building, and the Palm Jumeirah, an artificial archipelago created by Nakheel Properties, demonstrates the UAE's architectural prowess.

Tourism in the UAE is another sector experiencing rapid growth. A multitude of attractions, such as the world's most luxurious hotel, the Burj Al Arab, the largest mall globally, the Dubai Mall, and the cultural gem of the Sheikh Zayed Grand Mosque, draw millions of tourists to the country every year. According to the World Travel & Tourism Council, travel and tourism contributed significantly to the UAE's GDP and are expected to increase annually over the next decade.[4]

The UAE's logistics and infrastructure sectors have also seen significant growth. Dubai International Airport is among the busiest airports globally for international passenger traffic, while Jebel Ali port, operated by DP World, is the Middle East's largest marine terminal and one of the busiest ports worldwide.

Furthermore, the UAE's diversification strategy has been buttressed by considerable investment in education and healthcare.

The country is home to several esteemed universities and has attracted prestigious international institutions to establish campuses, such as New York University in Abu Dhabi. The healthcare sector has seen similar advancements, with state-of-the-art hospitals and facilities making the UAE an increasingly popular destination for medical tourism.

The UAE has seen significant growth and development as a result of its economic diversification efforts. However, as with any large-scale developmental strategy, challenges have emerged, two of which are the reliance on an expatriate workforce and the question of environmental sustainability.

Firstly, the expatriate issue. The rapid development and expansion of industries in the UAE have led to a significant influx of foreign workers to fill roles across many sectors. This has caused a demographic imbalance, with expatriates making up a substantial majority of the UAE's population. While this migrant workforce has been integral to the UAE's economic success, it also poses challenges. These range from social integration issues to the economic vulnerability associated with a reliance on foreign labour. In response, the UAE has launched Emiratisation initiatives aimed at increasing the number of Emiratis in the job market, particularly in the private sector. They have also been investing in education and vocational training for Emiratis to better equip them for the job market.

Secondly, the environmental sustainability issue. The UAE's rapid development has also had significant environmental impacts, including high levels of energy consumption, increased carbon emissions, and pressure on water resources. Recognising this, the UAE has taken a proactive stance on environmental sustainability. The UAE Vision 2021 emphasises a shift towards a green economy, promoting sustainable practices across sectors and making substantial investments in renewable energy. The UAE is home to one of the world's largest solar power plants, the Noor Abu Dhabi, which exemplifies this commitment. Similarly, the Masdar City project in Abu Dhabi is a planned city project that relies on renewable energy and aims to be a global model for sustainable urban development.

The UAE Centennial 2071 goes even further, laying out a long-term vision that looks towards the nation's 100th anniversary. It identifies key themes for this vision, including education, economy, government development, and community cohesion, all with a strong emphasis on sustainability and readiness for future challenges. It's particularly focused on moving towards a knowledge-based economy that's less dependent on oil and promoting innovation, research, and science.

So, while the UAE's diversification strategy has presented challenges, the country's leadership has shown a keen awareness of these and implemented initiatives to address them. They are working towards balancing the rapid growth and development with the need for social inclusion and environmental sustainability, aiming to ensure a prosperous future for generations to come. The leadership's proactive and forward-thinking approach, as seen in UAE Vision 2021 and UAE Centennial 2071, serves as proof of this commitment.

The UAE serves as an impressive model for economic diversification, particularly for countries reliant on natural resources, such as many nations on our continent of Africa. The UAE's strategy involved investing heavily in infrastructure, establishing world-class financial markets, attracting international business through favourable regulatory environments, and aggressively promoting tourism. African nations can draw several lessons from the UAE's experience.

Firstly, the UAE's diversification strategy was driven by a long-term vision led by strong and stable leadership. This provided the consistency and reliability necessary for large-scale investments in infrastructure, education, and healthcare. African nations would benefit from a similar level of long-term strategic planning and consistency in leadership to effectively diversify their economies.

Secondly, the UAE recognised the importance of creating a business-friendly environment to attract foreign direct investment (FDI). The establishment of free trade zones and financial hubs with independent regulatory and judicial systems, like the DIFC in Dubai, has been critical in attracting international business.

Lastly, the UAE placed considerable emphasis on building world-class infrastructure. This includes not just physical infrastructure, like airports, ports, and roads, but also social infrastructure, such as schools, hospitals, and universities. Investment in infrastructure can have a transformative effect, creating jobs, improving living standards, and fostering a more diversified economy.

Among African nations, again Rwanda presents an inspiring success story, particularly regarding economic diversification and development. Rwanda, under President Paul Kagame's leadership, has made remarkable strides in transforming its economy, as outlined in Vision 2020. This roadmap propelled the nation from an agriculture-based to a knowledge and service-oriented economy, targeting middle-income status with a focus on good governance, infrastructure, and private sector development.

Significant infrastructure investments like the Kigali Convention Centre have underpinned this growth, especially in the tourism sector. Business-friendly reforms have streamlined processes, leading to Rwanda's ranking as one of the easiest places to do business in Africa, per the World Bank's Doing Business report.[5]

The modernisation of agriculture and promotion of luxury tourism, utilising natural assets such as the Volcanoes National Park, are pivotal elements of this transformation. Kigali has emerged as a vibrant economic hub, with projects like the Kigali Innovation City catalysing Rwanda's shift to a knowledge-based economy.

Challenges remain, including land scarcity and the need for political stability. However, rwanda's model demonstrates the power of clear vision, strategic planning, and committed governance in achieving economic diversification and growth. International cooperation and foreign investment, bolstered by rwanda's stable political climate and anti-corruption stance, continue to be integral to its developmental success. President Kagame's consistent strategy, now extended into Vision 2050, maintains investor confidence, paralleling the UAe's diversification and innovation-driven approach.

While it's important to note that every country has a unique set of circumstances and challenges, and one size does not fit all, the UAE's successful diversification provides an example that African nations can analyse and draw lessons from as they shape their own diversification strategies. Similarly, Rwanda's success story provides another example of how focused leadership, a clear vision, and strategic reforms can drive economic diversification and growth, which in the African context serves as an encouraging model for other African nations to emulate.

Embracing Open Markets

Embracing open markets refers to the process of reducing barriers to trade and fostering an economy where foreign and domestic businesses can compete freely. This is a crucial step for many countries seeking to stimulate economic growth and enhance their global competitiveness. Reducing barriers to trade encourages domestic and foreign businesses to compete on an even playing field, which can lead to various economic benefits, such as increased competition, improved product quality, innovation, and enhanced consumer choice.

Singapore is a compelling example of a country that has embraced open markets to its advantage. As a small island nation with limited natural resources, Singapore has strategically positioned itself as a global trading hub. It has established a business-friendly environment, maintained low tariff rates, and participated actively in free trade agreements (FTAs). Singapore has more than 20 implemented FTAs with partners, including the United States, European Union, China, and India. As a result, the country has attracted substantial foreign investment and established itself as a global hub for finance, logistics, and services.[6]

Another example is Chile. Despite its geographical remoteness, Chile has become one of the most open economies globally due to its commitment to free trade. Chile has a strong global trade network, with 33 trade deals that cover 65 countries and make up 88 percent of the world's GDP. These deals come in various forms: 20 free trade agreements (FTAs), six economic association agreements, and five economic cooperation agreements, among others. Chile also has a specific trade agreement with India and a commercial protocol with the Pacific Alliance, which includes Colombia, Peru, and Mexico.[7]

Additionally, Chile was one of the original members of the Comprehensive and Progressive Agreement for Trans-Pacific Partnership (CPTPP), a trade agreement that includes ten other countries, including Australia, Canada, and Japan.[8]

Finally, Chile has joined the Digital Economy Partnership Agreement (DEPA) with Singapore and New Zealand. The partnership is a collaboration between member nations around digital issues brought on by ever-changing technology.[9]

The European Union (EU), a coalition of 27 European countries, represents a broader example of regional cooperation for mutual benefit. Initially established by six countries in the aftermath of two world wars, the EU has expanded over time with the intent to ensure peace, prosperity, fairness, and cultural diversity among its member nations. A notable characteristic of the EU is the principle of free movement, allowing its citizens, along with goods, services, and money, to move freely within the union. This, in turn, stimulates economic growth and cultural exchange.

Although there are still barriers between many African nations, the African Union (AU), a union of 55 African countries, is very similar to the EU. As such, the AU can learn several lessons from the EU's example to stimulate its own economic development. The EU's success underscores how regional integration can boost economic growth, maintain peace, and enhance the quality of life for its citizens. This suggests that deeper integration within the AU, achieved through reduced trade barriers, policy harmonisation, and the facilitation of people's free movement across borders, could be beneficial.

Political stability and peace, which the EU promotes through economic integration, are foundational for economic development. Therefore, the AU can potentially benefit from focusing on similar strategies to ensure stability and peace among its member nations. The concept of a shared currency, embodied by the euro within the EU, simplifies trade and cuts costs, although it also presents its own challenges. The AU has proposed the creation of an African Economic Community. One of the key aspects of this community is the introduction of a single continental currency.[10]

The idea behind a single currency is to promote economic integration and facilitate intra-African trade. This could simplify business transactions, eliminate currency exchange costs, foster price transparency, and facilitate comparative advantage – all of which can potentially boost trade and economic growth.

A single currency would also symbolise the unity of African countries and could foster a sense of shared identity and purpose. In a similar vein, the Euro in the EU not only serves an economic function but also represents a tangible symbol of European integration.

However, the road to a single African currency is fraught with challenges. Successful currency unions generally require member countries to have similar economic conditions, including inflation rates, fiscal policies, and business cycles. Given the economic diversity across Africa, meeting these preconditions would be a significant challenge.

Fiscal discipline is another critical requirement. Member countries would need to agree on, and adhere to, limits on budget deficits and national debt levels to avoid putting the common currency at risk. This would require significant political will and cooperation.

Moreover, a single currency implies a shared monetary policy, which would be set by a central African monetary authority. This means individual countries would lose the ability to use monetary policy, such as interest rates or money supply changes, to respond to national economic conditions.

The EU's experiences with the Euro provide both encouraging lessons and cautionary tales for the AU. The Euro has certainly facilitated trade and economic integration among Eurozone countries. However, the EU's challenges during the sovereign debt crisis, which began in 2009, highlighted the difficulties of maintaining a currency union in the face of significant economic differences and fiscal indiscipline among member countries.

In pursuing the goal of a single African currency, the AU will need to carefully consider these challenges and ensure that robust economic convergence criteria are met and appropriate fiscal and monetary institutions are in place to manage the currency effectively.

Furthermore, investments in cross-border infrastructure, research and development, and education have been significant within the EU. The AU could potentially boost its economic prospects by making similar investments, thereby enhancing productivity, fostering innovation, and building a skilled workforce. Good governance, democracy, and the rule of law are all emphasised within the EU, creating a business-friendly environment that attracts investment and promotes economic development. A strengthened focus on these areas within the AU could prove equally beneficial.

While there are valuable lessons to be learnt from the EU, the unique challenges and opportunities presented by the African context must also be recognised. Consequently, any lessons drawn from the EU should be adapted to suit this context. The AU's vision for the continent's development, articulated in Agenda 2063, incorporates many elements seen in the EU's journey, reflecting the AU's recognition of these lessons.

Agenda 2063 is Africa's master plan for achieving inclusive and sustainable development over the next 50 years, starting from 2013. Developed by the African Union, it marks a shift in focus from the earlier goals of political independence and anti-apartheid struggles to aims that include economic development, regional integration, and peace and security. The agenda aims to make Africa a dominant player on the global stage by leveraging ongoing structural transformations in the continent, such as renewed economic growth, social progress, and reduced conflict.

To achieve these lofty goals, African leaders signed the 50th Anniversary Solemn Declaration in May 2013, reaffirming their commitment to an integrated and prosperous Africa. Agenda 2063 not only outlines the continent's long-term aspirations but also specifies key flagship programmes to spur economic growth and development. It further includes a ten-year implementation plan detailing activities that will lead to both quantitative and qualitative transformational outcomes for Africa's people.

Agenda 2063 seeks to unlock new avenues of investment and development by focusing on areas such as agribusiness, infrastructure development, health, education, and value addition in commodities. Additionally, the agenda aims to ensure that growth benefits all segments of society by emphasising people-centred development, gender equality, and youth empowerment. It is positioned to capitalise on global trends like increased globalisation and the ICT revolution to make Africa a force to be reckoned with in the international arena. Overall, Agenda 2063 aims to catalyse Africa's development, turning the continent into a global powerhouse of the future.

Embracing open markets can, however, also pose challenges. It may expose domestic industries to competition from more efficient or better-resourced foreign competitors, potentially leading to job losses or business closures. Therefore, it's crucial for countries to balance the advantages of open markets with adequate support for their domestic industries and workers through measures such as skills development programmes, safety nets, and transitional support.

In a broader economic development strategy, these two concepts of diversifying economies and embracing open markets often go hand in hand. Diversifying economies often involves integrating new sectors into global markets. Embracing open markets can provide opportunities and incentives for economic diversification.

Need for Economic Diversification in Africa

As we already know, Africa is blessed with a rich abundance of natural resources that include oil, gas, precious metals, and an array of agricultural commodities. These resources have long played a central role in many African economies, often forming the backbone of their exports and revenue generation. However, this heavy reliance on raw material exports exposes these economies to the volatile nature of global commodity prices. The fluctuations in these prices can have a significant impact on economies that rely on a single or few commodities, leading to economic instability. Thus, the pursuit of economic diversification – or the expansion of the array of economic activities within a country – can serve as a viable strategy to counteract this vulnerability, fostering more balanced and resilient economies.

Risks Associated with Over-Reliance on a Single Commodity for Economic Sustenance

Nigeria, as one of Africa's most prominent oil producers, presents a compelling example of the risks associated with over-reliance on a single commodity for economic sustenance. The oil sector forms the backbone of the Nigerian economy, serving as a significant source of government revenues and foreign exchange earnings.

This heavy dependence on oil, however, has often left the nation at the mercy of the capricious global oil market. This vulnerability became acutely evident in 2014 when a dramatic decline in global oil prices plunged the Nigerian economy into a recession.[11] The oil price plunge from 2014 to 2016, one of the largest in modern history, had significant global repercussions and was particularly detrimental for oil-dependent economies such as Nigeria. A combination of factors led to this price drop, including increased supply due to efficiency gains in US shale oil production and declining demand. The US, as a significant player in the international oil market, was able to lower its break-even prices through advances in shale oil technology, thereby contributing to the oversupply.

In the context of Nigeria, this oil price collapse had dire consequences. When oil prices plummeted, the country experienced a sharp contraction in its economic growth, which led to a recession. The fallout from this economic downturn was severe, affecting various aspects of life in Nigeria, from public sector spending to employment and individual purchasing power. Nigeria's fiscal capacity was severely strained, leading to budget deficits. Additionally, the country's foreign exchange earnings suffered, causing a devaluation of the Nigerian Naira and a foreign exchange shortage that affected many sectors reliant on imports. This economic downturn underscores the risks of an over-reliance on a single commodity for national revenue and highlights the urgent need for economic diversification.

Countries with diversified exports and flexible exchange rates were better able to weather the oil price shock, underscoring the value of such economic strategies. This period reaffirmed the necessity for Nigeria to diversify its economy beyond oil, to provide a buffer against future commodity price shocks, and to create a more resilient and balanced economy.

Benefits of Diversification to Fuel Economic Development

As seen earlier, Botswana offers an excellent example of the principles of diversification in action. As mentioned earlier, the country is the world's largest diamond producer and has greatly benefited from open trade with global diamond markets. Unlike some other resource-rich countries, Botswana has effectively leveraged its diamond wealth to fuel economic growth and development.

A crucial factor in Botswana's success has been its partnership with De Beers, the international diamond company. As mentioned earlier, in 1969, shortly after gaining independence, Botswana entered into a 50-50 joint venture with De Beers to form Debswana Diamond Company. This partnership has facilitated the extraction, sorting, and marketing of Botswana's diamonds.

Through this partnership, Botswana has been able to move up the diamond value chain. In the past, diamonds were extracted in Botswana and then mostly exported for cutting, polishing, and sales. Now, through government policies and the De Beers partnership, Botswana has developed its own diamond cutting and polishing industry. This has allowed the country to capture more of the value from its diamond resources, leading to higher revenues and the creation of skilled jobs.

Moreover, Botswana has made conscious efforts to use the revenues from diamond mining for broad-based economic development. The government has invested heavily in infrastructure, education, and healthcare. The country has also established a sovereign wealth fund, known as the Pula Fund, to save and invest a portion of diamond revenues for future generations.

Botswana's story underscores the potential benefits of economic diversification using available natural resources. By integrating into the global diamond market and leveraging partnerships, Botswana has managed to transform its abundant natural resources into sustainable economic development.

Potential Challenges

The process of economic diversification and embracing open markets, while potentially beneficial, comes with its fair share of challenges. Countries embarking on this journey may face hurdles such as inadequate infrastructure, a lack of required skills, weak institutions, and vulnerability to foreign competition.

The African textile industry provides an illustrative example of these challenges. This industry has often found it difficult to compete with inexpensive imports, primarily from Asia, which have flooded local markets. This influx has occasionally led to the collapse of local textile industries, leading to job losses and compounding economic struggles.

For instance, in Nigeria, the textile industry was once the nation's second-largest employer after agriculture. In the 1970s and 80s, the country was home to thriving textile mills. However, a precipitous decline has occurred over the past few decades, leading to many factories being forced to shut down. This decline can be attributed to several intertwined factors. The liberalisation of trade policies resulted in a flood of cheap textile imports, primarily from China and other Asian countries. These lower-priced imports effectively undermined the competitiveness of Nigerian mills. At the same time, inadequate access to high-quality cotton significantly affected these mills' production. The challenge was compounded by agricultural underinvestment, leading to reduced cotton production, and the high cost and complexity of importing cotton. Frequent power outages and high energy costs also played a part in this industry's decline by dramatically increasing production costs, which further impaired the competitiveness of the local textile industry. Lastly, poor transport and logistics infrastructure contributed to these issues, inflating production costs and complicating market access.[12]

The Kenyan textile industry is struggling due to the prevalent import of second-hand clothes ('mitumba') that offer a cheaper alternative to local products, thus reducing the demand for domestically produced textiles. Additionally, the sector is hampered by the insufficient production of quality cotton, partly due to outdated farming practices and climate change effects, a challenge that mirrors Nigeria's situation. Kenyan producers also face stiff competition from inexpensive textiles from countries like China and Bangladesh, where production costs are lower, making it difficult for local manufacturers to remain competitive.

To revitalise their textile industries, both Nigeria and Kenya need comprehensive strategies addressing these multifaceted issues. These may include supporting cotton farmers, enhancing infrastructure, implementing trade protections, though this goes against open markets, and devising strategies for creating higher-value products to move up the value chain.

However, Ethiopia has managed to pivot the challenges of global competition into a unique opportunity for its textile sector.

It has drawn considerable foreign investment into this industry, transforming the country into a hub for textile manufacturing in Africa by offering attractive incentives.

One of the primary draws for foreign investors is Ethiopia's plentiful and relatively low-cost labour force. Given that labour costs are a significant factor in textile production, Ethiopia's competitive wages give it an edge over many other countries. This is particularly appealing to companies looking to diversify their supply chains away from more expensive labour markets.

In addition to its labour pool, Ethiopia has also attracted investment through favourable tax policies. The Ethiopian government has implemented tax breaks and duty-free privileges to companies investing in the textile sector. These fiscal incentives have made the country an even more attractive destination for foreign investment.

Perhaps most importantly, Ethiopia has been able to leverage its preferential access to major international markets. Thanks to trade agreements such as the Everything but Arms (EBA) initiative with the European Union, Ethiopian-made textiles can be exported duty-free to these markets. This preferential access to some of the world's largest consumer markets provides a significant advantage to companies operating in Ethiopia.

Lastly, the government has also heavily invested in infrastructure to support the industry. Industrial parks dedicated to textile and garment manufacturing, such as Hawassa Industrial Park, have been constructed. These parks offer ready-to-use factory shells, reliable power supply, and proximity to the Djibouti port, further easing operations for companies setting up manufacturing units.

All these factors combined have helped Ethiopia become an

attractive destination for foreign investment in the textile sector. Global brands like H&M, PVH (the parent company of Calvin Klein and Tommy Hilfiger), and Decathlon have already set up operations in the country. As a result, Ethiopia is not only gaining economic benefits from this investment but also creating thousands of jobs for its rapidly growing workforce.

Policy Implications

Governments have a crucial role to play in fostering diversification and helping domestic firms navigate the challenges of open markets. They can help pave the way for diversification through a range of initiatives, such as infrastructure development, bolstering education and skills development, advocating for research and innovation, and refining the overall business environment. Similarly, the formulation of trade policies needs careful consideration to ensure the benefits of liberalisation are widespread and not confined to a particular sector or demographic.

All in all, while diversifying economies and embracing open markets offer significant potential for boosting economic growth and development in Africa, these processes also present challenges. Therefore, carefully crafted policies and strategic investments are crucial to ensuring that the benefits of diversification and open markets are realised and broadly shared.

Economic diversification is crucial for Africa's long-term prosperity. As countries diversify their economies, they become more resilient to external shocks and better positioned to create jobs and reduce poverty. However, it's important to note that diversification is not an overnight process. It requires strategic planning, effective implementation, and a commitment to a long-term vision. The experiences of many developed and emerging economies suggest that those who manage to diversify their economies effectively often enjoy more sustainable growth and resilience to global economic shocks.

Nonetheless, diversification is not without its challenges. Constraints such as limited access to finance, a lack of skilled labour, and infrastructural gaps can impede diversification efforts. Addressing these challenges requires robust policies, improved education and training, and infrastructure development.

As Africa's economies continue to diversify, they are likely to experience increased economic stability, job creation, and a broadening of their economic base.

In Chapter 11, we will delve into the crucial role of innovation and technological advancements in fuelling economic growth across the continent. Investment in research, development, and a conducive environment for innovation can drive significant economic growth across Africa.

CHAPTER 11

INNOVATION AND TECHNOLOGICAL ADVANCEMENTS

For Africa, the journey to prosperity centres on innovation and technological advancements. This chapter focuses on the crucial role of innovation and technological advancements and how they can drive significant economic growth and prosperity across Africa.

Definition and Application of Innovation

The concept of 'innovation' varies widely depending on multiple factors, including the field in question, the level of analysis, and the specific type of change involved. In different disciplines and industries, what constitutes innovation can differ. For example, in technology sectors, innovation usually refers to the advent of new technologies or novel applications of existing ones. In social sectors, like healthcare or education, it may mean introducing new service delivery methods or strategies.

Additionally, the scope of innovation can change based on whether you're examining it at an individual, organisational, industry, or societal level. At the individual level, innovation might be about crafting new ideas or solutions, while at the societal level, it could concern sweeping changes in technology or institutions.

There are also multiple kinds of innovation, each with its distinct characteristics. Product innovation involves developing new products or enhancing existing ones, like a new smartphone model with upgraded features, or groundbreaking medication. Process innovation focuses on altering how products or services are produced and delivered, for example, the introduction of assembly line techniques in manufacturing.

Changes in the way a company functions to create, deliver, and capture value are termed business model innovations. For instance, some companies have transitioned from selling products outright to offering them as a service. Organisational innovation encompasses modifications to the way a company is managed or structured, such as the introduction of new employee evaluation systems or changes in corporate governance.

Social innovation relates to creative approaches to resolving societal issues. An example is the rise of microfinance institutions that extend small loans to individuals who are unable to access traditional banking services. Lastly, disruptive innovation represents a seismic shift in an industry, often creating new markets or drastically altering existing ones. The emergence of digital photography and online streaming services are classic examples of disruptive innovation.

Each of these types of innovation can bring about different kinds of change and may require different strategies and resources to achieve. Understanding the nuances of these different types of innovation can help organisations and policymakers better manage and promote innovation in various contexts.

However, while all the types of innovation mentioned are important, they eventually must lead to business model innovation to be useful and sustainable. In business model innovation, I like the simplified definition by the Global Innovation Management Institute (GIMI). GIMI provides a concise and insightful definition of business innovation, which it defines as the process of creating and capturing new value in new ways.[1] For a more comprehensive understanding, it's beneficial to dissect this definition into two key elements.

The first facet of innovation involves the generation of new value. This can be achieved by a myriad of strategies across the entire value chain, such as identifying new customer segments, implementing fresh delivery channels, devising innovative pricing models, forging new partnerships, and introducing unique product or service offerings. An important highlight from GIMI's perspective is that the novelty in value creation doesn't have to be globally unique; it simply has to be unprecedented within your organisation or society. This philosophy invites the potential to assimilate ideas from various industries or regions, recalibrating them to fit your company or region and your industry's or region's specific needs.

The second component of the innovation process, as outlined by GIMI, is seizing this new value in unconventional ways. An idea, regardless of how groundbreaking, doesn't qualify as an innovation until its value is effectively captured. This can manifest in multiple ways, such as driving revenue growth, achieving cost savings, securing strategic advantages, or unlocking new opportunities.

The practical implications and potential for driving organisational growth become clear when viewing innovation through this bifocal lens. The power of innovation lies not only in creating novel value but also in successfully leveraging it to fuel progress and success in unique and transformative ways.

Countries fostering an innovative environment tend to attract higher levels of foreign direct investment (FDI). Multinational corporations often prefer investing in innovative economies to leverage local capabilities, thereby enhancing their own competitiveness. Such investment not only brings capital into the host country but can also stimulate economic growth and job creation.

Furthermore, being innovative strengthens trade relationships. Countries leading in technological advancements generally produce goods and services that are in high demand globally. The use of innovative technologies can streamline production processes, making products more competitive and boosting exports. Innovation also increases productivity by creating more efficient methods of production, allowing a country to produce more with the same number of resources.

High-quality jobs are another byproduct of innovation, particularly in sectors like technology, biotech, and advanced manufacturing. These jobs usually pay well, enhancing the standard of living and contributing to a stronger middle class. A robust middle class can further spur economic growth through higher consumer spending. Additionally, innovative countries usually have diversified economies, making them more resilient to economic downturns and financial crises.

Innovation also plays a crucial role in sustainable economic development. Emerging technologies can address various environmental issues, such as reducing emissions and improving resource efficiency. This doesn't just benefit the environment; it also creates new economic opportunities in green industries.

Lastly, a nation with robust innovative capacities is often in a position to influence global policies and standards, especially those related to technology. This can give the country an advantage in global negotiations, enhancing its geopolitical influence. Therefore, innovation is not merely an economic driver; it's a multifaceted tool that can help a nation succeed on several fronts, from the economy to international relations and environmental sustainability. Innovation is therefore not just a driver of economic growth but also a critical component of a nation's overall development strategy.

Partnering with innovative nations can also boost a country's or organisation's global influence. Such alliances can help shape international norms, provide leverage in negotiations, and elevate a nation's standing in global affairs. Moreover, innovative nations frequently lead the way in tackling global challenges like climate change, pandemics, and food security. Collaborative efforts with these nations can facilitate a more effective and collective approach to solving these complex problems.

Another benefit is capacity building, especially for less technologically advanced countries. Collaborations can result in training local talent, strengthening institutions, and bolstering industries, all of which contribute to sustainable long-term development. The very act of partnering with an innovative nation can also inspire a culture of innovation within the partnering organisation or country. This influence and inspiration can serve as a motivational force, encouraging partners to innovate in their own practices and processes.

Finally, innovative nations tend to attract and retain talented individuals, who often aspire to live and work in environments that foster creativity and provide opportunities for personal and professional growth. This aligns with professor and entrepreneur Richard Florida's research, which suggests that innovative nations have a higher capacity to attract and retain creative talent.[2]

Certain nations stand out as hubs of opportunity due to their emphasis on cutting-edge research, innovative projects, and professional collaboration. These countries offer not just professional growth but also a superior quality of life characterised by robust healthcare, advanced infrastructure, and exceptional educational facilities. Additionally, their vibrant entrepreneurial ecosystems, rich in funding and mentorship, celebrate both achievements and learning from setbacks.

According to Florida's theory, such regions have a dense presence of the 'creative class' in fields like science and arts. This group attracts more of its kind, creating a self-sustaining circle of innovation and culture. Many of these nations host top-tier educational institutions, drawing global students, many of whom choose to stay post graduation, enriching the country's innovative capacity. Supported by immigrant-friendly policies, this talent adds diverse perspectives to the nation.

Networking in these settings, providing access to industry leaders and experts, further enhances their appeal, paving the way for more collaborations and opportunities. In essence, these innovative nations offer a blend of professional advancement, quality living, and vast networking opportunities. The combination of these premiums is a testament to why African countries focusing on innovation will witness sustained growth and prosperity.

Technological Advancements

On the other hand, technological advancements are related to the development and application of novel technologies, tools, or systems that augment capabilities, elevate efficiency, or offer innovative ways of performing tasks. These developments typically stem from research and development activities and can find application across various fields, including communication, manufacturing, agriculture, healthcare, and information technology.

Technological advancements can lead to the invention of new products or the improvement of existing ones. They can also result in more proficient processes or operational methods. Often, these advancements play a pivotal role in fuelling economic growth and productivity, while also having significant social and environmental impacts.

Looking at technology, as we forge ahead in the 21st century, the dynamic landscape of technology is an essential component for the development and transformation of societies. Technology cuts across various sectors.

Financial Services

As we saw earlier, digital financial services, such as mobile banking and digital wallets, are significantly transforming Africa's economic development landscape. These services have played a substantial role in promoting financial inclusion, especially for the traditionally unbanked population, enabling them to participate more effectively in the economy. As a result, various socio-economic benefits have ensued.

One of the key benefits is facilitating financial inclusion. By allowing individuals, typically excluded from formal banking systems, to access financial services, these digital solutions contribute substantially to economic empowerment and poverty alleviation. According to the World Bank's Findex Database from 2017, there was a notable increase in financial inclusion in Sub-Saharan Africa, with the share of adults with a financial institution account rising to 34 percent, while the share with a mobile money account almost doubled to 21 percent.[3]

Along with promoting financial inclusion, these services have also fostered a culture of savings. Mobile banking platforms have made it more efficient and secure for people to save, with users better equipped to weather financial shocks.[4]

The impact of these services extends to the remittance market as well, revolutionising the process of sending and receiving money, making it both cheaper and more convenient. This has significant economic implications, given that remittances often constitute a major portion of GDP in many of our African countries.

Another benefit of digital financial services is that they enhance transparency. Since digital transactions create records, they can help build credit history for unbanked individuals and businesses, thereby expanding access to finance.

Moreover, digital financial services have boosted ecommerce by offering a secure and efficient payment method. This development has been crucial for the growth of companies like Jumia, often referred to as 'the Amazon of Africa'.

Finally, digital financial services have supported the growth of micro and small enterprises in Africa by facilitating access to credit. A 2016 study found that the increased use of M-PESA in Kenya led to a wider choice of occupations and higher income for users, particularly for households led by women.[5] This underscores the significant role these services play in fostering economic development and social equity in Africa.

All in all, digital financial services are driving economic development in Africa by facilitating financial inclusion, fostering the growth of businesses, promoting savings, improving remittance services, enhancing transparency, and boosting ecommerce.

Agriculture

Agriculture is a critical sector in many African economies, and the innovative strides being made in AgriTech, or agricultural technology, are ushering in a new era for farming across the African continent. The introduction and adoption of technological innovations, such as precision farming, smart irrigation systems, and digital platforms, are enhancing agricultural productivity, profitability, and sustainability in unprecedented ways.

Precision Farming

Precision farming, a method that involves the use of technology to optimise crop yields and minimise waste, is an example of such innovation. In practice, precision farming could include the use of GPS technology and drones to analyse fields, guiding decisions on where and when to plant, or apply fertilisers and pesticides.

Precision farming in Africa is emerging, with pioneering projects showing significant potential. Kenya's UjuziKilimo uses sensors and analytics to offer tailored farming advice based on soil analysis. Nigeria's Zenvus uses sensors and machine learning to provide data on soil and crop health, aiding optimised farming. Another Nigerian venture, Hello Tractor, is a digital platform linking farmers with tractor owners, backed by GPS data for efficient machinery use. South Africa's Aerobotics employs drones and

AI for farm analytics, while Kenya's FarmDrive connects farmers to credit using data analytics to assess credit risks. However, challenges like high tech costs, limited digital literacy, and restricted internet access need addressing to fully unlock the potential of precision farming in Africa.

Smart Irrigation

Smart irrigation systems use sensors and data analytics to optimise water usage based on various factors, like weather, soil conditions, and plant water needs. These technologies can lead to significant water savings and improved crop yield, crucial for regions prone to droughts and water shortages.

The Water Efficient Maize for Africa (WEMA) project is a good example of this, having developed drought-tolerant maize using modern breeding techniques.

The WEMA project, led by the African Agricultural Technology Foundation (AATF) based in Nairobi, is a multi-country initiative focusing on developing drought-tolerant maize using advanced breeding techniques. Partnering with national research systems in countries like Kenya, Uganda, and Tanzania, the project aims to enhance maize's resilience to water scarcity, addressing a significant challenge due to climate change. As maize is vital for many Africans, its improved drought resistance can boost food security. By 2021, WEMA had released several drought-tolerant maize varieties, showing better yields in drought conditions. Distributed royalty-free to smallholder farmers, this project highlights the power of innovative technology and collaboration in addressing food security in a changing climate.

Digital Platforms for Market Access

Digital platforms are revolutionising market access for African farmers by linking them directly with consumers, reducing intermediaries, and increasing farmer profits. For instance, Nigerian startup Farmcrowdy offers a platform where individuals sponsor farming cycles, assisting farmers with funding, expert advice, and direct urban market access. In South Africa, Khula provides a 'fresh produce marketplace' for small-scale farmers to sell directly to businesses like restaurants. Khula also offers an input shop for farming essentials and a logistics app, creating a comprehensive support ecosystem for farmers. Meanwhile, Kenya's Twiga Foods connects smallholder farmers to urban vendors, ensuring fair prices by bypassing middlemen and optimising supply chains.

Information Services for Farmers

The advent of mobile phones and internet services has opened up a new world of possibilities for farmers in Africa, particularly when it comes to accessing critical, real-time information. Various applications and platforms now provide farmers with timely and localised information on weather, pest infestations, and best farming practices, which can significantly impact their productivity and efficiency.

A prime example of this can be seen in Kenya with the iCow app. The iCow app is transforming livestock care by providing farmers timely SMS information on veterinary and feeding practices, and tailoring advice based on each animal's specifics, such as age and milk production. Similarly, Malawi has embraced tech initiatives to support its agricultural sector. The Farmer Input Support Programme (FISP) offers a digital voucher system for farmers to access subsidised inputs like fertilisers. Another service, the

'321 service', launched by Human Network International in partnership with Airtel Malawi, gives farmers essential information, from farming techniques to weather forecasts, accessible even via basic phones. Esoko, originating in Ghana and now in Malawi, sends crucial market and weather updates to farmers via SMS and connects them directly with buyers. These tools underscore the transformative power of technology in Africa's agriculture and the continent's innovative approach to addressing local challenges.

Managing Climate-Related Risks

AgriTech can help farmers predict, monitor, and manage climate-related risks, such as droughts and flooding. One way AgriTech is addressing this challenge is through the development of sophisticated early warning systems. An initiative exemplifying this approach is the African Risk Capacity (ARC). ARC is an institution of the African Union designed to assist member states in improving their capacities to better plan, prepare, and respond to extreme weather events and natural disasters.

Improving Supply Chain Efficiency

Improving supply chain efficiency is a crucial aspect of enhancing the agricultural sector, and technologies such as blockchain have shown significant potential in this area. Blockchain technology, which is essentially a decentralised and secure ledger system, can offer improved traceability, transparency, and efficiency in agricultural supply chains.

Additionally, enhancing agricultural sustainability will help ensure food security for Africa's growing population, even in the face of climate change challenges. Finally, as agriculture is a major source of employment in Africa, innovations in this sector would lead to the creation of new types of jobs and opportunities for entrepreneurship.

Health

Given the vast healthcare needs and resource constraints on our continent of Africa, e-health technologies have great potential to address many of the health challenges Africa faces, improving healthcare delivery and, consequently, the continent's economic development.

Telemedicine

Telemedicine allows health professionals to evaluate, diagnose, and treat patients remotely using digital technology. This is particularly important in Africa, where many rural communities do not have access to quality healthcare services due to geographical distance. It enables patients to consult doctors without travelling long distances, thereby saving time and resources.

Digitising health records has become a critical aspect of improving the efficiency and effectiveness of healthcare delivery worldwide, and Africa is no exception. The transition to digital health records facilitates easy storage and retrieval of patient data, contributing to the continuity of care, reducing errors, and assisting in tracking disease trends and outbreaks.

In Kenya, CarePay's M-TIBA is leading the digital healthcare movement. It functions as a mobile health wallet, letting users manage their healthcare finances digitally. Beyond transactions, M-TIBA offers a digital record of medical and payment histories, giving healthcare professionals quick access to a patient's comprehensive health background. This insight not only aids better medical decision-making but also provides data on healthcare patterns and disease trends, proving instrumental for public health planning and prevention efforts.

Mobile Health Apps

Mobile health applications, often known as mHealth apps, are rapidly becoming an integral part of healthcare delivery across Africa, offering a wide range of services such as health information dissemination, patient monitoring, data collection, and health management. These applications play a significant role in improving healthcare access, particularly in remote or underserved areas, and in enhancing health outcomes.

For instance, Uganda's WinSenga, a brainchild of Makerere University students, is transforming maternal healthcare through mobile health technology. This affordable smartphone-based tool acts as an ultrasound, monitoring the mother and foetus during pregnancy. It captures sounds from the womb, analysing them to provide data on the baby's health, such as heart rate and expected delivery date. Besides foetal monitoring, it offers guidance on antenatal care. Especially beneficial for healthcare workers in remote regions, WinSenga identifies complications early, ensuring healthier maternal outcomes.

In South Africa, the MomConnect initiative by the National Department of Health enhances maternal and child health via mobile technology. Launched in 2014, it dispatches stage-specific health advice to pregnant women and new mothers through SMS. Beyond advice, MomConnect fosters two-way communication, allowing women to seek clarity and provide feedback, and even reminds mothers of medical appointments. The service's insights are also pivotal for health policy formulation. Challenges include ensuring message accuracy and user privacy. Both WinSenga and

MomConnect highlight the transformative potential of mHealth in African healthcare.

These apps are breaking down barriers to healthcare access, improving the quality of care, and enhancing health outcomes by leveraging mobile technology. However, challenges like ensuring data privacy, improving digital literacy, and expanding internet connectivity must be addressed to maximise the potential of mHealth applications in improving healthcare across Africa.

Data Analysis and Prediction

E-health technologies not only directly facilitate healthcare provision but also serve as critical tools for large-scale health data analysis. These analytics can provide valuable insights for predicting disease outbreaks, resource allocation, and the design of targeted healthcare interventions.

A significant player in this arena is BlueDot. Utilising artificial intelligence, BlueDot serves as a global early warning system for infectious diseases by analysing various data sources in real-time. While not African-developed, BlueDot's technology has crucial implications for Africa, given its battles with diseases like Ebola and malaria. Such systems can significantly aid in early detection and response, highlighting the value of e-health technologies in safeguarding public health.

Training Healthcare Professionals

The advent of e-learning platforms has been revolutionary for education, including the training of healthcare workers. Particularly in regions where training resources are scarce, e-learning offers a scalable solution to bridge this gap.

The African Medical Research Foundation (AMREF), Africa's

premier health development organisation, has advanced its training of health workers using an e-learning platform. This platform offers modular courses to healthcare professionals across Africa, including those in remote locations, allowing them to enhance their skills at their own pace. The initiative not only benefits individual health workers but also elevates the quality of healthcare services, positively impacting community health outcomes.[6]

The potential impact on Africa's economic development is also significant. Improved healthcare leads to a healthier workforce, which directly influences productivity and economic output. Moreover, the healthcare sector can also be a source of job creation, especially as the demand for digital skills increases. It also opens the opportunity for African tech entrepreneurs to develop solutions tailored to local needs, boosting the local tech industry.

In sum, e-health technologies offer a valuable tool in improving healthcare delivery on our continent of Africa, particularly in underserved rural areas. They contribute to expanding access to health services, improving the quality of care, and enhancing health information management. This progress in the healthcare sector will lead to substantial improvements in Africa's overall economic development.

Education

Educational technology, or edtech, has the potential to revolutionise education across Africa, addressing numerous challenges and contributing significantly to economic development.

One of the fundamental ways edtech enhances education is by expanding access, especially in remote or underserved areas. The eLimu app, developed in Kenya, is an outstanding example of how educational technology can enhance access to education. It is designed to provide interactive and engaging educational content to primary school learners, with a specific focus on making learning enjoyable and improving learners' retention and problem-solving skills.[7]

eLimu delivers content tailored to the Kenyan curriculum in both English and Swahili, enriched with multimedia elements like animations, videos, and quizzes. Covering core academic subjects, life skills, and even exam preparation materials, the platform makes education engaging and interactive. Especially valuable in Kenya's resource-limited, often rural settings, eLimu bridges educational gaps by offering quality content on mobile devices. By emphasising interactivity, the platform not only ensures accessibility but also engages students effectively, nurturing a genuine passion for learning.

Beyond enhancing access to education, another vital aspect of edtech's potential lies in its capacity to improve the quality of education. It fosters a more personalised and interactive learning experience by providing digital content that can be tailored to individual learning styles.

Siyavula, a South African edtech company, exemplifies this potential. The platform provides interactive learning materials for mathematics and science, primarily designed for high school learners. Siyavula's platform uses an adaptive, practice-oriented approach, where learners engage with the material through problem-solving.[8]

In the realm of education management, edtech introduces tools and platforms that streamline processes, enhance communication, and ultimately lead to more efficient and effective education delivery. Learning Management Systems (LMS), for instance, are one of the key innovations in this area. These digital platforms enable educators to manage course content, track learner progress, administer tests, and facilitate communication between all parties involved in the educational process.

Lastly, edtech also enriches educator training by providing platforms for professional development, leading to improved teaching practices and, consequently, enhanced learning outcomes. It holds immense potential to transform the education landscape on our continent of Africa, providing solutions to longstanding challenges and driving economic development.

Clean Energy

With many parts of our continent still lacking reliable access to electricity, clean energy technologies, such as solar and wind power systems, offer a sustainable solution. The transformative potential of clean energy technologies in Africa is immense and multifaceted. Particularly in regions where extending the traditional power grid is not economically feasible, clean energy technologies, such as solar power systems, present a viable solution.

Companies like ENGIE Energy Access in Southern Africa have turned to innovative solar power solutions to circumvent these barriers. ENGIE Energy Access is revolutionising energy access in Southern Africa with sustainable solar power solutions, addressing the electricity scarcity that plagues millions. Their solar systems, which serve as tools for socio-economic development, are accessible through a pay-as-you-go model, making energy independence attainable for many.

Understanding the limitations of traditional grid expansion, ENGIE Energy Access focuses on affordable, renewable alternatives that customers can easily adopt and manage. This approach not only provides immediate electricity but also helps customers build credit histories, changing the dynamics of energy financing and consumption.

Committed to long-term sustainability, ENGIE Energy Access prioritises comprehensive customer support, ensuring users are well-versed in operating and maintaining their solar systems, ready to tackle any subsequent challenges.

ENGIE Energy Access stands out as an innovator, not just offering energy solutions but also fuelling the region's progress and empowerment, panel by panel.[9]

The adoption of clean energy technologies also plays a crucial role in mitigating the effects of climate change through a reduction in carbon emissions. Given Africa's vulnerability to climate change impacts, this transition is particularly vital.

Reliable access to electricity, powered by clean energy technologies, will act as a catalyst for various economic activities, including small businesses and industries, and enhance public services like education and healthcare. This access will, in turn, stimulate economic growth, improve living standards, and enhance public health.

Lastly, the shift towards clean energy can be an attractive proposition for domestic and foreign investors, encouraging investment in renewable energy projects. This would foster technology transfer, boost local capacity, and stimulate economic growth.

It is therefore accurate to say that the transition to clean energy technologies offers a multifaceted and sustainable solution to Africa's energy challenges. The impact of this transition, from enhancing access to electricity and fostering energy independence to supporting economic activities and attracting investment, has the potential to create a more sustainable, prosperous, and resilient African economy.

Government

Technology can also enhance public service delivery and governance. The impact of technology in transforming public service delivery and governance, often referred to as e-governance, is becoming increasingly evident on our continent of Africa. E-governance initiatives are enhancing efficiency, increasing transparency, and fostering citizen engagement in ways that hold significant potential for boosting economic development.

The efficiency of public services has seen a significant improvement due to e-governance. The creation of online public service portals has the capacity to cut through bureaucratic red tape and expedite the delivery of services.

Rwanda's Irembo platform is a prime example of how technology can enhance the efficiency of public services. The IremboGov platform digitalises over 80 government services, offering quicker, transparent, and error-free processes, replacing old bureaucratic methods and reducing corruption. It has enhanced the government's oversight of service delivery and improved data-driven policymaking.

Kenya's eCitizen portal, launched in 2014, centralises various national government services online. The platform streamlines procedures, boosting transparency and accountability. It expedites services like passport applications and business registrations. Furthermore, it aids the government in collecting pertinent data for better policy decisions.

South Africa's GovChat platform allows direct communication between citizens and their representatives. It facilitates the reporting of service issues and provides news directly from the government. This innovative approach enhances public sector accountability and aids in performance evaluation.

Ghana's eServices platform, Ghana.GOV, digitises numerous public services. It offers online passport applications, tax services, and more, centralising access and promoting efficiency and convenience for Ghanaians.

Lastly, Nigeria's Budeshi platform links budget and procurement data to public projects, fostering transparency in public spending. It aids in monitoring corruption, enabling the public to demand accountability and engage in decision-making. This tool underlines the transformative power of tech in bolstering transparency, accountability, and good governance across Africa.

Furthermore, technology is paving the way for greater democratic participation by creating platforms for citizens to interact with their government. These platforms allow citizens to report issues, provide feedback, and contribute to decision-making processes. Kenya's Ushahidi platform provides a compelling example. Ushahidi, which translates to 'testimony' in Swahili, was developed in response to the post-election violence that rocked Kenya in 2008.[10]

As a crowdsourcing tool, Ushahidi was used to collect and map real-time reports of violence from citizens across the country. These reports were submitted through the internet and mobile phones, providing a dynamic picture of the situation on the ground. The visual mapping made the information easily accessible and comprehensible, which helped to raise awareness, prompt responses, and, ultimately, hold those in power accountable.

Globally, the platform has been pivotal in various emergencies. In 2010, it aided relief coordination in Haiti's earthquake and helped address Russia's wildfires. The same year, it helped Washington, DC manage 'Snowmageddon'. In 2011, Ushahidi supported response efforts for Japan's earthquake and tsunami and monitored Nigeria's elections for irregularities. It was instrumental in 2012 during Hurricane Sandy, directing relief measures, and, in 2015, it helped target relief during Nepal's earthquake. These instances highlight Ushahidi's adaptability in diverse crisis situations, from natural calamities to electoral affairs.

Overall, e-governance is playing a pivotal role in transforming public service delivery and governance on our continent of Africa, thereby facilitating economic development. It showcases the potential of technology in creating efficient, transparent, and accountable public systems that can drive Africa's progress.

The impact of these developments on Africa's economic development are substantial. Enhanced efficiency and transparency in public services leads to cost savings, improved business environments, and increased public trust, all of which are conducive to economic growth. Greater citizen engagement leads to more responsive and inclusive policies, improving social cohesion and stability. Finally, data-driven policymaking leads to more effective and targeted interventions, maximising the impact of public spending.

Entrepreneurship

Lastly, technological entrepreneurship is playing an increasingly critical role in economic development, particularly in the context of Africa. Tech startups are the harbingers of innovation, steering the development of new products, services, and business models that catalyse productivity and growth.

In addition to driving innovation, tech startups are potential job creators. As noted in the 2020 Global Startup Ecosystem Report, each tech job approximately generates five non-tech jobs.[11] The concept is based on the multiplier effect theory, which postulates that a single economic action, such as creating a job in the tech sector, will have a ripple effect leading to further economic activity.[12]

Tech startups, particularly those in high-growth areas, such as artificial intelligence, fintech, and biotechnology, often require a range of services to operate and expand. This creates direct employment opportunities not only for software engineers, data scientists, and other tech-focused roles but also for a host of non-tech positions. These might include roles in sales and marketing, human resources, finance, and administration.

Indirect jobs are also created in other sectors of the economy as the influence of the tech job extends outwards. For instance, the expansion of a tech startup might lead to increased demand for commercial real estate, benefiting those in the construction and property management industries. Moreover, the growth of tech startups can stimulate innovation and productivity improvements in other sectors.

Overall, the tech sector's growth can lead to substantial employment creation, boosting income levels and stimulating economic activity. However, this requires a conducive environment that supports tech startups, fosters innovation, and facilitates skills development. It also underscores the need for policies that ensure that the benefits of tech growth are widely shared, contributing to inclusive economic development.

Beyond job creation, tech startups foster economic diversification. They spur the growth of new industries by introducing new products, services, and business models. This is particularly significant for many African economies that have traditionally relied on a limited range of sectors, such as agriculture, mining, or oil. By fostering a vibrant tech sector, economies will diversify their sources of growth and become more resilient to shocks in any single sector.

However, for this vibrant tech ecosystem to thrive, a supportive environment is essential. This involves cultivating innovation hubs, attracting venture capital, creating regulatory sandboxes, and investing in education and skills training.

The Transformative Power of Innovation and Technology

The transformative potential of innovation and technology in fostering economic growth and social development is more significant than ever.

The idea of 'leapfrogging' is a potent concept in the context of Africa's development. It refers to the potential for developing nations to bypass, or 'leapfrog', over traditional stages of technological development and adopt newer technologies directly, thus accelerating their development process. It is a process that involves jumping ahead to the most efficient and effective systems without going through intermediary steps.

For instance, in the realm of financial services, Africa has seen significant leapfrogging thanks to digital technologies. Traditional banking infrastructures, such as physical bank branches and ATM machines, require substantial investments and are often inaccessible to people living in remote or underserved areas. However, the advent of mobile banking and digital wallets, epitomised by M-PESA in Kenya, has revolutionised financial inclusion. These digital solutions bypass the need for traditional banking infrastructure and provide financial services directly to individuals' mobile devices, wherever they are. As a result, a significant number of people who were previously unbanked now have access to financial services, accelerating economic participation and growth.

It's important to note, however, that while technology offers vast opportunities for leapfrogging, it needs to be coupled with supportive policies, adequate investment, and efforts to bridge the digital divide. Without these, the benefits of technology and leapfrogging risk being unevenly distributed, leading to further inequalities. Therefore, a holistic and inclusive approach is necessary to fully harness the potential of leapfrogging for Africa's development.

A Case Study – African Inventors

Other than the technologies and innovations mentioned earlier, there are a number of important inventions used globally that have been developed by Africans or people of African origin that need to be mentioned and appreciated. The following are the few I have picked as examples:

1. **Dr Thomas Mensah**, a Ghanaian-American engineer and inventor, has significantly influenced global technology with his contributions to fibre optics and nanotechnology. His innovations transformed the fibre optics manufacturing process, making it faster and more affordable, thereby democratising a critical technology for high-speed internet, telecommunication, and data storage. This has had ripple effects across sectors, enhancing telemedicine, global communication, financial trading, and even US military capabilities through laser-guided missile systems.

2. Cameroonian inventor **Arthur Zang** developed the Cardio Pad, a touch screen medical tablet designed to facilitate cardiac examinations in remote areas. Addressing

global cardiac care disparities, especially in regions with limited access to specialists, the Cardio Pad enables local healthcare workers to perform tests like electrocardiograms (ECGs). Crucially, it can wirelessly send this data to heart specialists globally for diagnosis and treatment recommendations, eliminating geographical and time barriers. This innovation boosts local healthcare quality, provides essential cardiac data from previously inaccessible areas, and reduces associated costs for patients by negating long travels for specialist care. Essentially, Zang's Cardio Pad is a revolutionary tool in telemedicine, showcasing how technology can bridge healthcare gaps and enhance accessibility in underserved communities.

3. Moroccan physicist **Rashi Kizami** revolutionised energy storage by developing a method for the reversible intercalation of lithium into graphite in electrochemical cells, paving the way for commercial lithium ion batteries with lithium graphite anodes. These batteries, crucial in devices like smartphones, laptops, and electric vehicles, can store more energy and have extended lifespans thanks to Kizami's innovation. His work has made electric vehicles more feasible and supported renewable energy storage, enhancing its competitiveness with fossil fuels. With the widespread use of lithium graphite anodes, battery technology has become affordable, fuelling various industries, from consumer electronics to sustainable transportation. In essence, many wireless devices today owe their functionality to Dr Kizami's pioneering efforts.

4. South African scientist **Sandile Ngcobo** invented the world's first digital laser, a monumental leap in optics and photonics with vast implications across sectors like communications, medicine, and manufacturing. Unlike traditional lasers that use fixed mirrors for a static beam, Ngcobo's innovation employs digital holograms for dynamic beam control, offering unparalleled flexibility. This innovation can enhance fibre-optic networks by optimising data transmission rates, revolutionise surgical procedures with adaptive lasers for precision, and elevate manufacturing processes such as laser engraving. Essentially, Ngcobo's digital laser pioneers a new era in laser technology, promising transformative applications and showcasing the potential of scientific innovation to redefine technological frontiers.

5. Malawian Professor **Landson Mhango** revolutionised the aviation sector with his high-speed motor invention, a device operating at 11,500 revolutions per minute, now integrated into most modern aircrafts, including those made by industry leaders like Boeing and Airbus. This innovation has enhanced air travel safety and efficiency on a global scale. Mhango's invention being embraced by top aerospace companies attests to its significance, as these corporations undergo rigorous testing before adopting new components. Each safe flight taken today owes a nod to Professor Mhango's pioneering work.

6. Professor **Mashudu Tshifularo**, a South African surgeon from the University of Pretoria, pioneered the world's first middle ear transplant using 3D printed titanium com-

ponents, marking a significant advance in treating hearing impairments. This innovative procedure, conducted at Steve Biko Academic Hospital, took under two hours and promises to revolutionise treatments for hearing disabilities, highlighting the potential of technologies like 3D printing in medical advancements.

The notable achievements of African inventors, including Dr Thomas Mensah, Arthur Zang, Rashi Kizami, Sandile Ngcobo, Professor Mhango, Professor Tshifularo, and many other African inventors, too numerous to mention, challenge misconceptions about Africa and position it as a hotbed of groundbreaking technological and scientific innovations.

Recognising the contributions of African innovators globally plays a crucial role in dismantling long-held stereotypes by highlighting the continent's intellectual prowess and sparking greater investment in its research and development sectors. Such acknowledgement serves as a powerful source of inspiration for the continent's youth, who, seeing successful role models from their own communities, are encouraged to pursue change and innovation. Moreover, many African innovators are focused on creating solutions specifically designed to meet the unique challenges faced by their home countries, often with potential global benefits. These contributions not only enrich the pool of global science but also foster a diverse and inclusive scientific community that enhances collaborative efforts and comprehensive problem-solving. Ultimately, this celebration of African ingenuity is a reminder that worldwide innovation thrives on the collective talents from all corners of the globe.

Bridging the Digital Divide: Challenges and Policy Considerations

However, the benefits of the digital revolution are neither automatic nor evenly distributed. While the digital revolution carries immense potential benefits, there exists a real risk that these advantages could elude those most in need, particularly if the digital divide isn't effectively addressed. This digital divide represents the disparity in access to digital technologies, influenced by factors such as geographical location, socio-economic status, and gender, among others.

A significant divide often exists between urban and rural areas. Urban areas typically enjoy better access to digital technologies, largely attributed to superior infrastructure. Thus, it is crucial to expand digital infrastructure into rural areas to prevent their further marginalisation.

Another critical aspect of the digital divide is the socio-economic disparity. Affordability plays a significant role in digital access. For low-income individuals and households, the high cost of digital devices and internet services can be prohibitive, severely limiting their access to and utilisation of digital technologies. Consequently, policies and initiatives designed to reduce the cost of devices and services, perhaps through subsidies or other mechanisms, will play a significant role in bridging this divide.

Gender disparity is also a pertinent issue in many African countries, where women generally have less access to digital technologies than men. This discrepancy is often driven by socio-cultural norms, lower income levels and education, and safety concerns. Initiatives focusing on empowering women both economically and socially, as well as those specifically promoting digital literacy and access among women, are key to addressing the gender digital divide.

Beyond mere access to digital technology, the ability to effectively utilise this technology, or digital literacy, is crucial. Without the necessary skills to use digital technologies effectively, individuals may not fully benefit from them, despite having access. This underscores the importance of education and training programmes in enhancing digital literacy.

As digital technologies become increasingly prevalent, the issues of privacy and data security grow in importance. It's critical that policies are put in place to safeguard users' data and ensure that individuals maintain control over their information. Additionally, users need to be made aware of how their data is being used and how they can protect themselves online.

As we continue our exploration of the pathways to prosperity in Africa, the next chapter will delve into the importance of social safety nets and inclusive growth in ensuring that the benefits of economic growth and development are widely shared.

CHAPTER 12

SOCIAL SAFETY NETS AND INCLUSIVE GROWTH

In looking into the journey to economic development and prosperity for Africa, we delve into an important aspect of economic development that often goes unnoticed: social safety nets and inclusive growth. In this chapter, the question of who benefits from economic development is as critical as the development process itself.

Social Safety Nets and Their Role in Poverty Reduction

The concept of social safety nets as public programmes aimed at protecting individuals and households from risks that could push them into extreme poverty is central to this discussion. These programmes offer financial and material aid, training, or services to the economically and socially disadvantaged segments of society, such as the unemployed, the disabled, the elderly, and children.

A study by Stephen Devereux and Rachel Sabates-Wheeler, 'Social Protection and Inclusive Growth in Africa', adds an important dimension to the conversation on social welfare policies on our continent of Africa. Rather than viewing social protection programmes merely as safety nets designed to alleviate immediate suffering due to poverty, the authors argue that these initiatives have broader implications for economic and social justice.[1]

In conventional economic discussions, social protection measures like unemployment benefits, disability allowances, and food assistance programmes are often seen as short-term solutions to address acute hardships. However, Devereux and Sabates-Wheeler suggest that social protection plays a more systemic role in reducing long-term inequality and fostering inclusive growth.

The authors emphasise that social protection can facilitate more equal distribution of resources and opportunities, enabling marginalised or vulnerable groups to participate in economic activities more fully. This, in turn, can contribute to more sustainable growth that benefits a larger segment of the population. By enhancing human capital through better health and education services or by providing the underprivileged with the necessary resources to engage in entrepreneurial activities, social protection programmes can stimulate economic productivity and innovation.

In the context of Africa, where inequality often exists along various axes, such as class, ethnicity, and geography, social protection mechanisms are particularly vital. These programmes act as a leveller, bringing about a more equitable society and, by extension, promoting social cohesion and stability.

Seeing social protection as an investment, rather than just a cost, is a perspective that can drive meaningful and long-lasting improvements within a country. By focusing on empowering people to be self-reliant, through healthcare and education for instance, the government can build a strong workforce. This, in turn, enhances the country's economic performance and standing in the world. So, in essence, when done right, social protection isn't just an expense; it's also a powerful tool for national development.

Investing in social protection does more than just help individuals; it strengthens the fabric of society as a whole. When the government provides a safety net for those who are most vulnerable, it helps to level the playing field and reduce income inequality. This fosters a sense of community and shared wellbeing, which can reduce social tensions and conflicts. A stable, peaceful society is not only better for its citizens, but it also becomes a more attractive place for investment. In this way, social protection is a key ingredient in creating a prosperous, harmonious nation.

Social protection programmes also encourage economic diversification and innovation. When people are not preoccupied with basic survival, they are more likely to take entrepreneurial risks or invest in furthering their skills. This can lead to the development of new industries or the enhancement of existing ones, contributing to economic resilience and adaptability.

Additionally, social protection can have intergenerational benefits. Children who grow up in households with sufficient income and access to social services are more likely to succeed in life, breaking the cycle of poverty. This ensures that the benefits of social protection are not just immediate but carry on to future generations, creating a cycle of positive development.

Moreover, well-designed social protection programmes can have a positive impact on labour market outcomes. These programmes help individuals transition between jobs more easily, adapting to changes in the economy by providing training and re-skilling opportunities. This is particularly crucial in times of economic downturns or structural shifts in the job market due to technological advancements.

Lastly, social protection programmes act as automatic stabilisers during economic downturns. When people continue to have some income through social benefits, they maintain their consumption levels to some extent, which helps to stabilise demand and, by extension, the economy. This mitigates the severity and duration of economic recessions, allowing for quicker recoveries.

Overall, when viewed as a long-term investment, social protection contributes to a myriad of factors that underpin a nation's comprehensive development, from economic productivity and innovation to social cohesion and intergenerational equity.

However, this only holds true if the political leadership uses these programmes to genuinely uplift people, not just to win votes. Furthermore, for social safety nets to effectively serve their functions, they must be well-designed, adequately funded, and effectively administered. They must also be responsive to changing social and economic conditions to meet the evolving needs of the individuals and households they are designed to support.

Overall, Devereux's and Sabates-Wheeler's work illuminates the crucial role that social safety nets play in poverty alleviation, inequality reduction, and the promotion of inclusive growth. Their insights underscore the importance of robust social protection programmes as integral components of a comprehensive strategy for sustainable economic development and social equity.

One of the most prominent examples of such a programme is Ethiopia's Productive Safety Net Programme (PSNP). Ethiopia's PSNP is an illustrative case of a social safety net that serves multiple purposes beyond immediate poverty alleviation. Initiated in 2005, it has become one of the largest social safety net programmes in Africa. While its core function is to act as an economic buffer by providing cash or food to vulnerable households, thereby reducing immediate vulnerability to financial shocks, its objectives and impacts are more multidimensional than merely offering a financial cushion.[2]

One key area where the PSNP has an extended role is in improving long-term resilience. By offering opportunities for public works employment, it helps to create community assets like roads, schools, and irrigation systems. This infrastructure development contributes to economic growth and increased community resilience against future shocks.[3]

The PSNP also intersects with educational and health outcomes. By providing a stable source of income, it enables families to invest in their children's education rather than sending them to work, thereby breaking the cycle of intergenerational poverty.[4] Similarly, the steady income alleviates the economic barriers to accessing healthcare services, contributing to better health outcomes for families enrolled in the programme.

The programme's cash or food transfers can also act as seed capital, enabling recipients to engage in micro-enterprises that would eventually become self-sustaining.[5] This is particularly vital for women, who, with the additional financial support, can invest in small-scale entrepreneurial activities, thereby gaining economic empowerment and improving the wellbeing of their families.[6]

Lastly, social safety nets like the PSNP contribute to social cohesion. By acting as a form of social insurance, they help in maintaining a sense of community and mutual help. Social safety nets can contribute to political stability by reducing the economic inequalities that often underlie social unrest.[7]

Social safety nets can also catalyse long-term change in two key ways: by promoting economic self-sufficiency and by contributing to social equity and inclusive growth.

Firstly, by promoting economic self-sufficiency, safety net programmes empower people and reduce the need for long-term financial aid. The PSNP, for example, includes a component dedicated to the creation of community assets and income-generating activities. This might include infrastructure projects, such as irrigation or road construction, which provide jobs for local residents and boost economic activity. It might also entail supporting individuals to develop small-scale businesses or agricultural activities. This is a better approach than just giving out regular handouts month after month, as it is based on the idea that providing people with the means to generate their own income is more effective and sustainable in the long term than merely giving them aid. It's an attempt to break the cycle of poverty by equipping people with skills and resources to stand on their own.

Secondly, by promoting social equity and inclusive growth, safety net programmes help reduce inequality and promote social inclusion. This is because they are typically targeted at the poorest and most vulnerable groups in society, who often face barriers to participation in economic activities. Safety net programmes can help level the playing field and ensure that the benefits of economic growth are shared more equitably by providing these groups with income support and opportunities to engage in productive activities. This aspect is crucial for fostering social cohesion and stability.

While the implementation of social safety nets can be challenging, requiring effective targeting, sufficient funding, and robust administration, they are crucial tools in the fight against poverty. They not only provide immediate relief from economic hardship but also contribute to broader development objectives, making them a vital component of poverty reduction strategies.

Another example is the South African grant system. The South African grant system is a vital component of the country's social support infrastructure, designed to alleviate poverty and offer aid to the nation's most vulnerable groups. It comprises a variety of grants, each aimed at distinct demographics, from the elderly and children to the disabled and those in need of care support.

The Older Person's Grant, also known as the Old Age Pension, is available to South African citizens, permanent residents, and refugees aged 60 years and above. It is means-tested to ensure that only those in real need receive it, supporting elderly individuals who may lack adequate income or savings.

The Child Support Grant helps parents and caregivers meet the basic needs of children under 18. It's available to South Africans who are in charge of a child or children, with a means-tested requirement and the stipulation that the child must live with the applicant.

The Care Dependency Grant is targeted towards caregivers of

children who need permanent and special care due to severe mental or physical disability. It aims to mitigate the financial strain on families who are caring for children requiring intensive support.

The Grant in Aid supports those who are already receiving a social grant but need additional financial assistance because they are reliant on someone else for their care. This is typically awarded to individuals unable to care for themselves due to old age or disability.

The War Veteran's Grant is set aside for veterans of World War I and II and the Korean War, who are 60 years or older, or are disabled. Eligible recipients must be South African citizens or permanent residents.

The Foster Child Grant is provided to foster parents caring for a child under the age of 18. This grant eases the financial burden of providing for a foster child, ensuring that they can access essential services.

Lastly, the Disability Grant is provided to South African citizens and residents who are temporarily or permanently disabled and cannot work as a result. This is offered to individuals aged between 18 and 59.

The South African grant system has seen several successes. It has been instrumental in poverty reduction, particularly among vulnerable populations, by providing a stable income to those who may have none. Additionally, grants such as the Child Support Grant have shown positive societal impacts, including improved school attendance rates and better health outcomes for children. The system's wide coverage, reaching over 18 million beneficiaries as of 2020, is another significant achievement.[8]

Despite these successes, the system has several shortcomings. While the grants have contributed to alleviating extreme poverty, the amounts often fall short of fully meeting recipients' basic needs, leading to questions about their long-term effectiveness in tackling poverty. The system is also plagued by administrative inefficiencies such as difficulties in processing applications, payment delays, and errors in the beneficiary database, which can prevent potential beneficiaries from receiving their grants on time or even at all. Furthermore, the system fails to cover individuals working in the informal economy or the unemployed who do not qualify for other grants. Given South Africa's high unemployment rate, this omission leaves a substantial part of the population without support. There are also concerns that the grant system could engender a culture of dependency, potentially discouraging recipients from seeking employment or improving their economic circumstances.

Crucially, the system predominantly funds consumption rather than production. In other words, while it helps beneficiaries meet immediate needs such as food, housing, and basic healthcare, it does little to foster productive investments that could enable recipients to become self-sustaining in the long term. Funding production could involve supporting recipients to acquire skills, invest in small businesses, or partake in income-generating activities. This approach could provide a more sustainable path out of poverty, encouraging economic independence and self-sufficiency.

To enhance the effectiveness of the South African grant system, improvements are required in administration, coverage, and transitioning from funding consumption to production. By refining administrative processes, expanding coverage to include overlooked demographics, and shifting the focus towards enabling beneficiaries to engage in productive, income-generating activities, the system could deliver far-reaching benefits. Not only would these changes help alleviate immediate poverty, but they could also empower recipients to break the cycle of poverty and sustainably improve their economic circumstances.

The Limits of Social Safety Nets and the Need for Inclusive Growth Strategies

Social safety nets, while important, have their limitations and are most effective when integrated into a broader inclusive growth strategy. Such a strategy must involve coordinated policies and investments that promote job creation, enhance access to quality services, and empower marginalised communities.

For instance, initiatives such as skills development and vocational training programmes should be employed to increase employment prospects, particularly for the youth and the long-term unemployed. By equipping individuals with in-demand skills, we increase their employability and potential income, providing a more sustainable solution than grants alone.

In a similar vein, programmes that aim to improve access to quality services such as education, healthcare, and housing are necessary. For example, investments in the public education system, particularly in low-income areas, can help ensure that all children, regardless of their socio-economic background, have access to a good education, enhancing their future employment prospects and potential for upward mobility.

The World Bank's 'World Development Report 2013: Jobs' emphasises that jobs are a cornerstone of economic development, not just as a means of earning income but also as a mechanism for broader societal progress. The report presents a nuanced argument that the value of jobs is multifaceted and has a far-reaching impact on several dimensions of development and poverty alleviation.[9]

Firstly, jobs are an instrument of social inclusion. When people have access to quality employment, they feel more integrated into society, which, in turn, enhances social cohesion.[10] Jobs create a shared sense of community and belonging that can reduce tensions and conflicts, thereby contributing to social stability.[11]

Secondly, jobs facilitate human capital development. Employment, especially when it provides opportunities for skills development, contributes to lifelong learning and human capital accumulation.[12] This increases individual productivity, which, in turn, contributes to economic growth.

Thirdly, jobs are critical for gender equity. They empower women by providing them with financial independence, thereby allowing them a greater say in household and societal decisions.[13] Employment opportunities for women also tend to have multiplier effects, including improvements in child health and education, which further fuels the cycle of economic development.[14]

In addition, jobs contribute to political stability. When a significant portion of the population is employed, especially youth, there is less likelihood of social unrest or political upheaval.[15] The sense of purpose and belonging that quality jobs provide can mitigate the factors that lead to instability.

Finally, jobs also play a role in shaping the social contract between citizens and their governments. When people are gainfully employed, they are more likely to have faith in their governing institutions and may be more willing to pay taxes, which are essential for the provision of public goods and services.[16]

The World Bank's report suggests that policy interventions aimed at job creation and improving job quality should be at the heart of strategies to promote development and reduce poverty.[17] This could include measures to enhance skills, promote entrepreneurship, improve labour market regulations, and ensure that workers can access the resources and support they need to find and maintain decent employment.

Overall, this report underlines the multifaceted role that jobs play in promoting development. While they are certainly vital as a source of income, their contributions to social cohesion, societal stability, and inclusive growth are equally important. This perspective underscores the importance of policies that support job creation and improve job quality as central components of development strategies.

Therefore, in designing and implementing social safety nets, it is essential to accurately identify the most vulnerable groups, ensure they receive adequate support, maintain programme integrity, and uphold beneficiaries' rights and dignity. Inaccurate targeting could lead to leakages, where resources intended for the most vulnerable end up benefiting those who are less needy.

Ensuring inclusivity implies creating opportunities for the underprivileged and marginalised, not merely for moral or ethical reasons but because it is a fundamental prerequisite for sustainable growth. Everyone should have the chance to contribute to and benefit from economic growth, and when this happens, societies will reap the rewards of enhanced productivity, a broader consumer base, increased socio-economic stability, and stronger social cohesion.

Therefore, while social safety nets are a crucial part of any strategy to reduce poverty and inequality, they must be complemented by more comprehensive and inclusive growth strategies. Only through this multipronged approach can we hope to address the root causes of poverty and inequality and build more equitable, inclusive, and prosperous societies.

As we transition to the next chapter, we will delve into the significance of fiscal responsibility and sound monetary policy. These factors form the cornerstone upon which economic development, inclusive of the maintenance and expansion of social safety nets, fundamentally depends.

CHAPTER 13

FISCAL RESPONSIBILITY AND SOUND MONETARY POLICY

Fiscal responsibility and sound monetary policy form the cornerstone of economic development for any nation. In this chapter, we delve into the pivotal role of fiscal responsibility and sound monetary policy in economic development. A nation's financial health is an essential element of its economic prosperity.

Fiscal Responsibility

Fiscal responsibility refers to a government's commitment to managing public resources efficiently, maintaining sustainable levels of public debt, and ensuring intergenerational equity, all of which are key to economic growth and stability. Transparency, accountability, and strategic planning are integral to this goal, with each element reinforcing the others.

Transparency in fiscal policy involves clear communication about government revenues, expenditures, and debt levels. This helps to build trust with citizens and international stakeholders, deter corruption, and ensure that resources are allocated efficiently and effectively. It's critical for governments to be transparent about their financial decisions so they can be held accountable.

Accountability, on the other hand, involves taking responsibility for fiscal decisions and their outcomes. This requires robust institutions and rule of law, with systems in place for oversight and audit of government activities. Accountability can help ensure that resources are used for their intended purposes and fiscal policy supports the public interest. For instance, in South Africa, the Auditor-General plays a crucial role in ensuring government accountability, particularly in terms of fiscal decisions and their outcomes. The office of the Auditor-General is a constitutionally established independent body that audits and reports on the use of public funds by the government.[1]

The Auditor-General's work involves auditing financial statements of all national and provincial departments and municipalities, as well as any other institution or business entity required by national legislation to be audited by the Auditor-General. In this capacity, the Auditor-General checks whether public funds have been used effectively, efficiently, and for their intended purposes. If there are discrepancies, mismanagement, or wastage, these are reported.

The reports of the Auditor-General are submitted to parliament and the respective provincial legislatures, providing a critical layer of oversight. These reports contribute to transparency in the public sector, as they are also made available to the public, thus empowering citizens to hold the government accountable.

The Auditor-General's role contributes to accountability by ensuring the rule of law in fiscal matters. Their work ensures that the government complies with legal requirements for fiscal management, aligns with budgetary objectives, and supports the public interest. This role is integral to promoting fiscal responsibility and intergenerational equity, as it helps to prevent the misuse of public funds, thereby securing resources for future generations.

Thus, the Auditor-General's work epitomises the concept of accountability in fiscal policy. By independently auditing and reporting on government spending, the office serves as a check and balance on the government's use of public funds, promoting efficiency, transparency, and accountability in public financial management.

Strategic planning is also crucial in fiscal policy. Governments need to carefully consider both the short-term and long-term impacts of their decisions on things like taxation and spending. Strategic planning allows governments to prioritise key areas for investment (like infrastructure or education), make adjustments in response to economic cycles, and ensure that public debt remains at sustainable levels.

Fiscal policy refers to government decisions about taxation and spending, which can influence economic activity, redistribute income, and provide public goods and services. Sound fiscal policy can help foster sustainable growth and reduce poverty, but it requires a balanced approach to prevent excessive debt accumulation and economic instability.

Monetary Policy

Monetary policy, on the other hand, involves central bank actions to control money supply and interest rates, aiming to manage inflation and stabilise the economy. A good example is the role the South African Reserve Bank (SARB) plays in maintaining effective monetary policy in South Africa. It is the central bank of the country, and its primary purpose is to achieve and maintain price stability in the interest of balanced and sustainable economic growth.[2]

To achieve these objectives, the SARB uses various monetary policy tools. Its key instrument is the repurchase rate (the repo rate), which is the interest rate at which it lends money to commercial banks. Changes in the repo rate affect the interest rates that banks charge for loans, impacting borrowing costs throughout the economy, thus influencing overall economic activity and inflation.

The SARB operates under an inflation targeting framework, aiming to keep inflation within a target range, currently at 3 to 6 percent. This approach provides a clear and transparent framework for monetary policy decisions, helping to anchor inflation expectations and providing certainty for households and businesses.

Furthermore, the SARB also plays a vital role in financial stability. It oversees the banking sector and the payment system, ensures the effective functioning of the national and international exchange of money, and acts as a lender of last resort to banking institutions.

However, the SARB, like other central banks in Sub-Saharan Africa, faces challenges due to fiscal dominance, volatility in commodity prices, and structural issues in the economy. Fiscal dominance occurs when high government debt and deficits limit the effectiveness of monetary policy. Volatility in commodity prices can lead to fluctuations in inflation and exchange rates. Structural issues, such as high unemployment and inequality, can also pose challenges for monetary policy.

Despite these challenges, the SARB has generally been praised for its independent and prudent monetary policy. It has played a key role in maintaining macroeconomic stability in South Africa, managing inflation, and supporting economic growth.

Central banks can play a key role in achieving macro-economic stability and fostering conditions for sustainable economic growth through the adoption of transparent, consistent, and responsive monetary policy frameworks. Thus, to boost economic growth and stability, African countries need to implement sound, effective fiscal and monetary policies, manage their public resources efficiently, maintain sustainable debt levels, and ensure intergenerational equity. This requires strong institutions, clear and transparent policies, and a commitment to accountability and strategic planning.

Monetary stability is crucial because it reduces uncertainty, fosters investment, and promotes economic growth. However, a sound monetary policy is not a panacea. It should be complemented with fiscal discipline, structural reforms, and prudent economic management.

Strategies to Ensure Fiscal Discipline and Sound Economic Management

One of the problems on our continent, and elsewhere in the world where you have multi-party democracy with varying ideologies, is the issue of using the state coffers to buy votes. This brings about fiscal indiscipline that leads to unmanageable national debt burdens.

Prime Minister Lee Hsien Loong's 2016 speech in the Singaporean Parliament certainly offers crucial lessons for African leaders aiming to stimulate economic development within their nations. His address puts emphasis on the protection of national reserves and the preservation of public service integrity, and provides a warning against 'auction' elections. These insights are instrumental to understanding Singapore's successful governance model.[3]

The necessity to protect national reserves was likened by PM Lee to safeguarding "oil in the ground." This asset, he argues, should be judiciously guarded to ward off any threats by a "profligate government" that could expend all the reserves, thus endangering the nation's future economic stability. This highlights the essentiality of fiscal discipline and sound economic management. African nations, many of which are abundant in resources, are thus reminded that natural resources and national reserves should be managed responsibly and preserved for future generations.

PM Lee's address imparts vital lessons on responsible governance, prudent economic management, and the necessity of institutional integrity. For African leaders, these principles could pave the way for more stable, sustainable economic development across the continent.

To prevent the misuse of national reserves, irresponsible election promises, corruption in public service, and a lack of checks and balances, our African nations need to implement strategies focused on promoting responsible governance and institutional integrity.

Firstly, our African nations must ensure the prudent management of national reserves through strict regulatory frameworks and oversight mechanisms. Sovereign wealth funds, similar to those in Norway and Botswana, can be a tool for managing resource revenues. The transparent management of these funds, with clear rules for withdrawals, will help prevent reckless spending.

Additionally, nations need to cultivate electoral integrity and transparency to avoid the peril of the 'auction elections' that PM Lee warned about. This refers to a scenario where political parties compete to promise increasing benefits to voters, potentially depleting the national treasury. An example from Australia was cited to stress the peril of short-term populism overshadowing long-term economic stability. African leaders are hence advised to ensure that election promises are grounded in sustainable policies instead of unsustainable spending, to avoid economic destabilisation or an accumulation of debt after elections.

Regulatory mechanisms could be developed to assess the fiscal feasibility of election campaign promises. Public awareness campaigns are also important to educate voters about the dangers of populist promises leading to economic destabilisation.

The discussion about the integrity of public service is another important aspect of Lee's speech. He emphasised the significance of integrity and competence in key public service positions and argued that a country's performance is largely dependent on these individuals. He also issued a stern warning about the drastic consequences of corruption, stating that it could permanently break the system. This point is especially relevant to African nations where public sector corruption often impedes economic development. Therefore, implementing strong anti-corruption measures, promoting transparency, and fostering a culture of integrity in public service are absolutely essential.

To accomplish this, our African nations should enforce strong anti-corruption measures, which include comprehensive legislation, stringent enforcement mechanisms, and severe penalties for corruption. Transparency in public service, perhaps achieved through public asset declarations, could also serve as a deterrent against corruption. Furthermore, the implementation of merito-cratic recruitment and promotion practices will assure that competent, integrity-driven individuals fill public service positions.

Building robust, independent institutions is also necessary to provide checks and balances against potential abuses of power and irresponsible fiscal policies. Such institutions may include independent judiciary systems, robust legislative bodies, and autonomous oversight agencies like anti-corruption commissions and ombudsman offices. Transparent public financial management mechanisms can also be an essential check on fiscal policy.

Finally, PM Lee spoke about the need for a "second key" in the system of governance. This second key serves to ensure checks and balances and reflects the importance of robust institutions capable of protecting against abuses of power or irresponsible fiscal policies. A good example of this in South Africa is the Independent Police Investigative Directorate (IPID). The IPID, as an autonomous body, is designed to investigate complaints of misconduct or offences committed by members of the police service. In this role, it serves as a critical check on the power of the police, ensuring that any potential abuses are thoroughly investigated and appropriate actions are taken.[4]

Like the 'second key' concept, the effectiveness of the IPID hinges on its independence and its ability to hold police officers accountable for their actions without interference. Its mandate to investigate serious complaints against the police, ranging from offences involving corruption to those involving serious harm or death, demonstrates its role as a vital safeguard within South Africa's governance system.

That said, it's important to note that the 'second key' is not just about having an independent institution but also about the effectiveness and trustworthiness of such an institution. For the IPID to fully function as a second key, it needs to operate independently, be adequately resourced, and its investigations need to lead to real consequences in cases of proven police misconduct. This will not only help maintain the rule of law but also build public trust in the police service.

Furthermore, while IPID provides a specific example related to law enforcement, the 'second key' concept applies to all areas of governance. It underscores the importance of having multiple, robust institutions that can hold various branches and agencies of government accountable, ranging from financial bodies that can check on fiscal policy, to judiciary systems that ensure legal accountability, to electoral commissions that safeguard the integrity of elections. Thus, the 'second key' concept is broad, encompassing a wide range of institutions and mechanisms that, together, ensure a balanced and accountable system of governance.

In essence, promoting public awareness and education can help foster a culture of accountability and transparency. Encouraging citizen participation in governance, perhaps through public consultations on major policies or budgetary decisions, can play a significant role in preventing abuses and fostering responsible governance.

Taken together, these measures provide a comprehensive and effective approach to prevent the issues outlined in PM Lee's speech and foster responsible, sustainable economic development.

As we continue our exploration in the subsequent chapters, we will look at how these macroeconomic fundamentals intersect with issues of environmental sustainability, regional cooperation, foreign investment, and economic diversification and resilience – all crucial aspects in the journey towards Africa's economic development and prosperity.

CHAPTER 14

ENVIRONMENTAL SUSTAINABILITY

In this chapter, the focus shifts to a pressing global concern – environmental sustainability. This is a complex, multifaceted issue that requires thoughtful and coordinated action at all levels, from local communities to international institutions.

Balancing economic growth with environmental conservation is one of the most critical challenges faced not just by African nations but by the world as a whole. This balancing act becomes even more challenging in developing regions like our continent, where the urgency to uplift millions from poverty often leads to increased pressure on the environment.

The challenge is twofold. On one hand, rapid economic growth is often associated with significant environmental degradation, including deforestation, pollution, loss of biodiversity, and increased greenhouse gas emissions. These environmental impacts, in turn, can threaten the very foundations of economic growth, as they degrade the natural resources upon which economies depend. For instance, deforestation can lead to soil erosion and reduced agricultural productivity, while pollution can lead to health problems that reduce human capital and productivity.

On the other hand, there is the challenge of ensuring that growth is inclusive and sustainable in the long term. This means moving away from growth that is solely based on the exploitation of finite natural resources and towards growth that is based on sustainable, renewable resources and technologies. It also means ensuring that the benefits of growth are widely shared, reducing inequalities and improving living standards for all.

The World Commission on Environment and Development (WCED), also known as the Brundtland Commission, captured this challenge succinctly in its 1987 report, 'Our Common Future'. The document came to be known as the 'Brundtland Report' after the Commission's chairwoman, Gro Harlem Brundtland. The report introduced the concept of sustainable development, defined as "development that meets the needs of the present without compromising the ability of future generations to meet their own needs."[1]

This concept of sustainable development provides a guiding principle for addressing the challenge of balancing economic growth with environmental conservation. It emphasises the need for a holistic approach, one that considers economic, social, and environmental dimensions together. For Africa, this means pursuing growth strategies that not only drive economic development and poverty reduction but also protect the environment and ensure the sustainable use of natural resources for future generations.

Implementing such strategies will require innovative thinking, strong governance, and cooperation at all levels. It will also require the integration of environmental considerations into all aspects of policy making and planning, from infrastructure development to education, health, and agriculture. This is a complex and challenging task, but it is essential for ensuring the long-term prosperity and resilience of Africa.

The Role of Local Participation in Conservation – Insights from Kenya

John Mbaria's and Mordecai Ogada's critique of conventional conservation approaches in 'The Big Conservation Lie: The Untold Story of Wildlife Conservation in Kenya' provides a profound perspective on how local communities can contribute to conservation efforts in Africa.[2]

The authors argue that conventional conservation efforts, often dictated by Western paradigms and driven by foreign NGOs, have failed to deliver meaningful and sustainable results in many cases. These conventional approaches frequently involve cordoning off vast tracts of land as protected areas or national parks, restricting access and use for local communities who have lived in and depended on these areas for generations.

This model, while perhaps well-intentioned, has been criticised for failing to consider the rights and needs of local people, sometimes leading to human rights abuses and exacerbating poverty. It has also been criticised for being ineffective at achieving its primary goal of conservation, as evidenced by continued biodiversity loss despite a growing number of protected areas.

Mbaria and Ogada propose an alternative approach that centres around local participation and indigenous conservation strategies.

They assert that local communities, who live closest to the land and rely on it for their livelihoods, are often the best stewards of the environment.

There are several reasons for this. First, these communities have a direct interest in the health and sustainability of their local ecosystems, as their livelihoods depend on it. Second, they possess deep, intimate knowledge of these ecosystems, gained through generations of interaction with the environment. This traditional ecological knowledge can be incredibly valuable in managing and conserving biodiversity, as it includes information about local species, ecosystems, and ecological relationships that may not be well-understood by Western science.

Lastly, local communities often have traditional practices and social norms that promote sustainable resource use and conservation. For instance, many indigenous cultures have taboos against overhunting or rules about resource use that help ensure sustainability.

Therefore, the authors argue, the active participation of local communities in conservation efforts is not just a matter of social justice but also a practical and effective strategy for conservation. By involving local people in decision-making, respecting their rights, and building on their knowledge and practices, conservation efforts are likely to be more successful and sustainable in the long run.

This argument has significant implications for how conservation is done in Africa and elsewhere. It suggests a need for a shift away from top-down, externally imposed conservation models towards more inclusive, participatory, and locally driven approaches. Such a shift could not only lead to better conservation outcomes but also help address some of the social and economic challenges faced by rural communities in Africa.

The proposition by Mbaria and Ogada, which emphasises local participation and indigenous strategies in conservation initiatives, is echoed globally by many scholars and practitioners. The importance of local and indigenous knowledge as well as the need for it to be integrated with scientific knowledge in managing ecosystems and conserving biodiversity has gained wider recognition.

Jules Pretty's and David Smith's 2004 work on the importance of local and indigenous knowledge in managing ecosystems and biodiversity, for example, opens up a significant discussion about the convergence of tradition and modernity in the realm of environmental conservation. At the heart of their argument is the recognition that indigenous communities, having lived in harmony with their surroundings for countless generations, possess a profound understanding of their environment that is deeply embedded in their cultural and social practices.[3]

Local and indigenous knowledge encapsulates not just empirical observations but also a philosophical orientation that often sees humans as part of the environment, rather than separate from or dominant over it. Such a perspective can offer a holistic approach to conservation, where the health of the ecosystem is intrinsically linked to the wellbeing of the people who inhabit it. This contrasts with some Western scientific traditions, which, though invaluable in their rigorous methodologies and global applicability, can sometimes miss the subtleties and interconnectedness that indigenous knowledge captures.

For instance, indigenous communities might possess detailed knowledge about the reproductive patterns of certain plants or the migratory behaviours of specific animals. Such insights, accrued over generations, often come from a continuous interaction with nature, where observations are made over long time frames and across different seasons. Western scientific studies, on the other hand, might be conducted over shorter durations and may miss these intricate patterns.

Additionally, local knowledge often encompasses sustainable management practices that have been refined over time to ensure that resources are not depleted. These practices might involve rotational farming, controlled hunting, or specific rituals that mandate the conservation of particular species or habitats. Such practices have ensured the survival of these communities over millennia and have maintained the ecological balance of their habitats.

There's also an ethical dimension to this. Recognising and integrating indigenous knowledge into mainstream conservation strategies respects and empowers local communities. It acknowledges their rights and contributions and can foster collaborative approaches that benefit both the environment and its indigenous inhabitants.

Similarly, Fikret Berkes's 2007 advocacy for a co-management approach in conservation echoes a rising understanding that sustainable environmental stewardship requires a convergence of diverse perspectives. Co-management, as Berkes conceptualises it, transcends traditional top-down governance structures, emphasising instead the harmonisation of multiple stakeholders' insights, from governmental bodies and scientists to local communities and NGOs. The result is an intricate collection of knowledge systems and decision-making strategies that converge to ensure the sustainable management of precious natural resources.[4]

Central to Berkes's argument is the recognition that no single knowledge system holds a monopoly on understanding complex ecosystems. While scientific methods can offer quantitative data and empirical insights, local and traditional knowledge, born from centuries of intimate interaction with the environment, brings qualitative depth and intricate detail that might be overlooked in purely scientific analyses. By weaving these varied strands of understanding together, co-management approaches can produce a richer, more holistic perspective on conservation, leading to strategies that are both ecologically sound and socially just.

The management of the Great Barrier Reef in Australia provides a sterling illustration of co-management in action. Given the Reef's global significance and the manifold challenges it faces – from climate-change-induced coral bleaching to industrial impacts – its conservation necessitates a broad-spectrum approach. The collaboration between different entities, such as government agencies and indigenous communities, ensures that management strategies are multifaceted, addressing not only ecological considerations but also social, economic, and cultural dimensions.[5]

For instance, the zoning plans devised as part of the reef's management are not mere bureaucratic dictums. Instead, they emerge from comprehensive consultations, balancing the interests of tourism operators, indigenous communities, conservationists, and fisheries, among others. By considering the aspirations and concerns of these diverse stakeholders, the zoning plans aim to be both ecologically sustainable and socially equitable. They demarcate areas for specific activities, thereby preventing overuse and ensuring that sensitive habitats remain undisturbed, all while allowing local industries and communities to benefit from the reef's resources.

Such an inclusive approach to governance also fortifies the legitimacy of management strategies. When stakeholders feel they have a voice in the decision-making process, they are more likely to respect and adhere to established guidelines, thus enhancing conservation outcomes.

Overall, these studies emphasise the need for a shift in conservation paradigms – a shift from top-down, externally driven approaches towards more inclusive, participatory, and knowledge-integrative strategies that engage local communities and respect and utilise their indigenous knowledge.

Several studies specific to Africa and other regions underscore the role of local communities in biodiversity conservation. These studies often focus on traditional practices, social norms, and community-managed resources.

One intriguing study by Colding and Folke delved into the role of 'taboos' in conservation among local communities in Madagascar. Taboos, or social prohibitions, have been identified in many traditional societies worldwide. In the context of Madagascar, certain taboos played a significant role in regulating the hunting of species and the harvesting of resources. For instance, some communities had taboos against hunting certain species or collecting certain plants at particular times, allowing these species to reproduce and thrive. By respecting these taboos, communities were effectively managing their resources sustainably. This example shows how social norms and cultural practices can contribute to effective conservation strategies.[6]

Local communities, with their intricate understanding of their environment and their deep stake in its wellbeing, can be powerful custodians of nature. Entrusting them with the agency to manage their resources can not only lead to better conservation outcomes but can also set a foundation for a more inclusive, equitable, and sustainable relationship between humanity and the natural world.

These studies emphasise the crucial role that local communities play in managing and conserving biodiversity. They also show that traditional knowledge and practices, community participation, and local management of resources can lead to effective and sustainable conservation outcomes. These findings resonate with the arguments made by Mbaria and Ogada and others, underscoring the need to integrate local participation and indigenous strategies in conservation efforts.

Thus, integrating local participation and indigenous strategies into conservation initiatives could be instrumental for African nations as the continent seeks to balance its growth trajectory with the preservation of its rich biodiversity. However, this requires a shift from externally imposed conservation paradigms towards more inclusive, participatory, and context-specific strategies that recognise and build upon local knowledge, practices, and institutions.

Case Study – The Green Belt Movement in Kenya

The Green Belt Movement in Kenya, founded by the Nobel laureate Wangari Maathai, stands as an exemplary model of grassroots conservation. Initiated in 1977, this movement empowers communities, particularly women, to conserve the environment by planting trees.[7]

Grassroots Conservation and Women Empowerment

The Green Belt Movement is primarily a community-based, grassroots organisation. Its principal objective is to engage ordinary people, especially women, in environmental conservation activities. The model developed by the Green Belt Movement is unique. Women's groups organise at the community level, plant trees, and manage public and private lands in their localities.[8] This grassroots model has resulted in the planting of over 51 million trees across Kenya, transforming landscapes and improving the environment significantly.[9]

Socio-Economic Impacts

Beyond its environmental impact, the Green Belt Movement also provides social and economic benefits to the participating communities. By creating income-generating opportunities, it addresses poverty at the grassroots level. The women involved in the tree-planting initiatives earn income, thereby improving their economic status and increasing their influence within the community.

The initiative also strengthens social cohesion. The communal activity of tree planting fosters a sense of community, mutual support, and shared purpose. By working together towards a common goal, participants build stronger social networks and bonds.[10]

The Interlinkage of Economic Growth and Environmental Sustainability

The success of the Green Belt Movement illustrates the possibility of pursuing economic growth and environmental sustainability concurrently, and that they can indeed reinforce each other. The initiative showcases how economic incentives can motivate environmental conservation and, conversely, how such conservation can generate economic benefits.[11]

Thus, the Green Belt Movement provides a practical and effective model for grassroots conservation that could be replicated in other contexts. The initiative has achieved significant environmental, social, and economic impacts by focusing on local participation, especially women's involvement, and combining environmental conservation with economic benefits.

Broader Aspects of Environmental Sustainability

Environmental sustainability transcends mere conservation and includes aspects such as the sustainable use of natural resources, energy efficiency, pollution control, and adaptation to climate change.

Sustainable Use of Natural Resources

Community-based natural resource management (CBNRM) is a people-centred approach to the management of natural resources, including forests, wildlife, water bodies, and others, in which local communities play a central role. This approach has been applied successfully in many parts of Africa to ensure the sustainable use of natural resources while also providing economic benefits to local communities.

For instance, the CAMPFIRE (Communal Areas Management Programme for Indigenous Resources) initiative in Zimbabwe is a well-known example of CBNRM. Under this programme, local communities are given the rights to manage and benefit from wildlife resources in their areas. Revenue from wildlife-based activities, such as hunting and ecotourism, is channelled back into the community to support local development projects. Studies have shown that CAMPFIRE has not only contributed to wildlife conservation by providing an economic incentive for communities to protect wildlife but has also generated significant income for rural communities.[12]

In the forests of the Congo Basin, community forestry initiatives have been implemented in countries like Cameroon and the Democratic Republic of Congo. These programmes fundamentally shift the dynamics of forest management by entrusting local communities with the stewardship of forest lands. Such empowerment stems from a profound understanding that local inhabitants, who have coexisted with these forests for generations, possess deep-rooted knowledge of its rhythms and intricacies. By formalising their rights to manage and utilise the forest resources, these initiatives tap into the communities' intrinsic motivation to ensure the forest's longevity – a longevity directly tied to their wellbeing and survival.

These community forestry initiatives have multifaceted benefits. Environmentally, they've ushered in more sustainable methods of resource utilisation. Economically, these initiatives have opened new avenues of income for the communities.

Sustainable timber harvesting provides a steady flow of income, while the collection and sale of non-timber forest products, such as medicinal herbs, resins, and fruits, often fetch premium prices in both local and international markets due to their organic and sustainable origins. Furthermore, the recognition of community rights over forests also leads to ecotourism opportunities, allowing communities to showcase their forests, traditions, and lifestyles to curious travellers, adding another layer of economic benefit.

However, the success of community forestry in the Congo Basin isn't just limited to environmental and economic outcomes. It's symbolic of a broader shift towards recognising the rights and knowledge of indigenous and local communities. It's proof of the idea that conservation efforts are most effective when they involve, respect, and empower those who are most intimately connected to the land.

These examples demonstrate how CBNRM strategies can lead to improved conservation outcomes and provide economic benefits to local communities. They underscore the importance of giving local communities a central role in the management of natural resources and highlight the potential of CBNRM as a strategy for sustainable development in Africa.

Energy Efficiency and Renewable Energy

Energy efficiency and the promotion of renewable energy are other key aspects of environmental sustainability. Africa, blessed with abundant renewable resources like solar, wind, and hydro, has a unique opportunity to leapfrog to a green economy, bypassing the environmentally damaging path of fossil fuel dependence that many developed countries have taken. Countries like Morocco and South Africa, as seen earlier, have made significant strides in this direction, with Morocco being home to one of the world's largest solar power plants, the Noor Complex.[13]

Pollution Control

Costa Rica, outside of Africa, is a recognised leader in environmental sustainability and has implemented robust policies for pollution control. The country's efforts provide valuable lessons for African nations seeking to reduce pollution and protect their natural environments.[14]

One of Costa Rica's notable initiatives is the 2018 National Decarbonisation Plan, which aims to modernise and decarbonise the country's transportation, energy, waste management, and agricultural sectors. By 2050, Costa Rica aims to have a net zero carbon footprint. Key components of the plan include the electrification of public and private transportation, a shift to clean and renewable energy sources, improved waste management and recycling programmes, and sustainable agricultural practices.[15]

Costa Rica's strong commitment to environmental sustainability is reflected in its rigorous air and water quality regulations. Recognising that pollution poses a significant threat to both public health and the environment, the country has enacted legislation that establishes maximum allowable limits for a range of pollutants. These standards apply to various sectors, including industry, agriculture, and transportation, and cover pollutants such as sulphur dioxide, nitrogen oxides, particulate matter, and various water contaminants.

Enforcement of these regulations is backed by regular monitoring and reporting of air and water quality, carried out by governmental bodies and environmental agencies. This allows for ongoing assessment of compliance, timely detection of issues, and the ability to gauge the effectiveness of policies and make necessary adjustments. In addition to this, Costa Rica has made significant investments in wastewater treatment infrastructure to reduce water pollution. By treating wastewater before it is discharged into rivers and coasts, the country has succeeded in protecting these critical water bodies, which, in turn, has led to Costa Rica having some of the cleanest water in Latin America.

Beyond pollution control, Costa Rica has demonstrated global leadership in its use of payment for ecosystem services (PES) schemes. The PES programme operates on the principle that those who provide ecosystem services should be compensated for their efforts. This includes services such as carbon sequestration (the absorption and storage of carbon dioxide), water filtration, and biodiversity conservation. In Costa Rica, landowners who agree to preserve forests on their property receive financial compensation. This incentive encourages conservation and sustainable land management practices.

The PES schemes have significantly contributed to Costa Rica achieving one of the highest forest cover rates in the world. Forests play a vital role in purifying water, preventing soil erosion, storing carbon, and providing habitat for a vast range of species, thus contributing to a reduction in water and soil pollution. The programme's success is evidence of the effectiveness of providing economic incentives for conservation.[16]

These strategies have contributed to making Costa Rica one of the greenest countries globally, with significant improvements in air and water quality. Our African countries can draw valuable lessons from Costa Rica's experience as they seek to implement pollution control measures. Lessons include the importance of comprehensive and integrated policies, strong regulatory frameworks, public investment in infrastructure, and innovative market-based mechanisms like PES.

Climate Change Adaptation

Africa is considered one of the continents most vulnerable to the impacts of climate change. Africa's vulnerability to climate change is a result of a myriad of challenges, from recurrent droughts and a reliance on rain-fed agriculture to widespread poverty. To counter these vulnerabilities, nations within the continent have actively embraced and implemented diverse strategies aimed at environmental sustainability and resilience against the changing climate.

In the agricultural sector, the emphasis has been on creating climate-resilient practices. Ethiopia, for instance, has been at the forefront with its Productive Safety Net Programme, as seen earlier, aiding farmers in drought-prone regions through initiatives such as terracing. This aids in water retention and soil erosion prevention. Niger provides another shining example, where farmer-led natural regeneration techniques have revitalised barren lands, leading to increased crop yields and greater resilience against droughts.

A focus on climate-resilient infrastructure is also of paramount importance. Mozambique, still reeling from the devastating floods of 2000 and 2007, has prioritised this by relocating communities to safer zones and embarking on the construction of more durable infrastructure, which includes schools and health centres designed to withstand extreme weather conditions. The coastal city of Beira, scarred by Cyclone Idai in 2019, took the initiative a step further. Its 'Master Plan for Urban Climate Resilience' encompasses strategies from improving drainage systems and constructing seawalls to safeguarding natural defences like mangroves and wetlands.

But infrastructure is not the only focus. Recognising the immediacy of certain climate threats, the establishment of early warning systems has gained prominence. Malawi offers a case in point. With the backing of the United Nations Development Programme, the country has set up weather monitoring facilities that send timely alerts regarding impending extreme weather phenomena. As a result, communities have been better equipped to face challenges such as floods, ensuring a reduction in both casualties and property damage.

These examples underscore the importance of embedding climate change adaptation strategies into development planning to enhance environmental sustainability and protect the most vulnerable populations.

Integration of Environmental Sustainability into Growth Pillars

Environmental sustainability is an essential aspect of any development endeavour, and this is particularly true for our continent of Africa, which is rich in natural resources and also particularly vulnerable to environmental challenges. Achieving environmental sustainability cannot be an isolated goal. Rather, it needs to be integrated across all aspects of development.

On a greater scale, achieving environmental sustainability in Africa requires embedding sustainability considerations into all areas of decision-making and development planning. As we delve into these interconnected topics in the upcoming chapters, the significance of regional integration and cooperation will underscore our discourse.

CHAPTER 15

REGIONAL COOPERATION AND INTEGRATION

In this chapter, we will explore the pivotal role of regional cooperation and integration in promoting shared prosperity. This notion is backed by an extensive body of literature suggesting that countries can achieve more working together than in isolation.

I would liken regional cooperation and integration to a relay race. A good example cited are the finals of the 2012 London Olympic Games on 11 August 2012 and the 4 x 100 m relay that the Jamaican team won. In the 2012 Olympic Games, Usain Bolt's individual 100 m world record stood at 9.58 seconds. At the same games, the Jamaican team (Nesta Carter, Michael Frater, Yohan Blake, and Usain Bolt) set a world record time of 36.84 seconds. If we divide the total time by four, we find that the average time per

100 m is 9.21 seconds. This is faster than the fastest member of the team could achieve on his own.

Of course, in reality, there are other factors at play in a 4 x 100 m relay. Relay races, such as the 4 x 100 m, involve four athletes each running 100 m. The total time is usually less than four times the world record for a single 100 m race. This is largely because three of the four runners in a relay race are already at or near their maximum speed when they receive the baton, thanks to the acceleration zone, which allows runners to start before the official exchange zone. This gives an advantage that athletes in individual races, who start from a standstill, don't have.

However, that's beside the point. The broader point is that teams can achieve feats that individuals, no matter how talented, cannot. This speaks to the power of synergy and is as applicable to the world of athletics as it is to regional integration and cooperation.

The Concept of Regional Integration

Regional integration has increasingly been recognised as a powerful strategy for economic growth, political stability, and social development. The process involves neighbouring states entering into agreements to improve cooperation through shared institutions and rules. This can be particularly advantageous for smaller economies, as it leads to larger market sizes, encouraging economies of scale, more significant investment inflows, and potentially improved global bargaining power.

Shared geographical, economic, and social traits can be used to establish a collective advantage, as countries that are geographically close often share similar natural resources, historical backgrounds, and sociocultural features. These shared characteristics can be used as a basis for fostering cooperation and building mutual trust among countries.

Economically, regional integration encourages trade by creating a larger, unified market that is more attractive to both local businesses and foreign investors. This results in increased production, job creation, and economic growth. Furthermore, regional integration can create a more stable and predictable business environment by harmonising policies such as trade tariffs and business regulations, thus attracting more foreign direct investment (FDI).

From a social perspective, regional integration can lead to improvements in social services and infrastructure as countries work together to achieve common social development goals. This leads to improvements in areas such as education, health, and social security.

Politically, regional integration improves stability by promoting peaceful relations among member states. The process of integration often involves negotiation and consensus-building, which reduces conflict and promotes peace.

The effectiveness of regional integration, however, depends on various factors, including the level of commitment from the member countries, the compatibility of their economies, and the effectiveness of the institutions set up to facilitate integration. It's also important to note that while regional integration brings many benefits, it can also pose challenges, including the potential for increased competition among local industries and the risk of economic contagion if one country in the region faces an economic crisis.

Regional Integration

Before looking at continental integration, let us look at the individual regional communities across the African continent.

Economic Community of West African States (ECOWAS)

The Economic Community of West African States (ECOWAS), established in 1975, serves as a powerful example of regional integration. It is an embodiment of a collective effort for regional growth. Comprising 15 countries – Benin, Burkina Faso, Cape Verde, Ivory Coast (Côte d'Ivoire), The Gambia, Ghana, Guinea, Guinea-Bissau, Liberia, Mali, Niger, Nigeria, Senegal, Sierra Leone, and Togo – ECOWAS was founded with the aim of promoting economic integration and cooperation among its members.

The first major achievement of ECOWAS was the creation of a free trade area in 1990, which removed customs duties and trade restrictions on goods originating from the ECOWAS region. This significantly facilitated intra-regional trade, fostering economic growth in the member countries.

The second major achievement was the introduction of the common external tariff (CET). Introduced by ECOWAS in 2015, the CET represents a harmonised tariff system on goods imported from outside the ECOWAS region. Before CET's adoption, each ECOWAS nation had individual tariffs, leading to complexities in intra-regional trade. CET ensures consistent import duties across member states, categorising goods into specific tariff bands to protect sensitive industries and promote products vital for economic growth. While aiming to shield regional sectors from external competition and support local industry growth, CET's uniform system means varied revenue outcomes for different countries. By standardising external tariffs, the CET boosts intra-regional trade, laying the groundwork for a potential full customs union within ECOWAS, thereby strengthening its collective economic presence globally.

The ECOWAS also introduced the ECOWAS Passport in 2000, a travel document that allows citizens of member countries to move freely within the ECOWAS region without requiring a visa. This is a significant step towards promoting the free movement of people and labour in the region. The member states are currently in the process of implementing a joint visa for non-ECOWAS citizens, the Eco-Visa, that covers the whole region.[1]

Additionally, ECOWAS has made strides in harmonising economic and monetary policies. The West African Monetary Institute (WAMI) is an institution of the West African Monetary Zone (WAMZ) and one of the specialised agencies of ECOWAS. The establishment of WAMI in 2001 represents ECOWAS's commitment to deeper economic integration among its member states. WAMI's creation was a decisive step towards achieving the ambitious goal of a unified monetary system in West Africa, reflecting the region's aspirations to harness the benefits of such integration similar to the European Union.[2]

WAMI's foundational members, which include Gambia, Ghana, Guinea, Nigeria, Sierra Leone, and later Liberia in 2009, have been striving towards the realisation of a single regional currency. The idea behind this unified currency is that it would eliminate the complexities of multiple exchange rates, reducing the cost of transactions and making the region more attractive for both local and foreign investment. This single currency would effectively reduce trade barriers, further facilitating intra-regional trade.

However, achieving this monetary union is not without its challenges. Diverging economic conditions, policies, and performance among the member states have sometimes made it difficult to align their economies to the criteria necessary for a currency union. Additionally, given the size and economic influence of countries like Nigeria within WAMI, ensuring that all members benefit equitably from such a union remains a concern.

The idea of transitioning from WAMI to a fully-fledged West African Central Bank indicates the region's direction. This transition would not only oversee the proposed single currency but would also be instrumental in formulating monetary policy for the entire region, influencing interest rates, inflation targeting, and other crucial economic indicators.

ECOWAS's commitment to regional peace and security is evident in its proactive initiatives, such as the Mechanism for Conflict Prevention, Management, Resolution, Peacekeeping and Security established in 1999. This mechanism exemplifies the organisation's evolving commitment to collective security and its readiness to act against threats to peace within its region. It underscores the principle that the stability of individual member states is deeply intertwined with the overall stability of the West African region.[3]

One of the most significant tests of ECOWAS's commitment to peace came with the civil wars in Liberia and Sierra Leone, both of which had devastating effects on their populations and posed risks to the broader stability of the region. The conflicts were characterised by brutal violence, with countless human rights abuses, including mass killings, mutilations, and the recruitment of child soldiers.

ECOWAS responded with its military arm, Economic Community of West African States Monitoring Group (ECOMOG), intervening in both nations. In Liberia, ECOMOG navigated a complex web of warring factions, enforcing ceasefires, and facilitating peace negotiations. In Sierra Leone, facing the notorious rebel group, the Revolutionary United Front (RUF), ECOMOG repelled advances on the capital, setting the stage for a combined

UN and British intervention to end the war. These interventions underscore ECOWAS's belief in regional security and its proactive role in conflict resolution, showcasing the potential of regional bodies in maintaining peace globally.

Despite these successes, ECOWAS faces numerous challenges, such as political instability in some member states, inadequate infrastructure, and disparities in levels of economic development among member countries. Nevertheless, the positive impacts of ECOWAS on the region highlight the immense potential of regional integration in promoting economic growth and stability.

Moving forward, ECOWAS continues to push for deeper integration among its member states. The success of ECOWAS provides a blueprint for other regions in Africa, underlining the importance of regional cooperation and integration in driving the continent's growth and prosperity.

East African Community (EAC)

The East African Community (EAC) is another notable example of regional integration in Africa. Established in 2000, the EAC consists of eight countries: Kenya, Uganda, Tanzania, Rwanda, Burundi, South Sudan, Democratic Republic of Congo, and Somalia. The community has made significant strides towards economic integration, with noteworthy developments in customs union, common market, and monetary union areas.[4]

The EAC's Customs Union, enacted in 2005, effectively dismantled internal tariffs on goods originating from member states and erected a common external tariff. This intervention significantly facilitated intra-regional trade, contributing to the economic advancement of member states.[5]

Furthermore, the Common Market Protocol, effective from

2010, stipulates the free movement of goods, labour, services, and capital among member countries. This provision further lubricates the engines of commerce within the region, allowing for increased economic activity and growth.[6]

Nonetheless, the EAC's journey towards complete integration is not without its hurdles. Notably, political cooperation and infrastructural development have been areas of challenge.

On the political front, Rwanda and Burundi's relationship is fraught with historical tensions, genocides, and mutual accusations of supporting rival rebel groups. This tension peaked in 2015 amid Burundi's political crisis. South Sudan, since joining the EAC in 2016, has also struggled with internal conflict and economic instability, complicating its EAC integration. Its ongoing strife, rooted in political and ethnic disputes, has ramifications for regional trade and cooperation. South Sudan's conflicts deter investments, affect regional economies, and burden neighbours with refugee influxes.

Infrastructural development in the EAC is pivotal for regional integration but has seen slow progress. The Mombasa-Nairobi-Kampala-Kigali railway project, vital for trade logistics, has faced setbacks, including funding shortfalls and skill deficits. However, there is hope, as Uganda recently partnered with Turkish company Yapi Merkezi to resume construction. This railway, over 1,500 kilometres, is a part of the Northern Corridor infrastructure project. Yet, due to financial constraints, as evident when Kenya couldn't secure funding from China, and bureaucratic hurdles, progress remains tentative.

To fully realise the benefits of regional integration, the EAC must address these challenges. This will require not only increased investment in infrastructure but also capacity building, policy harmonisation, and improved coordination among member states.

Additionally, while the EAC's Common Market Protocol envisages the free movement of people across borders, in practice, this is often hampered by inadequate transportation infrastructure. For instance, poor road networks and inefficient border crossing procedures often result in long delays for traders and travellers, impeding the flow of goods and people.

Lastly, disparities in infrastructure development among member states also create challenges. Countries like Kenya and Tanzania, which have more developed infrastructure, might benefit more from integration compared to less developed members like Burundi and South Sudan. This would lead to uneven benefits of integration and might cause tensions among member states.

To overcome these challenges, sustained commitment from all member states and strategic investments in key areas, such as infrastructure development and capacity building, are essential. The success of the EAC in achieving its integration goals will significantly depend on how effectively it can navigate these challenges.

The EAC's experiences underscore the complexity and multifaceted nature of regional integration – it is not merely an economic endeavour but a sociopolitical one as well.

Despite these challenges, member states continue to strive towards deeper integration. The EAC is progressively implementing its Monetary Union Protocol, which envisages a single currency for the region by 2024.[7] This effort, alongside ongoing initiatives to enhance political and infrastructural cooperation, signifies the EAC's commitment to the ideals of regional integration.

Overall, the EAC's experiences offer valuable lessons for other regional blocs in Africa and beyond. They highlight the importance of strong political commitment, robust institutions, adequate infrastructure, and harmonised policies in facilitating successful regional integration.

Southern African Development Community (SADC)

The Southern African Development Community (SADC) is another regional economic community in Africa, comprising 16 member states of Angola, Botswana, Comoros, Democratic Republic of Congo, Eswatini, Lesotho, Madagascar, Malawi, Mauritius, Mozambique, Namibia, Seychelles, South Africa, Tanzania, Zambia, and Zimbabwe. Established in 1980 as the Southern African Development Coordination Conference (SADCC) to reduce dependence on apartheid South Africa, it transformed into SADC in 1992.[8]

SADC has made strides in several areas of regional cooperation and integration, including trade and investment, infrastructure development, industrialisation, and peace and security.[9] A cornerstone of SADC's achievements in economic integration is the Free Trade Area, implemented in 2008.[10] This initiative substantially liberalised intra-regional trade, making it easier for member countries to trade goods with each other. The overall effect has been an increase in trade flows among SADC members, leading to economic growth and development in the region.

Complementing these efforts in trade and investment, SADC has also put in place coordinated policies in key sectors such as energy, water, tourism, and agriculture. SADC has facilitated shared benefits from the region's resources and has been able to address common challenges more effectively through the alignment of policies in these areas.[11] For example, through the SADC Regional Water Policy, member states have been able to manage shared watercourses in a manner that promotes equitable and sustainable use.

Infrastructure development, which is a fundamental enabler of economic activity, has also been a focus for SADC. The SADC Regional Infrastructure Development Master Plan, adopted in 2012, outlines strategic infrastructure development initiatives in sectors such as transport, energy, and ICT. The plan aims to provide a strategic framework for regional infrastructure development in order to enhance regional integration, promote trade, and ultimately improve the living standards of the people in the SADC region.[12]

Lastly, the SADC is not merely an economic bloc; it also has a pivotal role in ensuring that the Southern African region remains stable and secure. Given the interconnected nature of political dynamics in the region, instability in one member state can easily spill over into neighbouring countries, thus affecting the entire regional bloc. Recognising this, the SADC has prioritised peace and security as foundational elements of sustainable development and regional integration.

In his 2012 book, *Community of Insecurity: SADC's Struggle for Peace and Security in Southern Africa,* Laurie Nathan highlighted the importance of this regional approach and emphasised how the SADC's involvement in peace and security matters has contributed significantly to political stability in the region.[13] However, like all regional bodies, the SADC and its organs also face challenges, ranging from varying national interests of member states to resource constraints. Nonetheless, the commitment to a peaceful and secure Southern Africa remains a driving force behind the bloc's endeavours, reinforcing the belief that regional cooperation is crucial for addressing the continent's multifaceted challenges.

Yet, like other regional economic communities, SADC faces its own set of challenges, including economic disparities among member states, infrastructural deficits, and political hurdles in deeper integration.

The African Union

The African Union (AU) is an intergovernmental organisation comprising 55 member states of our continent of Africa. Established in 2002 as a successor to the Organisation of African Unity (OAU), the AU aims to promote unity and solidarity among African countries, uphold shared values, and drive social, economic, and political integration across the continent.[14]

The AU traces its roots to the postcolonial era's pan-Africanism, culminating in the formation of the Organisation of African Unity (OAU) in 1963. The OAU aimed to foster unity, support liberation movements, and represent Africa globally. However, its noninterference principle faced criticism, as it limited action on human rights abuses and conflicts. In response to evolving continental needs, the OAU was transformed into the AU in 2000, officially starting in 2002. Unlike the OAU, the AU adopted a stance of non-indifference, allowing interventions in grave situations and emphasising economic integration, peace, democratic governance, and human rights. With initiatives like the African Continental Free Trade Area, the AU, despite challenges, remains a beacon of unity and representation for African nations.

The AU works through several organs to achieve its objectives. The Assembly, composed of heads of states and governments, is the supreme decision-making body. The Executive Council, composed of ministers of member states, advises the Assembly on matters such as foreign trade, social security, and food agriculture. The

Commission acts as the secretariat of the AU and is responsible for the day-to-day management of the AU.

The African Continental Free Trade Area (AfCFTA)

The African Continental Free Trade Area (AfCFTA) is a key project under Agenda 2063, which is a framework for Africa's future development. The idea for the AfCFTA was approved by the Assembly of Heads of State and Government in Addis Ababa, Ethiopia, in 2012. The main goal of the AfCFTA is to increase trade within Africa and improve Africa's position in global trade by giving the continent a stronger voice in trade negotiations.[15]

The AfCFTA has several objectives. One of the primary aims is to create a single market for goods and services in Africa, thereby deepening the continent's economic integration. This aim aligns with the vision of an integrated, prosperous, and peaceful Africa, as outlined in Agenda 2063.[16]

Other objectives of the AfCFTA include liberalising the market for goods and services through continuous rounds of negotiations and promoting the movement of capital and natural resources to facilitate investments. It also aims to lay the groundwork for a Continental Customs Union to be established in the future.

The AfCFTA brings together a diverse group of countries with varying economic strengths. Notably, Nigeria, South Africa, and Egypt contribute about half of the continent's GDP, despite being only three out of 55 member nations. This economic disparity is evident when considering South Africa's dominance in trade. In 2020, African nations imported a massive US$20 billion worth of goods from South Africa, making it the sixth-largest supplier for the continent, trailing global giants like China, India, and the US.[17]

Such dominance by South Africa within the AfCFTA could lead to an imbalance. There's a risk that South African goods could saturate African markets, which might harm local industries in other African countries, leading to job losses. This will force more people from across the continent to trek to South Africa in search of better lives. This would in turn create tensions between people coming from outside and the local populace. If this happens, it could result in scepticism towards the AfCFTA, with doubts about its benefits for all member states.

Furthermore, the current trade structure often benefits urban areas more than rural ones. Cities are generally better connected to trade networks. If not managed properly, increasing trade could amplify the existing economic gap between urban and rural areas. This is particularly concerning when there's a shift from commodity exports, which might leave commodity-based rural economies at a disadvantage.

Lastly, while the AfCFTA has initiatives to support small and medium enterprises (SMEs), large companies still have an upper hand due to economies of scale. Given the high transportation costs within Africa, companies with larger trade volumes can distribute these costs more effectively, making them more competitive.

Addressing these economic inequalities might require provisions for special treatment for less developed economies, such as allowing longer time frames for tariff liberalisation. Meanwhile, political instability in some countries may also undermine the AfCFTA's progress, necessitating a strong political will, regional cooperation, and effective conflict resolution mechanisms to overcome these challenges.

The European Union (EU) provides an instructive example of how regional integration and open borders can be successfully managed, despite the complexity of coordinating policies among diverse member countries. This offers insights for the African Union (AU) as it seeks to foster greater intra-African trade and cooperation. The EU's robust institutions, such as the European Commission and European Court of Justice, have maintained stability and trust by ensuring adherence to regulations. By contrast, the AU might find it beneficial to reinforce its structures to effectively oversee the AfCFTA's provisions.

Infrastructure and connectivity have been pivotal to the EU, with significant investments like the Trans-European Transport Network bolstering the movement of goods and people. Africa would similarly benefit from enhancing its infrastructure.

In terms of migration and security, the EU has adeptly balanced the free movement of people through the Schengen Agreement while ensuring safety, an approach the AU could emulate.

On the economic front, the EU's European Structural and Investment Funds have been instrumental in addressing regional disparities, suggesting the AU might introduce analogous mechanisms to harmonise economic differences among its members.

Furthermore, the sense of a united European identity has proven crucial for EU integration, indicating the importance of nurturing a pan-African unity for the AU. Yet, the AU should also heed the challenges faced by the EU, from the complexities of the eurozone crisis to issues like Brexit, as they underscore the intricacies of regional integration. In sum, while the AfCFTA holds transformative promise for Africa, its successful realisation will necessitate learning both from the opportunities and challenges evidenced in the EU's experience.

What should be borne in mind is that while the AU can learn much from the EU's experience, it must also consider Africa's unique historical, political, and socio-economic context to develop an approach that is best suited to the continent's own needs and aspirations.

Monetary alignment within a trading bloc, exemplified by the eurozone's adoption of the Euro, offers significant benefits. It ensures exchange rate stability, eliminates currency risk, and promotes predictable trade, thereby stimulating intra-bloc investments. Such alignment fosters closer economic cooperation, boosts financial market efficiency, and cuts transaction costs as currency exchanges become redundant for internal trade.

In the current absence of monetary alignment across the African continent, individual nations rely on the use of the US Dollar, the world's most powerful reserve currency, as a medium for facilitating global and intra-African trade. However, over-reliance on the US dollar could have drawbacks for regional integration and intra-African trade. The value of African currencies against the dollar can be volatile, influenced by external factors such as changes in commodity prices, global financial conditions, and the monetary policy of the United States.[18] This volatility can increase the costs of trade and create uncertainty for African businesses.

Moreover, by transacting in dollars, African countries essentially peg their trade to the monetary policy of an external entity – the US Federal Reserve. This leaves African economies vulnerable to shocks from changes in US interest rates or shifts in global sentiment towards the dollar. An alternative could be the promotion of regional or continental currencies for intra-African trade.

AfCFTA could also consider the idea of a common African currency. However, the success of such initiatives requires robust macroeconomic convergence, strong institutions, and deep financial markets to absorb shocks.[19]

On another level, digital solutions like mobile money and pan-African payment and settlement systems can also provide alternatives for facilitating intra-African trade, reducing reliance on the US dollar.[20] Such innovations can lower transaction costs and increase the speed of commerce.

Among African leaders opposed to the use of the US Dollar for intra-African trade is Kenya's president, Dr William Ruto. President Ruto has called for African leaders to consider a pan-African payment system to facilitate trade within the continent and reduce reliance on the US dollar. This system would enable transactions to be conducted in local currencies, thereby minimising the need for foreign exchange conversions and enhancing economic sovereignty.

Transitioning to the pan-African payment system would have numerous benefits for Africa's economic development. Firstly, it would streamline and expedite cross-border transactions, reducing costs and improving efficiency. Secondly, it would foster regional economic integration and stimulate economic growth. Lastly, it could strengthen Africa's position in global trade by increasing the continent's financial autonomy.

For Africa, the implementation of the pan-African payment system could be a significant step towards achieving economic sovereignty and boosting the continent's economic development.

So, while the path to implementing the AfCFTA may be filled with hurdles, its potential benefits are substantial. However, realising its full potential will require considerable effort, strong political will, and cooperation among African nations.

The African Peace and Security Architecture (APSA)

Apart from economic integration, the AU has been active in promoting peace and security on the African continent, guided by the principles of non-indifference and noninterference.

The African Peace and Security Architecture (APSA) is a framework designed to promote peace, security, and stability across Africa. It was established under the AU, with its primary decision-making organ being the Peace and Security Council (PSC). The establishment of the PSC was finalised on 9 July 2002 in Durban, South Africa, with the protocol coming into force in December 2003 and the PSC becoming operational in early 2004.

APSA's role is critical in creating a stable environment that is conducive to economic development. When peace and security are assured, countries can focus on economic growth and development, attracting investment, and enhancing trade relationships both within Africa and globally. This promotes sustainable development, reduces poverty, and improves living standards for the African people.

The APSA is also essential in preventing and managing conflicts that could disrupt economic activities and cause humanitarian crises, which often result in significant economic costs. By promoting peace, security, and stability, the APSA plays a critical role in ensuring that Africa can achieve its economic potential and development goals.[21]

The African Governance Architecture (AGA)

Another critical area for the AU is human rights and governance. The African Governance Architecture (AGA) was launched in 2011 by the African Union. The initiative was motivated by recognising the need for a cohesive framework for promoting good governance across the continent, drawing on various instruments, principles, and values established by the African Union and its member states.

The AGA is a key initiative under the AU, primarily focused on promoting good governance and strengthening democracy across the African continent. It was inspired by the AU's commitment, as stated in its Constitutive Act, to foster human and people's rights, consolidate democratic institutions and culture, and ensure the rule of law.

The role of the AGA in promoting good governance and democratic principles is vital for Africa's economic development. Good governance is often seen as a prerequisite for economic growth and development. When governance is transparent, accountable, and participatory, it can help create a favourable environment for economic activities, attract investment, and facilitate the equitable distribution of resources. It can also help to prevent economic mismanagement, corruption, and other practices that hamper economic development.

To end this section, I would like to point out that, for its economic development, Africa needs to develop its own traditions and practices divorced from what was inherited from the colonial masters. African countries' reliance on practices from outside the continent, such as the use of the dollar and segregating each other based on the existing national borders, reminds me of a story about how traditions are born.

The story is about a commander who took over a new army camp. After being appointed, while inspecting the place, he saw two soldiers guarding a bench. He approached them and asked why they were guarding the bench. "We don't know," one of the soldiers replied. "The last commander told us to do so, and so we did. It's some sort of regimental tradition."

The new commander searched for the previous commander's phone number and called him to ask him why he placed guards on that particular bench. "I don't know. The previous commander had guards at that particular bench, and I kept the tradition," replied the previous commander.

Going back another three commanders, he found a now 100-year-old retired general. "Excuse me, sir. Sorry to bother you, my name is Jerry. I'm now the commanding officer of the camp you commanded 60 years ago. I've found two men assigned to guard a bench. Can you please tell me more about the bench?" asked the new commander.

"What?" responded the old general. "Is the paint still wet?"

This allegory illustrates the risks of adhering to practices or traditions without questioning their relevance or utility in the present context. In the African context, there are certain practices and customs that, while historically significant, could be obstructing regional integration and economic progress today.

One such tradition that has been cited in scholarly literature is the concept of political sovereignty rooted in the post-colonial era. The African state system, inherited from the colonial period, upholds the principle of absolute sovereignty and noninterference in the internal affairs of other states.[22] These are states that were created by outsiders who had no or very little knowledge of Africa and its people. While respecting national sovereignty is crucial, an overemphasis on this principle can hamper efforts towards deeper regional integration, as it often leads to reluctance among states to cede any form of sovereignty to supranational entities.

Another cultural factor impeding economic progress is the patronage system, or 'big man' politics, that prevails in many African societies.[23] In the past, our African leaders knew how to be servant leaders and what it meant to serve their people. The 'big man' politics system, characterised by the exchange of favours for political support, often results in corruption, poor governance, and mismanagement of resources. This system could hamper economic development by discouraging merit-based advancement and undermining the rule of law.

Additionally, some argue that African economies still adhere to colonial-era economic structures that primarily focus on the export of raw materials and agricultural produce, with less emphasis on manufacturing and value addition.[24] This reliance on a primary commodities export model leaves African economies vulnerable to global price fluctuations and hinders the development of diverse, resilient economies.

To overcome these barriers, it's crucial for African nations and societies to critically evaluate inherited practices and make necessary reforms. Embracing principles of good governance, promoting meritocracy, and transitioning towards more diversified, industrialised economies are vital steps towards enhancing regional integration and economic progress in Africa.

In the next chapter, we will go deeper into the role of foreign direct investment (FDI) in propelling economic growth and development on the African continent.

CHAPTER 16

ATTRACTING FOREIGN DIRECT INVESTMENT

Foreign direct investment (FDI) is when an investor, whether an individual or a company, puts money into a business located in another country. There is this notion that FDI is when developed countries invest in developing countries – but perish that thought. That's a wrong conception. FDI is not tied to whether the country is so-called developed or still developing. In fact, FDI can move between any set of countries, regardless of their financial status. FDI can flow from developed to developing nations, between developing countries, from developing to developed nations, or even between developed countries.

What is important to bear in mind is that FDI plays a crucial role in connecting the global economy. It's like a bridge that brings together both rich nations seeking new growth areas and emerging countries looking to tap into more advanced technologies or diversified markets. For example, a developed country might invest in a developing one because of its cheaper labour and new markets. On the other hand, a growing economy might invest in a developed country to access cutting-edge technology or due to any other factor that may be attractive to the investor. But a developed nation might also invest in a developing country to tap into technology that is cheaper.

The factors guiding FDI decisions are numerous, ranging from global politics to advances in technology. The digital boom and the push for green energy are some of the latest trends influencing these investments.

FDI isn't just about money changing hands; it impacts societies deeply. For the country receiving the investment:

1. New jobs are created, reducing unemployment.
2. Advanced technologies and business methods are introduced, which can boost productivity and train local workers in new skills.
3. Infrastructure often gets a boost. This could be direct, such as when an investment involves constructing new facilities, or indirect, such as when the presence of foreign businesses necessitates upgrades to local utilities, transportation, or public services. These improvements can have long-term benefits, as they enhance the host country's attractiveness for further domestic and foreign investments.

Nonetheless, while FDI brings opportunities, it also presents challenges, like becoming too dependent on foreign money or worrying about control in vital industries. Despite these challenges, the benefits often make FDI a welcome component in many nations' growth strategies.

However, it's important to note that the potential benefits of FDI are not automatic. They depend on various factors, including the sectors in which the investments are made, the policies of the host country, and the commitment of the investing firm towards responsible business practices. To maximise the benefits of FDI, host countries need to have strategic policies in place to ensure that these investments align with their development objectives, contribute to sustainable industrialisation, and foster inclusive economic growth.

The Role of Foreign Direct Investment in Economic Development

Foreign direct investment has proven to be a significant catalyst for economic development in several African countries. It often provides an infusion of capital, a transfer of skills and technology, and can contribute to job creation. In their seminal 1998 paper, 'How Does Foreign Direct Investment Affect Economic Growth?', Eduardo Borensztein, Jose De Gregorio, and Jong-Wha Lee argue that FDI has an essential role in enhancing economic growth in the host countries through the facilitation of technological diffusion. They emphasise, however, that the effectiveness of FDI is contingent on the host country's human capital stock.[1]

The authors argue that FDI does not just involve capital inflows, but it is also an avenue for more advanced technology and practices to be introduced to the host country. They proposed that the interaction between FDI and the human capital available in the host country significantly affects the country's ability to absorb new technologies, which, in turn, influences economic growth.

Furthermore, Miao Wang and M C Sunny Wong's 2011 paper, 'FDI, Education, and Economic Growth: Quality Matters!' underscores the crucial link between the quality of education in the host country and the full realisation of the benefits stemming from FDI. The research emphasises that it's not just the presence of education or its sheer quantity that matters, but rather its quality.[2]

Drawing from this research, one can infer that when a host country has a high-quality education system, it is better positioned to leverage the advanced technologies, business practices, and other resources brought in by foreign investors. A well-educated workforce that has undergone quality training can more effectively interact with, adapt to, and innovate upon the technologies and methodologies introduced by foreign entities. This means that the spillover effects of FDI – such as technology transfer, innovation, and productivity enhancements – become more pronounced when coupled with a robust educational foundation.

Moreover, quality education equips the local population with the necessary skills to take on more specialised roles in the ventures initiated by foreign investments. Instead of being limited to lower-skilled tasks, individuals in the host country are enabled to occupy positions that demand higher expertise, leading to better wages and a more diversified economy.

It's worth noting that, while these studies find a positive relationship between FDI, human capital development, and economic growth, they also underline that FDI is not a panacea. Each country must strategically manage FDI and ensure that domestic capacities are developed to maximise its benefits for sustainable development. While there are numerous examples, for the sake of illustration, let's focus on the cases of Ethiopia, Rwanda, and

Nigeria first.

Despite internal challenges, Ethiopia has become an FDI magnet, particularly in its burgeoning manufacturing sector, thanks to government-led industrialisation efforts like the establishment of the Hawassa Industrial Park, one of Africa's largest. Even after setbacks from the AGOA exclusion, signs of recovery in early 2023 indicate resilience and the importance of market diversification, with significant job creation potential.

In Rwanda, as mentioned earlier, the government has enacted reforms to create an investor-friendly climate, resulting in FDI growth across various sectors, including telecommunications and energy, with notable investments by companies like MTN.

Nigeria, with its sizeable economy, continues to draw FDI not just in its traditional oil and gas sector but also in tech, where the country is emerging as a hub. Startups such as Paystack and Flutterwave are drawing international investment, demonstrating Nigeria's widening appeal to foreign investors.

Other African countries can learn several lessons from Ethiopia, Rwanda, Nigeria, and others that have succeeded in attracting and managing FDI.

Firstly, the importance of having a stable, open, and transparent investment climate cannot be overstated. Countries like Egypt, Morocco, and South Africa have set clear regulations that encourage FDI. They've implemented reforms to reduce bureaucratic red tape, enhance the rule of law, and secure property rights. Therefore, other African nations can work towards fostering a conducive business environment that reassures foreign investors and minimises their perceived risks.

Secondly, these countries have made concerted efforts to develop their human capital. A minimum threshold of human capital is essential for reaping the full benefits of FDI, especially in terms of technology transfer.[3] Therefore, African countries can prioritise education and training to ensure their workforces effectively absorbs and utilises the knowledge and technologies brought by FDI.

Thirdly, infrastructure development is another crucial area. Ethiopia's Hawassa Industrial Park is a prime example of how good infrastructure can attract FDI. Hence, countries should aim to improve and modernise their infrastructure, including transport, utilities, and digital networks, to facilitate business operations and make their markets more accessible to foreign investors.

Lastly, it's crucial for these countries to align FDI with their development goals. They can identify sectors that are strategic for their economic development and channel FDI into those areas. Incentives need to be provided to foreign investors who invest in these prioritised sectors, like what Ghana did with its renewable energy sector.

It's also essential to remember that there isn't a one-size-fits-all approach to attracting FDI. Each country should consider its unique circumstances, including its development stage, resources, and socio-economic conditions, when formulating its FDI policies. A thoughtful and well-implemented approach can help African countries maximise the benefits of FDI, contributing to sustainable growth and development.

Factors Attracting FDI in Africa

According to Elizabeth Asiedu's research, 'Foreign Direct Investment in Africa: The Role of Natural Resources, Market Size, Government Policy, Institutions and Political Instability', several factors influence the influx of FDI into African nations.[4]

The study offers a multifaceted view of the determinants of FDI by examining data from 22 countries spanning a 16-year period between 1984 and 2000. The findings present an intricate mix of the push and pull factors affecting FDI flow, revealing that its determinants are not singular or straightforward.

At a primary glance, the presence of abundant natural resources and large markets within a nation seems to be a clear driver of FDI. While abundant natural resources and large markets are primary attractors for foreign direct investment, intangible factors also play a crucial role. Stable inflation, robust infrastructure, and an educated population create an environment conducive for business growth, with the latter ensuring a skilled workforce that can innovate efficiently. Equally vital is good governance. Countries that are open to FDI and have minimal corruption levels draw more investors. For instance, combating corruption can be as influential for FDI attraction as possessing valuable natural resources, as shown in comparisons between Nigeria and South Africa. Furthermore, political stability and a dependable legal system are essential, as they ensure investment safety and instil confidence in potential investors.

In the grand scheme of things, the study's revelations underscore a crucial message: while natural resources and market size are undeniable lures for FDI, the more abstract facets related to governance, infrastructure, and education play an equally vital role. This is particularly significant for our African nations, as it suggests a path forward: even if they lack in size or resources, by focusing on institutional reform, policy improvements, and infrastructure development, they can position themselves as attractive destinations for foreign investment.

Natural Resources

Natural resources play a significant role in attracting FDI. Many of our African nations are rich in natural resources such as oil, precious metals, precious stones, and various minerals. For instance, countries like Nigeria and Angola have attracted substantial FDI in their oil sector due to their vast reserves.

At a cursory glance, the presence of substantial natural resources, such as minerals or oil, in a country might be thought of as an unambiguous boon for attracting FDI. These tangible assets, after all, represent immediate profit opportunities. Yet, the research of Poelhekke and van der Ploeg showcases that the allure of these natural resources is a double-edged sword.[5] While they undoubtedly attract resource-specific FDI, they simultaneously repel non-resource FDI. This phenomenon, described as 'crowding out', highlights the paradox where the magnetism of one investment avenue can inadvertently discourage others.

However, the intriguing insights of the study don't end there. While it's intuitive to think that countries with ample natural resources are hotspots for investors, the research indicates that the situation is more intricate than it first appears.

One of the standout revelations from the study concerns the spatial distribution of these resources. In simple terms, it's not just the mere existence of resources that influences investment patterns but rather where these resources are physically located within a country. This geographical positioning can have unforeseen consequences on investment behaviours.

Imagine a country with vast mineral deposits situated in a specific region. This region might naturally become a focal point for investments, drawing in a surge of resource-driven FDI. Infrastructure may be developed, industries may be set up, and towns may expand in and around this resource-rich zone, such as where mines have been developed. This concentration of activity and investment can generate a magnetic effect, drawing even more attention and resources towards it.

However, the downside is that while this area thrives, other regions or sectors within the same country might get overlooked. We see a lot of this in several African countries. Investors, seeing the immediate profit potential in the resource-rich zone, might be less inclined to explore opportunities in, say, the country's agricultural, tech, or manufacturing sectors. This 'crowding out' effect indicates that the allure of one profitable sector can inadvertently lead to the neglect of others.

Furthermore, the geographical positioning can create other dynamics. For instance, if the resource-rich regions are remote or difficult to access, they might demand a lion's share of the country's infrastructure budget and attention, leaving less-developed areas further isolated. Conversely, if these areas are centrally located or near major trade routes, they could overshadow even the most promising sectors in proximity.

The overarching implication drawn from this study is profound. It reshapes how one might view the economic landscape of resource-rich countries. Instead of unequivocal magnets for total FDI, these nations, despite their resource wealth, might actually experience a net reduction in holistic foreign investments. Such findings place an onus on policymakers. They're tasked with the challenge of not just leveraging their natural assets but also crafting strategies to ensure that these assets don't overshadow or deter investments in other promising sectors.

In the broader perspective of economic development and planning, Poelhekke and van der Ploeg's research underscores the importance of a balanced approach. It's a reminder that while natural resources are invaluable, an over-reliance or focus on them can unintentionally stifle other sectors, leading to skewed development. The study serves as a clarion call for nations to diversify their investment portfolios and create an environment where both resource and non-resource sectors can coexist and flourish.

Market Size

Market size is a crucial factor for FDI, as it influences both the potential demand for goods and services and the capacity for economies of scale. When a country has a large population, it represents a sizeable pool of consumers for various goods and services, which can make it an attractive market for foreign investors. Moreover, a larger market size can provide companies with economies of scale, whereby the average cost of production decreases as the volume of output increases, thereby enhancing profitability.

The 1999 study by James R Markusen and Keith E Maskus, titled 'Discriminating among Alternative Theories of the Multinational Enterprise', explores this connection in detail.[6] Markusen and Maskus, through this research, present an insightful exploration into the dynamics of multinational enterprises and their predilection towards larger markets. At the heart of their study is the fundamental business desire to maximise profits, and larger markets inherently provide a conducive environment for this objective.

Larger markets, characterised by a vast consumer base, act as a beacon for firms. The sheer potential of reaching more customers directly translates to heightened sales opportunities. When assessing any market, the potential for revenue generation often takes precedence. While individual sales might yield modest profits, in voluminous markets, the cumulative effect results in impressive overall earnings, making them lucrative investment grounds for businesses.

But the allure of these expansive markets isn't just in their consumer numbers. The operational advantages they offer are equally significant. Consider the concept of economies of scale, which is a pivotal point in Markusen and Maskus's study. In business, some costs remain constant regardless of production volume, such as the cost of setting up a manufacturing plant. Larger markets allow firms to produce at an elevated scale, leading to the distribution of these fixed costs across a vast number of products. This results in a reduced cost per item, enhancing profitability. It's akin to buying in bulk; the more you produce, the cheaper each unit becomes.

Furthermore, the presence of large-scale production facilities in extensive markets can lead to further benefits like streamlined supply chains, efficient logistics, and more significant innovation due to higher competition. All of these facets contribute to reduced operational costs and heightened profitability.

The case of Egypt underscores these points. Egypt, with its substantial population of over 100 million, strategic geographical location, and concerted efforts towards economic liberalisation, provides an intriguing case study on the role of market size in attracting FDI.

The telecommunications sector is one of the key areas where Egypt has attracted significant FDI. Major multinational corporations, such as Vodafone and Orange, have invested heavily in the country, drawn by the potential of a market with over 100 million people. These investments have contributed to the development of Egypt's digital infrastructure, enabling the spread of mobile technology across the country and facilitating the growth of related industries such as ecommerce and digital services.

Egypt's large market has allowed these foreign companies to achieve economies of scale, reduce per-unit costs, and enhance their profitability. It has also contributed to job creation, technology transfer, and skill development within the country.

However, Egypt's success in attracting FDI is not solely due to its large market size. Other factors, such as economic reforms, investment-friendly policies, improved ease of doing business, and strategic location connecting Africa, Asia, and Europe, have also played crucial roles.[7] These factors illustrate that while market size is essential in attracting FDI, a conducive investment climate is equally important to fully harness the potential benefits of these investments.

Political Stability

Political stability also significantly impacts FDI. Investors tend to favour countries with stable political environments, as it reduces uncertainty and risk. In their study titled 'Political Risk, Institutions and Foreign Direct Investment', Matthias Busse and Carsten Hefeker detail the intricate relationship between political risk, institutional frameworks, and the attraction of FDI in developing countries.[8] Spanning over nearly two decades, from 1984 to 2003, and encapsulating data from 83 developing nations, the study presents a comprehensive analysis of how political factors influence investment decisions of multinational corporations.

A key revelation from Busse and Hefeker's research is the paramount significance of political stability in the realm of FDI. Like a beacon, nations that exhibit government stability, remain free from internal conflicts, diminish ethnic tensions, uphold democratic rights, and emphasise law and order become magnets for foreign investments. Such attributes create a hospitable environment for business activities, minimising potential operational disruptions and optimising conditions for profitability.

To break this down further, consider the perspective of a multinational corporation weighing potential investment locations. The longevity, success, and potential returns of their overseas ventures are closely tied to the stability of their chosen environment. An unstable political climate poses risks – from sudden changes in trade policies to potential civil unrest – that can jeopardise business operations and profitability. It's akin to building a house: just as one would prefer a solid foundation to ensure longevity and safety, businesses seek stable political environments to secure their investments.

Furthermore, the study reinforces an intuitive yet pivotal point: political risk is a primary consideration for investors. Even if a country offers abundant resources or market potential, if its political landscape is turbulent, investors might be deterred. The rationale is straightforward: political stability often translates to economic predictability. In a stable environment, businesses can more reliably forecast their operations, returns, and potential growth, making their investment decisions more informed and strategic.

In wrapping up this analysis, Busse and Hefeker's study provides empirical heft to the long-held notion that political stability is not just beneficial but crucial for attracting FDI. For developing nations aiming to attract foreign investments, the message is clear: fostering a stable political environment and strong institutions is not merely desirable but essential. A stable political climate doesn't just benefit the present; it also lays the groundwork for sustained economic growth and development in the future.

South Africa's case serves as a good example of this. Despite its challenges, South Africa has been relatively politically stable compared to many other African nations. It has a well-established legal framework, robust institutions, and a largely peaceful environment, making it attractive for foreign investment. The high level of FDI that South Africa consistently attracts can, in part, be attributed to these favourable political conditions.

However, the researchers also emphasise that political stability is not the only factor that affects FDI inflows. Asiedu's research agrees with this. As seen in her research mentioned earlier in this chapter, the significance of institutional quality, sound economic policies, and good governance in attracting FDI is essential. She underscores that while natural resources, market size, and political stability can draw in investors, they alone are not sufficient.[9]

Governance Infrastructure

Without robust institutions, sound governance, and reliable economic policies, these advantages might not fully translate into FDI.

The 2002 research by Steven Globerman and Daniel Shapiro, titled 'Global Foreign Direct Investment Flows: The Role of Governance Infrastructure', bolsters this argument. They argue that the quality of governance infrastructure, which includes factors like the reliability of legal systems, level of corruption, political stability, and effectiveness of regulatory systems, has a significant impact on FDI inflows.[10]

Their study found a strong correlation between the quality of institutions and FDI. Countries with better institutional quality are more likely to attract FDI, as they provide a more predictable and secure environment for foreign investors. This aligns with the broader understanding that while FDI is crucial for economic development, the presence of strong institutions and good governance is essential to ensure that FDI contributes positively to sustainable economic growth.

In the context of this discussion, Botswana serves as an excellent example. Even though it's a relatively small country, Botswana has been successful in attracting a significant amount of FDI. The country has leveraged its diamond resources effectively, but its success isn't just a result of resource wealth. Rather, it's a testament to its strong institutions, good governance, and sound economic policies.

Botswana has consistently ranked high on indices related to governance, political stability, and economic freedom. Its economic policies have been marked by fiscal discipline, open trade policies, and a business-friendly regulatory environment. Its strong institutions have ensured the rule of law, minimised corruption, and protected property rights. These factors have created a conducive environment for foreign investors, helping Botswana attract FDI despite its small market size.

Special Economic Zones

In North Africa, another success story in attracting FDI is Morocco. Morocco presents a prime example of how strategic positioning, political stability, and proactive government policies can boost a country's ability to attract FDI. The country has strategically leveraged its geographic location as a gateway to Europe, making it a crucial hub for businesses looking to access both African and European markets. Coupled with a stable political environment, these factors have made Morocco an attractive destination for FDI.[11]

A clear illustration of this success is the growth of Morocco's automotive industry, largely driven by significant investments from global car manufacturers such as Renault and Peugeot. With the establishment of manufacturing plants, Morocco has not only created thousands of direct and indirect jobs but also facilitated the transfer of technology and expertise in the automotive sector. Today, Morocco stands as Africa's leading car manufacturer, showcasing the transformative impact FDI can have on a country's industrial sector.[12]

In addition to these factors, the Moroccan government has proactively implemented policies to make the country more appealing to foreign investors. A notable strategy has been the establishment of special economic zones (SEZs). These zones are designed to attract investment by offering a combination of tax incentives, advanced infrastructure, and simplified administrative procedures.

One of the most prominent SEZs in Morocco is the Casablanca Finance City (CFC). The CFC is a significant strategic initiative by Morocco that underscores the country's success in attracting FDI. As an established SEZ, the CFC is designed to promote investment in the financial services sector, acting as a conduit between the financial markets of the North and the burgeoning markets of the South, particularly Africa.[13]

CFC's offerings are three-pronged, encompassing fiscal incentives, cutting-edge infrastructure, and a simplified administrative environment, each of which plays a crucial role in enhancing its appeal to foreign investors.

In their comprehensive study, 'Special Economic Zones: Progress, Emerging Challenges, and Future Directions', Thomas Farole and Gokhan Akinci, both of the World Bank, delve into the many benefits of special economic zones (SEZs) like Casablanca Finance City, while also highlighting the need for careful planning and implementation.[14] The authors highlight that SEZs can act as significant catalysts for increased trade. By offering fiscal incentives, such as duty-free importing and exporting or tax breaks, SEZs can make the involved trade activities more profitable. This economic advantage can spur businesses within the zones to increase their trade volumes, both import and export, thus fostering a more vibrant trade environment.

Employment is another critical area where SEZs can have a profound impact. With businesses attracted by the fiscal and infrastructural incentives, SEZs often become hubs of economic activity, creating numerous direct and indirect job opportunities. This job creation not only helps alleviate unemployment but also contributes to the growth of human capital, as workers often acquire new skills and expertise in the process.

Investment, both domestic and foreign, is also significantly influenced by the establishment of SEZs. The improved business conditions, coupled with potential high returns, make SEZs attractive destinations for investment. Thus, they can be magnets for FDI, as seen in the case of Morocco's CFC.

Despite these potential benefits, Farole and Akinci caution that SEZs are not a one-size-fits-all solution. They emphasise the importance of tailoring the design and implementation of SEZs to fit the specific context and needs of each country. Only when carefully planned and appropriately managed can SEZs fully realise their potential and contribute to broad-based and sustainable economic development.

Ultimately, the research by Farole and Akinci provides crucial insights into how SEZs, when executed correctly, can offer countries a viable strategy to stimulate economic growth, increase trade, and attract foreign direct investment.

The Moroccan experience provides valuable lessons for other African nations looking to attract FDI. Countries can enhance their appeal to foreign investors, stimulate industrial growth, and drive economic development by combining geographic advantages with political stability, proactive government policies, and the establishment of special economic zones.

Therefore, while natural resources, market size, political stability, sound governance, and SEZs can enhance a country's attractiveness to foreign investors, they need to be complemented by other positive factors to maximise FDI inflows.

Challenges in Attracting FDI

Attracting FDI can be a complex endeavour with a variety of challenges, from corruption to skilled labour shortages, that African nations must acknowledge and overcome.

Corruption

Corruption stands as a prominent, multifaceted challenge, erecting barriers in the path of attracting foreign direct investment. Its presence paints an uncertain and murky picture of the business landscape, magnifying both the risk and expenditure tied to conducting business. Some nations, blessed with bountiful natural resources, still wrestle with drawing FDI due to this very concern of pervasive corruption. The phenomenon isn't merely anecdotal; it's empirically rooted in research, particularly the 2002 study by Steven Globerman and Daniel Shapiro.[15]

In their illuminating paper titled 'Global Foreign Direct Investment Flows: The Role of Governance Infrastructure', Globerman and Shapiro peel back the layers of the intricate relationship between the quality of governance, corruption, and their combined impact on FDI. At its core, their argument pivots on a single premise: the calibre of governance is instrumental in a nation's allure and ability to not only attract but also extract value from FDI.

The authors' extensive analysis, spanning across a diverse set of countries, consistently underscored a fundamental truth: nations that exhibited superior governance traits – embodied in the rule of law, effective government functions, and minimal corruption – consistently attracted more FDI compared to their counterparts lagging in these areas.

The deleterious effects of corruption on FDI are emphasised profoundly in their study. By infusing uncertainty and elevating operational costs, corruption effectively repels foreign investors. This dynamic stands true even when other enticing attributes, such as a wealth of natural resources or expansive market sizes, are in play. Essentially, corruption, in its various manifestations, acts as a formidable deterrent, offsetting other advantages a country might possess.

Globerman and Shapiro's findings aren't merely academic; they're instructive. This research sheds light on the importance of adopting effective anti-corruption measures and improving overall governance to create an attractive investment climate. This insight is invaluable, especially for developing nations such as those on our continent that stand at crossroads, eager to magnetise foreign investments to fuel their future trajectories.

Bureaucracy

Bureaucracy is another critical impediment to FDI. Inefficient bureaucratic procedures can cause delays, increase the cost of business operations, and create uncertainty for investors. In their

2002 study titled 'The Regulation of Entry', Simeon Djankov and his colleagues explored how bureaucratic hurdles impact business operations, particularly concerning the entry of new firms. The study, which covered 85 countries, assessed the procedures, time, and cost involved in meeting government requirements for starting a business.[16]

Their findings indicate that countries with cumbersome and costly business registration processes tend to deter entrepreneurial activity, which could be extrapolated to foreign direct investment as well. Such bureaucratic inefficiencies could serve as significant barriers to entry for foreign investors, potentially discouraging them from entering the market. They found that more bureaucracy, measured by the number of procedures required to start a business, is associated with higher corruption and a larger unofficial economy.

Their work highlighted that an efficient, transparent, and predictable administrative system is a vital factor for attracting businesses and investment. Therefore, countries looking to attract more FDI should aim to reduce bureaucratic procedures, cut red tape, and streamline the process of doing business.

The research from Djankov and colleagues demonstrates that bureaucratic reforms are not just about attracting FDI but also about fostering a more vibrant private sector and encouraging entrepreneurship. These are all crucial elements for economic growth and development.

Lack of Adequate Skilled Labour

Additionally, the lack of adequately skilled labour is a significant challenge in many African countries. Investors need a competent and skilled workforce to operate efficiently and effectively. Countries that lack such a workforce may face difficulties in attracting FDI. For instance, despite its vast mineral resources, the Democratic Republic of Congo has struggled to attract FDI in sectors that require highly skilled labour. A study by Viviana V Roseth, Alexandria Valerio, and Marcela Gutiérrez titled 'Education, Skills and Labour Market Outcomes' delves into the importance of human capital, particularly education and skills, for economic development and FDI.[17]

The authors argue that a well-educated and skilled workforce is a crucial factor for attracting FDI, particularly for sectors that require specialised skills and knowledge. Foreign investors are likely to be attracted to countries where the local workforce has the necessary skills to support their business operations, contributing to the productivity and efficiency of these operations.

Furthermore, the authors emphasise that investments in education and training can help build this human capital. By developing a skilled workforce, countries can not only attract more FDI but also ensure that these investments contribute to sustainable economic growth.

In the context of the Democratic Republic of Congo, despite the country's vast mineral resources, the lack of a sufficiently skilled labour force has been a barrier to attracting FDI, particularly in sectors that require highly skilled labour.

In light of this, the study advocates for African countries and other developing economies to prioritise investments in education and skills development as part of their strategies to attract FDI and promote economic development. This can include measures such as improving the quality of education, expanding access to vocational and technical training, and strengthening the linkages between education and industry to ensure that the skills being developed meet the needs of the economy.

To surmount these challenges, African countries need to focus on improving governance, streamlining bureaucratic procedures, and enhancing their human capital. Good governance can reduce corruption and create a more transparent and predictable business environment. Streamlining bureaucratic procedures can make it easier and less costly for businesses to operate. Lastly, investing in education and training can improve the quality of the workforce and make the country more attractive to investors. Doing so not only fosters an environment conducive to FDI but also stimulates sustainable economic growth and development.

In the next chapter, we will discuss how cultivating global partnerships can open avenues to essential resources, cutting-edge technology, specialised expertise, and more.

CHAPTER 17

CULTIVATING GLOBAL PARTNERSHIPS

Global partnerships refer to alliances between countries, regions, or organisations across the globe with the shared goal of addressing common challenges or pursuing common objectives. Global partnerships have become the cornerstone of an increasingly interconnected world. These collaborations, steeped in shared aspirations, merge resources, expertise, and perspectives to confront mutual challenges and ambitions. For continents teeming with potential, like Africa, these alliances have the capacity to open avenues to essential resources, cutting-edge technology, and specialised expertise, while simultaneously ensuring they maintain decision-making autonomy and agency.

However, the effectiveness of these partnerships hinges on them being anchored on equal terms. This means that every nation, regardless of its developmental trajectory or economic power, must have an equal stake and a fair share in the results. This equitable approach challenges the archaic, often exploitative, dynamics where more powerful nations would wield their dominance to gain disproportionate advantages.

Mutual respect and trust are foundational for lasting collaborations, as seen in the partnership between the African, Caribbean, and Pacific (ACP) Group of States and the European Union (EU). The Cotonou Agreement underscores an equitable alliance, transcending traditional power dynamics and granting ACP nations a pivotal role in steering the partnership's direction. Central to this relationship is the continuous political dialogue, which ensures decisions are based on the diverse perspectives of all member states. Economic Partnership Agreements (EPAs) further highlight this dynamic, allowing ACP nations to set terms that reflect their specific developmental paths. In development cooperation, ACP countries actively decide where resources are best used, transitioning from mere recipients to active participants. Joint institutions like the ACP-EU Council of Ministers reinforce this essence, fostering policy collaboration and oversight. Cultural exchanges further enrich the partnership, highlighting the importance of shared human values.

Similarly, the US government's Millennium Challenge Corporation (MCC) compact with African nations epitomises mutual respect in development partnerships. The MCC selects nations that showcase good governance and citizen-centric investments, treating them as active partners in development rather than passive recipients. Projects are co-designed, ensuring alignment with a nation's strategic interests and the needs of its populace. This collaborative design empowers recipient countries, fostering a sense of ownership, effective implementation, and monitoring. The MCC approach also champions mutual accountability; both parties are held responsible for their roles, promoting a more equitable international aid landscape. Overall, the MCC's model signifies a shift in international development, emphasising genuine dialogue, collaboration, and mutual respect for impactful and sustainable outcomes.

This collaborative approach also sends a broader message to the international community about the evolving dynamics of international aid. Developing nations are no longer mere beneficiaries; they are equal stakeholders in a shared journey towards sustainable development.

What this means is that the MCC compact reshapes the narrative, proving that with mutual respect and collaboration, international development partnerships can be more impactful, sustainable, and harmonious. The model it offers goes beyond mere financial assistance, paving the way for a more equitable global order, where both developed and developing nations engage in genuine dialogue and collective action.

Furthermore, public-private partnerships (PPPs) in Africa are more than just contractual agreements between governments and private entities; they represent a transformative shift in how infrastructure development is approached on the continent. The synergy between public policy and private enterprise has paved the way for projects that are not only grand in scale but also innovative in execution.

Take, for instance, the road projects in Kenya. Historically, infrastructure projects would rely solely on government funding and expertise, which sometimes led to delays, inefficiencies, or designs that weren't always in line with global best practices. With the inclusion of international corporations through PPPs, there's an infusion of not just capital but also cutting-edge technology and sophisticated project management techniques. The Kenyan government benefits from the expertise and efficiency brought in by these corporations, ensuring that roads are not just built but also built to last and cater to future needs.[1]

Kenya, being an economic powerhouse in East Africa, has always had the challenge of linking its economic centres efficiently while ensuring rural regions are not left behind. The introduction of international corporations into this mix, via PPPs, brought several transformative changes.

Firstly, these projects exemplify how global standards and best practices can be integrated into local contexts. Before the adoption of PPPs in road infrastructure, many projects in Kenya faced challenges such as delays, cost overruns, and sometimes subpar quality due to various constraints, be it budgetary, technical, or expertise related. By collaborating with experienced international corporations, the Kenyan government is able to tap into a pool of knowledge, expertise, and advanced technologies. This means roads are designed and built with longevity in mind, incorporating features that cater to future traffic projections and environmental considerations.

Furthermore, the very involvement of these international entities brings about a degree of accountability and transparency that's essential for the public's trust. These corporations, operating on global scales, are accustomed to rigorous project management, reporting, and quality control standards. As a result, road projects executed under PPPs in Kenya often have meticulous planning, regular audits, and clear communication channels, ensuring all stakeholders, from policymakers to the general public, are kept informed and any concerns are addressed promptly.

But beyond the physical road lie the more intangible, yet equally significant, benefits. These partnerships are a hotbed for skills transfer. Kenyan professionals, be it engineers, project managers, or technicians, work alongside international experts, imbibing knowledge and skills that would otherwise be hard to access. Over time, this skills transfer ensures that Kenya builds a robust local cadre of professionals equipped with global best practices but tailored to local challenges and nuances.

For example, the Nairobi Expressway, a significant infrastructure project, is set to decongest traffic in the capital city by providing a faster route through the city, enhancing connectivity and reducing travel times. This project, involving international partnerships, serves as proof of Kenya's ambition and the potential of PPPs in transforming urban landscapes.

Beyond the tangible benefits – roads, ports, and other infrastructure – lies an even more crucial aspect of these partnerships: capacity building. The collaboration doesn't stop at the project's completion; there's a continuous exchange of knowledge, best practices, and technological advancements. Over time, this ensures that African nations are not perpetually dependent on external entities for their development needs. Instead, they gradually build a reservoir of knowledge, skills, and technology, allowing them to be self-sufficient in the long run.

Moreover, these collaborations set a precedent. They demonstrate to the world that African nations are not just passive recipients of aid or investment. They are dynamic partners, capable of negotiating, contributing, and ensuring the successful execution of large-scale projects. It underscores the idea that the continent is open for business, not charity.

However, the onus is on both parties to ensure that these partnerships genuinely serve the interests of the African populace. When international corporations respect the sovereignty, culture, and aspirations of their African partners, and when African governments ensure transparent, accountable collaborations, these projects can lead to sustainable growth, development, and empowerment. The potential of PPPs, then, is not just in bricks and mortar, but in building robust, self-reliant nations ready for the challenges and opportunities of the future.

The Importance of Global Partnerships

Global partnerships have an integral role in shaping the economic trajectory of African nations. They create bridges that facilitate the exchange of resources, knowledge, and technology among participating entities, fostering a cooperative approach to common developmental goals.

The Global Alliance for Vaccines and Immunisation (GAVI)

The Global Alliance for Vaccines and Immunisation (GAVI), established in 2000, is a public-private partnership aimed at 'immunisation for all'. It is a collaborative partnership with WHO, UNICEF, the World Bank, and the Bill & Melinda Gates Foundation. GAVI is a prime example of a successful global partnership contributing to sustainable development, specifically in the health sector.

GAVI's primary aim is to increase access to immunisation in low-income countries, which often lack the necessary infrastructure and financial resources to run comprehensive immunisation programmes. A significant part of GAVI's mission is to address the persistent inequality in vaccine access between developed and developing nations, a challenge that has historical roots and complex economic and logistical dimensions.[2]

The alliance's operational model is based on pooling demand for vaccines from developing countries, including many African nations, and negotiating lower prices with pharmaceutical companies. This approach creates a win-win scenario where pharmaceutical companies find incentives to invest in vaccine research and production for diseases prevalent in the developing world, and low-income countries get access to life-saving vaccines at affordable prices.

GAVI's work in Africa has been transformative, and its contribution towards the reduction of child mortality rates through increased immunisation is truly significant. This public-private partnership has successfully introduced underused, but critical, vaccines into healthcare systems that are often under-resourced, overcoming various logistical and financial challenges.

In countries like Kenya, Ghana, and Malawi, GAVI's support has enabled the introduction of the pneumococcal conjugate vaccine, which offers protection against pneumococcal disease. This disease is responsible for serious conditions such as pneumonia, meningitis, and sepsis, particularly in children under the age of five. By providing access to this vaccine, GAVI has contributed to a significant reduction in child mortality rates and the overall disease burden in these countries.[3]

Moreover, GAVI's impact extends beyond the health outcomes. Healthier populations mean more children can attend school, adults can work, and economies can thrive. Consequently, GAVI's work contributes to breaking the cycle of poverty and setting these nations on a path towards sustainable development.

It's also worth noting that GAVI's success in these countries has been underpinned by collaboration and cooperation. Its model of working with governments, international organisations, civil society, and the private sector has proven effective in addressing complex health challenges and should serve as a valuable lesson for other development initiatives. The partnership-based model emphasises the importance of shared goals, mutual trust, and a commitment to achieving sustainable health outcomes.

However, the work is far from over. While GAVI has made significant strides in expanding vaccine access, there are still many children on our continent of Africa and in other parts of the world whom routine immunisation services do not reach. The challenge of achieving universal immunisation is exacerbated by various factors, including conflicts, political instability, logistical difficulties, and vaccine hesitancy. Addressing these challenges will require concerted efforts from all stakeholders, including governments, international organisations, health workers, and communities.

Furthermore, GAVI's work goes beyond providing vaccines. The Alliance invests in strengthening health systems, improving vaccine delivery mechanisms, and building capacity for disease surveillance. These investments have long-term implications for public health, economic productivity, and social stability in African nations. A healthier population means fewer burdens on healthcare systems, more children attending school, and adults who can contribute productively to the economy.

Finally, GAVI's approach fosters sustainability. It gradually transitions financial responsibility for vaccines to the governments of the countries it supports. This transition is based on each country's increasing gross national income per capita, ensuring that countries take over vaccine financing in a way that is sustainable and does not compromise access.

The Paris Agreement on Climate Change

The Paris Agreement, established under the United Nations Framework Convention on Climate Change (UNFCCC), signifies a global commitment to mitigating the impacts of climate change and promoting sustainable and resilient development. Its adoption in 2016 marked a turning point in the global response to climate change, with the agreement's ambitious targets reflecting the scale of the challenge and the urgency of action.

In the context of Africa, the Paris Agreement holds particular significance. Many African countries are acutely vulnerable to the impacts of climate change, including increased droughts, floods, and heatwaves, all of which pose significant threats to livelihoods, economic stability, and development. In fact, the Intergovernmental Panel on Climate Change (IPCC) has highlighted Africa as a region that will be severely impacted, particularly in terms of water scarcity, agricultural productivity, and food security.[4]

The Paris Agreement, therefore, represents a critical opportunity for African nations to engage in climate-resilient economic growth and sustainable development. A key aspect of the Paris Agreement is its emphasis on the concept of 'nationally determined contributions' (NDCs), which are climate action plans developed by each country to reduce their greenhouse gas emissions and adapt to the impacts of climate change.[5]

The Paris Agreement also opens up avenues for international cooperation and financial support for climate action in developing countries. The agreement established the Green Climate Fund (GCF), aiming to channel significant financial resources to developing countries, including African nations, to support their climate mitigation and adaptation efforts. This funding is critical to help African countries transition towards low-carbon, climate-resilient development pathways.

The Paris Agreement represents a vital framework for African nations to pursue sustainable, climate-resilient economic development. They can safeguard their economies and societies against the impacts of climate change, while simultaneously reaping the benefits of sustainable development by aligning their development strategies with their commitments under the Paris Agreement. However, achieving these goals will require sustained political commitment, international cooperation, and substantial financial and technical support.

The Global Partnership for Education (GPE)

The Global Partnership for Education (GPE) is a leading global initiative committed to strengthening educational systems in developing countries. Recognising that education is a cornerstone of economic and social development, GPE employs a holistic approach to improving educational outcomes, focusing not only on enrolment but also on the quality of education and learning outcomes.[6]

On our continent of Africa, where many countries grapple with challenges such as poor school infrastructure, low literacy rates, gender disparities in education, and insufficient teacher training, the efforts of GPE have been particularly influential. GPE assists African nations in implementing comprehensive education sector plans designed to overcome these challenges by providing financial resources, technical assistance, and a platform for knowledge exchange.

Take, for example, the case of Burkina Faso, which, with the support of GPE, implemented a ten-year plan for the development of the education sector in 2012. As a result, Burkina Faso witnessed significant improvements in its education system. The gross enrolment rate in primary education rose from 45 percent in 2001 to 87 percent in 2021, while the completion rate in primary education increased from 25 percent in 2001 to 64 percent in 2021.[7]

In another instance, GPE played a significant role in the development of Sierra Leone's education sector. Following a devastating civil war and the Ebola epidemic, Sierra Leone faced immense challenges in rebuilding its education system. With GPE's support, the government of Sierra Leone developed and implemented an education sector plan that emphasised improved access to education, better learning outcomes, and system efficiency. The plan has resulted in increased school enrolment, reduced gender disparities in education, and improved learning outcomes in core subjects such as English and Mathematics.[8]

The work of GPE also extends beyond financial support and technical assistance. As a multi-stakeholder partnership, GPE facilitates dialogue and cooperation among diverse actors, including governments, civil society organisations, teacher associations, and the private sector. This inclusive approach encourages shared learning, policy coherence, and collective action, factors that are critical for sustainable improvements in education systems.

The economic implications of GPE's work are significant. By improving access to quality education, GPE contributes to the development of skilled and knowledgeable workforces in African countries, enhancing their competitiveness in today's knowledge-based global economy. Moreover, education, particularly of girls, leads to a wide range of social and economic benefits, including improved child health, increased female labour force participation, and greater gender equality.[9] As we look towards the future, it is clear that continued investments in education will be critical for Africa's sustainable development and the realisation of its vast potential.

The Sustainable Energy for All (SEforALL) Initiative

Launched by the UN in 2011, the Sustainable Energy for All (SEforALL) initiative aims to ensure universal access to modern energy services, promoting energy efficiency and renewable energy globally. The SEforALL initiative has been a major driver of change in the global energy landscape. Recognising the crucial role that energy plays in economic development and quality of life, the initiative seeks to address the global energy challenge through a three-pronged approach: ensuring universal access to modern energy services, doubling the rate of improvement in energy efficiency, and doubling the share of renewable energy in the global energy mix.[10]

The relevance of the SEforALL initiative to African countries cannot be overstated. As of 2021, Sub-Saharan Africa, home to more than half of the world's population without access to electricity, faces a critical need for increased energy access. Many of our African countries grapple with inadequate and unreliable energy supplies, which act as a significant constraint on economic development and poverty reduction efforts.

Under the SEforALL initiative, efforts are being made to enhance energy access in Africa through both grid expansion and the promotion of off-grid solutions, such as solar home systems and mini-grids. These efforts are not only improving living standards by facilitating access to vital services, such as healthcare and education, but also stimulating economic activity by providing the energy needed for businesses to operate and expand.

For instance, a programme in Rwanda, supported by the SEforALL initiative, has achieved significant progress in expanding access to electricity. In 2018, the Rwandan population's access to electricity was at 37.96 percent. By 2021, this had increased to 48.70 percent.[11] With the support of SEforALL, the Rwandan government implemented a comprehensive electrification strategy that focused on both grid expansion and off-grid solutions.

In addition to expanding access to energy, the SEforALL initiative also promotes energy efficiency and the use of renewable energy sources. These aspects of the initiative have significant economic implications. Energy efficiency measures can reduce energy costs for businesses and households, thereby freeing up resources for productive investments and consumption. At the same time, the transition to renewable energy sources offers opportunities for technological innovation and job creation, while addressing the climate change challenge.

Take, for instance, South Africa, where the government has implemented a renewable energy independent power producer procurement (REIPPP) programme that has added significant renewable energy capacity to the national grid. The programme has attracted substantial domestic and foreign investment, created jobs, and contributed to rural development.[12]

Overall, the SEforALL initiative is contributing significantly to Africa's economic development. It is creating conditions for sustainable and inclusive economic growth by addressing the energy challenge. As our African continent continues to strive for greater prosperity, initiatives such as SEforALL will be crucial in shaping a sustainable and equitable energy future.

China-Africa Cooperation

The China-Africa partnership has been pivotal for Africa's economic development. As Africa's largest trading partner, China invests heavily in infrastructure, manufacturing, and agriculture, providing Africa with financing, technology, and markets. The Sino-African partnership has seen a dynamic shift in the economic landscape of many African nations. China's direct investment in Africa goes beyond mere trade ties; it includes large-scale infrastructure projects, capital investments, and a strong cultural exchange, making it a comprehensive economic partnership. This cooperation presents opportunities for economic diversification, industrialisation, and development of the private sector in our African countries.[13]

The infrastructure projects that China finances and executes across the continent are part of its broader 'Belt and Road Initiative'. These projects span various sectors, including transport (railways, roads, and airports), energy (hydroelectric power plants, oil refineries), and real estate (housing projects). The Mombasa-Nairobi Standard Gauge Railway in Kenya, constructed by Chinese firms and financed by Chinese loans, is a prominent example of such projects. The railway line has boosted trade, tourism, and job creation in Kenya.[14]

In agriculture, China's investments focus on improving agricultural productivity and food security in Africa. These efforts not only ensure a stable supply of agricultural products for China but also contribute to rural development and poverty alleviation in African countries. Several African countries have become hosts to China-aided Agricultural Technology Demonstration Centres.

These centres are designed to provide local farmers with practical demonstrations of advanced and suitable farming techniques that can help increase productivity and, ultimately, income.[15]

For instance, in Zambia, the China-aided Agricultural Technology Demonstration Centre, operational since 2011, has been instrumental in enhancing local farmers' knowledge and practices. The centre, which is situated near Lusaka, focuses on promoting hybrid rice cultivation and has trained more than 1000 Zambian agricultural technicians and farmers, enabling them to grow high-yielding rice varieties that are well-suited to the country's climate and soil conditions.[16]

Similarly, in Mozambique, the China-aided Agricultural Technology Demonstration Centre focuses on promoting hybrid rice and vegetables, contributing significantly to local agricultural development. This centre has served as a pivotal platform for the exchange of agricultural technologies between China and Mozambique, benefitting over 10,000 local farmers since its inception in 2011.[17]

In Zimbabwe, the China-Zimbabwe Friendship Agricultural Technology Demonstration Centre, set up in 2012, has facilitated the adoption of advanced farming techniques among local farmers. The centre, based in Harare, primarily focuses on crop production, animal husbandry, and agricultural machinery use. Through various training programmes, the centre has reached thousands of Zimbabwean farmers, helping them improve their farming efficiency and productivity.[18]

The establishment of these centres marks a significant development in China's agricultural cooperation with Africa. They serve as valuable platforms for knowledge and technology transfer, contributing to agricultural development and food security in the host countries. These centres also play an important role in rural development and poverty alleviation by enhancing local farming capabilities.

The manufacturing sector also benefits from Chinese investments, with Chinese firms setting up manufacturing plants in Africa. This helps in transferring technology and skills to local workers, fostering industrial development, and creating jobs. The Eastern Industrial Zone (EIZ) in Ethiopia is an example of successful Sino-African cooperation in industrial development. Launched in 2007 and located in the Oromia region close to Addis Ababa, the EIZ has been a significant component of Ethiopia's industrialisation strategy.

The Sino-African partnership presents a unique model of South-South cooperation that has the potential to significantly contribute to economic growth and sustainable development in Africa.

Africa-European Union Partnership

As Africa's largest donor and key trading partner, the European Union has a substantial role in its economic development. The relationship between the European Union and Africa is deeply rooted in history, with the EU being a significant player in Africa's development journey. Over the years, the relationship has evolved from a mainly donor-recipient dynamic to a more partnership-based interaction, where the focus is not just on aid but also on sustainable development, economic growth, peace, and security.

For instance, under the framework of the Cotonou Agreement, signed in 2000, the EU has been aiding African countries in areas such as human rights, governance, and development cooperation.[19] It allows the EU to contribute to the poverty eradication efforts in African countries and supports their gradual integration into the global economy. Furthermore, it underscores the importance of dialogue, mutual respect, and shared responsibility.

Economic Partnership Agreements (EPAs) between the EU and ACP countries were designed to replace the non-reciprocal trade preferences that the EU had previously granted to these countries.

A significant aspect of these EPAs is that they provide African countries with fully duty-free and quota-free access to the EU market. The goal is to enhance market access, which can potentially stimulate economic growth, job creation, and overall development in African countries. For instance, African exporters can benefit from increased demand for their products, thereby boosting incomes and fostering growth in related industries.[20]

However, African countries are also expected to gradually open their markets to EU imports under the EPAs. This is a contentious point, as critics argue that this could expose domestic industries in African countries to intense competition from EU products. To mitigate these concerns, EPAs include long transition periods for tariff reductions, exclusion of sensitive products from liberalisation, and 'safeguard measures' to protect African industries from sudden import surges.

Furthermore, EPAs incorporate 'development cooperation' provisions. These are designed to help African countries take advantage of the EPAs, such as through building trade capacity, infrastructure, and improving regulatory frameworks. This component is crucial, as many African countries lack the resources and capacities to fully leverage the opportunities provided by the EPAs.

All in all, EPAs represent a significant shift in EU-ACP trade relations towards a more reciprocal and comprehensive framework. While they offer potential opportunities for African countries, their successful implementation requires careful consideration of potential challenges and proactive efforts to address them.

Furthermore, the EU's commitment to supporting peace and security in Africa has been instrumental. The African Peace Facility (APF), established by the European Union in 2004, represents a critical element of the EU's engagement with Africa on peace and security. Recognising the need for African-led solutions to African problems, the APF provides financial support to operations led by the African Union or African regional organisations, emphasising African ownership and regional solutions to conflict.

An example of APF's impact can be seen in its funding of the African Union Mission in Somalia (AMISOM). This mission, active since 2007, has been crucial in pushing back the extremist group Al-Shabaab and stabilising the country. Without APF funding, which covers allowances for troops, police, and civilian personnel, along with operational costs, the mission would struggle to maintain its operations.[21]

The EU's financial commitment through the APF demonstrates a recognition that peace and security are prerequisites for sustainable development. However, the APF's approach also acknowledges that lasting peace and security in Africa can only be achieved if African nations themselves lead and own the processes.

The EU-Africa partnership continues to play an integral role in driving economic development and fostering sustainable and inclusive growth in African countries through these varied yet interconnected mechanisms.

The Power Africa Initiative

Power Africa is an innovative partnership designed to increase access to electricity in Sub-Saharan Africa where more than 600 million people currently lack access. The Power Africa initiative was launched by President Barack Obama in Tanzania during his Africa Tour in July 2013. The initiative aims to support economic growth and development by increasing access to reliable, affordable, and sustainable power on the African continent. It is designed as a multi-stakeholder partnership among the governments of the United States of America, Tanzania, Kenya, Ethiopia, Ghana, Nigeria, and Liberia, the US and the African private sector, international institutions, nongovernmental organisations, and other partner countries. Its approach involves a blend of technical assistance, capacity building, and leveraging finance to remove the systemic barriers to private sector investments in energy.[22]

One significant achievement of Power Africa has been its 'Beyond the Grid' programme, which focuses on off-grid and small-scale energy solutions that are essential for reaching populations in remote areas. By facilitating partnerships between investors, entrepreneurs, and governments, this programme has helped catalyse private investment in off-grid and small-scale renewable energy projects.

Tanzania is an excellent example of how Power Africa's strategy can foster sustainable change. The country's energy sector has faced numerous challenges, including insufficient generation capacity, a lack of reliable and affordable electricity in rural areas, and heavy reliance on non-renewable energy sources.

Power Africa has addressed these issues by supporting various off-grid solar projects across Tanzania, directly aligning with the country's Power System Master Plan, which emphasises the importance of off-grid solutions for rural electrification. One innovative strategy has been to foster partnerships with private sector companies, which are well-positioned to implement technological solutions and manage the commercial aspects of electricity distribution.

One such partnership is with Off Grid Electric, a private company that specialises in providing cost-effective solar energy solutions. With Power Africa's support, Off Grid Electric has been able to scale up its operations in Tanzania, offering solar home systems on a pay-as-you-go model, which makes them affordable for low-income households. The solar home systems include solar panels and lithium ion batteries, along with energy-efficient appliances like LED lights and radios.

These solar home systems have had significant impacts on the lives of Tanzanians. Households with access to reliable electricity can extend their productive hours into the evening, children can do their homework after dark, and businesses can operate more efficiently and for longer hours.

Additionally, access to clean energy means reduced reliance on harmful fuels like kerosene for lighting, creating health benefits. The shift from non-renewable energy sources to solar power also contributes to climate change mitigation efforts, aligning with the environmental sustainability objectives of both Tanzania and the broader international community.

This example demonstrates how Power Africa leverages partnerships to support sustainable economic and social development in Africa. By doing so, it not only increases electricity access but also facilitates the transition to clean, renewable energy, providing a robust model for other countries in the region and beyond.

Challenges and Opportunities

Global partnerships, despite their potential for facilitating economic development and growth in African nations, can also present challenges that need to be delicately managed. These range from issues of economic disparity and debt sustainability to maintaining policy space for national development.

Economic disparity is a significant challenge in global partnerships, particularly in those involving developed and developing nations. For instance, trade agreements, while fostering access to markets, may sometimes lead to unfair competition due to the disparity in economic strengths between partnering nations. African countries, with their developing economies, may find it challenging to compete with more advanced and industrialised economies, leading to imbalances in benefits derived from such agreements.[23]

Debt sustainability is another critical issue, particularly in partnerships that involve substantial financial lending or investment, such as the China-Africa partnership. While Chinese investments in Africa's infrastructure have brought considerable economic benefits, they have also raised concerns about increased debt levels in several African nations, potentially leading to debt distress. For instance, Zambia's debt to China is a clear illustration of the concerns associated with debt sustainability in the context of global partnerships. Over the past few decades, Zambia, like many African countries, engaged in significant borrowing from China to finance infrastructure projects, which are crucial for the country's development. These investments, while playing a key role in improving the country's infrastructure, have also resulted in a substantial accumulation of debt.[24]

By 2017, Zambia's external debt stock stood at approximately $8.7 billion.[25] The situation escalated when in 2020, amid the economic stress caused by the COVID-19 pandemic, Zambia became the first African country to default on its sovereign debt in the pandemic era. This raised questions about debt sustainability not just in Zambia but also in other heavily indebted low-income countries.

The potential consequences of debt unsustainability are severe. Overwhelming debt burdens can divert resources from much-needed public services, such as health and education, to service debt. Additionally, in cases of default, countries may face reputational damage, making it more difficult and costly to access international capital markets in the future. There are also concerns about the potential implications for national sovereignty, given the need to comply with the conditions set by creditor countries or institutions.

In response to this situation, initiatives like the G20's Debt Service Suspension Initiative (DSSI) and the Common Framework for Debt Treatments have been established to provide temporary debt relief and restructure unsustainable debt, respectively. However, addressing the underlying issues of debt sustainability in global partnerships will require more systemic and long-term solutions. This includes ensuring responsible lending and borrowing practices, improving debt transparency, and enhancing debt management capacities in borrowing countries.

Finally, preserving policy space for national development is another challenge that needs to be carefully managed in global partnerships. Preserving policy space for national development is about enabling countries to devise, implement, and adjust policies in response to their specific development needs and goals. It involves the ability to control and regulate economic sectors, protect nascent industries, and prioritise local over foreign investments when necessary. However, in the context of global partnerships, this policy space can sometimes be limited, as conditions tied to financial aid or trade agreements may require policy concessions or adherence to international norms and standards.

A notable example is the Economic Partnership Agreements (EPAs) between the African, Caribbean, and Pacific (ACP) countries and the European Union (EU). While these agreements aim to promote trade and development, critics have argued that they can limit the policy space for ACP countries. For instance, the EPAs require the progressive elimination of tariffs on a substantial number of imports from the EU, which could limit the ability of ACP countries to use tariffs as a tool for industrial development and for protecting local industries from competition from European products.[26]

To ensure that global partnerships contribute to sustainable development, it's important that they are designed and implemented in a way that respects and preserves policy space. This could involve providing flexibility in agreements, promoting policy dialogue and knowledge exchange, and strengthening capacities for negotiation and policy implementation.

While global partnerships undoubtedly offer immense opportunities for Africa, the challenge lies in managing these partnerships in ways that ensure equity and contribute to sustainable development. Policymakers in our African nations and their global partners must continuously work towards a mutually beneficial equilibrium, ensuring that these partnerships promote not just economic growth but also sustainable and inclusive development.

Future Directions

Our African nations need to strategically cultivate their global partnerships to ensure they align with their development objectives. Strategically cultivating global partnerships necessitates a nuanced understanding of both the opportunities and challenges associated with these collaborations. Africa, with its array of different nations and contexts, must aim to forge partnerships that align with its unique development goals and socio-economic circumstances.

For instance, in the context of China-Africa relations, African nations need to strive for more balanced trade relations and ensure the investments contribute to local employment creation and technology transfer. To this end, African nations could negotiate investment contracts that include provisions for local content requirements, joint ventures, or technology-sharing agreements. Such arrangements would allow our continent to not only benefit from financial investment but also gain from skill development and technological advancements.[27]

Similarly, in the partnerships with the EU or US, Africa could focus on maximising benefits from trade preferences and aid. For instance, it could aim to diversify its export basket to the EU or US markets to reduce over-reliance on a few primary commodities and move up the value chain.[28] Additionally, aid should be utilised strategically to build capacities in key sectors, such as education, health, and infrastructure, which can provide a strong foundation for long-term development. Honestly speaking, I would prefer that our African nations totally move away from aid in preference of trade.

Moreover, in climate-change-related partnerships, such as those associated with the Paris Agreement, African countries could leverage global climate finance opportunities. They could attract international funding from the Green Climate Fund or other climate finance mechanisms by developing robust and viable projects and programmes for climate change adaptation and mitigation. This would not only help them address climate vulnerabilities but also foster sustainable economic development.[29]

It's also crucial for African nations to ensure that the policy space for national development is maintained in these partnerships. This means being able to regulate foreign investments, protect local industries if needed, and design policies that best meet their development needs. A strong institutional framework and a well-informed negotiating strategy would be instrumental in preserving this policy space.[30]

In essence, strategic cultivation of global partnerships involves aligning partnerships with national development goals, negotiating terms that ensure mutual benefits, leveraging opportunities offered by partnerships, and maintaining policy space for national development.

Even with strong global partnerships, the path to a prosperous and thriving Africa will be fraught with challenges and setbacks. In the following chapter, we will discuss the necessity of exercising adaptability and resilience in the face of adversity, and how African nations have done this in the past.

CHAPTER 18

ADAPTABILITY AND RESILIENCE

This chapter places emphasis on the necessity for adaptability and resilience in the face of various challenges. In a continent often beset with various economic, environmental, and health crises, the ability to pivot, adapt, and rise stronger is a key determinant of progress.

Resilience in Health Crises

In *The Next Pandemic: On the Front Lines Against Humankind's Gravest Dangers*, Dr Ali S Khan, a former director of the Office of Public Health Preparedness and Response at the Centers for Disease Control and Prevention in the US, with decades of experience in epidemiology, examines the global challenge of pandemics and the critical role that preparation and response strategies play in mitigating their impact.[1] Particularly noteworthy is Khan's recognition of the resilience shown by several African countries in the face of such threats, despite resource constraints and other challenges.

Over the years, African nations have contended with numerous disease outbreaks, including HIV/AIDS, Ebola, and, more recently, COVID-19. These public health crises have posed immense challenges, but they have also led to significant advances in Africa's public health policies and response systems. Often working with limited resources, African countries have had to innovate and develop new strategies to track disease outbreaks, manage cases, and prevent further spread.

Ebola Outbreak

For example, the 2014–2016 Ebola outbreak in West Africa stands as a stark reminder of the toll pandemics can take, especially in regions with less resilient health systems. This outbreak, caused by the Zaire Ebola virus, resulted in over 28,000 cases and 11,000 deaths, significantly impacting Guinea, Liberia, and Sierra Leone both socially and economically.[2]

The initial response was largely inadequate due to a variety of factors. This included weak health systems, a lack of trained health professionals, limited laboratory capacity for diagnosing Ebola, and poor infection prevention and control practices in many health facilities. However, as the outbreak continued, the scale of international support increased, and domestic response strategies improved.

The World Health Organization (WHO), Doctors Without Borders (MSF), the Centers for Disease Control and Prevention (CDC), and numerous other international partners collaborated to support the affected countries. These efforts included setting up Ebola treatment centres, providing laboratory support for diagnosing cases, training health workers, conducting contact tracing, and implementing safe burial practices.

This Ebola outbreak in West Africa also brought to light the significance of community engagement in handling health crises. Communities played a substantial role in curbing the spread of the disease, with various local groups, including traditional and religious leaders, youth groups, and women's associations, becoming instrumental in the fight against Ebola.[3]

In Sierra Leone, the revered 'Sowei' leaders, central to women's secret societies, significantly influenced the fight against Ebola by modifying traditional burial practices that spread the disease. They play crucial roles in rites of passage for young girls and have sway in community ceremonies and decisions.

In Liberia, religious leaders, commanding vast respect, were instrumental during the Ebola crisis. They disseminated accurate health information during services, dispelling myths and integrating prevention measures into religious teachings. They also advocated for safer burial practices, respecting cultural and religious sensitivities. Simultaneously, youth volunteers connected with community or religious groups spread health messages door to door, supporting disease tracking. Women's associations, recognising women's increased risk as primary caregivers, actively promoted Ebola awareness.

HIV/AIDS Epidemic

Similar resilience and innovation have been demonstrated in the fight against HIV/AIDS. HIV/AIDS has been one of the most devastating epidemics of the late 20th and early 21st centuries, particularly affecting Sub-Saharan Africa. In response to the dire need for comprehensive intervention, the United States initiated the President's Emergency Plan for AIDS Relief (PEPFAR). Although the US has been involved in efforts to address the global AIDS crisis since the mid-1980s, the creation of PEPFAR in 2003 marked a significant increase in funding and attention to the epidemic. Twenty years in, PEPFAR reported saving more than 25 million lives and is currently providing HIV prevention and treatment services to millions.[4] PEPFAR represents the largest commitment by any nation to combat a single disease internationally and has been instrumental in changing the trajectory of the HIV/AIDS epidemic.

For example, South Africa has made considerable progress in combating its HIV/AIDS epidemic, aided by initiatives like PEPFAR. The country has notably increased access to HIV testing and prevention methods and significantly scaled up the provision of antiretroviral therapy (ART) through its national programme, which is the largest globally. This expansion of ART has transformed HIV/AIDS into a manageable chronic illness, decreased AIDS-related deaths, and reduced new infections. South Africa has also been a leader in HIV research and has implemented a variety of prevention strategies to cater to the diverse needs of its population, contributing to the international efforts against HIV/AIDS.

South Africa's experience with HIV/AIDS illustrates how a combination of political commitment, international cooperation, robust health systems, and community engagement can tackle a major public health crisis. While challenges remain, the country's achievements in combating HIV/AIDS are a testament to the resilience and potential of African countries in the face of formidable health threats.

COVID-19 Pandemic

The COVID-19 pandemic is another notable example where African countries showed resilience and adaptability. The COVID-19 pandemic presented an unprecedented global challenge, but many African nations responded rapidly and effectively. Drawing upon their experiences from past epidemics, including HIV/AIDS, Ebola, and malaria, these countries showcased their resilience and adaptability.

Early implementation of lockdowns and travel restrictions played a significant role in controlling the virus's spread. Several countries imposed strict measures, such as closure of schools and businesses, curfews, and stay-at-home orders, even before a high number of cases were detected. They also restricted international travel and established rigorous screening procedures at airports and other points of entry.

Public health measures were swiftly put in place, including widespread promotion of mask-wearing, hand hygiene, and social distancing. The public was continuously informed about these measures through various media platforms, including radio, television, and social media, and even through the involvement of community leaders. This ensured that even remote communities were aware of the necessary preventative actions.

Many African nations also leveraged their existing health infrastructure for COVID-19 testing and contact tracing. Senegal, Nigeria, and South Africa demonstrated the importance of local capacity in disease response, with Senegal producing its own COVID-19 testing kits, enabling swift and extensive testing. This self-sufficiency allowed Senegal to avoid global shortages and maintain a steady testing supply, even during supply chain disruptions, showcasing the benefits of local manufacturing and innovation in healthcare.

South Africa repurposed its extensive HIV and TB healthcare infrastructure for COVID-19 testing, quickly adapting diagnostic tools and leveraging community healthcare networks to expand testing and contact tracing. This strategic use of existing health systems facilitated rapid and effective pandemic response.

Nigeria, building on its experience with Ebola, utilised its established network of laboratories to enhance COVID-19 testing capabilities. The existing lab infrastructure, intended for other infectious diseases, was swiftly adapted for COVID-19, significantly increasing Nigeria's testing capacity and strengthening its pandemic management.

These examples underline the crucial role that robust local health systems and past experiences play in addressing new public health challenges, emphasising the need for continued investment in health infrastructure and preparedness.

However, while these examples demonstrate the adaptability and resilience of African health systems, they also highlight the challenges faced due to inadequate health infrastructure and resources. For sustained health security, there is a need for continued investment in strengthening health systems across the continent.

Moreover, lessons from previous epidemics underscored the importance of clear communication. Misinformation and rumours can exacerbate a health crisis, so government authorities, health professionals, and even community leaders took steps to ensure clear, accurate, and timely information was disseminated to the public.

Community engagement was another crucial strategy employed.

Involving community leaders in messaging helped to increase public trust and ensure adherence to health regulations. They played a key role in disseminating health messages, enforcing lockdowns, and even helping in the distribution of aid and supplies.

Cross-border collaboration was also critical. Given the interconnectedness of many African nations, collaboration was necessary to manage the spread of the virus. Organisations such as the African Union and Africa Centres for Disease Control and Prevention (Africa CDC) played key roles in coordinating responses, sharing resources and information, and advocating for the continent on an international stage.

From this, we can see how many African countries demonstrated that lessons learned from previous health crises could be effectively applied to new challenges. Their rapid and proactive responses to the COVID-19 pandemic highlight the significant strides made in their public health sectors, providing valuable lessons for other nations in managing such crises.

Adaptability Amid Economic Uncertainty

However, this chapter extends beyond health crises and examines the broader capability of African countries to adapt and show resilience in other contexts. African countries, such as Ethiopia, have shown remarkable resilience in the face of economic uncertainties induced by global economic shifts and volatile commodity prices. Central to this resilience has been their strategic efforts to diversify their economies.

Ethiopia, traditionally a hub for agriculture and, notably, coffee, has been steering its economy in new directions. The government initiated the Growth and Transformation Plan (GTP) to diversify and build a sustainable economy with the aspiration of achieving middle-income status by 2025. There are two phases of the GTP: GTP I (2010/11–2014/15) and GTP II (2015/16–2019/20).

GTP I laid the foundation for structural transformation and growth across different sectors, such as agriculture, manufacturing, and construction. It aimed to expand physical infrastructure (like roads, railways, and energy), improve access to quality education and health services, and enhance food security and social safety nets.

GTP II built upon the achievements of GTP I and aimed to consolidate the gains in infrastructure development while focusing more on industrialisation, particularly light manufacturing. It prioritised areas like textiles and garments, leather products, and agro-processing, sectors where Ethiopia has a comparative advantage. GTP II also sought to enhance competitiveness and productivity, improve the domestic private sector's capacity, and promote innovation and technology.

A key sector that has seen significant growth in Ethiopia is manufacturing. In the past decade, Ethiopia has sought to position itself as a leading manufacturing hub in Africa. For instance, it has successfully attracted large-scale foreign investment in the textile and garment industry. Industrial parks, like the Hawassa Industrial Park mentioned in earlier chapters, have been set up to facilitate this growth. They provide a complete ecosystem for garment manufacturing, including factories, worker accommodation, and related infrastructure. These parks have attracted big-name brands like H&M and Calvin Klein, turning Ethiopia into a significant player in global supply chains.

The country has also taken steps to develop its service sector, with an emphasis on tourism. Ethiopia boasts diverse cultural heritage and stunning natural landscapes that appeal to international and domestic tourists. The government has capitalised on these assets by investing in tourism infrastructure and promoting Ethiopia as a top tourist destination. The World Travel & Tourism Council (WTTC) reported that the direct contribution of travel and tourism to Ethiopia's GDP was nearly 9.5 percent in 2018.[5]

Furthermore, Ethiopia has made efforts to develop its Information Communication Technology (ICT) sector. The government's Digital Ethiopia 2025 strategy aims to transform the country into a digital economy, with plans to expand digital infrastructure, promote digital skills, and foster digital innovation and entrepreneurship.[6]

These efforts towards economic diversification have not only helped Ethiopia navigate global economic shifts and volatile commodity prices, but they have also generated jobs, reduced poverty, and set the country on a path of sustainable and inclusive growth.

Resilience Against Environmental Challenges

African nations have also shown commendable resilience in addressing environmental challenges, particularly those related to climate change. As the impacts of climate change intensify, these countries have adopted innovative strategies to mitigate and adapt to changing environmental conditions.

Kenya, for instance, has been at the forefront of afforestation efforts to combat deforestation and climate change. The Green Belt Movement (GBM) in Kenya is an excellent example of a grassroots, community-led initiative that simultaneously addresses environmental, economic, and social challenges. The late environmentalist, who was ahead of her time, and Nobel Peace Prize laureate Wangari Maathai started the movement in 1977. Her idea was to counteract the deforestation that was stripping

Kenya of its natural resources while also empowering women economically.

The movement's approach is holistic. The tree-planting initiative is its most known aspect, which contributes to combating climate change, conserving the environment, restoring biodiversity, and promoting sustainable use of natural resources. As mentioned earlier, GBM has planted over 51 million trees since its inception, helping restore degraded environments.

However, the GBM goes beyond just planting trees. It has a strong socio-economic dimension as well. It empowers communities, particularly women, by teaching them to sustainably cultivate and care for tree nurseries. The women are then paid a small stipend for their work, contributing to local economic development and promoting gender equality.

Additionally, the Green Belt Movement also advocates for environmental conservation at the policy level. They engage with governments, international organisations, and civil society to promote legislation and strategies that protect the environment and ensure sustainable land use.[7]

In addition to the Green Belt Movement, the Kenyan government has undertaken its initiatives to increase forest cover. In line with its commitment under the Paris Agreement on climate change, the government aims to increase forest cover to at least 10 percent of the country's total land area. As part of this, they have launched initiatives like the 'Panda Miti, Penda Kenya' (Plant Trees, Love Kenya) campaign to encourage Kenyans to actively participate in tree planting.

These initiatives demonstrate how environmental resilience can be built through community participation, policy action, and international cooperation. They underline the potential of inclusive, sustainable strategies in creating environmental, economic, and social benefits.

Further south, in South Africa, the country has become a global leader in energy efficiency and demand-side management. Despite current challenges of power outages (locally termed 'load shedding'), through its national utility, Eskom, South Africa has implemented one of the world's most successful energy efficiency demand-side management programmes, reducing peak demand and preventing or minimising power outages.

Simultaneously, various African nations have adopted climate-smart agriculture (CSA). CSA has become an increasingly crucial strategy for African nations as they seek to build resilience within their agriculture sector amid the looming threat of climate change. The CSA approach intertwines the three main objectives of sustainably increasing agricultural productivity, adapting and building resilience to climate change, and reducing or removing greenhouse gas emissions where possible.[8]

Agriculture is a predominant part of many African economies, contributing significantly to food security, employment, and gross domestic product (GDP). However, the effects of climate change, including erratic rainfall patterns, prolonged droughts, and increasing temperatures, threaten this vital sector. The integration of CSA techniques offers a way to manage these challenges while maintaining agricultural productivity.

One such technique is agroforestry, the intentional integration of trees into crop and animal farming systems. The benefits of agroforestry are manifold, including improving soil fertility, reducing soil erosion, diversifying farm produce, and sequestering carbon, thus mitigating climate change.

A case in point is Zambia. Zambia, grappling with environmental degradation and climate-induced threats to agriculture, collaborated with the World Agroforestry Centre (ICRAF) to establish the Conservation Farming Unit (CFU). The CFU promotes agroforestry among smallholder farmers to enhance productivity, bolster climate resilience, and boost environmental sustainability. Through training and extension services, farmers learn techniques like integrating the nitrogen-fixing African winter thorn (*Faidherbia albida*) with maize, which enriches the soil and minimises competition for light. The initiative, impacting over 160,000 Zambian farmers, has led to increased yields, climate resilience, diversified produce, and additional income streams. The CFU exemplifies how collaborations can foster sustainable agriculture and rural advancement.

Another popular CSA practice is conservation agriculture (CA). Conservation agriculture has emerged as a promising climate-smart agricultural practice due to its potential to mitigate climate change impacts, especially in regions characterised by erratic rainfall patterns, such as Zimbabwe. CA is based on three primary principles: minimal soil disturbance (no tillage), permanent soil cover (mulching), and crop diversification (rotations and intercropping). Together, these principles contribute to improved soil health, enhanced water retention, and increased crop productivity – all critical under changing climate conditions.[9]

In Zimbabwe, the application of conservation agriculture practices has been shown to increase agricultural resilience and productivity. A study conducted by Frédéric Baudron and colleagues demonstrated the positive impact of CA on maize production, a staple crop in Zimbabwe.[10] The study was carried out across several seasons, which provided valuable insights into CA's role in buffering against weather variability induced by climate change.

The study found that, compared to conventional tillage methods, CA plots consistently yielded more maize. This was attributed to the better water-holding capacity of the soil under CA, resulting from minimal soil disturbance and the organic matter provided by crop residues used as mulch. These conditions were found to be particularly advantageous during seasons with low or erratic rainfall, enhancing crop resilience to drought.

Additionally, the study reported reduced yield variability in CA plots across seasons, a critical feature for farmers facing unpredictable weather patterns. This steadiness offers farmers a more predictable output, contributing to their food and income security under changing climate conditions.

Lastly, it was also noted that the benefits of CA accrued over time, as the continuous application of CA principles led to improved soil health, further emphasising the sustainability of CA practices.

The case of Zimbabwe demonstrates the potential of conservation agriculture as a strategy for climate resilience in African agriculture. It offers a practical, cost-effective, and sustainable solution for smallholder farmers in the face of climate change.

Finally, drought-resistant crops are a crucial component of CSA, especially in areas that face frequent and prolonged periods of low rainfall. The use of these crops is increasingly being recognised as a practical and effective way of ensuring food security in the face of climate change.

In Kenya, the introduction and widespread adoption of drought-tolerant maize varieties have proven beneficial in maintaining and enhancing productivity under drought conditions. Maize is a staple food for the majority of Kenya's population, and the country's agriculture is predominantly rain-fed. Hence, periods of low rainfall significantly impact maize production and, consequently, food security.

A 2015 study by Monica Fisher and colleagues (2015) documented the benefits of adopting drought-tolerant maize in Kenya.[11] According to their research, farmers who grew drought-tolerant maize varieties were able to harvest more maize than those who cultivated non-drought-tolerant varieties. This higher yield was particularly noticeable during drought seasons, thus reducing the vulnerability of farmers to climatic shocks.

In addition to the direct benefits of enhanced yield, the use of drought-tolerant maize also offered indirect benefits. It improved farmers' food and income security, reduced the need for riskier and more expensive coping strategies (like selling off assets), and allowed for greater investment in health and education. Furthermore, it fostered a sense of resilience and empowerment among farmers, as they were better equipped to deal with the effects of climate change.

The experience of Kenya underlines the potential of drought-resistant crops as a practical and effective CSA strategy. It demonstrates how these varieties can contribute to building resilience and enhancing food security under changing climate conditions.

Thus, CSA techniques represent a viable approach for African countries to build resilience in their agricultural sectors, securing food supply, livelihoods, and economic stability in the face of climate change.

These examples demonstrate the innovative strategies that African nations are implementing in response to climate change. However, these efforts often face challenges, including limited financial resources, lack of technical expertise, and institutional constraints. Addressing these challenges will be crucial in ensuring the sustainability and effectiveness of these resilience-building measures.

Conclusively, this chapter underscores that adaptability and resilience are invaluable assets for the progress of African nations. Whether in the face of health crises, economic shocks, or climate change, Africa's capacity to adjust, endure, and bounce back plays a significant role in its journey towards prosperity.

Moving on to Chapter 19, we will take a deep dive into health and wellness development and discuss why a robust and comprehensive healthcare system is crucial to any nation's future and development.

CHAPTER 19

HEALTH AND WELLNESS DEVELOPMENT

Health and wellness development in Africa has the potential to bring about transformative societal change. A healthy society is not only happy but also productive.

The Importance of Robust Health Systems

Robust health systems play a pivotal role in shaping the socio-economic fabric of a society. In our continent of Africa, where many nations grapple with a plethora of health challenges, the emphasis on health and wellness development is paramount. By focusing on comprehensive healthcare, disease prevention, and overall wellbeing, there's an opportunity to significantly improve the quality of life for people on the continent, leading to a ripple effect of positive outcomes in various societal domains.

Comprehensive Healthcare

Comprehensive healthcare refers to a health system that encapsulates the entire spectrum of medical needs, ranging from preventive measures to critical care services. Such an all-encompassing approach ensures that individuals receive timely care throughout their lives, from routine check-ups and vaccinations to specialised treatments for severe illnesses. A prime illustration of the benefits of comprehensive healthcare is seen in Rwanda, where the nation has made considerable strides in improving its healthcare delivery.

As mentioned several times in this book, in the early 2000s, Rwanda was grappling with the aftermath of its devastating genocide and faced numerous health challenges, including a high burden of infectious diseases and limited access to medical services. However, the country recognised that strengthening its healthcare system was imperative for its broader socio-economic revival.

To this end, Rwanda introduced community-based health insurance schemes. Known locally as 'Mutuelles de Santé', these schemes were designed to make healthcare more affordable and accessible to the general populace. Instead of individuals bearing the brunt of medical expenses out of pocket, which often deterred them from seeking care, these community-backed funds ensured that a majority of the costs were covered, making healthcare services more accessible to all, regardless of their economic status.[1]

The implementation of these insurance schemes had a transformative effect. For example, there was a noticeable increase in institutional deliveries, which is crucial for reducing maternal and neonatal mortality. Mothers who might have given birth at home without professional medical assistance due to financial constraints could now afford to do so in healthcare facilities, ensuring safer deliveries and immediate medical intervention if complications arose.

Additionally, with the new-found financial protection from these schemes, many Rwandans began accessing preventative care services, such as regular health check-ups and screenings. This shift is particularly significant in the context of diseases like malaria and HIV, where early detection and treatment can make a world of difference.

Furthermore, Rwanda's commitment to comprehensive healthcare was not limited to just financing. The nation also invested in strengthening its primary healthcare network, training community health workers, and ensuring that even remote villages had access to essential health services. These health workers played a pivotal role in promoting preventive healthcare measures, providing basic treatments, and referring more complicated cases to larger health facilities.

The impact of these concerted efforts has been profound. By 2012, Rwanda had witnessed substantial improvements in health outcomes. Child mortality rates plummeted, and there was a significant decline in deaths from preventable diseases.[2] The success story of Rwanda underscores the immense potential of comprehensive healthcare and serves as a beacon for other nations striving to optimise their health systems for the wellbeing of their citizens.

Then there's Botswana, which has been at the forefront of the battle against HIV/AIDS in Africa, as mentioned in earlier chapters. In the early 2000s, the country faced a crisis – close to 25 percent of its adult population was infected with HIV. The implications of this high infection rate were profound, from strained healthcare facilities to declining life expectancy.

Realising the magnitude of the crisis, the Botswana government, in collaboration with international partners, initiated a comprehensive response. One of the earliest and most significant interventions was the launch of a universal free antiretroviral treatment (ART) programme in 2002. Before this, antiretroviral therapy was mainly accessible to those who could afford it, creating disparities in treatment access. However, Botswana's move to provide these treatments free of charge ensured that all HIV-positive citizens could access life-saving medication, regardless of their financial standing.

Coupled with the provision of free ART, Botswana invested in extensive testing campaigns. The goal was to ensure that everyone knew their HIV status. Early detection meant early initiation of treatment, which not only improved the life expectancy of those infected but also reduced the chances of transmission to others. For instance, the 'Treat All' strategy, endorsed by the World Health Organisation, was adopted by Botswana, allowing all HIV-positive individuals to receive treatment regardless of their CD4 count, thus accelerating treatment access.

Robust public education efforts were another cornerstone of Botswana's strategy. The government, with support from organisations like UNAIDS and the World Health Organisation, launched public campaigns that emphasised the importance of regular testing, safe sexual practices, and adherence to medication. These campaigns played a pivotal role in destigmatising the disease, which, in turn, encouraged more people to get tested and seek treatment.

The combination of these interventions bore fruit. By the mid-2010s, there was substantial evidence that the HIV epidemic in Botswana was stabilising, with the widespread provision of ART being associated with significant reductions in HIV/AIDS-related mortality. As a result, life expectancy, which had plummeted due to the epidemic, began to rise again.

Furthermore, the 'Botswana Combination Prevention Project', a study funded by the US President's Emergency Plan for AIDS Relief (PEPFAR), highlighted that comprehensive HIV prevention and treatment interventions, like the ones employed in Botswana, led to a significant decline in new HIV infections.[3]

Botswana's proactive and holistic approach to the HIV/AIDS epidemic is a testament to what can be achieved when there's political will, robust public health interventions, and international collaboration. The nation's successes serve as a model for other countries grappling with similar public health challenges.

Each of these countries, in their unique ways, highlights the transformative power of comprehensive and community-focused healthcare strategies. While challenges persist, the strides made by these nations serve as a testament to what is possible with the right policies, investments, and community engagement in the realm of public health in Africa.

Disease Prevention

Disease prevention, as a fundamental pillar of public health, holds profound implications for the health and economic wellbeing of populations. Not only does it help reduce morbidity and mortality rates, but prevention is often found to be more cost-effective than treatment. This economic argument for prevention resonates even more in regions with strained healthcare systems and limited resources, such as many countries on our continent of Africa.

One of the remarkable triumphs in preventive medicine has been vaccination campaigns. The impact of vaccination campaigns on public health cannot be overstated.

Another standout example is the fight against meningitis in the African meningitis belt, which spans from Senegal in the west to Ethiopia in the east. This vast region faced severe challenges due to this disease, often witnessing thousands of cases each year. These outbreaks not only had health implications but also resulted in significant economic and social impacts. For communities in the meningitis belt, the recurring epidemics disrupted daily life, impacted economies, and put immense stress on already over-stretched healthcare systems.

The introduction of the MenAfriVac vaccine in 2010 marked a turning point in the fight against meningitis in the region. Developed specifically for Africa, MenAfriVac targeted the meningococcal group A bacteria – the predominant cause of meningitis epidemics in the region. Unlike previous vaccines, MenAfriVac was designed to provide longer-lasting protection, was more affordable, and could be stored without refrigeration for up to four days, making it particularly well-suited to the conditions in many parts of Africa.[4]

With a concerted effort from international and local health agencies, large-scale mass vaccination campaigns were launched. These campaigns aimed to inoculate people, especially those between ages 1 and 29, across the meningitis belt. The results were nothing short of remarkable. Within a short span of time after the introduction of the vaccine, there was a dramatic drop in the number of meningitis A cases. By 2015, just five years after the vaccine's introduction, the WHO reported that countries that had conducted these mass vaccination campaigns with MenAfriVac saw a staggering 99 percent reduction in confirmed meningitis A cases.[5]

Yet, the importance of prevention isn't limited to infectious diseases alone. Non-communicable diseases (NCDs), such as heart disease, diabetes, and cancer, are increasingly prevalent in Africa. Strategies like promoting healthy diets, encouraging physical activity, and anti-smoking campaigns can play an instrumental role in curbing the rise of NCDs. A study titled 'Tackling NCD in LMIC: Achievements and Lessons Learned from the NHL-BI-UnitedHealth Global Health Centers of Excellence Programme', published in the *Global Heart* journal in 2016, underscored the value of multifaceted interventions in preventing and controlling NCDs in low- and middle-income countries. Recognising that a single approach wouldn't be sufficient, the Centres of Excellence adopted a multi-pronged strategy. This included community engagement, knowledge dissemination, capacity building, and evidence-based interventions.[6]

For example, in addressing heart diseases, interventions didn't just focus on medical treatments. Instead, they emphasised the importance of lifestyle changes, such as adopting healthier diets and encouraging more physical activity. Similarly, for diseases like diabetes, awareness campaigns were launched to educate communities about the risks of excessive sugar intake and the importance of regular health check-ups.

One of the pivotal findings of the study was the importance of localising interventions. While NCDs might be a global challenge, the specific conditions, cultural practices, and socio-economic realities of each country or region influence how they manifest and how they can be best addressed. Thus, interventions tailored to local contexts, leveraging local expertise, and in collaboration with local communities were found to be most effective.

Another significant takeaway was the value of collaboration and capacity building. The NHLBI-UnitedHealth initiative brought together experts from various fields, creating a cross-disciplinary approach to tackle NCDs. This collaborative ethos extended beyond just experts; there was also an emphasis on community engagement and empowerment, ensuring that solutions were not just imposed but collaboratively crafted.

From this, we can see that while treating diseases is essential, focusing on preventive strategies often yields long-term benefits, both in terms of health outcomes and economic savings. The successes of vaccination campaigns and lifestyle interventions in Africa underscore the importance of a proactive approach to public health.

Quality Over Quantity

A health system's success isn't merely about the number of hospitals or doctors but also the quality of care provided. The emphasis on quality over quantity in healthcare systems underscores the idea that the mere presence of numerous medical facilities or a vast number of professionals does not necessarily translate to optimal health outcomes for the population. Instead, it's the calibre of care they provide that's paramount. South Africa, for instance, has been acutely aware of this dynamic and has taken notable steps to elevate the standard of care in its healthcare establishments.[7]

The introduction of the National Core Standards for Health Establishments by the South African Department of Health in 2011 was a milestone in this pursuit. These standards were formulated to set a clear benchmark for healthcare quality in the nation, ensuring that every establishment, regardless of its size or location, adheres to a baseline level of care that ensures patient safety and wellbeing.

One tangible example from the National Core Standards pertains to the 'Patient Rights' domain. This domain emphasises the importance of treating patients with respect and dignity, ensuring that their privacy is maintained and that they are well-informed about their health conditions and treatment options. By focusing on such rights, the standards aim to foster a patient-centric healthcare environment where individual needs and concerns are given paramount importance.

Another critical aspect detailed in the standards is the 'Clinical Governance and Clinical Care' domain. This segment of the standards focuses on the proper management of clinical risks, the efficacy of clinical services, and ensuring that clinical care is evidence-based. For instance, healthcare facilities are encouraged to have protocols in place for critical conditions like sepsis or heart attacks, ensuring that every patient receives consistent, evidence-backed care. References to such evidence-based protocols can be found in international journals such as *The Lancet* and the *Journal of Clinical Epidemiology*.

Moreover, to ensure that these standards are more than just ink on paper, the South African Department of Health established the Office of Health Standards Compliance (OHSC). This body is tasked with inspecting health establishments to verify their adherence to the National Core Standards. The OHSC's work and its impact on enhancing healthcare quality in the country have been explored in various academic articles, such as those published in the *South African Medical Journal*.

Thus, South Africa's proactive approach, as exemplified by the introduction of the National Core Standards for Health Establishments, highlights the global shift in healthcare – moving from a quantitative benchmarking system to one that prioritises qualitative outcomes. Such endeavours not only enhance the immediate patient experience but also pave the way for better overall health outcomes for the broader population.

Impacts on Quality of Life and Longevity

A direct consequence of improved healthcare is increased life expectancy. Life expectancy, often used as an indicator of the health and wellbeing of a population, has risen in many countries around the world. One of the most dramatic improvements has been observed in developing countries, including those on our own continent of Africa, where various healthcare interventions have been employed to combat widespread diseases and conditions. A remarkable example of this is Kenya.

Kenya's rise in life expectancy from 53 years in 2000 to 66 years in 2019 serves as proof of the power of targeted healthcare initiatives.[8] In just under two decades, Kenya has experienced a significant near 13-year increase in life expectancy. Several factors contribute to this commendable achievement.

The substantial increase in life expectancy can be heavily attributed to marked reductions in childhood mortalities. An evident testament to this advancement is the dramatic decline in under-five mortality rates, which plummeted by 58 percent from 1990 to 2019, as highlighted by UNICEF.[9]

This decline is not merely a numerical victory; it signifies countless young lives spared and family units sustained. Crucial to this transformation have been immunisation campaigns. These programmes, often championed by international organisations and governments, have broadened the scope of routine vaccinations against prevalent diseases like measles, polio, and tuberculosis. By making these vaccines accessible even in the remotest of regions, numerous children have been shielded from diseases that were once lethal.

Alongside this, maternal healthcare has seen significant enhancements. The intertwined health of the mother and child has been given prime attention, with improvements in prenatal, delivery, and postnatal care practices. With more skilled birth attendants, better healthcare facilities, and a greater emphasis on antenatal visits, both mothers and their babies now have an increased survival rate. In addition, tackling malnutrition has been a priority. By focusing on nutritional programmes for children and expectant mothers, stressing the importance of breastfeeding, providing vital vitamin supplements, and advocating for balanced diets and clean water, children now have a more robust foundation for a healthy future.

Kenya's struggle with HIV/AIDS over the years resembles the daunting challenge faced by many African countries. This health crisis prompted swift and comprehensive interventions that have since reshaped the HIV/AIDS landscape in Kenya. A cornerstone of this transformation has been the expansive provision of antiretroviral treatment (ART) programmes. These drugs, which are crucial for managing the virus's progression, have seen increased availability and affordability, thanks to collaborations between the Kenyan government, the WHO, and the Global Fund. By 2018, a remarkable two-thirds of Kenyans living with HIV had access to ART. Alongside treatment, vast awareness campaigns have been instrumental in debunking myths about the virus, underlining the need for testing and elucidating transmission modes. High-profile personalities have supported these initiatives, amplifying their impact. On the prevention front, strategies such as promoting condom use, harm reduction for drug users, and medical male circumcision have been employed. Significant efforts have also been made to curb mother-to-child transmission, granting pregnant women the necessary testing and medication. International organisations like PEPFAR have played a pivotal role in funding these initiatives. Today, the decrease in new HIV infections and HIV-related deaths in Kenya stands as a beacon of hope, demonstrating the might of collaborative health endeavours.

Malaria, a longstanding health challenge in Kenya, has also seen remarkable control and management in recent years. A multipronged strategy has been deployed against this disease. One of the primary defences has been the distribution of insecticide-treated nets (ITNs). With backing from international entities like the Global Fund and WHO, there have been extensive campaigns to distribute these nets, especially in high-risk areas. Coupled with this has been health education, ensuring people understand the significance of these nets and their maintenance. Additionally, indoor residual spraying (IRS) has been introduced in high-transmission regions. This technique, which involves spraying home interiors with insecticides that kill mosquitoes, offers an added layer of protection against malaria when combined with ITN use.

Kenya's commendable rise in life expectancy is, therefore, a combination of multiple interventions, collaborations, and persistent efforts across various health challenges.

Lastly, advances in the pharmaceutical domain have been pivotal in the fight against malaria in Kenya. The introduction of effective antimalarial drugs, such as artemisinin-based combination therapies (ACTs), has radically transformed the approach to managing malaria cases. The unparalleled efficacy of these drugs in eradicating the malaria parasite assures swifter recovery for patients, mitigating the progression into severe disease stages.

In tandem, the advent of rapid diagnostic tests has expedited the detection and treatment of malaria. To bolster these achievements, the Kenyan government, hand in hand with healthcare associates, has prioritised the frequent training of health workers and community health volunteers, ensuring malaria patients receive timely and appropriate care. In addition, there's a community-based test, treat, and track (T3) surveillance and response mechanism.[10] Furthermore, Kenya began its distribution campaign for long-lasting insecticide treated mosquito nets (LLINs) in November 2023.

Moreover, maternal health has been a focal point in the global health sphere, and Kenya's journey in enhancing this sector has been both significant and transformative. The maternal mortality rate serves as a paramount indicator of a country's health infrastructure and its dedication to women's health. Over the years, Kenya has registered a marked decline in this rate, attributable to thoughtful interventions, collaborative efforts, and policy implementation. Antenatal care stands as a protective shield, bolstering both maternal and neonatal health. By attending regular antenatal check-ups, women allow healthcare professionals to vigilantly monitor the health of both the mother and the unborn child, pre-emptively identifying potential complications. With the WHO's recommendation of a minimum of four antenatal visits during pregnancy, Kenya has heightened its efforts to urge more expectant mothers to adhere to this guideline. These consultations are comprehensive, encompassing nutritional guidance, malaria prophylaxis in endemic areas, tetanus immunisations, and HIV screenings. It's noted that nearly 5000 women and girls die annually from pregnancy and childbirth complications.[11] However, the country has seen some progress, with access to skilled birth attendance increasing from 62 percent to about 70 percent over a seven-year period. There are also local initiatives being developed to improve transportation to health facilities for pregnant women.[12]

The importance of having skilled personnel during childbirth cannot be overstated, as their presence drastically reduces the risk of maternal mortality. These professionals, whether they are doctors, nurses, or midwives, bring to the table a wealth of expertise, crucial for managing standard deliveries and detecting complications necessitating advanced interventions. A concerted effort in Kenya aims to escalate the number of births supervised by such skilled attendants. This initiative is complemented by the introduction of mobile health clinics, community-centric programmes, and equipping traditional birth attendants with knowledge to redirect complex cases to better-equipped facilities. Furthermore, acknowledging the unforeseeable intricacies of childbirth, there's a pronounced focus on making emergency obstetric care services widely available. Such services, adept at managing severe complications like postpartum haemorrhage or eclampsia, have become more accessible as health institutions across Kenya bolster their capabilities. The collective endeavours in these areas, championed by both the Kenyan government and global allies, are testimony to the monumental progress in maternal health. Reinforcing this commitment, policies have been rolled out to offer free maternal services in public health establishments, effectively eliminating financial impediments.

Beyond the realms of medicines and treatments, the metamorphosis of healthcare is deeply intertwined with the quality of infrastructure and the proficiency of healthcare providers. In Kenya, an integrated approach to ameliorate healthcare infrastructure and professional training has been instrumental in augmenting both the reach and calibre of care, translating to better health outcomes for its residents. Fundamental to this transformation has been the augmentation and modernisation of healthcare facilities. This not only includes the inception of new medical establishments but also the rejuvenation of existing ones, aligning them with the evolving needs of the populace. Such enhancements permeate both urban and rural landscapes of the country.

Parallelly, initiatives focusing on the education and skill development of medical professionals underscore the belief that the strength of a healthcare system is mirrored by its workforce. The digital wave, too, has lapped the shores of Kenya's healthcare, with telemedicine emerging as a beacon of hope. By leveraging technology, geographical and logistical barriers are dissolved, enabling patients in remote locations to seek expert advice, procure diagnoses, and even receive prescriptions. This digital bridge not only conserves time and resources but also facilitates early medical interventions, potentially life-saving in critical scenarios. It also serves as a conduit for continuous learning for medical professionals, keeping them abreast of the latest medical breakthroughs and methodologies.

In summation, this comprehensive approach to infrastructure, professional training, and technological integration offers a glimpse into the bright future of Kenya's healthcare. These strides, grounded in strategic policymaking and collaborations, are vital in ensuring that each Kenyan, irrespective of their geographical location, is entitled to exemplary healthcare, laying the groundwork for a thriving nation.

In the larger scheme of economic development, the symbiotic relationship between health and economic growth is unmistakable. A healthy populace forms the bedrock of a thriving economy. When individuals are liberated from the shackles of severe diseases and enjoy a commendable quality of life, they become active contributors to economic endeavours. This intricate correlation becomes evident when one evaluates the economic ramifications of health interventions, like those targeting malaria prevention. The narrative of Kenya epitomises how sustained, targeted healthcare strategies can revolutionise the lives of countless individuals, laying the foundation for a prosperous future generation.

Mental Health

Mental health, a once sidelined aspect of healthcare, has in recent years gained the recognition it rightfully deserves as an essential facet of holistic wellbeing. Historically, many cultures and societies, due to a combination of stigma, lack of awareness, and inadequate resources, did not address mental health issues with the urgency and sensitivity they warranted. However, the contemporary global health narrative underscores the importance of mental wellbeing, resonating with the understanding that the mind and body are intrinsically linked and one cannot be truly healthy without the other.

Nigeria's evolving approach to mental health offers a compelling case study of this shift in perspective. A nation with diverse cultures and a rich history, Nigeria, like many other countries, has had its challenges in confronting and addressing mental health concerns. The weight of traditional beliefs, sociocultural misconceptions, and a paucity of specialised care facilities and professionals has often made the mental health landscape challenging.[13]

However, recognising the critical nature of mental health, Nigeria has started to prioritise it at both the policy and grassroots levels. The Mental Health Action Committee stands as a testament to this new-found focus. This initiative aims at not just bringing mental health into mainstream health discussions but also ensuring that actionable and sustainable strategies are in place. One of its core objectives is to raise awareness about mental health issues, dispelling myths and destigmatising mental illnesses. Such endeavours are vital, especially in regions where misconceptions can often lead to ostracisation or harmful treatments.[14]

Furthermore, the committee focuses on improving care for those with mental health issues. This is not just about providing medical interventions but also ensuring a supportive ecosystem. It involves training more mental health professionals, creating accessible and culturally sensitive care centres, and fostering community support networks. Emphasising community involvement ensures that mental health care is not just clinical but also inclusive, compassionate, and tailored to the unique cultural nuances of the diverse Nigerian populace.

The efforts in Nigeria mirror a broader global trend, where mental health is finally getting the attention and resources it has long deserved. As more countries prioritise mental wellbeing, recognising its critical role in societal development, the hope is for a future where mental health issues are approached with the same urgency, understanding, and compassion as any other health challenge.

Community Engagement

Active involvement of community members in health and wellness programmes isn't just a progressive strategy but also a necessity for the success of such programmes. The rationale behind this is straightforward: when communities have a stake in their health initiatives, when they are not mere recipients but active participants, they are more invested in the programme's success, understand its intricacies, and can better adapt it to suit their unique contexts.

Ethiopia's Health Extension Programme (HEP), mentioned earlier, offers a textbook example of the efficacy of community-led health interventions. Traditionally, the vast geographical expanse of Ethiopia combined with varied terrains, diverse populations, and limited resources made it challenging to provide uniform healthcare access across the nation. To address this disparity and enhance grassroots healthcare delivery, Ethiopia rolled out the HEP, an innovative initiative that fundamentally banked on the power of community engagement.[15]

Central to the HEP's design was the training of local women, chosen from their communities, to become health extension workers (HEWs). By focusing on women, especially those with respect and influence within their communities, the programme tapped into a potent force of change. These women underwent rigorous training that equipped them with skills to provide a range of basic health services, from maternal and child health advice to sanitation practices and disease prevention.

This community-centric approach had manifold advantages. First, being from the community themselves, HEWs understood the cultural, social, and logistical nuances that outsiders might overlook. Their advice, therefore, wasn't generic; it was tailored to the unique needs and challenges of their community, making it more likely to be accepted and acted upon.

Secondly, as trusted members of the community, HEWs faced less resistance. Their interventions were not viewed with scepticism, which can often be the case when external agents try to introduce new health practices. Instead, their recommendations were more readily embraced, leading to more profound and sustained behavioural changes.

The results of this programme have been nothing short of transformative. Health indicators across regions that implemented the HEP witnessed notable improvements. Rates of immunisation, antenatal care attendance, and adoption of hygienic practices saw significant upticks. Similarly, there was a notable decline in preventable diseases and conditions, testament to the programme's success in enhancing preventive healthcare.[16]

To sum it all up, the success of Ethiopia's HEP underscores the pivotal role that community engagement and participation play in health interventions. By leveraging the local knowledge, trust, and influence of community members, health programmes can achieve results that are not only statistically impressive but also sustainable and deeply ingrained in the community's fabric. Such initiatives serve as beacons, illuminating the path for other nations striving to improve their healthcare outcomes through community-led strategies.

Nutrition and Lifestyle

Nutrition and lifestyle choices are often fundamental determinants of overall health and wellbeing. As societies worldwide grapple with the growing burden of non-communicable diseases (NCDs) like diabetes, hypertension, and cardiovascular disorders, the importance of early intervention becomes evident. Good nutritional habits formed during childhood not only foster immediate health benefits but also serve as a bulwark against future health complications.

Ghana's school feeding programme is an apt demonstration of this principle in action. Recognising the dual challenges of malnutrition and the looming threat of NCDs, the Ghanaian government initiated the Ghana School Feeding Programme (GSFP). It was started in 2005 as an initiative of the Comprehensive Africa Agricultural Development Programme (CAADP) Pillar 3, which seeks to enhance food security and reduce hunger in line with the UN Millennium Development Goals (MDGs) on hunger, poverty, and malnutrition.

The immediate objectives of the GSFP were to increase school enrolment, attendance, and retention, reduce short-term hunger and malnutrition among kindergarten and primary school children, and boost domestic food production. The long-term objectives of the programme were to contribute to poverty reduction and improving food security. By 2016, the programme had achieved feeding 1.69 million children, which is 37.4 percent of national coverage. The government also approved to expand the programme to 3 million school children by July 2016.[17]

Another initiative called the Food for All Ghana School Feeding programme was started in 2016, establishing school feeding kitchens in the poorest and unreached primary schools in order to provide a daily, hot, nutritious meal to students throughout the school year.

These programmes' primary objective is to provide school children with balanced, nutritious meals, ensuring that they receive the necessary nutrients for growth, cognitive development, and overall health.

The impact of such programmes isn't limited to immediate nutritional benefits. When children have access to nutritious food, it sets a foundation for healthy eating habits that can last a lifetime. By instilling these habits at an early age, there's a higher likelihood that children will make healthier food choices in adulthood, reducing the risk of NCDs. Additionally, well-nourished children are more attentive and perform better academically, which can have positive long-term socio-economic repercussions.

Turning our gaze to Central Africa, Rwanda presents an example of similar success. Rwanda's school health and nutrition programme, supported by various international organisations, seeks to provide children with micronutrient-rich meals, health check-ups, and nutrition education. This multifaceted approach ensures that children not only receive nourishing meals but are also educated about the importance of nutrition and healthy living.[18]

The Rwandan programme emphasises locally sourced foods, which not only guarantees freshness but also supports local farmers and boosts the domestic agricultural sector. This integrated approach has several cascading benefits. It not only nourishes the young but also stimulates the local economy, ensuring sustainability and community support.

Furthermore, Rwanda's school nutrition initiative incorporates deworming and health check-ups. These integrated health interventions ensure that children are free from common ailments that might inhibit nutrient absorption or overall wellbeing, further amplifying the programme's impact.

Coming to Southern Africa, South Africa, with its diverse population and economic might within the African continent, has recognised the pivotal role of nutrition and lifestyle in shaping the health outcomes of its citizens. As a result, the country has initiated a myriad of programmes and policies to improve nutritional status and promote healthier lifestyles, especially among its younger population.

But South Africa's battle with nutrition and lifestyle challenges isn't confined to the younger generation. The country has seen a surge in non-communicable diseases, primarily linked to lifestyle choices. Recognising this, the Department of Health launched the

Strategic Plan for the Prevention and Control of Non-Communicable Diseases. This comprehensive plan targets issues like obesity, diabetes, and hypertension, which are increasingly prevalent in the South African population.[19]

Integral to this strategic plan is the focus on nutrition and active living. The government has initiated campaigns to reduce salt and sugar intake, promote the consumption of fruits and vegetables, and emphasise the dangers of excessive alcohol and tobacco use. To support active lifestyles, there's been a drive to create more public spaces like parks and recreation centres, allowing citizens to engage in physical activity.

Furthermore, South Africa's approach to health and nutrition has been collaborative. The government has actively sought partnerships with civil society, the private sector, and international organisations. These collaborations aim to widen the reach of health campaigns, increase resources for public health programmes, and share best practices.

A focus on health and wellness development in Africa will bring about transformative societal change. By ensuring that health systems are robust, comprehensive, and efficient, there's an opportunity to elevate not only the quality of individual lives but also the socio-economic trajectory of nations.

In the next chapter, we will focus on Enterprising Africa Regional Network (Pty) Ltd (EARN), our own South African purpose-driven but for-profit organisation and its role in developing the next generation of successful African agripreneurs. We will explore EARN's 360-degree agripreneur development programme and how it equips young people with the skills and knowledge needed to establish and manage successful businesses.

CHAPTER 20

A CASE STUDY: FOSTERING ENTREPRENEURSHIP IN AFRICA

In our journey through this book, Chapter 3 highlighted Africa's vast natural resources, and Chapter 4 introduced us to Africa's young and dynamic demographic. Together, these strengths present an opportunity for Africa to soar. But, for this to happen, they need to intertwine with the pillars of economic development we explored from chapters 5 to 19. As the world progresses deeper into the 21st century, there's an urgency to prepare our youth for an ever-evolving economic world, especially in Africa where over 60 percent are aged under 25. Harnessing the power of this youthful demographic means equipping them with the right skills and creating economic participation avenues.

To bring these concepts to life, let's delve into the story of Enterprising Africa Regional Network (Pty) Ltd, commonly known as 'EARN'. EARN was established in September 2014, and it stands as a beacon of what's possible, being a purpose-driven, profit-oriented entity with a mission: shaping the young African generation into prosperous entrepreneurs. EARN's focus is on empowering a new generation of young Africans to run thriving, sustainable businesses that contribute to job creation and prosperity in South Africa, and later across the continent.

With a rapidly growing young population, Africa holds the key to a wealth of expertise and a vast market for products and services. While EARN has developed commercial business entities in **agriculture, technology, real estate,** and **business support solutions,** EARN's primary objective remains the development of young entrepreneurs. In just over nine years, EARN has grown from a nascent idea to 150 people operating across five EARN Group subsidiaries. Through organisations like EARN and working with other like-minded people and organisations across Africa and elsewhere in the world, we envision building a future where these young minds foster businesses that not only thrive but also boost job creation and wealth, starting in South Africa and eventually rippling across the entire African continent.

Through our work, we aim to create a world where young women have the same opportunities as their male peers to access resources, information, and networks. We believe that by empowering young women in agriculture, we can drive economic growth, reduce poverty, and promote sustainable development across Africa. We are deeply committed to building a more equitable and sustainable

Africa, and we believe that empowering young men and women is essential to achieving this goal.

Background

Upon acquiring the 8.5-hectare (21-acre) farm in Centurion, Gauteng Province of South Africa, in 2012, our initial plan was to construct a residential estate. But by 2014, we saw a looming issue of rising unemployment in South Africa. We recognised then that the problem was bigger than any single entity and that this newly acquired farm could serve as a beacon of hope, so we changed the original plan.

Data from Statistics South Africa painted a sombre picture. From 2008 to 2014, despite the modest growth in employment, the unemployment rate continued to increase.[1] This imbalance, coupled with educational disparities, led to an alarming spike in unemployment, especially among the youth. By 2014, a staggering half of the country's young populace was jobless, struggling to find roles that matched their skill sets. As we fast-forward to 2023, this predicament has further intensified, with about two-thirds of the job-seeking youth still unemployed.

Though this situation might seem unique to South Africa, similar narratives can be found across the African continent. However, in adversity often lies the seed of opportunity. So, in 2014 as we pondered potential solutions, the idea of channelling the untapped entrepreneurial potential of the youth began to emerge. Thus, amid these challenges, the vision for EARN was born. Our goal became clear: to cultivate the entrepreneurial ambitions of the youth, providing them with the tools and knowledge to forge their paths, thereby addressing the unemployment crisis at its root.

The Fourth Economy

At the time I had just finished reading *The Fourth Economy: Inventing Western Civilization* by Ron Davison. After studying a 700-year progression of Western history, a pattern in the world economy became evident. Davison charted three major economic periods that held significant influence. Between 1300 and 1700, spanning 400 years, the agricultural revolution dominated, with land as its primary constraint. Once this limitation was surpassed, the 18th century, from 1700 to 1900, experienced the industrial revolution for 200 years, where capital became the central bottleneck. The 20th century, from 1900 to 2000, marked a 100-year-long knowledge era, emphasising the constraints of knowledge and skills. Davison then projected that we would move into the fourth economy, potentially lasting until 2050, which would pivot around entrepreneurship.[2] I realised at that moment that the reason for the rising unemployment was that despite the fact that we were in the fourth economy, our country and much of the world was operating in the wrong economy – that is, the third economy.

It was intriguing to observe that each economic phase's duration seemed to halve from its predecessor, indicating an accelerating pace of global transformation. The knowledge era, particularly, had catalysed a mass movement towards higher education in the 20th century. However, this surge also posed challenges, as the job market began to saturate with knowledge workers. Many found their academic qualifications misaligned with evolving market needs. Moreover, while technology advancements brought numerous benefits, automation and the impending emergence of various technologies threatened to intensify unemployment issues further.

I notice that Africa, with its burgeoning youth demographic, is confronted with an amplified version of this challenge. Despite the global shift towards entrepreneurship, Africa continues to contend with its unique struggles. There are evident disparities in quality education across regions, leading to a variance in skill acquisition. Young African entrepreneurs also face hurdles in getting proper entrepreneur training and development, including securing initial capital, given the lack of supportive financial structures on our continent.

Delving deeper into these economic epochs, I discerned a recurring theme. At the brink of every economic shift, persisting in the investments of the fading era yielded diminishing returns. The prevalent unemployment, particularly among the youth, as observed earlier, seems to be a consequence of this transitional friction between the knowledge-based third economy and the emerging entrepreneurship-driven fourth economy.

The implication is clear: pouring more resources into an outdated model would no longer produce desired outcomes. As knowledge becomes widely accessible due to technological advancements, the focus must shift from mere knowledge acquisition to entrepreneurial endeavours. If the world economy is to advance, fostering entrepreneurship becomes paramount.

According to Statista, employment numbers from one of Europe's economic giants, Germany, further underlines this assertion. In 2018, small and medium enterprises (SMEs) employed 63.2 percent of the German workforce. Between 2011 and 2018, the contribution of SMEs to the German economy surged from 745 billion Euros to 968 billion Euros.[3] These figures are revelatory. African nations that can discern this global economic trend, emulate models like Germany, and cultivate an environment conducive to entrepreneurship, stand to gain immensely.

Considering Africa's vast diversity, entrepreneurship appeared as a potent catalyst for change. Entrepreneurs inherently recognise local issues and innovate tailored solutions. By fostering entrepreneurship, Africa could potentially transition from relying on a few significant employers to a broader landscape speckled with SMEs, thereby significantly alleviating unemployment. These insights were seminal. Recognising the patterns of global economic shifts, the tangible promise entrepreneurship held for Africa, and the continent's unique challenges, I was inspired. It became evident that championing the entrepreneurial spirit was pivotal not just for addressing immediate concerns but also for positioning Africa to seize the vast opportunities the future held.

Massive Transformative Purpose

However, dealing with any challenge effectively in any organisation requires a clear purpose to unify and drive the team. This should not be any purpose; you must have a strong Massive Transformative Purpose or MTP. The term Massive Transformative Purpose was coined by Salim Ismail, founder of OpenExO, and popularised by Peter H Diamandis, founder and chairman of the XPRIZE Foundation and Singularity University. The concept of MTP is about defining a clear and compelling goal that inspires and drives a team or organisation to achieve significant and positive transformational change in the world. It is a guiding principle that helps focus efforts and resources towards a meaningful and impactful objective.

An MTP goes beyond the scope of regular business goals; it provides a clear direction for personal and organisational growth, ignites passion, and aligns with an individual or company's deepest values.

For an initiative to succeed, particularly one that aims to address substantial challenges, it requires a purpose that's not just clear but also ambitious and motivational. The concept of an MTP is drawn from the belief that having a higher purpose, particularly one that is centred on transforming the world or a sector of it, can serve as a powerful motivator. It guides decision-making, fosters resilience, and provides a consistent, overarching goal that drives long-term efforts. Having a clear MTP helps individuals and organisations sustain their motivation and keep their focus, even in the face of obstacles, setbacks, and pivots.

An MTP has several key attributes: it is unique, feels true, is driven by emotional energy, and is something to which one is willing to commit a significant portion of one's life.

Consequently, drawing from the profound understanding of the fourth economy, we established Enterprising Africa Regional Network (Pty) Ltd, not for monetary gain, but to create global impact. Our MTP is: **Developing the African youth into successful entrepreneurs that would grow profitable and sustainable businesses to increase levels of employment and prosperity.** Currently, our entrepreneur development focus is on agriculture, which adds another dimension of ensuring food security.

On 1 September 2014, EARN began its journey with a goal to mould young minds into cutting-edge entrepreneurs, thereby boosting Africa's economic development and prosperity. The objective was to cultivate entrepreneurs, aligning them with the prevailing global economic context, ensuring a thriving and resilient African economy for years to come. EARN's goal was, and still is, to create an enabling environment for the young African entrepreneurs to create and grow profitable, sustainable businesses that would compete regionally, nationally, and internationally. This would enable our youth to EARN a decent living, EARN independence and respect, and EARN dignity and pride, and that would, in turn, EARN the continent the respect it deserves.

EARN stands as a testament to the power of MTP. The name itself encapsulates the organisation's essence. By fostering an enterprising spirit across Africa, EARN would enable individuals to become self-reliant, emphasising earning through effort rather than relying on aid. Our transformative purpose isn't just about economic independence; it's also about instilling a sense of purpose, pride, and empowerment among our African youths.

This clarity of purpose, of developing African youth into successful entrepreneurs, is what sets EARN apart. It's **massive** in its aspirations, as it dreams of a continent where the youth lead in creating sustainable and profitable businesses. It's **transformative**, envisioning a future where these young business leaders redefine Africa's global economic stance. And, most importantly, it's **purposeful**, with a clear 'why' propelling every action and decision.

The reason for EARN's success in realising this vision lies in its unwavering commitment to its MTP. At EARN, we ensure that we stay on course, inspiring action and unity, prioritising growth strategies, and fostering organisational agility through the adherence to our MTP. Our MTP guides, empowers, and inspires us. It helps us decide what to do and, more importantly, what *not to do*. It's thus both our **fuel** and our **filter**. We aren't in this endeavour for mere financial gains, but to create a ripple effect of positive societal impact.

Moonshot Thinking

A moonshot concept is an ambitious and transformative idea or project inspired by the monumental Apollo 11 mission that landed the first humans on the moon in 1969. Such a mission was a significant leap in technological advancement and human capability at the time. Like this historic venture, moonshot concepts aim to address massive challenges or achieve goals that may seem near impossible at the outset. These projects stand out because they require groundbreaking innovation and a departure from traditional thinking. While they inherently come with higher risks due to their ambitious nature, the rewards, if successful, can be immense and transformative. Committing to a moonshot requires a long-term vision, persistence, and a readiness to invest substantial resources, even when faced with potential failures.

At EARN, we use both the massive transformative purpose and moonshot concept to help us better focus on any project we embark on for effective results.

Our Agriculture Training and Development Moonshot aims to establish EARN as a leading centre of excellence that will lead the development of at least 5 million agripreneurs across various countries in Africa by 2033.

EARN's Focus Area and Its Training and Development Operating Model

EARN proudly aligns its operations with the 17 UN Sustainable Development Goals (SDGs). Taking a deep dive into SDG 2, which targets zero hunger, our agricultural subsidiary, African Greeneurs (Pty) Ltd (AG), is committed to moulding Africa's youth into forward-thinking agripreneurs. These young visionaries will be empowered to establish and oversee thriving agribusinesses that are primed for growth. But our vision doesn't stop there. Recognising agriculture's impact on climate change, we instil in these budding entrepreneurs the essence of eco-friendly farming. By doing so, we're championing a future where food is produced sustainably, and our planet is cherished.

Why Agriculture?

As we saw in Chapter 4, our continent of Africa has the advantage of a growing young population that would be a source of ongoing expertise and a market for various food products if properly engaged. Thus, Africa stands at the brink of an agricultural revolution. With this growing young population and the warmth of Africa's climate allowing for extended growing seasons, the continent is primed for agricultural greatness. The fact that Africa holds 65 percent of the world's untapped arable land isn't just a statistic; it's a promise. A promise that, though we currently face hunger issues, we have the innate ability to not only provide for ourselves but also to nourish other parts of the world.

However, challenges exist. Socio-economic roadblocks, occasional political turbulence, and limited advancements in farming technologies have kept Africa's people from reaching full potential. The fading number of older, skilled farmers is a significant concern. The narrative that farming is old-fashioned and physically taxing has deterred many young people from replacing the older agripreneurs, even causing traditional farmers' children to choose other careers. Therefore, the age-old tradition of passing down farming wisdom from generation to generation is waning.[4]

Yet, in this narrative of challenge lies opportunity – a chance to redefine and rejuvenate African agriculture. That's where EARN steps in. To attract the youth to the agricultural sector, we recognise that the young people are drawn to modern farming with high levels of technology and have a deep-rooted passion for the environment. So, we invite them to a modern, eco-friendly farming world powered by the latest technology. We're not just teaching farming; we're unveiling a future where agriculture meets innovation. At EARN, through a rigorous selection process, we handpick potential leaders, nurturing them in our state-of-the-art training facilities, introducing them to groundbreaking farming technologies, and immersing them in time-tested agricultural best practices. Together, we're not just cultivating land; we're cultivating the future.

EARN's 360-Degree Agripreneur Development Programme

We also noted that although there are several agriculture training centres and programmes out there, these programmes are still based on rote learning, which is not very different from what has led to the increased number of unemployed youths in the first place. These programmes lack an exit strategy. To overcome this, EARN has developed a 360-degree agripreneur development programme.

Selection Process

At the heart of EARN's Agripreneur Development Programme is a detailed and thorough process for selecting candidates. This is what has led to the programme's success. We firmly believe that everyone has an innate genius that shines brightest when they're in their element. This is why we focus on finding those individuals who have a genuine love for agriculture, a knack for entrepreneurship, and the readiness to dive headfirst into sustainable agribusiness.

Our selection journey starts with an open call, inviting all potential candidates to apply. Through this competitive application, we're able to pinpoint those who not only have a keen interest in agriculture but also the ambition to carve a niche for themselves in agribusiness.

Of course, succeeding in agribusiness isn't just about a love for farming; it's also about having the entrepreneurial spirit. We evaluate this spirit in each candidate, identifying those with the potential to thrive in the dynamic world of agribusiness.

Another crucial aspect we assess is their readiness to embrace agribusiness in a sustainable manner. This involves understanding their commitment to the long haul, their ability to bounce back from setbacks, and their zeal for continuous learning in the agripreneur journey.

After this comprehensive evaluation, we then handpick the most promising candidates. It's these individuals we believe will benefit the most from our Agripreneur Development Programme and will go on to make a significant, positive difference in the agricultural sector and their communities. This is proof that this programme is not for everyone.

The Training and Development Programme and Exit Strategy

At EARN, the journey of our agripreneurs doesn't stop with mere selection; it's only the beginning. Once we've identified the most promising candidates, as part of the training and development programme, we introduce them to seasoned coaches and mentors from the agribusiness realm. These coaches and mentors, armed with years of experience, become invaluable guides, helping our candidates navigate the intricate pathways of the industry. They're not just guiding lights; they also foster an environment for skill sharing, insights, and passing down tried-and-tested methodologies.

Recognising the uniqueness of each individual, we shun the cookie-cutter approach. Instead, we curate bespoke training sessions, aligning them with the distinct needs and dreams of each agripreneur. Our goal is to equip them with tools tailored for their specific agricultural ambitions.

But learning isn't confined to just classrooms and modules. At EARN, we believe in the power of firsthand experience. We plunge our candidates into the very heart of agricultural operations, letting them feel the soil, grapple with challenges, and find solutions on the go. This tangible interaction with the farming world cements their theoretical knowledge.

Success in agribusiness isn't just about knowledge and experience; it's also about connections. We pave the way for our candidates to mingle with the who's who of the industry, investors, and fellow agripreneurs. These networking forays are more than just meet and greets; they're platforms to forge alliances, collaborations, and partnerships.

Throughout their journey with us, we keep a keen eye on their evolution. Through consistent evaluations and feedback loops, we ensure that our agripreneurs are always on an upward trajectory, tweaking their strategies and approaches as needed.

EARN's commitment is unwavering, and it extends beyond the duration of the programme. As our candidates step confidently into the agribusiness arena, we remain by their side, providing them with resources, guidance, and support. Be it securing capital, business consultancy, or creating market inroads, we're with them, every step of the way.

EARN's Agripreneur Development Programme is more than just a training initiative. It's a commitment, a promise, to nurture and support every budding agripreneur, ensuring they're not just ready for the world of agriculture but poised to revolutionise it.

Our holistic approach combines cutting-edge training facilities with practical tools, creating a nurturing environment for budding agripreneurs in our our country and region.

Our 12-month signature Agripreneur Development Programme is split into two main phases: Activate and Accelerate. Both are crucial for equipping our trainees with the necessary skills to own and operate their farms.

In the Activate Phase, our trainees undergo a three-month intensive course, focusing both on the theoretical and the practical aspects of the programme. About a quarter to a third of their time is spent in classrooms, while the remainder is dedicated to hands-on fieldwork. This ensures they're not only knowledgeable but also ready to handle the realities of agribusiness.

Following this, they transition to the Accelerate Phase, a nine-month journey of real-world farming. Under the watchful eyes of experts, trainees go through the full cycle of agriculture, from planting seeds to selling their harvested produce. This phase embodies our belief in '**earning while learning**', where they reap the rewards of their efforts in real time.

EARN's trainee agripreneurs at EARN's Training and Development Centre.

But EARN's support isn't confined to just training. We also assist our trainees in finding their own piece of land, which they'll eventually call home after completing our programme. This is our exit strategy. We recognise that thriving in agribusiness isn't solely about knowing how to farm.

To ensure our trainees' success, we connect them to a network of ecosystem enablers – from funding sources and infrastructure providers to seasoned industry mentors and market links. We guide every step, from produce sorting and packaging to market access. Our overarching goal is to set up our trainees for long-term success, equipping them to meet the high standards of today's agribusiness landscape.

Community Clustering

EARN is deeply committed to the growth and sustainability of the agribusiness sector, going beyond individual empowerment. Our primary focus also encompasses community unity, shared growth, and regional development. This commitment shines brightly through our community clustering approach. Rather than benefits accruing to our trainees alone, we design our approach in such a way that the entire community should feel the positive impacts.

Central to this strategy is the principle of mutual growth and shared success. When we group agripreneurs from the same community, a natural synergistic environment forms. This collaboration means that the combined efforts of these agripreneurs far exceed what they could achieve individually. This synergy is instrumental in the accelerated growth and success of our programme.

Additionally, the culture within these community clusters encourages continuous learning. Our seasoned coaches and mentors would generously share their expertise with newcomers, facilitating a smooth and efficient transfer of knowledge and skills. This environment ensures new agripreneurs are well-prepared to meet industry challenges head-on.

Farming and agribusiness, by nature, present many uncertainties, from erratic weather to market volatility. Yet, within the safety of our community clusters, our trainees have a ready-made support system. They can pool resources and brainstorm collective solutions during tough times, significantly reducing the risks they might face as individuals.

From a market perspective, clustering offers a unique advantage. Agripreneurs within a cluster can present a unified brand for their products, which enhances marketability and builds trust among consumers. This unity ensures product consistency and high standards, further solidifying their position in the market.

The cultural dimension of EARN's community clustering cannot be overlooked. By bringing together agripreneurs from the same background, local agricultural practices, valuable heirloom seeds, and traditional farming methods are preserved and celebrated. This not only safeguards our rich agricultural heritage but also introduces distinctive products to the market.

Furthermore, as communities grow and thrive, leaders will naturally rise to the forefront. Our programme doesn't just nurture agricultural talent; it also identifies and supports these emerging community leaders. With EARN's backing, they would take on vital roles in steering their communities towards a brighter, unified future.

In the grand scheme of things, EARN's community-based clustering approach isn't just about economic metrics. It embodies unity, shared objectives, and collective growth, ensuring individual triumphs are magnified to benefit the entire community.

EARN's Agriculture Training and Development, and Commercial Infrastructure and Facilities

EARN has established a state-of-the-art training centre in Centurion, Gauteng Province, South Africa, under our subsidiary AG. Built from the ground up, this centre serves as a hands-on learning ground where aspiring agripreneurs and emerging farmers are trained in the art of modern farming. Every bit of fresh produce cultivated here is directed towards commercial sale.

One of the farm's standout features is its self-sufficiency. We source our water independently, drawing from both boreholes and harvested rainwater. Additionally, our bioactive water treatment system efficiently manages grey and black water, ultimately producing pure water as a by-product. Powering the farm is mainly our robust solar power generation system. Although we remain connected to the main power grid, we predominantly rely on our solar resources, ensuring uninterrupted power supply, free from outages.

Agriculture Training and Development Centre in Centurion.

This farm offers everything that agripreneurs need to model and practise their learned skills in order to succeed. We are planning to expand our training facilities and infrastructure to further enhance our training programmes and accommodate more agriculture trainees.

Our goal is to continue to refine and improve our model, ensuring that our agriculture trainees have access to the best training and resources to build successful and sustainable agribusinesses as agripreneurs. We also aim to ensure gainful employment for other trainees seeking agriculture knowledge and experiential training.

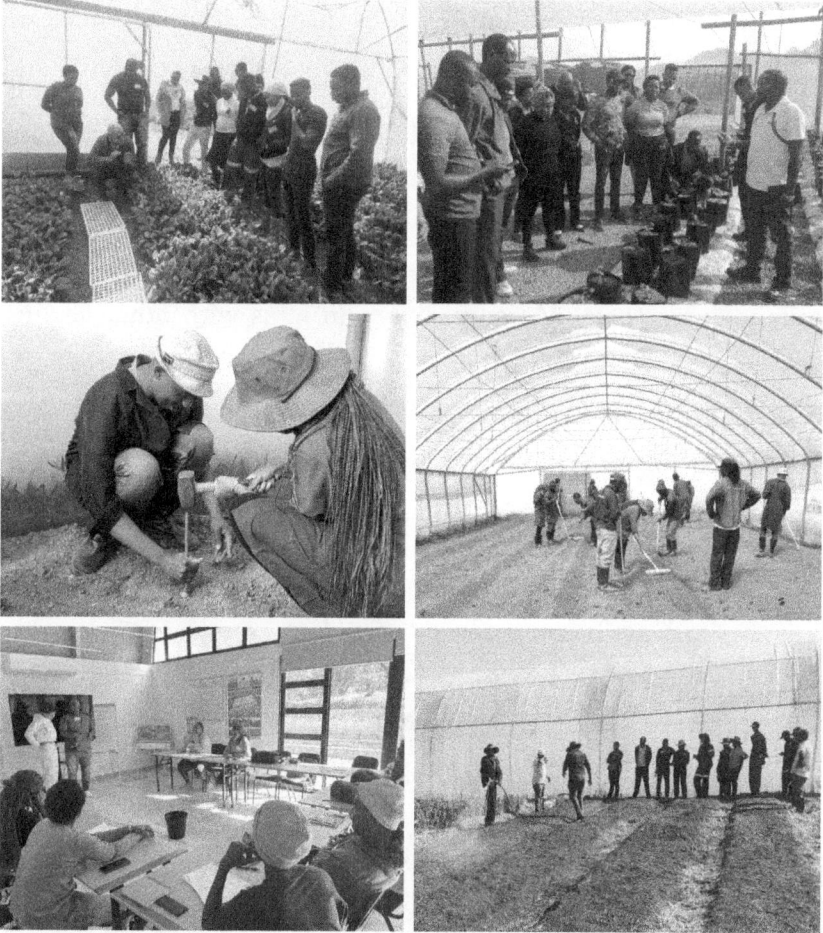

Practical technical skills training in Centurion.

AG Horticulture (Pty) Ltd, better known as AGH, is our commercial primary agriculture subsidiary. Located in Ekurhuleni, also in Gauteng Province, AGH manages a bustling 100-hectare farm. On this expansive property, we currently cultivate fresh produce using nine multi-span, fully equipped, high-tech greenhouses, each covering 0.7 hectare. We've also recently introduced three experimental dual-span greenhouses that, combined, span 0.2 hectare, along with a 0.7-hectare shade net house.

Our commitment to ensuring the quality of our produce is evident from our in-house built, 2000-square-metre, medium care fresh produce packhouse. It meets all food safety standards and primarily packages peppers, tomatoes, cucumbers, and other leafy products for supermarket distribution.

At present, AGH's fresh produce finds its way to the shelves of the major supermarkets and food manufacturers, thanks to our offtake agreements. Moreover, we're in talks with other leading supermarket chains to further expand our distribution both locally and for export. An important future objective is to collaborate with the agripreneurs we train. By facilitating the packing of their fresh produce, we aim to help them tap into these established market outlets.

Commercial primary agriculture 100-hectare farm in Ekurhuleni.

Our farm is more than just land and infrastructure; it's a thriving hub of activity operated and managed by approximately 120 team members. Looking ahead to 2024, we're planning to introduce more multi-span greenhouses. Additionally, we're also envisioning a 6-hectare shade net house and a 1000-square-metre high care packhouse. The latter is specially designed to cater to our offtakers' requests for leafy fresh produce, including microgreens and herbs, and it will be fully equipped with modern machinery. These developments are expected to further boost our workforce.

AGH team and fresh produce grown at AGH's farm in Ekurhuleni.

Our success in the commercial agricultural sector stands as a testament to our expertise and commitment. For our trainees, it serves as a vivid, tangible demonstration of what they can achieve with the right guidance. As they undergo training to become cutting-edge agripreneurs, they can draw inspiration from our accomplishments. Remember, people don't listen to what you say; they listen to what you do. Our success gives them confidence in the quality of their training and reinforces their belief in what they can achieve under our mentorship. After all, seeing is believing, and, at EARN, we show them what's truly possible in the realm of agribusiness.

Enhanced Food Value Chain

EARN's vision for Africa transcends the traditional model of merely exporting primary agricultural produce. Instead, we advocate for a shift towards local beneficiation, which involves adding value to raw materials by processing them into finished products ready for consumption. This paradigm shift isn't just about economic growth; it's also about reshaping Africa's role in the global market and ensuring sustainable development for its communities.

When countries rely heavily on exporting raw materials, they often miss out on a wealth of opportunities presented by the value addition process. For instance, converting raw cocoa into chocolate or turning cotton into textiles not only increases the product's value manifold but also provides job opportunities at various stages of production, processing, marketing, and distribution. This means that by promoting local beneficiation, Africa could substantially increase employment opportunities and, in turn, uplift numerous communities from poverty.

Moreover, producing finished products ready for consumption places African industries in a better position in the global market. Instead of being at the mercy of fluctuating global prices for raw materials, adding value locally can stabilise income streams, leading to more predictable and sustainable economic growth.

Furthermore, by focusing on local beneficiation, Africa can reduce its dependency on imports. Producing finished products domestically would decrease the need to import those same goods, ensuring that a more significant portion of the profit remains within the continent. This also enhances Africa's trade balance, making it more resilient to global economic shocks.

Local beneficiation will also drive innovation and technological advancement. When industries move beyond primary production into processing and manufacturing, they are often compelled to innovate, adopt new technologies, and upskill their workforce. This not only makes the continent more competitive but also fosters an environment where knowledge and technological growth thrive.

Through our agriculture subsidiary companies, **AG** and **AGH**, we seek to build capacity and develop competitiveness aimed at achieving meaningful participation in the mainstream food supply value chain for the majority of the population in Africa. An important future objective is to construct more commercial agrihubs across the country, and continent, in partnership with local partners and communities..

Our AG Agripreneur Development Model (AG Model) and EARN Business Development Process (EARN Process) are the two models that we use to provide the holistic training and development of our young people into cutting-edge entrepreneurs.

Our dream is not about having a big bank account; it's about creating business opportunities that make a big difference to the lives of the majority of our people. We are committed to creating opportunities for job creation, skills development, value creation, and increasing levels of prosperity in historically disadvantaged communities.

Partner Strategy

EARN's Partner Strategy is multifaceted and focuses on building a robust network that covers every aspect of nurturing future agripreneurs. One of its central tenets is collaborating with capability partners, which include both private sector entities and esteemed educational and research institutions, both locally and on an international scale. This collaboration seeks to continuously enrich and enhance the capabilities and programmes within the agricultural sector, making them more attractive to the younger generation. Such partnerships will ensure that the training is current, relevant, and of the highest standard, thereby promising a higher chance of success for the young agripreneurs.

Additionally, securing sponsorships from government agencies, international organisations, or private sector partners is pivotal. These sponsors play a crucial role by financially backing trainees, most of whom are from poor financial backgrounds. This financial support can make the difference between a passionate individual having the means to undergo training or being left out. Such sponsorships also underline the importance and potential of the agricultural sector, making it more credible and appealing to potential agripreneurs.

Land is, of course, a fundamental resource in agriculture. Partnering with landowners, be it public entities or private individuals, who are willing to allocate their land for the use of trained agripreneurs on a long-term lease basis, is vital. This gives these budding entrepreneurs a tangible platform to put their skills into practice, converting theory into real-world agribusinesses. Without access to suitable land, even the best training would remain under-utilised.

Lastly, the importance of funders, including development finance institutions (DFIs) and commercial banks, cannot be understated. Once trained, agripreneurs need financial resources to kick-start their ventures, purchase necessary equipment, and handle initial operational costs. EARN ensures that its trainees have the monetary backing needed to transform their dreams into thriving businesses by collaborating with these financial entities.

All in all, EARN's Partner Strategy is about weaving a comprehensive support system for future agripreneurs. Every partner, from those offering knowledge and skills to those providing financial support or tangible resources like land, is a pillar on which the success of the next generation of agripreneurs rests. This holistic approach ensures that trainees are not only well-equipped with knowledge but also have the practical means to manifest their vision, which is paramount for the sustainable growth of the agricultural sector in Africa.

At EARN, we recognise the vastness of the challenges we face on our continent of Africa. While our contributions might seem small in the grand scheme of things, especially when compared to entities with vast resources, we believe deeply in the value of our endeavours. Every effort counts, no matter its size. Drawing inspiration from Mother Teresa's words, she eloquently remarked, "We know only too well that what we are doing is nothing more than a drop in the ocean. But if the drop were not there, the ocean would be missing something." In a similar spirit, our work, though seemingly modest, fills a crucial void. It's proof of the belief that every single effort, big or small, collectively contributes to a more promising and hopeful tomorrow.

EPILOGUE

Africa, often referred to as the birthplace of humanity, holds a unique and pivotal position in the annals of human history. Within the pages of *It's Time for Africa*, we journeyed back to these ancient roots, taking a moment to understand and appreciate the deep connections that unite us all, regardless of our current geographical or cultural distinctions.

Yet, while this shared ancestry is a vital part of our story, it's only a chapter. Today's Africa is a thriving mosaic of cultures, ideas, and potential. To get fixated solely on its past would mean overlooking the vibrant energy and progress the continent is currently experiencing.

Every sunrise in Africa shines on cities bustling with innovation, landscapes echoing with age-old traditions adapting to modern times, and a people filled with hope and aspiration. The continent, once primarily seen through the lens of its ancient history, is now carving out a modern narrative filled with promise and anticipation for what the future holds.

From the rhythmic beats of Kinshasa's rhumba music to the bustling markets of Marrakech, every corner of Africa resonates with stories of triumph over trials. Its vast deserts, lush rainforests, and overflowing rivers echo tales not just of survival but of thriving against all odds.

The continent, with its vast array of languages and cultures, also showcases unity in diversity. Take, for instance, Zambia's peaceful transitions of power, setting a gold standard for democratic processes. Or the solar innovations lighting up villages in Tanzania, bringing a new dawn of sustainable energy. South Africa's journey from the shackles of apartheid to a rainbow nation underlines the power of reconciliation and healing. The growth of Nigeria's Nollywood, now a global cinematic phenomenon, speaks volumes of the creativity and talent that abounds.

Every river, mountain, and plain in Africa tells a story. From Egypt's rich history as an ancient civilisation to Uganda's progressive efforts in wildlife conservation, Africa continuously moulds its narrative, embracing its past while fearlessly charting a path to the future.

The agricultural revolutions in Malawi, turning famine into feast, or the digital leaps in tech hubs like Nairobi and Cape Town, reflect the continent's versatility and forward-thinking. Mozambique's recovery and rebuilding post natural disasters, and Botswana's fiscal discipline and good governance, illustrate the continent's holistic approach to growth.

Just as the Nile River encounters numerous bends and obstacles on its journey to the Mediterranean, yet never loses its force or direction, Africa too has faced its share of hurdles, yet remains undeterred. There are undeniable scars left by colonialism, socio-political upheavals, and economic disparities. Nonetheless, these scars, instead of being mere reminders of a painful past, also exemplify the continent's ability to endure, heal, and emerge stronger.

In cities like Kigali and Cairo, young entrepreneurs are harnessing the power of technology to create solutions tailored for African contexts, showcasing that innovation isn't just about global trends but also about local relevance. In places like Zimbabwe and Zambia, community-driven initiatives are working towards sustainable agriculture and conservation, highlighting the blend of tradition and modernity in crafting a brighter future.

The energy of Africa's youth, constituting a significant portion of its population, is another proof of its forward momentum. They're not just the leaders of tomorrow but active change-makers today, advocating for transparent governance, equal rights, and a sustainable environment.

Moreover, Africa's approach to its challenges and opportunities has garnered global attention. International collaborations are no longer merely about aid but about mutual growth and shared objectives. From Asia to Europe, from the Americas to Oceania, there's a growing recognition that Africa's success story is integral to the global narrative of progress and development.

In the cultural realm, African art, music, and literature are receiving worldwide acclaim, bridging gaps and fostering understanding. This cultural renaissance, echoing from the vibrant festivals of Accra to the art galleries of Tunis, is evidence of Africa's profound influence on global aesthetics and thought.

As the rhythms of African drums resonate far and wide, so does the continent's potential to be a beacon of hope, innovation, and progress. Every individual, whether residing in the heart of Lilongwe or in the bustling streets of New York, holds a part of the

African narrative within them. The diversity, tenacity, and resilience that Africa represents are qualities that the world desperately needs in these rapidly changing times.

The stories we've traversed in *It's Time for Africa* are more than mere chronicles of a continent; they are tales of humanity, evolution, and the shared dreams of a world bound together by common aspirations. As Africa rises, it brings with it lessons of community, the importance of harmony with nature, and the profound understanding that our destinies are intricately interwoven.

To the businesses eyeing the next big opportunity, Africa is not just a market but a hub of creativity and innovation. To educators and thinkers, it offers insights into ancient wisdom and the future of learning. And to the youth, it stands as proof that change can be spearheaded by the fervour and passion of those willing to believe in a brighter tomorrow.

It is this belief in tomorrow that the world must hold on to. The challenges we face today, from climate crises to socio-economic disparities, are not insurmountable. Africa's journey is proof of that. A continent that has faced centuries of exploitation and adversity is now emerging as a leader in sustainable growth and holistic development.

As we look ahead, envisioning a world where every individual has access to opportunities, where every dream is valid, where every effort is recognised, we must remember the strength that lies in unity. Our planet's future hinges on our ability to come together, to share knowledge, resources, and dreams. Africa's ascent serves as an inspiration and a reminder that when we uplift one another, we rise together.

So, as the sun sets on one chapter and dawns on another, let it illuminate a world where borders are mere geographical constructs, and our hearts and minds are aligned in purpose. For in this unity, in this shared vision, lies our path to a world that not only celebrates Africa's glory but also recognises the infinite potential that humanity holds when united in purpose.

ACKNOWLEDGEMENTS

My deepest appreciation goes to the Dean Publishing team, with a special note of gratitude for Susan Dean and Natalie Deane. Your unwavering support, insightful guidance, and editorial prowess have been instrumental in transforming my experiences and thoughts into the pages of this book. Your belief in my story has not only nurtured its growth but has also been a source of personal inspiration.

I would like to extend my heartfelt thanks to every individual who has crossed my path, leaving indelible marks of wisdom and insight. This book has been enriched by the myriad of perspectives and knowledge shared with me. To the authors and researchers whose works are referenced, your scholarly contributions have profoundly shaped my understanding and interpretation of the complex tapestry of life, culture, resources, business, and economic development in Africa.

To my dedicated team at Enterprising Africa Regional Network (Pty) Ltd (EARN), your commitment and tireless efforts form the backbone of our organisation. It's more than just work; it's a mission to foster positive change in society. This book is a reflection of our shared vision and collective endeavour towards building a better world. Your passion and hard work are not just transforming lives but are also shaping a brighter future for our continent.

And to you, the readers, who have chosen to embark on this journey with me, your engagement with this book transcends the act of reading. It represents a step towards meaningful dialogues and actionable steps that can catalyse economic and social prosperity, not just in Africa but also globally. Your interest, thoughts, and actions are integral to the realisation of the visions and solutions proposed in these pages. Together, through shared knowledge and collaborative efforts, we can forge pathways to a more prosperous, equitable, and sustainable world.

Thank you all for being part of this journey, for your contribution to the narrative of progress, and for your commitment to making a difference. This book is not only a testament to what has been achieved but is also a beacon of hope for what we can accomplish together.

ABOUT THE AUTHOR

Joshua Chimakula Ngoma is a serial social entrepreneur, entrepreneur development specialist, engineer, project specialist, and dedicated family man.

Born on 17 August 1960, he was inspired by his father, an ex-soldier turned entrepreneur, and began his own business journey at age 8 after his father's death. With ventures in vegetable sales, photography, and import-export by age 18, Joshua's early life set the stage for his remarkable future.

His academic pursuits took him from Zambia to England, earning a Bachelor of Engineering with Honours in Mining Engineering from the Camborne School of Mines, followed by a Master of Engineering in Project Management from the University of Pretoria, South Africa.

Joshua's extensive three-decade career in mining in key positions

435

in Zambia and South Africa laid a foundation for his leadership skills. In the late 90's he joined a group of emerging mining entrepreneurs that formed Eyesizwe Mining, which played a pivotal role in the formation of Exxaro Resources. His entrepreneurial acumen flourished in 2007 when he became the founding CEO of Tranter Holdings, a venture he co-owned with former colleagues from Eyesizwe Mining. Under his leadership, Tranter Holdings grew rapidly, expanding to over 300 employees with four subsidiaries and a presence in three countries by 2009. The company's success in mineral exploration and engineering manufacturing cemented his reputation as a dynamic entrepreneur.

After retiring from mining in 2012, Joshua's passion for entrepreneurship led him to 'refire' a year later, founding Enterprising Africa Regional Network (Pty) Ltd (EARN) in 2013. EARN, which started operations on 1 September 2014, focuses on nurturing young African entrepreneurs, particularly in agriculture and food sectors. His commitment to EARN underscores his dedication to leveraging Africa's youthful population for continental growth and global impact.

Beyond his business ventures, Joshua has served on a number of engineering professional bodies and voluntary associations. Outside the engineering field, he served on the Evian Group@IMD in Lausanne, Switzerland – an international coalition of corporate, government, and opinion leaders, committed to fostering an open, inclusive, equitable, and sustainable global market economy.

A dedicated family man, married to Susan Nyirenda since 1991, and father to Daliso and Natasha, Joshua infuses strong family values and the ethos of giving back into all aspects of his life. His belief in the power of knowledge and generosity manifests in his support for the education of extended family members and his commitment to lifelong learning.

Joshua's journey is a testament to the power of vision, entrepreneurship, and education in creating a positive global impact, making him a renowned social entrepreneur and mentor.

www.earninternational.net
www.itstimefor.africa

TESTIMONIALS

"From the moment I met Joshua at Singularity University, it was evident he was no ordinary thinker. His blend of profound wisdom and infectious humour transcends conventional storytelling, offering readers a unique lens through which to view Africa's future potential.

Through his narrative, I was afforded my inaugural insight into the African continent, viewed through the perspective of someone deeply rooted within it. His fervour for his homeland and the wider continent was thoroughly infectious. It was, indeed, a privilege to be approached by him to review his manuscript prior to its publication.

Joshua's narrative is a testament to the vibrant spirit of Africa, united with a language that lightens the gravity of the subjects he tackles. His book is not just a call to action; it is an invitation to reimagine Africa through the eyes of someone who knows it intimately.

He challenges the narrative, echoing Shakira's anthem (quite impossible not to sing this book title in my head as I read it) with a twist – this time, it's an assembling cry from within, urging us to see Africa's brightness among its complexities. What sets this book apart is Joshua's ability to make you hopeful while simultaneously compelling you to think deeply about the issues at hand.

As a Brazilian used to witnessing the untapped potential of my country, I am well aware of the opportunities awaiting the African continent upon addressing its significant challenges. This book unveiled several facets of Africa previously unknown to me, ranging from its abundant natural resources and rich cultural heritage as the cradle of human civilisation to the origins of slavery.

Two years ago, I participated in Antler's program, a venture capital (VC) fund that had recently expanded to Brazil. I was initially surprised to learn of their African chapter, not entirely common for VC funds. However, this book shifted my perspective, dispelling prior prejudices. Joshua presents a thorough exploration of the continent, emphasising its entrepreneurial potential with clarity and insight; therefore – all of a sudden – the investment in the African continent made extraordinary sense.

This book is a journey – a passage through time and thought, leaving you with a sense of hope and a smile on your face. In a world filled with literature that often paints Africa in broad, dark strokes, Joshua's book emerges as a symbol of hope. It's a must-read for anyone, anywhere in the world, who seeks to understand the continent beyond the headlines.

Through passion and wisdom, Joshua invites us to join him in believing in Africa's boundless potential. In essence, *It's Time for Africa* is more than a book; it's a movement. A movement that champions the continent's dynamism, resilience, and spirit, all while reminding us that the path to understanding and progress can be paved with joy. Joshua Ngoma doesn't just tell a story; he invites us to be part of Africa's unfolding narrative, one filled with hope, humour, and heart."

Fabio Ivatiuk
São Paulo, Brazil
Co-Founder and CEO of Rhevolut

UNDERSTANDING AFRICA'S RICH HISTORY AND CULTURAL DIVERSITY

I had no background in Africa's history. So, in this chapter, I gained a much better understanding that there are multiple Africas, each with distinct social, economic, and cultural aspects. It was brief but helped me realise that we should always talk about each country separately.

THE IMPACT OF RACISM, SLAVERY, AND COLONIALISM ON AFRICA

I had a brief schooling on European colonialism in Africa and how it shaped the current conflicts in the region. This part helped me understand the conflicts better. I appreciated how the chapter transitioned from the negative aspects of colonialism to the opportunities it created, introducing the next chapter.

AFRICA'S NATURAL RESOURCES AND ECONOMIC POTENTIAL

This chapter was one of the most interesting for me. It provided insights into the opportunities and potential of each country, with a specific focus on the mining industry. It gave me a big picture of the available natural resources and how they are currently utilised.

AFRICA'S YOUTH DEMOGRAPHIC AND THE CHALLENGE OF YOUTH UNEMPLOYMENT

In this chapter, I gained a good overview of the demographic aspects and challenges Africa faces, particularly regarding the youth population. We share a similar challenge in Brazil concerning credit, job opportunities, and investment.

LEADERSHIP ESSENTIAL FOR ECONOMIC DEVELOPMENT

This chapter creates a broad understanding of leadership and how key aspects play many roles in contributing to economic development. It provides multiple examples of leaders who were able to create an impact.

UNVEILING AFRICA'S CULTURAL RENAISSANCE

This chapter shows how culture plays a crucial role in society's development across various sectors, like tourism, the film industry, and medicine. It introduced me to multiple aspects of Africa that I had no idea about before. I liked how it connects the previous chapter with the next one.

INFRASTRUCTURE DEVELOPMENT

This chapter takes a deep dive into Africa's infrastructure aspects, mainly digital, telecom, water/sanitation, energy, and transportation, with multiple successful examples. It also highlights some of the challenges that need to be addressed.

EDUCATION AND HUMAN CAPITAL DEVELOPMENT

This chapter provides an overview of the education sector in Africa, emphasising the importance of inclusive, creative, digital, critical thinking, and relevant education. It mentions multiple examples of successful initiatives and how they contributed to improving the life of the population. It also outlines some of the challenges that should be addressed.

RULE OF LAW AND GOOD GOVERNANCE

This chapter discusses the importance of having a legal system that works alongside a governance system to ensure fair and equal investments, holding responsible parties accountable. I appreciated the example of Porto Alegre in Brazil regarding participatory budgeting, but we also face bad examples of corruption and governance issues (Car Wash operation, for instance). The challenges, in this aspect, are very similar to Brazil's, mainly due to weak institutions, laws, and low accountability. It's good to see World Bank initiatives addressing this issue.

DIVERSIFYING ECONOMIES AND EMBRACING OPEN MARKETS

This chapter emphasises the importance of diversification and open markets to improve the economy. It highlights examples like the UAE and Rwanda, showing that such initiatives can lead to economic growth. The challenge is that most of the continent relies on commodity exports, which fluctuate and create risks and vulnerabilities. The Nigerian example emphasises how critical this economic aspect can be.

INNOVATION AND TECHNOLOGICAL ADVANCEMENTS

It was great to see how many technological innovations were created in the last few years, mainly mobile banking initiatives, agtech, climate, supply chain, health, education, clean energy, and govtechs. The section on African inventors also shows how strong technological inventions are in Africa. Again, I had no idea about those aspects of technology, and it was a great chapter to demonstrate this.

SOCIAL SAFETY NETS AND INCLUSIVE GROWTH

This chapter presents the concept of safety nets and their importance in inclusive growth and poverty reduction, highlighting some examples, such as PSNP in Ethiopia. It should be noted that safety nets should always be accompanied by other initiatives that enable the population to increase their wages and leave the safety net.

FISCAL RESPONSIBILITY AND SOUND MONETARY POLICY

This chapter highlights the importance of fiscal responsibility for governments and a strong and intelligent monetary policy to make economies more stable. It also showcases some good examples, such as the SARB tools, to keep inflation within a target. This is very similar to Brazil's Central Bank, which is independent from the government and has very similar goals.

ENVIRONMENTAL SUSTAINABILITY

This chapter shows the importance of sustainable development regarding environmental issues and how local communities are crucial to developing a longstanding environmental plan that can create and distribute wealth. I had no idea Africa was one of the continents most vulnerable to climate change and that many initiatives are in place to improve infrastructure and create early warning systems.

REGIONAL COOPERATION AND INTEGRATION

This chapter demonstrates the importance of cooperation and integration among countries in Africa. I also had no idea that there were so many economic blocks inside Africa, such as the African Union, with free trade among the participants. The comparison between the EU and AU also offers some crucial insights into how many challenges this cooperation faces, mainly corruption and poor governance practices of current countries.

ATTRACTING FOREIGN DIRECT INVESTMENT

This chapter communicates the amount of foreign investment being made into African countries and its importance in the development of societies. It also highlights the importance of political stability and governance to attract those investments, showing some interesting examples such as Botswana, which attracts a lot of FDI even though it has a small market size. The challenges African countries face to attract FDI are very similar to Brazil's.

CULTIVATING GLOBAL PARTNERSHIPS

I was able to learn in this chapter about the importance of global partnerships in Africa and also how PPPs are playing an important role in improving many aspects, which is very similar to Brazil in this sense. It was also interesting to see the role China and Europe are playing in Africa, which is leading, in some cases, to an increase in the debt ratio of those countries, which can be a challenge in the future, leading to unbalanced commercial relations, which can be bad. I also agree with the author on this topic, and China is also trying to do the same FDIs here in Brazil to buy our assets for a very low price.

ADAPTABILITY AND RESILIENCE

This chapter talks about many challenges that Africa faced and is facing, but also how resilient the countries are becoming, showing multiple examples. It is interesting how African countries are adapting to resist commodity crises by diversifying their economic activities. It was great to see how strong the societies in these countries are and how resilient to disasters, climate change, and crises they are.

HEALTH AND WELLNESS DEVELOPMENT

It was really interesting to see how the health sector works in Africa and the many innovative initiatives the countries are adopting to fight diseases, childhood mortality, and to ensure healthy nutrition to the people. We also face some of these challenges in Brazil, mainly in some parts of the country that are not very well-developed.

A CASE STUDY: FOSTERING ENTREPRENEURSHIP IN AFRICA

Joshua knows I am a huge fan of him and the work he is doing with EARN; this chapter was incredible for me to really understand how transformative it is, exactly how it works, and its impact on African entrepreneurship.

LAST FEW WORDS

Reading this book made me travel into Africa and discover how superficial my knowledge was. Starting from natural resources, technologies, government, economics, entrepreneurship, and many other areas, I was able to understand a lot better Africa's opportunities and challenges. It was also very interesting to see how comparable and similar Brazil's challenges and opportunities are to some African countries. The language was very easy to understand, and the chapters were very well-connected. Great job!

Rafael Libardi
São Paulo, Brazil
CEO, NoLeak Defence Technologies Inc.

"*It's Time for Africa* comes at a time when Africa's consciousness is rising. The author senses and captures the awakening of the giant that is Africa. The message has breadth and depth, starting from way back when the human race was trickling out of Africa to populate the world. That opening tells the reader that the author has a lot to go through. The book ends in contemporary issues of Africa's growing approaches to regional integration and cooperation as a major part of what the author envisions as the desired prosperous tomorrow. The clarion call is for Africans to take time to fully understand, embrace and love their past as the main gateway for energising the unfolding African renaissance.

The book delves into Africa's economy more than most books of this nature do. A most enriching aspect of the book is treatment of future economic fortunes by addressing social, technological and physical infrastructure. The author laments, for instance, how the residual education system continues to produce 'thinkers' not 'doers'. There is good substance in addressing the need for diversifying economies in Africa through innovation and technology development among other interventions.

The author is self-evidently committed to Africa's youth bulge and dedicates his final message to EARN's 360-Degree Agripreneur Development Programme. A creation and investment of the author, this is a life-transforming programme for Africa's youth. The programme is indeed a microcosm of what the author sees clearly in an advanced, future Africa."

Professor Mandi Rukuni
Harare, Zimbabwe
Director, BEAT Afrika Doctoral Academy

"Get ready to be inspired, informed, and motivated to be part of Africa's transformative narrative. *It's Time for Africa* is a must-read! Through engaging storytelling and insightful analysis, Joshua Chimakula Ngoma inspires readers with a captivating journey that delves into the rich tapestry of Africa's past, present, and future.

The book also paints a vivid picture of a continent brimming with cultural diversity, innovation, and untapped potential through a blend of historical insights and contemporary narratives while also offering a great opportunity to reflect on Africa's past struggles, while celebrating its vibrant present and promising future."

Jones Mpakateni
Lusaka, Zambia
Advocacy and Communications Consultant, Africa Union (AU)

"Joshua Ngoma's seminal book, *It's Time for Africa*, is a compelling narrative on Africa's imminent transition from a casually known continent to a 55-nation powerhouse. The author gives a panoramic overview of Africa's role as the 'cradle of humanity', where the first Homo sapiens lived, to emphasise that *the entire human race is ultimately of African descent, and we all share a common ancestry.* Any notions of racial inferiority or superiority are completely misplaced.

It is commendable that the author's references to the injustices suffered by the peoples of Africa over the centuries are not with a view to lament or apportioned blame, but to highlight the current state of poverty and underdevelopment, and to show how the new generations are resolutely overcoming the legacy of history to carve a new path – focusing only on the future they can have and should have.

Ngoma provides an indisputable rationale to drive home that multiple nations on the continent are well-positioned to become the pivotal new sources of growth for the entire world. With brilliant analysis and insights, he outlines five transformational revolutions that are rapidly unfolding the enormous potential of the entire continent.

The book will leave every reader with a firm conviction that this continent, with 60 percent of its population under the age of 25, has already taken off on a high-growth trajectory. The question hereafter for political and corporate leaders is not whether to engage with Africa; it is how to evolve a unique strategy to engage with each nation of Africa. This outstanding book unambiguously answers all these questions. It is the right book at the right time. Very aptly, *It's Time for Africa*."

Ravi Chaudhry
New Delhi, India
Author of *Quest for Exceptional Leadership: Mirage to Reality*
Former Chairman, Tata Group Companies

"*It's Time for Africa* is an inspirational delight. It offers a rich tapestry of information that leaves no stone unturned in the uniqueness of the African continent and her people.

Joshua Ngoma gives us a peek into the brain of a man whose drive to be a catalyst for change saw him shrug off serious illness. His quest to leave a legacy led to the creation of the EARN business model – a business model set to revolutionise the way business is conducted in Africa and beyond.

The book delves into the continent's history, examining cultural, social, and economic factors, specifically addressing the challenges and opportunities for sustainable growth in Africa.

The strategic perspective of this book offers insights into the economic dynamics and resource exploitation in Africa. Additionally, it explores the integration of lessons and experiences, shedding light on the importance of collaboration, cooperation and shared value.

Ngoma offers perspective on sustainable development, environmental practice, and the role of education as a catalyst for change. His thoughts and insights on the importance of alternative strategies for economic growth are much needed as we sit on the precipice of the new age.

It's Time for Africa provides a fountain of wisdom and knowledge, with a well-rounded understanding of Africa and Southern Africa.

The valuable insight, strategic guidance, thought leadership and the integration of key lessons make this a must read for policy makers, business leaders and entrepreneurs that wish to boldly tread where few have walked before."

Dr Nirmala Reddy
Johannesburg, South Africa
Strategy Specialist: Enterprise Development, Commercial Banking at Nedbank

ENDNOTES

Introduction

1   Economist Intelligence Unit 2022, 'Mining in Africa: The Benefit of Elevated Prices Amid Inflationary Pressures', viewed 20 November 2023, https://www.eiu.com/n/campaigns/mining-in-africa-amid-inflationary-pressures/.

2   Karkee, V & O'Higgins, N 2023, 'African Youth Face Pressing Challenges in the Transition from School to Work', *International Labour Organization*, viewed 20 November 2023, https://ilostat.ilo.org/african-youth-face-pressing-challenges-in-the-transition-from-school-to-work/.

3   Food and Agriculture Organization of the United Nations 2022, 'Chapter 2: Food Security and Nutrition around the World', viewed 20 November 2023, https://www.fao.org/3/cc0639en/online/sofi-2022/food-security-nutrition-in-dicators.html.

Chapter 1

1   White, F 1987, *The Overview Effect: Space Exploration and Human Evolution*, Houghton Mifflin, Boston.

2   Guthrie, M 1967, *Comparative Bantu: An Introduction to the Comparative Linguistics and Prehistory of the Bantu Languages*, Greg Press.

3   Eyo, Ekpo & Willett, F 1980, *Treasures of Ancient Nigeria*, Knopf/Detroit Institute of Arts.

4   Haynes, J 2016, *Nollywood: The Creation of Nigerian Film Genres*, University of Chicago Press, Chicago.

5   Bhorat, H & Tarp, F 2016, *Africa's Lions: Growth Traps and Opportunities for Six African Economies*, Brookings Institution Press. Washington DC.

6   Jack, W & Suri, T 2016, 'The Long-Run Poverty and Gender Impacts of Mobile Money', *Science*, vol 354, no 6317, pp 1288-1292, viewed 16 November 2023, doi.org/10.1126/science.aah5309.

7   African Development Bank 2012, *African Economic Outlook 2012: Promoting Youth Employment*, OECD Publishing, Paris, doi.org/10.1787/aeo-2012-en.

8   Friederici, N, Ojanperä, S, & Graham, M 2017, 'The Impact of Connectivity in Africa: Grand Visions and the Mirage of Inclusive Digital Development', *Electronic Journal of Information Systems in Developing Countries*, vol 79, no 2, pp 1-20, viewed 16 November 2023, doi.org/10.1002/j.1681-4835.2017.tb00578.x.

Chapter 2

1   Brewer, MB 1979, 'In-Group Bias in the Minimal Intergroup Situation: A Cognitive-Motivational Analysis', *Psychological Bulletin*, vol 86, no 2, p 307, viewed 16 November 2023, doi.org/10.1037/0033-2909.86.2.307.

2   Allport, GW 1954, *The Nature of Prejudice*, Addison-Wesley, Boston.

3   Bavel, JJV & Packer DJ 2021, *The Power of Us: Harnessing Our Shared Identities to Improve Performance, Increase Cooperation, and Promote Social*

Harmony, Little, Brown Spark, Boston.

4   Duello, TM, Rivedal, S, Wickland, C, & Weller, A 2021, 'Race and Genetics Versus "Race" in Genetics: A Systematic Review of the Use of African Ancestry in Genetic Studies', *Evolution, Medicine, and Public Health*, vol 9, no 1, pp 232-245, viewed 16 November 2023, doi.org/10.1093/emph/eoab018.

5   Grosfoguel, R 2016, 'What Is Racism?', *Journal of World-Systems Research*, vol 22, no 1, pp 9-15, viewed 16 November, doi.org/10.5195/jwsr.2016.609.

6   Nunn, N 2008, 'The Long-Term Effects of Africa's Slave Trades', *Quarterly Journal of Economics*, vol 123, no 1, pp 139-176, viewed 16 November 2023, doi.org/10.1162/qjec.2008.123.1.139.

7   Eltis, D 2000, *The Rise of African Slavery in the Americas*, Cambridge University Press, Cambridge.

8   Rodney, W 1972, *How Europe Underdeveloped Africa, Bogle-L'Ouverture Publications*, London; Beckles, H 2013, *Britain's Black Debt: Reparations for Caribbean Slavery and Native Genocide*, University of the West Indies Press, Kingston, Jamaica.

9   Duignan, P & Gann, LH 1897, *The United States and Africa: A History*, Cambridge University Press, Cambridge.

10 Wikipedia 2023, 'Congo Pedicle', viewed 16 November 2023, https://en.wikipedia.org/wiki/Congo_Pedicle.

11 Wikipedia 2023, 'Caprivi Strip', viewed 16 November 2023, https://en.wikipedia.org/wiki/Caprivi_Strip.

12 Laskow, S 2017, 'The True Origin of The Gambia's Bizarre Borders', *Atlas Obscura*, viewed 16 November 2023, https://www.atlasobscura.com/articles/the-true-history-of-the-gambias-bizarre-origin-story.

13 Elkins, C 2005, *Imperial Reckoning: The Untold Story of Britain's Gulag in Kenya'*, Henry Holt and Company, New York City.

14 Davidson, B 1992, *The Black Man's Burden: Africa and the Curse of the Nation-State*, James Currey.

15 Johnson, DH 2003, *The Root Causes of Sudan's Civil Wars*, Indiana University Press, Bloomington, Indiana.

16 Forsyth, F 1969, *The Biafra Story: The Making of an African Legend*, Penguin, London.

17 Adichie, CN 2006, *Half of a Yellow Sun*, Knopf, New York City.

18 Gourevitch, P 1998, *We Wish to Inform You That Tomorrow We Will Be Killed with Our Families: Stories from Rwanda*, Farrar, Straus and Giroux, New York City.

19 Dallaire, R 2003, *Shake Hands with the Devil: The Failure of Humanity in Rwanda*, Arrow Books, London.

20 Rodney, W 1972, *How Europe Underdeveloped Africa*, Bogle-L'Ouverture Publications, London.

21 Fraser, A & Larmer, M 2010, *Zambia, Mining, and Neoliberalism: Boom and Bust on the Globalized Copperbelt*, Palgrave Macmillan, London.

22 Autesserre, S 2012, 'Dangerous Tales: Dominant Narratives on the Congo and their Unintended Consequences', *African Affairs*, vol 111, no 443, pp 202-222, viewed 16 November 2023, doi.org/10.1093/afraf/adr080.

23 Ngũgĩ wa Thiong'o 1986, *Decolonising the Mind: The Politics of Language in African Literature*, James Currey.

24 Mandela, N 1995, *Long Walk to Freedom: The Autobiography of Nelson Mandela*, Little, Brown and Company, Boston.

Chapter 3

1   African Development Bank 2019, 'Feed Africa', viewed 17 November 2023, https://www.afdb.org/fileadmin/uploads/afdb/Documents/Generic-Documents/Brochure_Feed_Africa_-En.pdf.

2   International Trade Administration 2022, 'Rwanda – Agriculture Sector', viewed 17 November 2023, https://www.trade.gov/country-commercial-guides/rwanda-agriculture-sector.

3   Cioffo, GD, Ansoms, A, & Murison, J 2016, 'Modernising Agriculture through a "New" Green Revolution: the Limits of the Crop Intensification Programme in Rwanda', *Review of African Political Economy*, vol 43, no 148, pp 277-293, viewed 17 November 2023, doi.org/10.1080/03056244.2016.1181053.

4   World Nuclear Association 2023, 'Uranium in Niger', viewed 18 November 2023, https://world-nuclear.org/information-library/country-profiles/countries-g-n/niger.aspx.

5   World Nuclear Association 2023, 'Uranium Production Figures, 2013-2022', viewed 18 November 2023, https://www.world-nuclear.org/information-library/facts-and-figures/uranium-production-figures.aspx.

6   Extractive Industries Transparency Initiative 2022, 'Democratic Republic of the Congo', viewed 18 November 2023, https://eiti.org/countries/democratic-republic-congo.

7   Trading Economics 2023, 'Zambia Exports', viewed 18 November 2023, https://tradingeconomics.com/zambia/exports.

8   Deloitte 2016, 'Mozambique's Economic Outlook: Governance Challenges Holding Back Economic Potential', viewed 18 November 2023, https://www2.deloitte.com/content/dam/Deloitte/uk/Documents/international-markets/deloitte-uk-mozambique-country-report.pdf.

9   Frühauf, A 2014, 'Mozambique's LNG Revolution: A Political Risk Outlook for the Rovuma LNG Ventures', *The Oxford Institute for Energy Studies*, viewed 18 November 2023, https://www.oxfordenergy.org/wpcms/wp-content/uploads/2014/04/NG-86.pdf.

10 Zainudeen, NM, Mohammed, L, Nyamful, A, Adotey, D, & Osae, SK 2023, 'A Comparative Review of the Mineralogical and Chemical Composition of African Major Bauxite Deposits', *Heliyon*, vol 9, no 8, viewed 18 November 2023, doi.org/10.1016/j.heliyon.2023.e19070.

11 International Trade Administration 2022, 'Tanzania - Country Com-

mercial Guide', viewed 18 November 2023, https://www.trade.gov/
country-commercial-guides/tanzania-mining.

12 Wikipedia 2023, 'Mining Industry of Ghana', viewed 18 November 2023,
https://en.wikipedia.org/wiki/Mining_industry_of_Ghana.

13 GlobalData 2016, 'Diamond Mining in Botswana to 2020', viewed
18 November 2023, https://www.globaldata.com/store/report/
diamond-mining-in-botswana-to-2020/.

14 Galal, S 2023, 'Oil Production in Africa as of 2022, by Country', *Statista*,
viewed 18 November 2023, https://www.statista.com/statistics/1178514/
main-oil-producing-countries-in-africa/.

15 Weny, K, Snow, R, & Zhang, S 2017, 'The Demographic Dividend Atlas for Africa: Tracking the Potential for a
Demographic Dividend', *United Nations Population Fund*,
viewed 12 December 2023, https://www.unfpa.org/resources/
demographic-dividend-atlas-africa-tracking-potential-demographic-dividend.

Chapter 4

1 UNICEF 2017, 'Generation 2030 Africa 2.0: Prioritizing Investments in Children to Reap the Demographic Dividend', viewed 18 November 2023, https://
www.unicef.org/reports/generation-2030-africa-20.

2 UNICEF n.d., 'Education', viewed 18 November 2023, https://www.unicef.
org/rwanda/education.

3 The World Bank 2023, 'Government Expenditure on Education, Total (% of
Government Expenditure)', viewed 19 November 2023, https://data.world-
bank.org/indicator/SE.XPD.TOTL.GB.ZS.

4 CIA n.d., 'Field Listing – Literacy', viewed 19 November 2023, https://www.
cia.gov/the-world-factbook/field/literacy/.

5 NHIS n.d., 'Brief Intro to the NHIS', viewed 19 November 2023, https://
www.nhis.gov.gh/about.

6 NHIS 2018, 'National Health Insurance Authority 2018 Annual Report',
viewed 19 November 2023, https://www.nhis.gov.gh/files/2018%20Annu-
al%20Report.pdf.

7 Rwanda Social Security Board 2023, 'Community-Based
Health Insurance Scheme Receives Financial Boost from
AHF', viewed 19 November 2023, https://www.rssb.rw/
community-based-health-insurance-scheme-receives-financial-boost-from-ahf.

8 World Health Organization 2019, 'Rwanda: the Beacon of Universal Health
Coverage in Africa', viewed 19 November 2023, https://www.afro.who.int/
news/rwanda-beacon-universal-health-coverage-africa.

9 Karkee, V & O'Higgins, N 2023, 'African Youth Face Pressing Challenges
in the Transition from School to Work', viewed 19 November 2023, https://
ilostat.ilo.org/african-youth-face-pressing-challenges-in-the-transition-from-
school-to-work/.

10 Choi, J, Dutz, MA, & Usman, Z 2019, 'The Future of Work in Africa:

Harnessing the Potential of Digital Technologies for All', *The World Bank*, viewed 19 November 2023, https://openknowledge.worldbank.org/entities/publication/9213ac4b-01ed-5d3b-b146-832fadb09d34.

11 Pitan, OS & Adedeji, SO 2012, 'Skills Mismatch Among University Graduates in the Nigeria
    Labor Market', *US–China Education Review*, pp 90-98, viewed 12 December 2023, https://www.researchgate.net/publication/305280818_Skills_Mismatch_Among_University_Graduates_in_the_Nigeria_Labor_Market.

Chapter 5

1 Sinek, S 2011, *Start with Why: How Great Leaders Inspire Everyone to Take Action*, Portfolio.

2 Mohler, A 2014, *The Conviction to Lead: 25 Principles for Leadership That Matters*, Bethany House Publishers, Bloomington, Minesota.

3 World Bank 2023, 'School Enrollment, Primary (% Gross) – Rwanda', viewed 19 November 2023, https://data.worldbank.org/indicator/SE.PRM.ENRR?locations=RW.

4 Rwanda Social Security Board 2023, 'Community-Based Health Insurance Scheme Receives Financial Boost from AHF', viewed 19 November 2023, https://www.rssb.rw/community-based-health-insurance-scheme-receives-financial-boost-from-ahf.

5 International Monetary Fund 2010, 'Press Release: IMF and World Bank Announce US$4.6 Billion Debt Relief for Liberia', viewed 19 November 2023, https://www.imf.org/en/News/Articles/2015/09/14/01/49/pr10267.

6 Dr. Brad Hounkpati 2017, *Former President Thabo Mbeki on African Leadership*, video, YouTube, viewed 19 November 2023, https://youtu.be/rNkLGhjqSDI.

Chapter 6

1 Wikipedia 2023, 'Orisha', viewed 19 November 2023, https://en.wikipedia.org/wiki/Orisha.

2 Lawal, B 1996, *The Gelede Spectacle: Art, Gender, and Social Harmony in African Culture*, University of Washington Press, Seattle.

3 Coast, E 2002, 'Maasai Socioeconomic Conditions: A Cross-Border Comparison', *Human Ecology*, vol 30, no 1, pp 79-105, viewed 19 November 2023,

4 Wikipedia 2023, 'Cinema of Nigeria', viewed 19 November 2023, https://en.wikipedia.org/wiki/Cinema_of_Nigeria.

5 Onuzulike, U 2007, 'Nollywood: the influence of the Nigerian Movie Industry on African Culture', *Human Communication*, vol 10, no 3, pp 231-242, viewed 19 November 2023, https://www.academia.edu/2537401/Nollywood_The_Influence_of_the_Nigerian_Movie_Industry_on_African_Culture.

6 Kelley, RDG 2000, *Freedom Dreams: The Black Radical Imagination*, Beacon Press, Boston; Neal, MA 2002, That's the Joint!: The Hip-Hop Studies Reader, Psychology Press, London.

7   The World Bank 2019, 'Record High Remittances Sent Globally in 2018', viewed 20 November 2023, https://www.worldbank.org/en/news/press-release/2019/04/08/record-high-remittances-sent-globally-in-2018.

8   AIMS n.d., *AIMS South Africa – African Institute of Mathematical Sciences (South Africa)*, website, viewed 20 November 2023, https://aims.ac.za/.

9   Institute of International Education n.d., 'Carnegie African Diaspora Fellowship Program', viewed 20 November 2023, https://www.iie.org/programs/carnegie-african-diaspora-fellowship-program/.

10 African Diaspora Network n.d., *Home – African Diaspora Network*, website, viewed 20 November 2023, https://africandiasporanetwork.org/.

11 Garrity, DP, Akinnifesi, FK, Ajayi, OC, Weldesemayat, SG, Mowo, JG, Kalinganire, A, Larwanou, M, & Bayala, J 2010, 'Evergreen Agriculture: A Robust Approach to Sustainable Food Security in Africa', *Food Security*, vol 2, no 3, pp 197-214, viewed 20 November 2023, doi.org/10.1007/s12571-010-0070-7.

12 Fernandes, EC & Nair, PK 1986, 'An Evaluation of the Structure and Function of Tropical Homegardens', *Agricultural Systems*, vol 21, no 4, pp 279-310, viewed 20 November 2023, doi.org/10.1016/0308-521X(86)90104-6.

13 Lin, BB 2011, 'Resilience in Agriculture through Crop Diversification: Adaptive Management for Environmental Change', *BioScience*, vol 61, no 3, pp 183-193, viewed 20 November 2023, doi.org/10.1525/bio.2011.61.3.4.

14 Griscom, BW, Adams, J, Ellis, PW, Houghton, RA, Lomax, G, Miteva, DA, Schlesinger, WH et al. 2017, 'Natural Climate Solutions', *Proceedings of the National Academy of Sciences*, vol 114, no 44, pp 11645-11650, viewed 20 November 2023, doi.org/10.1073/pnas.1710465114.

15 Dawson, IK, Carsan, S, Franzel, S, Kindt, R, van Breugel, P, Graudal, L, & Jamnadass, R 2014, 'Agroforestry, Livestock, Fodder Production and Climate Change Adaptation and Mitigation in East Africa: Issues and Options', *World Agroforestry Center*, Nairobi, Kenya, viewed 20 November 2023, doi.org/10.5716/WP14050.PDF.

16 Hobbs, PR 2007, 'Conservation Agriculture: What Is It and Why Is It Important for Future Sustainable Food Production?', *Journal of Agricultural Science*, vol 145, no 2, pp 127-137, viewed 20 November 2023, doi.org/10.1017/S0021859607006892.

17 Kassam, A, Friedrich, T, Shaxson, F, & Pretty, J 2009, 'The Spread of Conservation Agriculture: Justification, Sustainability and Uptake', *International Journal of Agricultural Sustainability*, vol 7, no 4, pp 292-320, viewed 20 November 2023, doi.org/10.3763/ijas.2009.0477.

18 Giller, KE, Witter, E, Corbeels, M, & Tittonell, P 2009, 'Conservation Agriculture and Smallholder Farming in Africa: The Heretics' View', *Field Crops Research*, vol 114, no 1, pp 23-34, viewed 20 November 2023, doi.org/10.1016/j.fcr.2009.06.017.

19 World Health Organization 2002, 'Traditional Medicine Strategy 2002-2005', viewed 20 November 2023, https://www.who.int/publications/i/item/

WHO-EDM-TRM-2002.1.

20 Tu, Y 2011, 'The Discovery of Artemisinin (Qinghaosu) and Gifts from Chinese Medicine', *Nature Medicine*, no 17, no 10, pp 1217-1220, viewed 20 November 2023, doi.org/10.1038/nm.2471.

Chapter 7

1 Transnet National Ports Authority 2021, 'Durban Port Development Framework Plan', https://www.transnetnationalportsauthority.net/CorporateAffairs/EnvironmentalPublic/Durban%20Port%20Development%20Framework%20Plan.pdf.

2 Addis Fortune 2019, 'Bole Airport expansion inaugurated', https://addisfortune.news/bole-airport-expansion-inaugurated/.

3 Climate Investment Funds n.d., 'Ouarzazate Lighting up the Sky', viewed 12 December 2023, https://www.cif.org/CIF10/morocco/ouarzazate.

4 Imbali, F 2020, 'A Different Wind of Change – Harnessing Africa's Largest Wind Project for Climate Action', *Rapid Transition Alliance*, viewed 12 December 2023, https://rapidtransition.org/stories/a-different-wind-of-change-harnessing-africas-largest-wind-project-for-climate-action/.

5 International Hydropower Association n.d., 'Ethiopia - Grand Ethiopian Renaissance Dam (GERD)', viewed 12 December 2023, https://www.hydropower.org/sediment-management-case-studies/ethiopia-grand-ethiopian-renaissance-dam-gerd.

6 Benti, NE, Woldegiyorgis, TA, Geffe, CA, Gurmesa, GS, Chaka, MD, & Mekonnen, YS 2023, 'Overview of Geothermal Resources Utilization in Ethiopia: Potentials, Opportunities, and Challenges', *Scientific African*, vol 19, https://doi.org/10.1016/j.sciaf.2023.e01562.

7 Jeffreys Bay Wind Farm 2020, 'Benefiting the Environment & Creating a Cleaner, Brighter Future', viewed 12 December 2023, http://jeffreysbaywindfarm.globeleq-projects.co.za/wp-content/uploads/sites/2/2020/01/Jeffreys_Bay_Wind_Farm_fact_files_2018.pdf.

8 Kathu Solar Park n.d., *Kathu Solar Park*, website, viewed 12 December 2023, https://www.kathusolarpark.co.za/.

9 Hitachi Energy n.d., 'Inga Kolwezi', *Hitachi Group*, viewed 12 December 2023, https://www.hitachienergy.com/about-us/customer-success-stories/inga-kolwezi.

10 Schneider Electric 2020, 'Schneider Electric to Build Four Control Centers for Egypt's National Energy Grid', viewed 12 December 2023, https://www.se.com/ww/en/about-us/newsroom/news/press-releases/schneider-electric-to-build-four-control-centers-for-egypt%E2%80%99s-national-energy-grid-5f0ece5929490d6702214d3a.

11 Prüss-Ustün, A, Bartram, J, Clasen, T, Colford, JM Jr, Cumming, O, Curtis, V &, Bonjour, S et al., 'Burden of Disease from Inadequate Water, Sanitation and Hygiene in Low- and Middle-Income Settings: A Retrospective Analysis of Data from 145 Countries', *Tropical Medicine & International Health*, vol 9,

no 8, pp 894-905, viewed 12 December 2023, doi.org/10.1111/tmi.12329.

12 International Coalition for Trachoma Control 2016, 'One WASH – the Implementation of Ethiopia's National Programme', viewed 12 December 2023, https://www.trachomacoalition.org/sites/default/files/content/resources/files/Ethiopia%20-%20One%20WASH.pdf.

13 MacLeod, NA 2018, 'Increasing Financial Flows for Urban Sanitation', *World Water Council*, viewed 12 December 2023, https://www.worldwatercouncil.org/sites/default/files/2018-03/IFFS_Durban%20eThekwini_case_study.pdf.

14 GSMA 2021, 'The Mobile Economy Sub-Saharan Africa 2021', viewed 12 December 2023, https://www.gsma.com/mobileeconomy/wp-content/uploads/2021/09/GSMA_ME_SSA_2021_English_Web_Singles.pdf.

15 Nigerian Communications Commission 2023, 'Industry Statistics', viewed 12 December 2023, https://ncc.gov.ng/statistics-reports/industry-overview#monthly-4.

16 Cowling, N 2023, 'Total Number of Mobile Connections in South Africa from 2017 to 2023', *Statista*, viewed 12 December 2023, https://www.statista.com/statistics/1347388/number-of-mobile-connections-south-africa/.

17 Baller, S, Dutta, S, & Lanvin, B 2016, 'The Global Information Technology Report 2016', *World Economic Forum*, viewed 12 December 2023, https://www.wsj.com/public/resources/documents/GITR2016.pdf.

18 Jack, W & Suri, T 2016, 'The Long-Run Poverty and Gender Impacts of Mobile Money', *Science*, vol 354, no 6317, pp 1288-1292, viewed 12 December, https://www.jefftk.com/suri2016.pdf.

19 Aker, JC 2011, 'Dial "A" for Agriculture: A Review of Information and Communication Technologies for Agricultural Extension in Developing Countries', *Agricultural Economics*, vol 42, no 6, pp 631-647, viewed 12 December 2023, doi.org/10.1111/j.1574-0862.2011.00545.x.

20 Amoah, B, Anto, EA, Osei, PK, Pieterson, K, & Crimi, A 2016, 'Boosting Antenatal Care Attendance and Number of Hospital Deliveries among Pregnant Women in Rural Communities: A Community Initiative in Ghana Based on Mobile Phones Applications and Portable Ultrasound Scans', *BMC Pregnancy and Childbirth*, vol 16, no 141, viewed 12 December 2023, doi.org/10.1186/s12884-016-0888-x.

21 Calderón, C & Servén, L 2010, 'Infrastructure and Economic Development in Sub-Saharan Africa', *World Bank*, Washington DC, viewed 13 December 2023, https://openknowledge.worldbank.org/entities/publication/2d680660-d5ec-5b81-9037-976840d352d8.

Chapter 8

1 Hanushek, E 2020, 'Quality Education and Economic Development', in B Panth & R Maclean (eds), *Anticipating and Preparing for Emerging Skills and Jobs: Key Issues, Concerns, and Prospects*, Springer, Singapore, pp 25-32, http://hanushek.stanford.edu/sites/default/files/publications/Hanushek%202020%20QualityEducation.pdf.

2   The World Bank 2023, 'Literacy Rate, Adult Total (% of People Aged 15 and Above)', viewed 14 December 2023, https://data.worldbank.org/indicator/ SE.ADT.LITR.ZS.

3   The World Bank 2023, 'Literacy Rate, Adult Total (% of People Aged 15 and Above)', viewed 14 December 2023, https://data.worldbank.org/indicator/ SE.ADT.LITR.ZS.

4   The World Bank 2023, 'Literacy Rate, Adult Total (% of People Aged 15 and Above)', viewed 14 December 2023, https://data.worldbank.org/indicator/ SE.ADT.LITR.ZS.

5   Trading Economics n.d., 'Germany Youth Unemployment Rate', viewed 14 December 2023, https://tradingeconomics.com/germany/ youth-unemployment-rate.

6   International Labour Organization 2022, 'National TVET Policies and Systems in Ethiopia', viewed 14 December 2023, https://www.ilo.org/wcmsp5/ groups/public/---africa/---ro-abidjan/---sro-addis_ababa/documents/publica-tion/wcms_863440.pdf.

7   Educate! n.d., 'Impact Evaluation Results', viewed 14 December 2023, https:// www.experienceeducate.org/results.

8   United Nations n.d., 'The 17 Goals', viewed 14 December 2023, https://sdgs. un.org/goals.

9   Department of Basic Education n.d., 'Inclusive Education', *South African Government*, viewed 14 December 2023, https://www.education.gov.za/Pro-grammes/InclusiveEducation.aspx.

10   Miller, JP 2007, *The Holistic Curriculum*, University of Toronto Press, Tornto.

11   Kingcombe, C 2012, 'Lessons for Developing Countries from Experience with Technical and Vocational Education and Training', *International Growth Centre*, London, viewed 14 December 2023, https://www.theigc.org/sites/ default/files/2014/09/Kingombe-2014-Working-Paper.pdf.

12   Piper, K 2020, 'What Kenya Can Teach Its Neighbors — and the US — about Improving the Lives of the "Unbanked"', *Vox*, New York City, viewed 14 December 2023, https://www.vox.com/future-perfect/21420357/ kenya-mobile-banking-unbanked-cellphone-money.

13   Korosec, K 2022, 'Zipline Is Now the National Drone Service Provider for Rwanda', *TechCrunch*, San Francisco, viewed 14 December 2023,

14   Meindl, L 2022, 'Jumia's 3 Keys to Reaching Profitability', *The Motley Fool*, Alexandria, Virginia, viewed 14 December 2023, https://www.fool.com/ investing/2022/02/05/jumias-3-keys-to-reaching-profitability/.

15   Wikipedia 2023, 'Mo Ibrahim', viewed 14 December 2023, https://en.wikipe-dia.org/wiki/Mo_Ibrahim.

16   Nsehe, M 2013, 'Five Lessons from Zimbabwe's Richest Man, Strive Masiyiwa', *Forbes*, Jersey City, viewed 14 December 2023, https://www.forbes.com/sites/mfonobongnsehe/2013/02/24/ five-lessons-from-zimbabwes-richest-man-strive-masiyiwa/.

17 Hanushek, E & Woessman, L 2015, *The Knowledge Capital of Nations: Education and the Economics of Growth*, MIT Press Academic, Cambridge.

Chapter 9

1 South African Government n.d., 'Promotion of Access to Information Act 2 of 2000', viewed 14 December 2023, https://www.gov.za/documents/promotion-access-information-act.

2 Federal Government of Nigeria 2011, 'Freedom of Information Act', *Laws of the Federation of Nigeria*, viewed 14 December 2023, https://www.cbn.gov.ng/FOI/Freedom%20Of%20Information%20Act.pdf.

3 Aristotle 1998, *Politics*, E Barker (trans), OUP, Oxford.

4 Dicey AV 1885, *Introduction to the Study of Law of the Constitution*, Liberty Classics, Indianapolis, https://files.libertyfund.org/files/1714/0125_Bk.pdf.

5 Leiter, B & Sevel, M n.d., 'Philosophy of Law', *Encyclopaedia Britannica*, Chicago, viewed 14 December 2023, https://www.britannica.com/topic/philosophy-of-law/Realism; Krygier, M 2005, 'Review: [Untitled]', *Journal of Law and Society*, vol 32, no 4, pp 657–666, viewed 14 December 2023, https://www.jstor.org/stable/3557257.

6 The World Bank n.d., 'Doing Business', viewed 14 December 2023, https://archive.doingbusiness.org/en/doingbusiness.

7 The Independent Commission Against Corruption of Mauritius n.d., 'About the ICAC', viewed 14 December 2023, https://www.icac.mu/about-the-icac/.

8 The Editors of Encyclopaedia Britannica 2023, 'Civil Rights Act: United States [1964]', *Encyclopaedia Britannica*, Chicago, viewed 14 December 2023, https://www.britannica.com/event/Civil-Rights-Act-United-States-1964.

9 South African History Online n.d., 'Truth and Reconciliation Commission (TRC)', viewed 14 December 2023, https://www.sahistory.org.za/article/truth-and-reconciliation-commission-trc-0.

10 BBC News 2012, 'Rwanda "Gacaca" Genocide Courts Finish Work', *BBC*, London, viewed 14 December 2023, https://www.bbc.com/news/world-africa-18490348.

11 Abers, R, King, R, Votto, D, & Brandão, I 2018, 'Porto Alegre: Participatory Budgeting and the Challenge of Sustaining Transformative Change', *World Resource Institute*, viewed 14 December 2023, https://www.wri.org/research/porto-alegre-participatory-budgeting-and-challenge-sustaining-transformative-change.

12 The World Bank 2008, 'Brazil: Toward a More Inclusive and Effective Participatory Budget in Porto Alegre', viewed 14 December 2023, https://openknowledge.worldbank.org/entities/publication/ca9f0984-5ad0-5435-ad75-828abaf06d4d.

13 The World Bank n.d., 'Governance', viewed 15 December 2023, https://www.worldbank.org/en/topic/governance.

14 African Union n.d., 'AGA', viewed 15 December 2023, https://au.int/en/aga.

15 Integrity & Anti-Corruption Commission n.d., 'Home Page - Integrity &

Anti-Corruption Commission', viewed 15 December 2023, https://www.jiacc.gov.jo.

16 Transparency International 2021, 'Corruption Perceptions Index', viewed 15 December 2023, https://www.transparency.org/en/cpi/2021/index/aus.

17 Wikipedia 2023, 'Economic and Financial Crimes Commission', viewed 15 December 2023, https://en.wikipedia.org/wiki/Economic_and_Financial_Crimes_Commission.

Chapter 10

1 Wikipedia 2023, 'Zayed bin Sultan Al Nahyan', viewed 15 December 2023, https://en.wikipedia.org/wiki/Zayed_bin_Sultan_Al_Nahyan.

2 Wikipedia 2023, 'Khalifa bin Zayed Al Nahyan', viewed 15 December 2023, https://en.wikipedia.org/wiki/Khalifa_bin_Zayed_Al_Nahyan.

3 Wikipedia 2023, 'Mohammed bin Rashid Al Maktoum', viewed 15 December 2023, https://en.wikipedia.org/wiki/Mohammed_bin_Rashid_Al_Maktoum.

4 World Travel and Tourism Council 2023, 'UAE Travel & Tourism Sector Set to Recover This Year, Says WTTC', viewed 15 December 2023, https://wttc.org/news-article/uae-travel-and-tourism-sector-set-to-recover-this-year-says-wttc.

5 The World Bank n.d., 'Doing Business', viewed 17 December 2023, https://archive.doingbusiness.org/en/doingbusiness.

6 Ministry of Trade and Industry Singapore n.d., 'Free Trade Agreements', viewed 17 December 2023, https://www.mti.gov.sg/Trade/Free-Trade-Agreements.

7 International Trade Administration 2023, 'Trade Agreements', viewed 17 December 2023, https://www.trade.gov/country-commercial-guides/chile-trade-agreements.

8 Department of Foreign Affairs and Trade n.d., 'Comprehensive and Progressive Agreement for Trans-Pacific Partnership (CPTPP)', Australian Government, viewed 17 December 2023, https://www.dfat.gov.au/trade/agreements/in-force/cptpp/comprehensive-and-progressive-agreement-for-trans-pacific-partnership.

9 Ministry of Trade and Industry Singapore n.d., 'Digital Economy Partnership Agreement (DEPA)', viewed 17 December 2023, https://www.mti.gov.sg/Trade/Digital-Economy-Agreements/The-Digital-Economy-Partnership-Agreement.

10 Ntembe, A 2022, 'A Single Currency for Africa: Challenges and Possibilities', in AA Amin, RN Tawah, & A Ntembe (eds), Monetary and Financial Systems in Africa, Palgrave Macmillan, London, pp 395-417, https://doi.org/10.1007/978-3-030-96225-8_17.

11 Hou, Z, Keane, J, Kennan, J, & te Velde, DW 2015, 'Shockwatch Bulletin: The Oil Price Shock of 2014: Drivers, Impacts and Policy Implications', ODI, viewed 17 December 2023, https://odi.org/en/publications/shockwatch-bulletin-the-oil-price-shock-of-2014-drivers-impacts-and-policy-implications/.

12 This Day 2021, 'The Demise of Nigerian Textile Industry', viewed 17 December 2023, https://www.thisdaylive.com/index.php/2022/05/02/the-demise-of-nigerian-textile-industry.

Chapter 11

1 GIMI n.d., *Global Innovation Institute – GIMI*, website, viewed 17 December 2023, https://www.giminstitute.org/.

2 Florida, R 2002, *The Rise of the Creative Class*, Basic Books, New York.

3 Demirgüç-Kunt, A, Klapper, L, Singer, D, Ansar, S, & Hess, J 2017, 'The Global Findex Database 2017', World Bank Group, viewed 17 December 2023, https://documents1.worldbank.org/curated/en/332881525873182837/pdf/126033-PUB-PUBLIC-pubdate-4-19-2018.pdf.

4 Suri, T, Jack, W, &, Stoker, TM 2012, 'Documenting the Birth of a Financial Economy', *Proceedings of the National Academy of Sciences of the United States*, vol 109, no 26, pp 10257-10262, viewed 17 December 2023, doi.org/10.1073/pnas.1115843109.

5 Matheson, R 2016, 'Study: Mobile-Money Services Lift Kenyans out of Poverty', *MIT*, Cambridge, Massachusetts, viewed 17 December 2023, https://news.mit.edu/2016/mobile-money-kenyans-out-poverty-1208.

6 Amref Health Africa n.d., *Amref Health Africa*, website, viewed 17 December 2023, https://amref.org/.

7 eLimu n.d., *eLimu World*, website, viewed 17 December 2023, https://www.e-limu.org/.

8 Siyavula n.d., *Siyavula: Technology-Powered Learning*, website, viewed 17 December 2023, https://www.siyavula.com/.

9 ENGIE Energy Access n.d., 'Our Solutions', viewed 17 December 2023, https://engie-energyaccess.com/solutions.

10 Ushahidi n.d., *Ushahidi – Crowdsourcing Solutions to Empower Communities*, website, viewed 17 December 2023, https://www.ushahidi.com/.

11 Startup Genome 2020, 'Global Startup Ecosystem Report 2023 (GSER2020)', viewed 17 December 2023, https://startupgenome.com/reports/gser2020.

12 Ganti, A 2023, 'What Is the Multiplier Effect? Formula and Example', *Investopedia*, viewed 17 December 2023, https://www.investopedia.com/terms/m/multipliereffect.asp.

Chapter 12

1 Devereux, S & Sabates-Wheeler, R 2017, 'Social Protection and Inclusive Growth in Africa', *Journal of Social Policy*, vol 47, no 1, pp 153-171.

2 ODI n.d., 'Productive Safety Net Programme (PSNP), Ethiopia', viewed 18 December 2023, https://odi.org/en/about/our-work/productive-safety-net-programme-psnp-ethiopia/.

3 Hoddinott, J, Berhane, G, Gilligan, DA, Kumar, N, & Taffesse, AS 2012, 'The Impact of Ethiopia's Productive Safety Net Programme and Related Transfers on Agricultural Productivity', *Journal of African Economies*, vol 21,

no 5, pp 761-786, viewed 18 December 2023, doi.org/10.1093/jae/ejs02.

4   Woldehanna, T 2010, 'Productive Safety Net Program and Children's Time Use between Work and Schooling in Ethiopia', in J Cockburn & J Kabubo-Mariara (eds), *Child Welfare in Developing Countries*, Springer, New York, doi.org/10.1007/978-1-4419-6275-1_6.

5   Coll-Black, S, Gilligan, D, Hoddinott, J, Kumar, N, Taffesse, AS, & Wiseman, W 2011, 'Targeting Food Security Interventions When "Everyone Is Poor": The Case of Ethiopia's Productive Safety Net Programme', *International Food Policy Research Institute*, Washington, DC, viewed 18 December 2023, https://ebrary.ifpri.org/digital/collection/p15738coll2/id/124855.

6   Holmes, R & Jones, N 2010, *Gender and Social Protection in the Developing World*, Zed Books, London.

7   Sabates-Wheeler, R & Devereux, S 2010, 'Cash Transfers and High Food Prices: Explaining Outcomes on Ethiopia's Productive Safety Net Programme', *Food Policy*, vol 35, no 4, pp 274-285, viewed 18 December 2023, doi.org/10.1016/j.foodpol.2010.01.001.

8   Orlandi, N 2021, 'Social Grant Performance as at End March 20/21', *Parliament of the Republic of South Africa*, viewed 18 December 2023, https://www.parliament.gov.za/storage/app/media/PBO/National_Development_Plan_Analysis/2021/june/03-06-2021/May_2021_Social_Grant_fact_sheet.pdf.

9   The World Bank 2012, 'World Development Report 2013: Jobs', viewed 18 December 2023, http://hdl.handle.net/10986/11843.

10 Sen, A 1999, *Development as Freedom*, Oxford University Press, Oxford.

11 Fukuyama, F 2001, 'Social Capital, Civil Society and Development', *Third World Quarterly*, vol 22, no 1, pp 7-20, viewed 18 December 2023, doi.org/10.1080/01436590020022547.

12 Becker, G 1964, *Human Capital: A Theoretical and Empirical Analysis*, Columbia University Press, New York.

13 Duflo, E 2012, 'Women's Empowerment and Economic Development', *Journal of Economic Literature*, vol 50, no 4, pp 1051-1079, viewed 18 December 2023, doi.org/10.1257/jel.50.4.1051

14 The World Bank 2012, 'World Development Report 2012: Gender Equality and Development', viewed 18 December 2023, http://hdl.handle.net/10986/4391.

15 Collier, P 2007, *The Bottom Billion: Why the Poorest Countries are Failing and What Can Be Done About It*, Oxford University Press, Oxford.

16 Birdsall, N & Londono, JL 1997, 'Asset Inequality Matters: An Assessment of the World Bank's Approach to Poverty Reduction', *The American Economic Review*, vol 87, no 2, pp 32-37, viewed 18 December 2023, https://www.jstor.org/stable/2950879.

17 The World Bank 2012, 'World Development Report 2013: Jobs', viewed 18 December 2023, http://hdl.handle.net/10986/11843.

Chapter 13

1   Auditor-General of South Africa n.d., *Auditor General South Africa*, website, viewed 18 December 2023, https://www.agsa.co.za/.

2   South African Reserve Bank n.d., 'Monetary Policy', viewed 18 December 2023, https://www.resbank.co.za/en/home/what-we-do/monetary-policy.

3   Prime Minister's Office, Singapore 2016, *Parliamentary Debate on President's Address,* YouTube video, viewed 18 December 2023, https://youtu.be/Q6Gce5wEue0.

4   GovLine n.d., 'Department of IPID | Independent Police Investigative Directorate', viewed 18 December 2023, https://www.govline.co.za/department-ipid-independent-police-investigative-directorate/.

Chapter 14

1   World Commission on Environment and Development 1987, 'Report of the World Commission on Environment and Development: Our Common Future', *United Nations,* viewed 18 December 2023, https://sustainabledevelopment.un.org/content/documents/5987our-common-future.pdf.

2   Mbaria, J & Ogada, M 2016, *The Big Conservation Lie: The Untold Story of Wildlife Conservation in Kenya*, Lens & Pens Publishing.

3   Pretty, J & Smith, D 2004, 'Social Capital in Biodiversity Conservation and Management', *Conservation Biology*, vol 18, no 3, pp 631-638, viewed 18 December 2023, doi.org/10.1111/j.1523-1739.2004.00126.x

4   Berkes, F 2007, 'Community-Based Conservation in a Globalized World', *Proceedings of the National Academy of Sciences*, vol 104, no 39, pp 15188-15193, viewed 18 December 2023, doi.org/ 10.1073/pnas.0702098104.

5   Great Barrier Reef Marine Park Authority 2014, 'Great Barrier Reef Region Strategic Assessment: Program Report', *Australian Government,* viewed 18 December 2023, https://elibrary.gbrmpa.gov.au/jspui/bitstream/11017/2860/1/GBR%20Region%20SA_Program%20Report_FINAL.pdf.

6   Colding, J & Folke, C 2001, 'Social Taboos: "Invisible" Systems of Local Resource Management and Biological Conservation', *Ecological Applications*, vol 11, no 2, pp 584-600, viewed 18 December 2023, doi.org/10.1890/1051-0761(2001)011[0584%3ASTISOL]2.0.CO%3B2.

7   Maathai, W 2007, *Unbowed: A Memoir*, Anchor Books.

8   The Green Belt Movement 2018, 'Annual Report 2018', viewed 18 December 2023, http://www.greenbeltmovement.org/sites/greenbeltmovement.org/files/2018%20Annual%20Report.pdf.

9   The Green Belt Movement n.d., *The Green Belt Movement,* website, viewed 18 December 2023, http://www.greenbeltmovement.org/.

10 Maathai, W 2004, *The Green Belt Movement: Sharing the Approach and the Experience*, Lantern Books.

11 United Nations Environment Programme & United Nations Development Programme 2008, *World Resources 2008: Roots Resilience - Growing the Wealth of the Poor,* World Resources Institute, Washington, DC, https://wed-

ocs.unep.org/20.500.11822/28261.

12 Pacey, P 2020, 'CAMPFIRE (Communal Areas Management Programme for Indigenous Resources)', *Whole Earth Education*, viewed 18 December 2023, https://wholeeartheducation.com/campfire-communal-areas-management-programme-for-indigenous-resources/.

13 Independent Evaluation Group 2015, 'Publication: World Bank Group Support to Electricity Access, FY2000-2014: An Independent Evaluation', *World Bank Group*, viewed 18 December 2023, http://hdl.handle.net/10986/22953.

14 United Nations Environment Programme 2019, 'Costa Rica Named 'UN Champion of the Earth' for Pioneering Role in Fighting Climate Change', *United Nations*, viewed 19 December 2023, https://www.unep.org/news-and-stories/press-release/costa-rica-named-un-champion-earth-pioneering-role-fighting-climate.

15 Government of Costa Rica 2018, 'National Decarbonization Plan', viewed 19 December 2023, https://unfccc.int/sites/default/files/resource/NationalDecarbonizationPlan.pdf.

16 Porras, I, Barton, DN, Miranda, M, &, Chacón-Cascante, A 2013, 'Learning from 20 Years of Payments for Ecosystem Services in Costa Rica', *International Institute for Environment and Development*, viewed 19 December 2023, https://www.iied.org/sites/default/files/pdfs/migrate/16514IIED.pdf.

Chapter 15

1 United Nations Economic Commission for Africa n.d., 'ECOWAS - Free Movement of Persons', viewed 19 December 2023, https://archive.uneca.org/pages/ecowas-free-movement-persons.

2 West African Monetary Institute n.d., *West African Monetary Institute*, website, viewed 19 December 2023, https://www.wami-imao.org/.

3 Meyer, I 2009, 'ECOWAS: The Protocol Relating to the Mechanism for Conflict Prevention, Management, Resolution, Peace-Keeping and Security', *Grin*, viewed 19 December 2023, https://www.grin.com/document/157548.

4 East African Community n.d., 'Overview of EAC', viewed 19 December 2023, https://www.eac.int/overview-of-eac.

5 East African Community n.d., 'Customs Union', viewed 19 December 2023, https://www.eac.int/customs-union.

6 East African Community n.d., 'Common Market', viewed 19 December 2023, https://www.eac.int/common-market.

7 East African Community n.d., 'Monetary Union', viewed 19 December 2023, https://www.eac.int/monetary-union.

8 African Union n.d., 'Southern African Development Community (SADC)', viewed 19 December 2023, https://au.int/en/recs/sadc.

9 Hartzenberg, T 2011, 'Regional Integration in Africa', *World Trade Organization*, viewed 19 December 2023, doi.org/10.2139/ssrn.1941742.

10 SADC n.d., 'FTA Brochure', viewed 19 December 2023, https://tis.sadc.int/french/regional-integration/tifi/sadc-free-trade-area/fta-brochure/.

11 Mandaza, I & Phiri, M 2017, 'An Overview of Regional Integration in SADC: Macroeconomic Convergence and Sectoral Cooperation', *African Journal of Economic and Sustainable Development*, vol 6, no 1, pp 1-16.

12 SADC 2012, 'Regional Infrastructure Development Master Plan Executive Summary (2012)', viewed 19 December 2023, https://sadc-eu.sardc.net/regional-infrastructure-development-master-plan-executive-summary-2012/

13 Nathan, L 2012, *Community of Insecurity: SADC's Struggle for Peace and Security in Southern Africa*, African Books Collective.

14 African Union n.d., 'About the African Union', viewed 19 December 2023, https://au.int/en/overview; Murithi, T 2005, *The African Union: Pan-Africanism, Peacebuilding and Development*, Ashgate.

15 African Union n.d., 'The African Continental Free Trade Area', viewed 19 December 2023, https://au.int/en/african-continental-free-trade-area.

16 African Union n.d., 'Agenda 2063: The Africa We Want', viewed 21 December 2023, https://au.int/en/agenda2063/overview.

17 Tayo, T 2021, 'Gains from Africa's Single Market Must Be Equitable', *Institute for Security Studies,* viewed 21 December 2023, https://issafrica.org/iss-today/gains-from-africas-single-market-must-be-equitable.

18 Reinhart, CM & Rogoff, KS 2004, 'The Modern History of Exchange Rate Arrangements: A Reinterpretation', *The Quarterly Journal of Economics*, vol 119, no 1, pp 1-48, viewed 21 December 2023, doi.org/10.3386/w8963.

19 Masson, P & Pattillo, C 2005, 'Monetary Union in West Africa (ECOWAS): Is It Desirable and How Could It Be Achieved?', *International Monetary Fund*, viewed 21 December 2023, https://www.imf.org/external/pubs/nft/op/204/.

20 Ndemo, B & Weiss, T 2017, *Digital Kenya: An Entrepreneurial Revolution in the Making,* Palgrave Macmillan, London.

21 African Union n.d., 'African Peace and Security Architecture (APSA)', viewed 21 December 2023, https://au.int/en/apsa.

22 Clapham, C 1996, *Africa and the International System: The Politics of State Survival*, Cambridge University Press, Cambridge.

23 Van de Walle, N 2001, *African Economies and the Politics of Permanent Crisis*, Cambridge University Press, Cambridge, pp 1979-1999.

24 Rodney, W 1972, *How Europe Underdeveloped Africa*, Bogle-L'Ouverture Publications, London.

Chapter 16

1 Borensztein, E, De Gregorio, J, & Lee, JW 1998, 'How Does Foreign Direct Investment Affect Economic Growth?' *Journal of International Economics*, vol 45, no 1, pp 115-135, viewed 21 December 2023, doi.org/10.1016/S0022-1996(97)00033-0.

2 Wang, Miao & Wong, MC Sunny 2011, 'FDI, Education, and Economic Growth: Quality Matters!', *Atlantic Economic Journal*, vol 39, no 2, pp 103-115, viewed 21 December 2023, doi.org/10.1007/s11293-011-9268-0

3   Borensztein, E, De Gregorio, J, & Lee, JW 1998, 'How Does Foreign Direct Investment Affect Economic Growth?' *Journal of International Economics*, vol 45, no 1, pp 115-135, viewed 21 December 2023, doi.org/10.1016/S0022-1996(97)00033-0.

4   Asiedu, E 2005, 'Foreign Direct Investment in Africa: The Role of Natural Resources, Market Size, Government Policy, Institutions and Political Instability', *SSRN*, viewed 21 December 2023, doi.org/10.2139/ssrn.717361.

5   Poelhekke, S & van der Ploeg, F 2010, 'Do Natural Resources Attract FDI? Evidence from Non-Stationary Sector-Level Data', *CEPR*, viewed 21 December 2023, https://ssrn.com/abstract=1711092.

6   Markusen, JR & Maskus, KE 1999, 'Discriminating among Alternative Theories of the Multinational Enterprise', *National Bureau of Economic Research*, Cambridge, viewed 21 December 2023, https://www.nber.org/system/files/working_papers/w7164/w7164.pdf.

7   Lloyds Bank 2023, 'Foreign direct investment (FDI) in Egypt', viewed 21 December 2023, https://www.lloydsbanktrade.com/en/market-potential/egypt/investment.

8   Busse, M & Hefeker, C 2005 'Political Risk, Institutions and Direct Foreign Investment', *HWWA*, viewed 21 December 2023, doi.org/10.2139/ssrn.704283.

9   Asiedu, E 2005, 'Foreign Direct Investment in Africa: The Role of Natural Resources, Market Size, Government Policy, Institutions and Political Instability', *SSRN*, viewed 21 December 2023, doi.org/10.2139/ssrn.717361.

10 Globerman, S & Shapiro, D 2002, 'Global Foreign Direct Investment Flows: The Role of Governance Infrastructure', *World Development*, vol 30, no 11, pp 1899-1919, viewed 21 December 2023, doi.org/10.1016/S0305-750X(02)00110-9.

11 Lloyds Bank 2023, 'Foreign Direct Investment (FDI) in Morocco', viewed 21 December 2023, https://www.lloydsbanktrade.com/en/market-potential/morocco/investment.

12 Wilson, G 2021, 'Morocco: Africa's Leading Automotive Manufacturing Hub', *Manufacturing Digital Magazine*, viewed 21 December 2023, https://manufacturingdigital.com/smart-manufacturing/morocco-africas-leading-automotive-manufacturing-hub.

13 Upsilon Consulting 2021, 'Casablanca Finance City (CFC): What You Should Know', viewed 21 December 2023, https://www.upsilon-consulting.com/en/2021/03/casablanca-finance-city-cfc-what-you-should-know/.

14 Farole, T, Akinci, G 2011, 'Special Economic Zones: Progress, Emerging Challenges, and Future Directions', *World Bank*, viewed 22 December 2023, http://hdl.handle.net/10986/2341.

15 Globerman, S & Shapiro, D 2002, 'Global Foreign Direct Investment Flows: The Role of Governance Infrastructure', *World Development*, vol 30, no 11, pp 1899-1919, viewed 22 December 2023, doi.org/10.1016/S0305-750X(02)00110-9.

16 Djankov, S, La Porta, R, LopezdeSilanes, F, & Shleifer, A 2000, 'The Regulation of Entry', *NBER*, viewed 22 December 2023, doi.org/10.3386/w7892.

17 Roseth, VV, Valerio, A, & Gutiérrez, M 2016, 'Education, Skills and Labour Market Outcomes', *World Bank*, viewed 22 December 2023, https://openknowledge.worldbank.org/bitstream/handle/10986/24276/Education-00ski0reas0in0120countries.pdf.

Chapter 17

1 Kenya Urban Roads Authority n.d., 'Private Public Partnership', viewed 22 December 2023, https://kura.go.ke/private-public-partnership/.

2 Gavi Staff 2022, 'Gavi impact in Africa since 2000', *Gavi*, viewed 22 December 2023, https://www.gavi.org/vaccineswork/gavi-impact-africa-2000.

3 Hotez, P 2014, 'Vaccine Diplomacy: Historical Perspectives and Future Directions', *PLoS Neglected Tropical Diseases*, vol 8, no 6, viewed 22 December 2023, doi.org/10.1371/journal.pntd.0002808.

4 Trisos, CH, Adelekan, Em, Totin, A, Ayanlade, J, Efitre, A, Gemeda, K, Kalaba, C, Lennard, C, Masao, Y, Mgaya, G, Ngaruiya, D, Olago, NP, Simpson, & S, Zakieldeen 2022, 'Africa', in HO Pörtner, DC Roberts, M Tignor, ES Poloczanska, K Mintenbeck, A Alegría, M Craig, S Langsdorf, S Löschke, V Möller, A Okem, & B Rama (eds), *Climate Change 2022: Impacts, Adaptation and Vulnerability*, Cambridge University Press, Cambridge, pp 1285-1455, viewed 22 December 2023, doi.org10.1017/9781009325844.011.

5 UNFCCC n.d., 'Nationally Determined Contributions (NDCs)', viewed 22 December 2023, https://unfccc.int/process-and-meetings/the-paris-agreement/nationally-determined-contributions-ndcs.

6 GPE n.d., 'GPE Impact', viewed 22 December 2023, https://www.globalpartnership.org/results/gpe-impact.

7 The World Bank 2023, 'School Enrollment, Primary (% Gross) - Burkina Faso', viewed 22 December 2023, https://data.worldbank.org/indicator/SE.PRM.ENRR?locations=BF.

; The World Bank 2023, 'Primary Completion Rate, Total (% of Relevant Age Group) - Burkina Faso', viewed 22 December 2023, https://data.worldbank.org/indicator/SE.PRM.CMPT.ZS?locations=BF.

8 GPE n.d., 'Education in Sierra Leone', viewed 22 December 2023, https://www.globalpartnership.org/where-we-work/sierra-leone.

9 Klasen, S 2002, 'Low Schooling for Girls, Slower Growth for All? Cross Country Evidence on the Effect of Gender Inequality in Education on Economic Development', *World Bank Economic Review*, vol 16, no 3, pp 345-373, viewed 22 December 2023, https://doi.org/10.1093/wber/lhf004.

10 SEforALL n.d., *Sustainable Energy for All*, website, viewed 22 December 2023, https://www.seforall.org/.

11 Macrotrends 2023, 'Rwanda Electricity Access 1992-2023', viewed 22 December 2023, https://www.macrotrends.net/countries/RWA/rwanda/electricity-access-statistics.

12 Baker, L, Newell, P, & Phillips, J 2014, 'The Political Economy of Energy Transitions: The Case of South Africa', *New Political Economy*, vol 19, no 6, pp 791-818, viewed 22 December 2023, doi.org/10.1080/13563467.2013.849674.

13 The Economist 2022, 'The Chinese-African Relationship Is Important to Both Sides, but Also Unbalanced', viewed 22 December 2023, https://www.economist.com/special-report/2022/05/20/the-chinese-african-relationship-is-important-to-both-sides-but-also-unbalanced.

14 Jennings, R 2021, 'Charting the Future of China's Infrastructure Projects in Africa After a Decade of Lending', *VOA*, viewed 22 December 2023, https://www.voanews.com/a/charting-the-future-of-china-s-infrastructure-projects-in-africa-after-a-decade-of-lending-/6355784.html.

15 Sun, HL 2011, 'Understanding China's Agricultural Investments in Africa', *SAIIA*, viewed 22 December 2023, https://saiia.org.za/research/understanding-chinas-agricultural-investments-in-africa/.

16 Chen, X, Zhang, F, Zhang, J, & Zhou, Q 2018, 'China's Agricultural Technology Demonstration Centres in Africa: Overview and Assessment', *African Studies Quarterly*, vol 18, no 1, pp 73-91.

17 Jiang, H, Zhou, L, & Tang, M 2016, 'The Effects of China's Aid to Africa Agricultural Technology Demonstration Centres: Evidence from Mozambique', *Journal of International Development*, vol 28, no 7, pp 1038-1056.

18 Zhang, H & Smith, G 2020, 'China's Agricultural Aid to Africa: Policy Evolution and Features', *International Journal of Agricultural Sustainability*, vol 18, no 3, pp 264-277.

19 Knoll, A & de Weijer, F 2016, 'Understanding African and European Perspectives on Migration: Towards a Better Partnership for Regional Migration Governance?', *European Centre for Development Policy Management*, viewed 22 December 2023, https://ecdpm.org/application/files/5116/5546/8821/DP203-Understanding-African-European-Perspectives-Migration-November-2016.pdf.

20 Morrissey, O & Zgovu, E 2009, 'The Impact of Economic Partnership Agreements on ACP Agriculture Imports and Welfare', *University of Nottingham*, viewed 22 December 2023, https://ideas.repec.org/p/not/notcre/07-09.html.

21 Elowson, C 2019, 'The African Peace Facility: Evaluating a Decade of EU Assistance to Peace in Africa', *Nordic Africa Institute*.

22 African Development Bank Group n.d., 'Power Africa Initiative', viewed 22 December 2023, https://www.afdb.org/en/topics-and-sectors/initiatives-partnerships/power-africa-initiative.

23 Rodrik, D 2018, 'New Technologies, Global Value Chains, and Developing Economies', *National Bureau of Economic Research*, viewed 22 December 2023, doi.org/10.3386/w25164.

24 Brautigam, D 2020, *Will Africa Feed China?* Oxford University Press, Oxford.

25 Simumba, T 2018, 'He Who Pays the Piper: Zambia's Growing China Debt Crisis', *Centre for Trade Policy and Development*, viewed 22 December 2023, https://www.asienhaus.de/uploads/tx_news/He_Who_Pays_The_Piper-_

Zambia_s_Growing_China_Debt_Crisis-1.pdf.

26 Bilal, S & Szepesi S 2005, 'How Regional Economic Communities Can Facilitate Participation in the WTO: The Experience of Mauritius and Zambia,' in P Gallagher, P Low, & AL Stoler (eds), *Managing the Challenges of WTO Participation: 45 Case Studies*, Cambridge University Press, Cambridge.

27 Brautigam, D 2011, 'Chinese Development Aid in Africa: What, Where, Why, and How Much?', in J Golley & L Song (eds), *Rising China: Global Challenges and Opportunities*, Australian National University Press, Canberra.

28 Morrissey, O 2005, 'Imports and Export Performance in Developing Countries', *Review of World Economics*, vol 141, no 2, pp 219-241.

29 Betzold, C & Weiler, F 2017, 'Allocation of Aid for Adaptation to Climate Change: Do Vulnerable Countries Receive More Support?', *International Environmental Agreements: Politics, Law and Economics*, vol 17, no 1, pp 17-36.

30 Gallagher, KP 2005, *Putting Development First: The Importance of Policy Space in the WTO and IFIs*, Zed Books, London.

Chapter 18

1 Khan, AS 2017, *The Next Pandemic: On the Front Lines Against Humankind's Gravest Dangers*, PublicAffairs, New York.

2 World Health Organization n.d., 'Ebola: West Africa, March 2014-2016', viewed 23 December 2023, https://www.who.int/emergencies/situations/ebola-outbreak-2014-2016-West-Africa.

3 Li, ZJ, Tu, WX, Wang, XC et al. 2016, 'A Practical Community-Based Response Strategy to Interrupt Ebola Transmission in Sierra Leone', *Infect Disease of Poverty*, vol 5, no 74, viewed 23 December 2023, doi.org/10.1186/s40249-016-0167-0.

4 HIV.gov 2023, 'PEPFAR', *U.S. Department of Health & Human Services*, viewed 23 December 2023, https://www.hiv.gov/federal-response/pepfar-global-aids/pepfar/.

5 Knoema n.d., 'Ethiopia - Contribution of Travel and Tourism to GDP as a Share of GDP', viewed 23 December 2023, https://knoema.com/atlas/Ethiopia/topics/Tourism/Travel-and-Tourism-Total-Contribution-to-GDP/Contribution-of-travel-and-tourism-to-GDP-percent-of-GDP.

6 Yonas, H 2022, 'Digital Ethiopia 2025 Hopes to Streamline Ethiopia's Economy', *The Borgen Project*, viewed 23 December 2023, https://borgenproject.org/digital-ethiopia-2025/.

7 Green Belt Movement n.d., 'Our History', viewed 23 December 2023, https://www.greenbeltmovement.org/who-we-are/our-history.

8 Braimoh, A 2018, 'Climate-Smart Agriculture: Lessons from Africa, for the World', *World Bank*, viewed 23 December 2023, https://blogs.worldbank.org/nasikiliza/climate-smart-agriculture-lessons-from-africa-for-the-world.

9 Nyamangara, J, Nyengerai, K, Masvaya, EN, Tirivani, R, Mashingaidze, N, Mupangwa, W, Dimes, J, Hove, L, & Twomlow, S 2014, 'Effect of Conser-

vation Agriculture on Maize Yield in the Semi-Arid Areas of Zimbabwe', *Experimental Agriculture*, vol 50, no 2, pp 159-177, viewed 23 December 2023, doi.org/10.1017/S0014479713000562.

10 Baudron, F, Thierfelder, C, Nyagumbo, I, & Gerard, B 2015, 'Where to Target Conservation Agriculture for African Smallholders? How to Overcome Challenges Associated with its Implementation? Experience from Eastern and Southern Africa', *Environments*, vol 2, pp 338-357, doi.org/10.3390/environments2030338.

11 Fisher, M, Abate, T, Lunduka, RW, Asnake, W, Alemayehu, Y, & Madulu, RB 2015, 'Drought Tolerant Maize for Farmer Adaptation to Drought in Sub-Saharan Africa: Determinants of Adoption in Eastern and Southern Africa', *Climatic Change*, vol 133, pp 283-299, viewed 23 December 2023, doi.org/10.1007/s10584-015-1459-2.

Chapter 19

1 Rwanda Social Security Board n.d., 'CBHI Scheme', viewed 23 December 2023, https://www.rssb.rw/scheme/cbhi-scheme.

2 Lu, C, Chin, B, Lewandowski, JL, Basinga, P, Hirschhorn, LR, Hill, K, & Binagwaho, A 2012, 'Towards Universal Health Coverage: An Evaluation of Rwanda Mutuelles in Its First Eight Years', *PLoS One*, vol 7, no 6, viewed 23 December 2023, doi.org/10.1371/journal.pone.0039282.

3 Ussery, F, Bachanas, P, Alwano, MG, Lebelonyane, R, Block, L, Wirth, K, Ussery, G, Sento, B, Gaolathe, T, Kadima, E, Abrams, W, Segolodi, T, Hader, S, Lockman, S, & Moore, J 2022, 'HIV Incidence in Botswana Rural Communities With High Antiretroviral Treatment Coverage: Results From the Botswana Combination Prevention Project, 2013-2017', *Journal of Acquired Immune Deficiency Syndromes*, vol 91, no 1, pp 9-16, viewed 23 December 2023, doi.org/10.1097/QAI.0000000000003017.

4 Zeitvogel, K 2016, 'MenAfriVac Vaccine Slashes Meningitis Cases in Africa', *Fogarty International Center*, viewed 23 December 2023, https://www.fic.nih.gov/News/GlobalHealthMatters/may-june-2016/Pages/menafrivac-meningitis-vaccine.aspx.

5 Trotter, CL, Lingani, C, Fernandez, K, Cooper, LV, Bita, A, Tevi-Benissan, C, Ronveaux, O, Préziosi, M, & Stuart, JM 2017, 'Impact of MenAfriVac in Nine Countries of the African Meningitis Belt, 2010–15: An Analysis of Surveillance Data', *The Lancet Infectious Diseases*, vol 17, no 8, pp 867-872, viewed 23 December 2023, doi.org/10.1016/S1473-3099(17)30301-8.

6 Elorriaga, N 2016, 'Tackling NCD in LMIC: Achievements and Lessons Learned From the NHLBI-UnitedHealth Global Health Centers of Excellence Program', *Global Heart*, vol 11, no 1, pp 5-15, viewed 23 December 2023, doi.org/10.1016/j.gheart.2015.12.016.

7 National Department of Health 2011, 'National Core Standards for Health Establishments in South Africa', *The Republic of South Africa*, viewed 23 December 2023, https://static.pmg.org.za/docs/120215abridge_0.pdf.

8   World Health Organization n.d., 'Kenya: Health Data Overview for the Republic of Kenya', viewed 24 December 2023, https://data.who.int/countries/404.

9   UNICEF n.d., 'Health: Reducing Maternal, Newborn and Child Mortality', viewed 24 December 2023, https://www.unicef.org/kenya/health.

10 Olingo, A 2023, 'Test, Treat and Track: China's Surveillance System Promising to End Malaria in EA', *MSN*, viewed 24 December 2023, https://www.msn.com/en-xl/africa/ghana/csir-sari-s-improved-yam-variety-produces-high-yield/ar-AA1m3tky.

11 UNFPA n.d., 'Maternal Health', viewed 24 December 2023, https://kenya.unfpa.org/en/topics/maternal-health-16.

12 Yuen, E 2022, 'Kenya and Maternal Health: Delivering Results', *Think Global Health*, viewed 24 December 2023, https://www.thinkglobalhealth.org/article/kenya-and-maternal-health-delivering-results.

13 Gureje, O, Lasebikan, VO, Kola, L, & Makanjuola, VA 2006, 'Lifetime and 12-Month Prevalence of Mental Disorders in the Nigerian Survey of Mental Health and Well-Being', *The British Journal of Psychiatry*, vol 188, pp 465-471, viewed 24 December 2023, doi.org/10.1192/bjp.188.5.465.

14 Atilola, O 2015, 'Level of Community Mental Health Literacy in Sub-Saharan Africa: Current Studies Are Limited in Number, Scope, Spread, and Cognizance of Cultural Nuances', *Nordic Journal of Psychiatry*, vol 69, no 2, pp 93-101, viewed 24 December 2023, doi.org/10.3109/08039488.2014.947319.

15 Tefera YG 2022, 'Community-Based Health Extension Policy Implementation in Ethiopia: A Policy Experience to Scale-Up', *Journal of Public Health in Africa*, vol 13, no 3, viewed 24 December 2023, doi.org/10.4081/jphia.2022.2074.

16 Medhanyie, A, Spigt, M, Dinant, G, & Blanco, R 2012, 'Knowledge and Performance of the Ethiopian Health Extension Workers on Antenatal and Delivery Care: A Cross-Sectional Study', *Human Resources for Health*, vol 10, no 44, viewed doi.org/10.1186/1478-4491-10-44.

17 Ghanaian Ministry of Gender, Children and Social Protection 2017, 'Ghana School Feeding Programme (GSFP) Secretariat', viewed 24 December 2023, https://www.mogcsp.gov.gh/ghana-school-feeding-programme-gsfp/.

18 Rwandan Ministry of Education 2019, 'National Comprehensive School Feeding Policy', viewed 24 December 2023, https://planipolis.iiep.unesco.org/sites/default/files/ressources/rwanda_school_feeding_policy.pdf.

19 South African Non-Communicable Diseases Alliance 2020, 'National Strategic Plan for the Prevention and Control of Non-Communicable Diseases 2020-2025', viewed 24 December 2023, https://www.sancda.org.za/wp-content/uploads/2020/05/17-May-2020-South-Africa-NCD-STRATEGIC-PLAN_For-Circulation.pdf.

Chapter 20

1   Statistics South Africa 2015, 'Labour Market Dynamics in South Africa, 2014

Report', viewed 24 December 2023, https://www.statssa.gov.za/?p=4445.

2   Davison, R 2011, The Fourth Economy: Inventing Western Civilization, Figment.

3   McEvoy, O 2023, 'Number of Small and Medium-Sized Enterprises (SMEs) in Germany from 2008 to 2022, by Size', Statista, viewed 24 December 2023, https://www.statista.com/statistics/818691/small-and-medium-sized-enterprises-germany/.

4   Geza, W, Ngidi, M, Ojo, T, Adetoro, AA, Slotow, R, & Mabhaudhi, T 2021, 'Youth Participation in Agriculture: A Scoping Review', Sustainability, vol 13, no 16, viewed 24 December 2023, https://doi.org/10.3390/su13169120.